Political Values and the Educated Class in Africa

Political Values and the Educated Class in Africa

ALI A. MAZRUI, D.Phil.(Oxon)

*Department of Political Science
and Center for Afro-American and African Studies,
The University of Michigan, Ann Arbor*

London

HEINEMANN

Ibadan   Nairobi   Lusaka

Heinemann Educational Books Ltd
48 Charles Street, London W1X 8AH
P.M.B. 5205 Ibadan.   P.O. Box 45314 Nairobi
P.O. Box 5205 Lusaka
EDINBURGH MELBOURNE TORONTO AUCKLAND NEW DELHI
KINGSTON SINGAPORE HONG KONG KUALA LUMPUR

ISBN 0 435 96522 0 (cased)
ISBN 0 435 96523 9 (paper)

Set in 10 on 11 point Compugraphic Baskerville
Printed in Great Britain by
Biddles Ltd, Guildford, Surrey

'To Makerere! You, who were built for the future, must now await the future to rebuild you.'

CONTENTS

Preface   ix

Introduction: Educated Africans in Politics and Society   1

PART ONE: A STUDY OF ORIGINS   21

1 Education and the Quest for Salvation   23
2 Education and the Quest for Sovereignty   42
3 The Emergence of Modern Orators   64

PART TWO: EXPANDING INTELLECTUAL HORIZONS   79

4 Ancient Greece in African Thought   81
5 Mahatma Gandhi and Black Nationalism   103
6 Rousseau and the African Legacy of the French
   Revolution   120
7 Islam and Radicalism in African Politics   134
8 Christianity and Humanitarianism in African
   Diplomacy   153
9 The USSR and China as Models of Innovation   170

PART THREE: THE SEARCH FOR RELEVANCE   185

10 Education and Political Change   187
11 Education and Nationalist Aspirations   202
12 Education and Developmental Goals   218

PART FOUR: HIGHER EDUCATION AND NATION-BUILDING   233

13 The Meaning of Higher Education   235
14 The Environment of Higher Education   252
15 The Political Functions of Higher Education   268

PART FIVE: EDUCATION, DEPENDENCY AND LIBERATION 283

16 The African University as a Multinational Corporation 285
17 The African Computer as an International Agent 320
18 The African Intellectual as an International Link 343
19 Cultural Liberation and the Future of the Educated Class 368

Index 387

PREFACE

This book is an accumulation of experience, rather than merely a collection of essays. Both as an educated African and as an African educator I have lived through many of the issues raised in the coming pages — ranging from socialization in a colonial situation to the tensions of nation-building after independence. My early education was in Mombasa, Kenya, against the background first of the Second World War and later of the Mau Mau war within Kenya itself. My university training involved two western countries — England (where I obtained my first and last degrees) and the United States (where I acquired my master's qualification). Approximately two-thirds of my education was in Africa and one-third in the western world. As a student I also had a brief spell at the University of Mexico in Mexico City — my first exposure to the wider politics of what later came to be known as the 'Third World'.

Since then I have taught in many lands. I have certainly interacted with, or lectured to, university audiences in five continents of the world. But my most concentrated area of university experience as a teacher was in East Africa. My base was Makerere University, where I served as a teacher, as a researcher and as an academic administrator. There were times when almost every episode was at least a paragraph in the great book of experience. Let me illustrate with one such episode.

One day in the course of 1968 Mr Y. K. Lule, then Principal or head of Makerere University College, sent for me. It was after five o'clock in the afternoon. He asked me whether I had ever written an article comparing President Obote of Uganda with Thomas Hobbes' sovereign. Obote was then in power. It will be remembered that Hobbes, the English political philosopher of the seventeenth century, was a champion of absolute government. He favoured strong centralized authority, and has been interpreted as an advocate and defender of political dictatorship. If I was comparing Obote with Thomas Hobbes' concept of the sovereign, I could be interpreted as implying that Obote was an absolute dictator.

Had I ever written an article comparing Obote with Hobbes' sovereign in that manner? I tried to think, but I could not remember any such comparative adventure. I explained to Mr Lule that I wrote a good deal, and could not remember immediately a reference of the kind he had in mind. But I could provide him with a full list of my publications. Whoever had submitted the report about my comparing Obote with Hobbes' sovereign in that manner could therefore consult my list of publications, and draw my attention accordingly.

Mr Lule then explained why he needed to know. He was acting in response to a complaint from 'very high quarters' in Uganda.

The situation captured a number of important issues which will be discussed more fully in the coming pages. First, there was the political nearness between the campus and the national structure of power. A comparative exercise in political philosophy by a scholar could become an issue with direct implications for the wider polity.

Secondly, the name Thomas Hobbes was symbolic in the circumstances. In that very conversation between Mr Lule and myself Hobbes signified and represented the intellectual presence of the western academic heritage in our midst. We shall later explore more fully the implications of two factors which profoundly affect educational and academic work in Africa as a whole to the present day — the nearness of domestic politics in the life of the educator, and the nearness of a Eurocentric world culture in the system of education as a whole. If I had indeed compared Thomas Hobbes with Milton Obote, I had brought these two factors together. Hobbes was part of the Eurocentric world culture in our lives; Obote's apparent reaction to a Hobbesian analogy on campus illustrated the relative proximity of practical politics to academic concerns.

Some months later I was in the Presidential Lounge of Parliament Building in Kampala engaged in a discussion with President Obote and some of his Ministers. In the course of the conversation President Obote referred to a diagram I had drawn on the blackboard in my first-year class at Makerere. In that lecture I had been discussing the relationship between class formation and the ethnic structure of African societies. I had asserted in the course of the lecture that tribalism in Africa could not be eliminated without at the same time creating new classes. I also implied that the emergence of new social classes, criss-crossing with tribal boundaries, could itself reduce the dangers of ethnic confrontations in Uganda and help to promote nation-building. To illustrate this idea of criss-crossing loyalties I must have drawn a diagram on the blackboard for the first-year under-graduates. That was supposed to be in the privacy of my own class at Makerere. And yet here was the Head of State of Uganda complaining to me in the calmness of his Presidential Lounge that he had not been able to understand the diagram I had drawn on the blackboard in my class at Makerere! It then dawned upon me that the President was taking a special interest in what I said to my students in my classes, and that he had informers in my classroom.

In my own mind I related this discussion of the diagram on the blackboard to the previous complaint about a comparison between Milton Obote and Thomas Hobbes' *Leviathan*. I realized that the complaint submitted to Mr Lule was not really about something I had written in an article but must have been about something I had said in a lecture. I still could not remember having published an article comparing Obote to a Hobbesian dictator, but in my lectures I often extemporized and might well have drawn attention to points of similarity between the absolutism championed by Thomas Hobbes and the ideas of strong and centralized government favoured by President Obote.

Both through direct government policy and through informers, the university was thus penetrated by the wider system. What should not be overlooked is the fact that the wider political system had in turn been deeply penetrated by the influence of the university over the years.

Makerere was indeed a kind of political institution from quite early on. By the very act of producing some of the leaders of thought and political organization, the college contributed to the ferment of nationalist forces leading up to independence. But during the colonial period the college was not as yet intended to produce the *ultimate* decision-makers in the political system. British administrative officers were expected to remain the major decision-makers for quite a while to come, and the ambition of the college was primarily to train a second-level administrative cadre, a pool of teachers for schools in the region as a whole, and a community of intellectuals generally.

In 1963 the federal University of East Africa came into being with a campus in Kampala, another in Nairobi and a third in Dar es Salaam. This was also the year when Kenya became independent following Uganda (1962) and Tanzania (1961). The University of East Africa as a post-independence institution had a more direct political impact since the products of the university were no longer excluded a priori from the commanding heights of the political systems. Makerere products like Milton Obote and Julius Nyerere did indeed finally get to the top in any case. But at the time of their education Makerere was not consciously producing rulers. Its ambition was the more modest one of producing 'native' leaders.

As the base of the educated class in Africa as a whole has expanded, it has become less and less automatic that every graduate would attain a position of even modest leadership. Progress in education must gradually lead to the production of educated followers, as well as educated leaders. But while it is true that a graduate might now conceivably have to settle for a lower position than he might have done during the colonial period, he also stands a chance of attaining a higher position than was reasonable to expect in the colonial government. In other words, the range of jobs for graduates has been expanding in both directions. And the new national universities of Africa are now more conscious of contributing to the commanding heights of the administrative and political structure than they were when they were first built.

A related phenomenon is the issue of bonding students for government service. A number of African countries have already devised an elaborate bonding system to ensure that nationals who emerge from the universities are available to be channelled into specific positions determined by the government. During the colonial period many students who received government scholarships to study abroad were bonded to serve the local colonial government for three years or so on their return. But students going to local universities were not subject to the same obligation. On completion of their education they could join government service or the private sector or go abroad as they deemed fit. This latitude has been shrinking since independence. And the careers of graduates emerging from Africa's institutions became determined more directly at the political level than they ever were before. But there did remain the question of what proportion of the graduates the government services could in fact absorb.

The bonding of university students itself is part of the broader phenomenon of a change in the nature of administration. In a sense, the universities of independent Africa are now more political as institutions than colonial colleges used to be. This is partly because a bigger sector of life in Africa is now politically determined. Administration during the colonial period was, to some extent, minimalist. The bureaucratic ethos was oriented more towards stability than development. Law and order was a higher ideal than rapid economic transformation. It was to this system that colonial colleges were contributing educated personnel. By its very nature a law-and-order minimalist system is less politically sensitive than a developmental ethos. By thus contributing to a less politicized system, the old colonial college was itself less of a political institution. The difference is dramatized in the case of Tanzania. Tanzania today is more of a politicized system than it ever was as a 'stable' trusteeship leisurely administered by Britain. An educational institution which serves Tanzania today is therefore more directly contributing to political processes than an institution which served the old trusteeship adminstration.

What the universities of Africa now produce is a major factor in the calculations and projections of development plans. Many of the graduates would, in due course, be taking up key positions in the whole complex process of social and economic change. Some of the changes that they might help to precipitate are bound to have major political repercussions as well. We might therefore say that the influence of the universities on the life of the continent has now wider ramifications than it might have had within a political ethos which was less consciously oriented towards development.

In the coming pages we shall examine these processes of politicization both before and after independence. We shall look not merely at educational institutions but at education itself. But ultimately our focus will be on the educated class itself — the product of the modern school in Africa, with all its strengths and deficiencies.

We describe the intellegentsia in this book as an educated *class* partly because we are convinced that, whatever Karl Marx might have surmised about the role of economic factors in class formation in nineteenth-century Europe, class formation in twentieth-century Africa has been profoundly affected by western education.

The colonial impact transformed the natural basis of stratification in Africa. Instead of status based on, say, age, there emerged status based on literacy. Instead of classes emerging from the question 'who owns what?', class formation now responded to the question 'who *knows* what?'. The knowledge may be merely literary, but the colonial impact certainly distorted reality both in a Marxist materialist sense and in an African normative sense. The very process of acquiring aspects of the imperial culture came to open the doors first of influence and later of affluence itself.

The following pages should help reveal one person's view of this process, seen partly from the inside. In the ultimate analysis, this book is a product of participant observation extending over many years. But almost by definition a participant observer is not an island unto himself. I owe a great debt both to institutions and to individuals. I cannot do justice to them all here.

Institutionally, my most stimulating experience in this field of study continues to be my ten years as a teacher at Makerere University in Uganda. I still draw new insights from that experience to understand newer aspects of life. But Makerere was part of a system of academic life in East Africa, and shared aspects of cultural and intellectual experience with Africa as a whole. My debt must therefore fundamentally include my ancestral continent in all its stimulating power.

McGill University in Canada and the American University in Cairo played a part in getting me to reflect on education as a subject of study fit for a political scientist. Both universities (in 1968 and 1970 respectively) invited me to give lectures not on politics in Africa, as so many other institutions had done, but on higher education in East Africa. In responding to their challenge I started laying the foundations of this book.

The final phases of research and the writing of the final versions of the manuscript were supported by the Center for Advanced Study in the Behavioral Sciences, Stanford, the Hoover Institution on War, Revolution and Peace, Stanford, and the Center for Afro-American and African Studies at the University of Michigan, Ann Arbor.

To the Rockefeller Foundation I am grateful for the funding of some of the earlier phases of this enterprise when I was still a professor at Makerere.

Many individuals have played a part in the process which has produced this book. I am especially indebted to colleagues at Makerere University and at the Universities of Nairobi and Dar es Salaam for both the stimulation of quiet conversations and the shock-treatment of ideological debates.

For copy editing before the final manuscript left for the publishers I owe sincere thanks to my students at the University of Michigan with special reference to David F. Gordon and Darryl Thomas.

Valerie Ward and Casandra Collins came to the rescue with their typing skills in the final preparation of the manuscript for publication. I am grateful for their capacity to combine patience with speed: the patience was extended to the author, the speed to the enterprise!

Three of the chapters in this collection were co-authored in their original forms. I am grateful to Dent Ocaya-Lakidi as co-author of the original version of the first chapter, to Geoffrey Engholm as co-author of the original joint essay on Rousseau, and to Rovan Locke as co-author of the original piece on Russia and China as models of innovation. But I have modified those three essays to suit the structure of this book. If the quality of the essays has suffered as a result, the fault is entirely mine.

Is it really true that behind every male author there is a woman? I am not sure about the generalization. What I do know is that behind every book, every article and every lecture of mine since 1962 there has always been Munā, my wife. When the western professors finished with me as a student, Munā took over as a loving mentor. This book bears strong traces of her influence over the years — for better or for worse.

Ali A. Mazrui

INTRODUCTION:
Educated Africans in Politics and Society

There can be little doubt that education and politics affect each other in quite profound ways. The impact of politics on education is clear enough. How much money is allocated to education, how teachers are recruited, what kind of values are transmitted in the system, how fast indigenous headmasters replace expatriate headmasters, whether more money is spent on the armed forces than on schools, or whether the Minister of Education is on speaking terms with the Minister of Finance, are all political issues which could profoundly affect education.

On the other hand, political life and the political system of the country are in turn affected by the educational process. The quality of leaders who find their way to responsible political positions, the kind of political values which activate policy and behaviour, the class structure in the country, the system of occupational rewards and social prestige, are all factors deeply influenced by the educational system of a country.

During the colonial period in Africa, education served the purpose of creating not only a reservoir of qualified people which the government could use, but also a pool of potential qualified nationalists who came to challenge the colonial presence itself. As one political analyst put it more than fifteen years ago:

> Western education has been the most revolutionary of all influences operating in Sub-Saharan Africa since the imposition of European rule. It has been the instrument of the creation of a class indispensable for imperial rule, but one which invariably has taken the leadership in challenging and displacing that rule.[1]

As we shall elaborate later, Christian missionary influence was an important factor in the promotion of education during the colonial period. The missions were interested in spreading the Christian gospel—but in due course a new secular gospel captured the imagination of many young Africans. This was the gospel of nationalism and its commitment to the liberation of the continent.

Sometimes it was touch-and-go whether a particular educated African became a priest or a politician. Kwame Nkrumah of Ghana

1

did seriously consider the possibility of becoming a priest, and studied theology when he was in the United States. But he gradually drifted away from the gospel of Christianity towards the secular gospel of Pan-African commitment and some kind of socialism. In the words of Nkrumah in his autobiography: 'I am a Marxist-socialist and a non-denominational Christian and I see no contradiction in that.'[2]

Sometimes the tougher the conditions under which Africans suffered, the closer became the contact between religion and politics. To the present day there are occasions when nationalism itself takes on a direct religious form. These are occasions when neo-Christian or other separatist churches assert themselves. In the words of a French sociologist, Georges Balandier:

> New Christian movements must come to the attention of the sociologists in so far as they are reactions against the colonial situation . . . these movements lead above all to the study of the origins of nationalism, and in so doing, confront the sociologist with one of the most important problems of our time.[3]

The influence of Christianity on nationalism has by no means been limited to those who have risen as 'prophets' in a religious sense. On the contrary one of the striking aspects of nationalist leadership in English-speaking central Africa and in South Africa is how often modern political leadership seems to carry a religious influence as well. In Zambia, Kenneth Kaunda, the son of an African missionary, is himself a devout Christian. In Malawi, Hastings Banda, now a more controversial figure, was in his older days of anti-colonial agitation for Nyasaland a revered figure, partly because of his position as an elder in the Church of Scotland. In Zimbabwe, the radical nationalists for a while included Reverend Ndabaningi Sithole and Bishop Abel Muzorewa. In South Africa the late Albert Luthuli, winner of the Nobel prize for peace and symbol of non-violent resistance to South African apartheid, was a deeply devout Christian. But the trend more recently in Africa has been towards the secularization of politics and of nationalism itself. The link between religious tendencies and political ambition has become weaker with the years. An assessment of the future might therefore usefully include a probable continuation of this secularizing tendency.

Another tendency in much of Africa was the extent to which politics attracted teachers away from schools into public careers. While in places like the United States it is still from the legal profession that politics have attracted a particularly disproportionate occupational segment, in Africa it was the educational profession which was often hit hard by the lure of politics.

The extent of legal representation in the United States has sometimes been a subject of criticism for those who believe that the legislature should to some extent be a microcosm of the composition of the country as a whole. I remember reading a campaign speech by Nikita Khrushchev in 1958 in which Khrushchev attacked the relatively unrepresentative nature of the composition of the American Congress. He asserted that Congress had no workers and no ordinary farmers. Out of 531 Congressmen, Khrushchev noted, more than half were lawyers. The black population which was more than ten per cent of the national population, had a representation in Congress of less than one per cent. The women of the land, presumably about half the total national composition, had only three per cent of the composition of Congress.

Khrushchev's attack was in some ways unfair since the composition of Congress was not intended to be purely a microcosm of the national population. Representation in this case was in terms of people elected to represent diverse interests in specific geographical areas. A lawyer was not representing lawyers, but was representing a geographical unit, a geographical constituency. Within that constituency he represented all the men and women residents there — the workers, the farmers, the bankers, the teachers. And yet the interesting point about Khrushchev's analysis was this reference to the highly disproportionate weighting in Congress on the side of the legal profession.

In those parts of Africa still under civilian rule, the representation of the teaching profession in politics has not been as striking as that of the law in the United States. While a person can quite easily combine the law with a political career, a person cannot easily combine a teaching profession with a political career. The teachers mobilized into African politics are in fact a collection of ex-teachers, or teachers who have interrupted their educational careers for the time being in pursuit of a political career.

As Africa entered the first decade of independence in the 1960s, the number of politicians with experience in teaching was striking. In Ghana and Nigeria thirty per cent of the members of the legislatures were teachers. Most of them were drawn from rural areas. An observer of the Ghanaian scene argued that this heavy representation of teachers was 'mainly attributable to the fact that the primary school teacher enjoys a position in the bush village which gives him a high social standing and great influence.'[4] Coleman has argued that the same was true of Nigeria at that time. The high prestige inherent in the new western-style secular education, as well as the prerequisite of the English language for a national political career, converted teachers into highly eligible parliamentarians.[5]

On the eastern side of Africa the Ugandan experience at the time of independence was even more striking. Among the candidates put forward by the Democratic Party in the 1961 and 1962 elections nearly half were teachers. Among the candidates put up by the Uganda People's Congress in those elections almost exactly one-third were candidates from this same profession. The Democratic Party had relied more on the Catholic Mission schools for some of its candidates than the UPC had relied on Protestant schools. But there was substantial recruitment, by all political groups, from the educational profession for parliament.[6]

In fact all over Africa, the 1940s and the 1950s were the years of the prestige of politics. Many young people started dreaming about active participation in political activities and some vowed full commitment to a political career. With independence on the horizon in different parts of the continent, the romance of politics was at its most sparkling.

But colonial education did not merely produce teachers, politicians and administrators. It also produced a new literate culture which affected a much wider range of social variables. One aspect of the rise of the new literate culture was the newspaper – an institution which provided yet another arena of interaction between politics and the educated class. It is to this institution and its meaning for the new Africa that we must briefly turn.

Journalism and Political Education

The origins of African journalism lie in dry official publications issued by colonial governments. The word for newspaper in Swahili is *Gazeti* – derived from *Government Gazette*. The ancestry of the Fourth Estate, or the Press, in Africa is therefore decidedly political, at least in part. But also important as part of the origins of African journalism is the role of Christian missionaries. A de facto alliance grew up between colonial administration and missionary activity, both interested in promoting literacy and propaganda, though for different motives. The colonial governments were eager to consolidate their authority partly through propaganda and partly through power. The missionaries were eager to spread the gospel partly through propaganda and partly through service.

The first newspaper in Swahili in East Africa came barely three or four years after the full establishment of German rule in Tanganyika. *Msimulizi* (News-Bearer) came into being in 1888, and *Habari za Mwezi* (News of the Month) probably came into being in 1894. The missionaries were especially active in these early endeavours to make Swahili an effective language both for missionary work and for administration. Later there emerged *Pwani na Bara* (The Coast and the Hinterland), the first issue of which consisted of four pages, with an article in an early issue on the Kaiser's birthday and a note on the Nyamwezi Chief, Mirambo. The newspaper also contained statistics on the number of lions and leopards killed.

But although the origins of East African journalism lie in these colonial and missionary publications, history came to indulge her ironic sense of humour when newspapers formed part of the medium for agitation against colonialism itself. Jomo Kenyatta's journalistic experience goes back to the 1920s in this regard. As General Secretary of the old Kikuyu Central Association, Kenyatta started and edited what was probably the first Kikuyu journal, the *Muigwithani*, from 1928 to 1930.

As a generalization we might even say that in many countries of Africa the role of the press changed from being essentially governmental to being essentially opposed to the colonial establishment as it had then evolved. Even the settler press in Kenya was often a press of dissent, tending to be recurrently critical of the colonial government's position on this or that issue. The settler press was on the whole critical from the right of the political spectrum. But at least it had the vigour and sense of independence which comes with being sceptical of officialdom.

As independence approached, and literacy spread more widely, the habit of reading newspapers began to take deeper roots. In black Africa as a whole Kenya comes second only to Nigeria in the number of newspapers the country has been able to sustain over the years. The number has fluctuated, but somewhere in the region of half a dozen daily newspapers has been more the rule than the exception for several years. In fact, per head of population, Kenya is perhaps more of a 'newspaper-reading' country than Nigeria. But in absolute terms Nigeria, in spite of the vicissitudes of political tensions and the aftermath of a civil war, has remained a particularly rich country in journalism. Sometimes the number of newspapers in Nigeria has gone up to nearly two dozen.

In general, we might observe that English-speaking countries in sub-Saharan Africa are greater newspaper readers than their Francophone counterparts. A high proportion of French-speaking African countries have no daily newspapers at all. They may have a publication which comes out twice a week or something like that. And often these publications consist more of government announcements than of news as such. In this latter case newspapers in French-speaking Africa may be said to continue the role of the government gazette. Some of these publications have never gone beyond their rudimentary official origins.

The three countries of Kenya, Uganda and Tanzania for a while precariously maintained an economic partnership called the East African Community. At least theoretically the Community included not only special trade relationships among the three countries but also shared services, jointly run. At one time these included railways and harbours, joint currency, postal services, income tax and excise duties. But in addition to these officially shared institutions, journalism has also played a part in regional integration. There was a time when a chain of newspapers in East Africa as a whole existed as a regional institution in the private sector. The leading English-language daily newspapers in Kenya, Uganda and Tanzania were once commercially and professionally connected as a chain. Since independence the forces of narrower nationalism in each of the countries have led to the loosening of these commercial chains. But newspapers from Tanzania can still be bought in Kenya and vice versa. Uganda has now retreated into a fortress of journalistic isolation.

Perhaps even now, the capital of East African journalism remains Nairobi. Certainly the most sophisticated and widely-read newspapers come from Nairobi. *The Standard* and the *Daily Nation* are widely read not only in their home country but also among policy-makers in both Tanzania and, in secret, perhaps even in Uganda. Perhaps the most East African of all newspapers now is no longer the former *East African Standard*, but the *Sunday Nation*. The *Sunday Nation* is certainly the most elaborate newspaper produced in East Africa, and is on sale in the streets of Dar es Salaam and Arusha, as well as Nairobi, by Saturday evening.

We mentioned earlier that in Tanganyika under German rule newspapers were partly intended to spread the Christian gospel. But in Tanzania under President Nyerere's rule, newspapers are intended to spread the socialist gospel. To this extent Tanzania has gone further than either Uganda or Kenya in utilizing the press after independence as a medium of political mobilization. This has been attempted both in Swahili and in the English language. For a while *The Nationalist* was a voice of political militancy. In the early years of its existence it did face a professional rival, far more sophisticated in many ways, in the other English-language newspaper of Dar es Salaam, *The Standard* of Tanzania. *The Standard* was part of the colonial journalistic heritage, and had constituted an element in the regional chain of newspapers which included at one time the *East African Standard* in Nairobi, the *Mombasa Times* of the Kenya Coast, and the *Uganda Argus* in Kampala. But Nyerere's government in the end decided to nationalize *The Standard*, and make it a government newspaper, as distinct from a party newspaper. *The Nationalist* remained the party organ while the voice of the government sought to express itself through *The Standard*, though with considerable latitude allowed to editorial initiative. *The Standard* newspaper as newly nationalized was not intended to be merely an outlet for government notices, but was designed originally to be a forum of socialist debate, as well as a sounding board for official policies.

The politically effervescent Miss Ginwala, who was once in Tanzania and was deported in the early years of independence, came back. Miss Ginwala, a South African of Indian origin, a Marxist by conviction and British national by convenience, was invited by President Nyerere to return to Dar es Salaam and edit *The Standard*. The paper did acquire a new liveliness under her editorship. But in 1971 she was dismissed by President Nyerere, seemingly because of a precipitate editorial condemning President Numeiry of the Sudan following the execution of Sudanese communists. This editorial embarrassed the government, as Nyerere was not yet ready to take a public stand on Sudanese affairs. The fact that *The Standard* was a government newspaper carried the risk of having its editorial mistaken for a concrete governmental policy on the Sudanese question. But on balance Miss Ginwala's dismissal might have been a case of cumulative dissatisfaction with her initiatives and the tone of her editorials. She had created a number of enemies in positions of power and influence. Her precipitous condemnation of the Numeiry regime was apparently the last straw which broke the patience of the President.

Across the border an experiment in mobilization through the media had been attempted under the rule of Dr A. Milton Obote while it lasted. Obote had started *The People* as the equivalent of *The Nationalist* of Tanzania. But for quite a while *The People* was permitted greater editorial independence by Dr Obote as party leader than *The Nationalist* under Dr Nyerere. This was particularly so when *The People* was a weekly newspaper under the de facto leadership-editorship of a trusted Englishman, Danny Nelson. One found in *The People* criticism of government policy that one would not normally find in an independent newspaper in Uganda. But from 1969 Milton Obote began his move to the left, and the strategy of mobilization through the mass media began to demand greater conformity. *The People* lost some of its earlier independence and initiatives. After Amin seized power it continued for a couple of years, and then collapsed. The *Uganda Argus* became *The Voice of Uganda*. And the Luganda newspaper, *Munno*, was periodically and sometimes brutally harassed.

Of these three countries of East Africa it is Kenya that has shown the least interest in inaugurating a party newspaper, or in adopting a strategy of mass mobilization through mass media. Jomo Kenyatta himself had once been an amateur journalist both in Kenya and during his many years in England. And yet the country which has an ex-journalist for President is the one which has shown least inclination to have a special newspaper for either the government or the ruling political party.

There is recognition in much of Africa of the connexion between the press and political stability. The governments of the new African states have often seen their countries as being in a kind of state of emergency, comparable to a war situation. In this case the emergency concerns the two crises of stability and underdevelopment. There is a feeling that an irresponsible use of the mass media could quickly plunge an African country into a serious political convulsion.

The question which now arises is whether newspapers in independent Africa are about to resume their earliest role in the history of colonialism, and become government gazettes, or *magazeti ya serikali*, all over again. In at least some African countries what were once vigorous newspapers have indeed been reduced to official gazettes or government bulletins. With regard to at least this particular aspect of Africa's new literate culture, the political wheel seems to have come full circle. The educated class is represented in the government which censors, in the press which is being censored, and in the reading public which is a semi-deprived clientele.

The Politics of the Literary Elite

But the most central of all members of a literate culture are surely the creative writers themselves. Modern · novelists and playwrights in contemporary Africa are certainly another product of colonial education. They are, by definition, members of the educated elite. Like other intellectuals, they have of course been profoundly conditioned by the imperial politics of the twentieth century.

One of the more striking things about African literature as it has evolved so far is the extent to which it is still disproportionately concerned with social and political issues. Even when it focuses attention on an individual, African literature is very often an attempt to see the impact of social forces on that individual. This tendency towards a socially oriented literature may have its roots both in the old traditions of Africa and in the impact of the colonial experience. From the African traditions comes the sharp awareness of the community — what Nyerere identified as *Ujamaa*. A tribal affinity, loyalty to the group, kinship ties, the social factors having a bearing on the evolution of the person, the admission of the person through initiation or circumcision into membership of society — all these are factors which intimately weave the life and spirit of the individual into the fabric of his community.

When, therefore, young, newly educated Africans turned to the modern pen to express themselves, perhaps their entire attitude was affected by this tradition of collective awareness. The matters that affected the community assumed extra importance to the artist. And so the modern pen, responding to an ancestral urge, analysed social forces rather than personal, individual concerns. We see the artist looking at culture change and culture conflict. He looks at the nature of relations between the conquerors and conquered. He looks upon the resilience of certain social habits and the fight that some traditionalists put up to preserve and conserve what was imperilled. All these issues have tended to give us in the main a literature of social involvement, rather than a literature of personal intimacy.

But another factor which has emphasized the social dimension in African creativity for the time being is the nature of the colonial impact. The colonial impact is inevitably a question which involves political and cultural issues. The response to that impact and the attempts to analyse its ramifications help to force the artist out into the glare of social and public issues. And so here again, when a poet laments the alienation of a particular individual in a situation of cultural denial, there is always contact with wider issues of the community as a whole. The alienation is alienation from the community, and the rebellion is a rebellion against major cultural and sometimes military challenges from the outside. Occasionally it is also a rebellion against the ancestral lethargy which comes with rejection of the new and obstinate attachment to the old. It is this old pervasive social awareness which has given African literature as it has evolved so far a major political dimension. African literature has, in fact, been a meeting point between African creativity and African political activity at large. Much of the literature, especially prose but including poetry, is in fact political literature. The politics come in sometimes directly as protest. Here then you have art being invoked as a method of registering political grievance and asserting a militant objection. But there are occasions when the political component in African literature is merely an exercise in political observation and recording.

The most persistent of the socio-political themes in much of this literature can be reduced to the following five strands. First, there is protest against alien control — colonial or neo-colonial. This is a comprehensive protest and tends to be discernible in the literature of all parts of the African continent. Secondly, protest against the cultural arrogance of the alien rulers. This actually is somewhat distinct from the first strand. Not all anti-imperialism is, in fact, a protest against cultural arrogance as such. It may simply be a protest against political domination. Objection to cultural prejudice is perhaps pre-eminently observable in the literature of French-speaking Africa. In much of the literature of English-speaking Africa nostalgia for the old African traditions is not quite as overpowering. There is less preoccupation with the survival of African culture, less rebellion against imported cultural innovation. This relative acceptance of the western cultural impact in English-speaking Africa is in contrast to some of the literary passions of Francophone Africa. Thirdly, there is protest against racial prejudice. Again, this is not necessarily to be confused with the other two. It is true that all these forms of protest overlap. It may even be true that sometimes all three are observable in a single work of art. But these are different forms of protest. Protest against racial prejudice and racial discrimination is pre-eminently a feature of the literature of Southern Africa. In this case the artist is not kicking against colonial domination, or indeed even against cultural humiliation. What is more paramount is the simple matter of skin colour. There is an awareness of difference in colour, regardless of similarity of acquired cultural traits. Fourthly, there is the literature of detached observation — observation of culture contact and the process of culture change. This too is of course a matter of political significance. But in this case the artist is not necessarily protesting. He may be merely an observer, noticing the realities of the situation with some concern. Chinua Achebe's first novel, *Things Fall Apart*, is perhaps of this category. There is a deep acceptance of history and its demands. There is a sense of human bewilderment which history is exacting. But this consciousness of costs is not accompanied by angry protest, but more by profound lament. In his first novel Chinua Achebe is essentially a concerned observer rather than a fighter. Fifthly, there is the literature of protest against Africa itself — or at least against the current generation of Africans. The beautiful ones are not yet born — the continent stinks of political excreta. Achebe's *A Man of the People* was in fact one of the first African novels to set this tone of political disenchantment. But Ayi Kwe Armah's *The Beautyful Ones are not Yet Born* is a greater book than Achebe's *A Man of the People* from that point of view. In East Africa Ngugi wa Thiongo has been getting angrier with every new work. *Petals of Blood* and *The Trial of Dedan Kimathi* are in the same tradition of indignation and disillusionment. Okot p'Bitek is also an angry artist. Given half a chance he would dance himself into a frenzy of anger. Sometimes his art is a case of suppressed violence. Frantz Fanon must have had Okot p'Bitek in mind when he said:

> We have seen how violence is canalized by the emotional outlets of dance and possession of the spirits. Now the problem is to lay hold of this violence and help it to change direction — from dance to revolution!! [7]

These five strands of politicized literature vary partly according to differing colonial experiences in the different parts of Africa. But that is only part of the picture. The rest lies in the individual artist's own response to political situations. Nevertheless, it is worth taking a closer look at the effect which differing colonial experiences have had on African literary preoccupations.

There are occasions when what is dirty and perhaps even smelly becomes an essential prerequisite for the creation of what is beautiful or valuable. The standard example is that of manure and its role in increasing the fertility of the land. And out of land manured emerges either a grain of wheat or a bud. There are occasions when a rose owes the bloom of its beauty to cow-dung. To some extent the cow-dung of African literature is the phenomenon of European arrogance. Many Africans writers have been reacting against or responding to the arrogance of their masters, or former masters. Out of the depths of European prejudice and contempt have emerged here and there the plants of African inspiration.

But this phenomenon of arrogance itself differs from one imperial power to another. A case can be advanced to the effect that what the French were ultimately guilty of was cultural arrogance — whereas, the greatest fault of the British conqueror was racial arrogance. The two forms of arrogance can be seen as distinct phenomena. The British did not mix much with local people in Africa or India. They insisted a little more readily than the French on segregated areas of residence and segregated places in cinemas, segregated schools, segregated restaurants and hotels. In this lay their racial arrogance. However, in the cultural field the British were more tolerant and broadminded than the French. The British permitted the survival of many local institutions. In Uganda, for example, kings sometimes retained a resilience well into independence. Other cultural factors were also permitted a continuing life. Vernacular languages kept a role for themselves in the educational systems of British colonies. The British even started organizations specifically entrusted with tasks of preserving and, if possible, improving local languages. The Inter-territorial Languages Committee of East Africa was one such organization with this specific task of ensuring a meaningful survival of local languages in the region. The East African Literature Bureau is another organization with a colonial ancestry, but entrusted with the preservation and promotion of indigenous creativity. These kinds of organizations, and even the concessions to vernaculars in schools, were much less common in French colonies. There was less toleration of local cultures and local institutions. The French might have been less racially exclusive, less segregated in their areas, less horrified by miscegenation and mixed marriages: they were, therefore, less racially arrogant in the pure pigmentational sense. But they were also more culturally arrogant in their attitudes to local African traditions in their colonies. They stood for assimilation as far as possible. They were not consistent in this, but in essence they regarded their mission in Africa to be the dissemination of French culture — with as few concessions to local cultural peculiarities as possible.

What were the effects of these differences in forms of arrogance? What implications did they have for the types of creativity which the colonial impact fostered in these two language sectors of colonized Africa? It has often been suggested that a striking difference between English-speaking and French-speaking Africans is that for two decades the latter were, on the whole, the more culturally creative of the two groups. It has been pointed out often enough that Léopold Senghor of Senegal was a poet, Kéita Fodéba of Guinea a producer of ballets, Bernard Dadié of the Ivory Coast a novelist, and Cofi Gadeau a playwright before they held office in their respective states. One reason advanced to explain this is that the Africans who were ruled by France were more exposed than their British counterparts to collective humiliation in the cultural field. Their earlier literary creativeness was thus a response to the assimilationist assumption that African culture was inferior to that of France. African creative writers were, in other words, attempting to invalidate French contempt for African cultures.

Yet somehow there was a certain illogicality in the method used by Francophone African writers for this exercise. It was assumed that in order to disprove the claim that African societies were culturally impoverished you need only prove that African individuals have a capacity for cultural excellence. It was almost as if one were saying that since the French were denying African culture the right to a distinctive excellence of its own, modern Africans ought to prove to the French that they as individual minds could be intellectually creative in terms intelligible to their French masters. The African writers were also faced with the dilemma of trying to prove themselves culturally eqûal by invoking the device of cultural imitation. Many leading Francophone African intellectuals have continued to retain a sense of pride in French culture itself. Although the Francophone Africans were the more culturally humiliated of the two major linguistic sectors of contemporary Africa, there is in fact far less talk of 'our British heritage' among English-speaking Africans than of 'our French cultural background' among at least the more conservative groups of former French subjects. Their rebellion against French cultural arrogance has not yet taken the form of a determined attempt to tear away from French influence — in spite of Senghor's homage to negritude. Theirs, in fact, is less a rebellion than the paradox of rebellious emulation.

Nevertheless it remains arguable that the greater volume of poetry, prose, drama, ballet and other forms of artistic expression in French-speaking Africa in those early days was in part a reaction to the arrogance that the French colonial rulers displayed in their exercise of power. It was certainly not for nothing that negritude as a movement of glorifying traditional values in Africa tended to be pre-eminently a Francophone phenomenon in its literary form. To rebel against French cultural arrogance was to romanticize African roots through cultural media, or so it was assumed.

This explanation of early literary behaviour in French-speaking Africa has a lot of evidence to support it. But other factors ought always to be borne in mind. It is arguable that the difference lay not in the colonial policies of Britain and France but in the total national characteristics of the British and the French. The French have a greater preoccupation with expressing themselves through artistic and philosophical media. It is a total national orientation. Okot p'Bitek should approve of the French, for they more easily burst into song than the British; the French more easily burst into poetic lamentation. If then these two colonial powers bequeathed to their possessions abroad the essence of their own ways of life it was not surprising that French-speaking Africans tended, as least for a while, to be more culturally expressive than their English-speaking counterparts. Both groups of Africans might therefore be regarded as reflections of the total cultural orientations of the countries which ruled them.

The Spectre of Cultural Dependency

The fact that westernized African artists reflect their colonial background is itself part of a much wider phenomenon — the phenomenon of cultural dependency in all its ramifications.

The educated class has already grasped at least the basic fact that sovereignty implies both self-reliance and autonomous power. Much of Africa outside southern Africa has already acquired political sovereignty in the sense of the right to exercise political power over one's own citizens, for better or worse. The educated class has at last begun to realize the need for economic sovereignty in the sense of the right to exercise power over one's own economic resources. That is what the struggle for a New International Economic Order is all about. But unfortunately very few educated Africans are even aware that they are also in cultural bondage. All educated Africans to a man (and to a woman) are still cultural captives of the West. The range is from Samora Machel (a captive of Marxism as a western ideology) to Léopold Senghor (a captive of French philosophical traditions), from Charles Njonjo (a profoundly anglicized Kenyan) to Wole Soyinka (the angry westernized rebel with a Yoruba accent). And every morning when Ali Mazrui shaves before a mirror, he bears witness to the visage of yet another cultural captive of the West. The differences among educated Africans do not lie in whether we are cultural captives but in the extent to which we are. We vary in degrees of bondage but not in the actual state of being enslaved. We shall return to these themes later.

But how do we measure degrees of cultural dependency? One measurement is objective — how far an African has become a black European in dress, language, ideology and style. The other measurement of dependency is subjective — how far the slave realizes he is a slave at all and seeks to rebel against his condition.

By objective criteria President Senghor is one of the most deeply westernized of all African intellectuals. In many ways he is indeed a black Frenchman. But by the subjective criterion of realizing the dangers of western cultural imperialism, Senghor has been trying to contribute to the reafricanization of Africa. At a private ceremony in Dakar in October 1976, I presented to President Senghor what was then my latest book just off the press, *A World Federation of Cultures: an African Perspective*. In my speech to the President I addressed him as '*Professor* Senghor' — and I said to him 'This book owes more to you than it acknowledges'. Senghor has inspired many others into taking African cultures seriously.

Also in Dakar at that time was the President of Zaire. In his speech in Dakar in honour of Senghor's seventieth birthday, President Mobutu Sese Seko made one brilliant distinction between his own idea of authenticity and Senghor's negritude. Mobutu observed that negritude was a rebellion against the arrogance of others; authenticity was a rebellion against one's own dependency and imitativeness. Negritude as a Francophone literary movement was certainly born as reaction against French cultural arrogance. Writers like Césaire, Damas and Senghor were out to demonstrate to Europeans that black culture had a validity of its own.

Mobutu, on the other hand, seemed shocked by how far Africans themselves continued to act as if their own cultures were indeed inferior. In his own non-intellectual and sometimes inconsistent way, Mobutu was shocked less by the white man's arrogance than by the black man's acceptance of cultural inferiority. One can almost say that the only sense in which twentieth-century Africans are apes is the sense in which we are cultural imitators, apeing the behaviour of the white homo sapiens.

Mobutu's speech in Dakar was in some respects embarrassing to the man he had come to honour. Mobutu attacked the habit of naming African streets and institutions after imperialist heroes—and Senegal is full of such streets! He attacked our preoccupation with dressing up like Europeans—and Dakar is very strict on an antiquated European form of etiquette concerning dark suits and bow-ties for a night at the opera. Indeed I have never seen a single photograph of President Senghor in anything but an impeccable western suit, in spite of all his homage to negritude. In a sense, Mobutu in Dakar was echoing an old dictum sometimes associated in the Anglophone world with a character in Shakespeare's *Hamlet*. Polonius advised his son that 'the apparel oft proclaims the man'. It is less true in the twentieth century than it was in Shakespeare's day that dress or 'apparel' can really reveal at a glance a man's social class or national origins. But Mobutu is right that the triumph of the western suit from Tokyo to Timbuktu is a symbol of the domination of western civilization itself over the rest of the world.

I remember a speech in Nairobi by Eliud Mathu during the colonial period. As a pioneer African member of Kenya's Legislative Council, Mathu became for a while the main spokesman for the African masses in the national politics of colonial Kenya. Mathu was sick and tired of being told that Europeans had brought civilization to Kenya. In a dramatic symbolic move before an enthusiastic African audience Mathu tore off his own European jacket, asserting that if civilization meant western culture he was ready to pawn it in return for his freedom. The apparel may not always proclaim the social class of a man, but it often proclaims the relative status of cultures in a given society. Both Mathu and Mobutu have been justified in treating it seriously as an aspect of colonization. But Mathu (like most educated Africans outside Zaire) treated western dress as a measure of colonization rather than the enduring substance. Mathu soon returned to his western wardrobe. Zaireans under Mobutu, on the other hand, are experimenting with new forms of attire. Is Mobutu in danger of mistaking the trappings of western colonization for the essence? Dress and names are the outer covering of culture. In the years ahead a lot would depend upon how far Zaire transforms its educational system, adopts a language policy of relevance to African culture, pursues an ideology which puts a premium on autonomy, and builds a political system which gives weight to the culturally more authentic peasants.

But cultural emancipation must not be used merely as an end in itself. It must also serve as means of securing economic independence and consolidating political sovereignty. Most African countries are still intricately linked with the metropolitan economies of the western world. What all their societies need is the kind of additional insight which would establish a link between culture as a style of life and economics as a means of livelihood, between authenticity as a basis of civilization and autonomy as a condition of self-reliance, between negritude as a struggle to reafricanize Africa and social justice as the basis of a new domestic as well as international economic order. We shall address ourselves in later chapters more fully to the required strategies of such liberation.

From Meritocracy to Militocracy

But meanwhile the very juxtaposition of soldier Mobutu Sese Seko with philosopher-poet Léopold Senghor raises the question of yet another primordial tension for Africa's educated class—the tension between warrior and sage, soldier and intellectual. It is to this theme of militocracy versus meritocracy that we must now turn.

The warrior is an older phenomenon in Africa than the writer. Indeed there are many African societies which until recent times had no writing at all, but there are hardly any societies with no military experience of one kind or another. The defence of the tribe was always one important area of public concern in traditional African societies. The warrior, complete with initiation which went towards producing such a fighter, featured prominently in the organization of African political life well before colonial control.

What all this means is that the art of defending oneself with a spear is very old in Africa. But the art of defending oneself with a pen is, on the whole, an innovation. In between written warfare and physical warfare lies oral warfare. Written warfare is the utilization of the pen in a fighting spirit. Physical warfare is a literal confrontation in combat. Oral warfare is the use of the spoken word—as distinct from the written word—for militant purposes. On the eve of independence many Africans rose to political prominence partly through the utilization of oratorical skills. Those who rose to the very top as Africa was emerging from colonial rule owe a good deal of their success to the gift of the gab in the imperial language. The first African Presidents were disproportionately good public speakers in the language of the colonizer. We shall return to this oratorical theme later, but what we should note for the time being is how the warrior tradition in Africa was undermined by this new culture of words.

Certainly one process which helped to reduce the prestige of the warrior tradition concerned the intellectualization of African political culture under the impact of a more literate civilization. The coming of the written word in many African societies, the establishment of missionary and state schools, and the rise of a white-collar class — all these competed effectively against the old indigenous prestige of warriorhood, and pulled young men in their millions towards classrooms indoors, away from war dances in village compounds.

Another relevant process behind the decline of warriorhood concerned the economic diversification of African societies. Many of these societies no longer felt that the ultimate economic roles for young people lay either in settled agriculture or in herding cattle. There were now the additional opportunities of urban employment, work in the mines, jobs as domestic servants and farm assistants, and the whole range of white-collar occupations available to those who had acquired some of the literary skills of the new metropolitan culture.

Against this background of new opportunities, a job as a soldier even in a modern uniform and with guns rather than spears or bows and arrows, was now seldom at the top of the scale of preferences for ambitious young men. Those who could go to school and move on towards white-collar jobs normally preferred such prospects to the opportunities of being recruited into the army. The colonial armed forces therefore increasingly turned to the most disadvantaged sector of society for their soldiers.

There was a related factor which made colonial recruiting officers inclined more towards the less literate of their subjects for use in the armed forces. This was simply the conviction among many colonial administrators that illiterate or semi-literate Africans made better soldiers than the better educated. The better educated were sometimes distrusted as 'cheeky' and not adequately inclined towards the level of obedience that the armed forces required. An illiterate tribesman could, it was assumed, be trusted to be more automatically obedient than a product of a secondary school.

The less educated Africans were in their general orientation and attitude more rural than the educated. Indeed, western education in African conditions was a process of psychological deruralization. The educated African became in a fundamental sense a misfit in his own village. His parents were often people who had made sacrifices to improve the career opportunities of their child. When he graduated from school, his parents did not expect him to continue living with them, tending the cattle, or cultivating the land. Many parents assumed that the whole purpose of education was occupational improvement. They were therefore inclined to regard any insistence on the part of their educated son to remain with them in their village as something approaching filial betrayal. If their son was going to remain in the rural areas, why were all those sacrifices necessary? White-collar jobs in the villages were few and far between, and precisely because of that their son would become a rural misfit.

The illiterate or semi-literate village boy, on the other hand, maintains compatibility with his rural environment. And upon being recruited into the army, he takes into the armed forces many of the predispositions, attitudes and even superstitions that are characteristic of the rustic community from which he springs.

It is true that once the young rustic is himself in the army, he becomes subject to certain westernizing influences. After all, as we indicated, the army is still substantially organized on the basis of a western model, utilizes western military technology, and is partly influenced by western military values. Lucian Pye compares the acculturative impact of military training with the acculturative influences involved in the urbanization process. On balance, Pye regards the army as a more potent influence for culture change within individuals than living in a city.

On this issue Pye is less than persuasive. The range of influences at work in urban centres, partly because of their very diffuseness, might constitute a more potent force for psychological reorientation than military training per se. This is particularly so when the urbanization process is combined with formal education in a western type of school. The peasant boy who goes to the barracks and receives military training is primarily being inducted into new skills, and secondarily into new values. And even these new values are often limited to a small area of experience, the values of combat and military co-ordination, with a few derivative normative tendencies. Even after years of experience in the army, the semi-literate or illiterate African soldier is much further from a secondary-school graduate living in a city in his level of westernization than Pye's assumptions might imply. The urbanized secondary-school graduate is simply more comprehensively, and perhaps even more deeply, acculturated than the peasant warrior in uniform in the barracks.[8] As for secondary-school graduates who enter the armed forces, and later receive additional training, these in turn are on balance at a lower level of normative westernization than civilian university graduates in Africa.

Many of the first waves of African rulers were in some sense products of the intellectualization of political culture in the colonies. A few of those leaders, including such figures as Kwame Nkrumah and Milton Obote, were basically intellectuals in their capacity to be fascinated by ideas and in their ability to handle some of those ideas effectively. Some of the soldiers who have replaced them bear a more modest impact of western intellectualization than they did.

From the point of view of the immediate risks to rational policy making, and the utilization of careful intellectual criteria in determining policy choices, the fact that most military leaders are less intellectual than their civilian predecessors might have a political cost. On the other hand, from the point of view of the long-term reduction of intellectual dependency in Africa and the partial resurrection of indigenous cultural ways, the soldiers might prove to be greater agents for the re-Africanizing of Africa than their civilian predecessors.

Scholars like Aristide R. Zolberg have therefore been mistaken in their refusal to recognize any significant differences between military and civilian rulers in African conditions:

> Beneath their uniforms, the Gowons, Lamizanas, Bokassas, and Mobutus are men with the same range of virtues and vices, wisdom and foolishness as the Balewas, Olympios, Yameogos, and Nkrumahs they replaced. . . . As a category, the military governors of Africa are unlikely to rule better, or more justly, or more effectively than their civilian predecessors.[9]

In fact the range of vices and virtues has not been identical. On balance, the level of political brutality and violent sanctions against offenders has been higher under military rule in countries such as the Central African Republic, Uganda, and in a special sense even Nigeria. The invocation of physical force has tended to increase in such countries. It is therefore not clear why we should not regard this as a moral cost when men specialized in a profession of violence and combat assume supreme authority. On the other hand, the potential influence of the soldiers on the process of re-Africanizing African political culture might be regarded as a moral benefit. What is important is to stop the facile equation of relatively less educated soldiers with relatively westernized African intellectuals in power. Idi Amin of Uganda is simply not Milton Obote, nor is Achiempong of Ghana either Busia or Nkrumah.

In the struggle to give aspects of African culture greater respectability, young Africans themselves might have to start with the most ambitious of the tasks — the prior struggle to conquer African self-contempt. This in turn requires the growing toleration of some of the least respected, in western terms, of those aspects of indigenous culture. If an African intellectual can begin to concede dignity to the physical nakedness of the Karamojong men, or to the use of red ochre on the skin of the Masai, or the invocation of supernatural forces to help determine an election, that African intellectual is on his way to transcending his own cultural self-contempt.

Some of the soldiers in power provide precisely that kind of challenge to the new generation of westernized and semi-westernized Africans. Field Marshal Idi Amin has been a particularly severe test for large numbers of African intellectuals. Many seem to have been more ashamed of Amin's 'superstitions' than of his political brutality, more worried by Amin's distance from normal western diplomatic style, than by how many Ugandans he has detained or eliminated, even more ashamed of Amin's 'brazen poligamy' than his political arbitrariness.

David Martin, in his book on General Amin, has drawn attention to the prevalent nature of witchcraft and sorcery among Africans in different parts of the continent. Martin has also reminded us that it is not unusual to find 'highly educated Africans visiting witch-doctors' in a bid to ensure promotion to better jobs. But, according to Martin, Amin had 'taken his belief in occult powers to a ridiculous extent'. He refers to a Zambian seer, Dr Ngombe Francis, who claimed to have predicted the overthrow of President Milton Obote. After the coup the Zambian prospered significantly, and became Amin's soothsayer and prophet. There was also the Ghanaian mystic who claimed power to raise people from the dead. The mystic was flown to Uganda, and Amin later asserted that he had had an opportunity to talk to a man who had risen from the dead. As for Amin's innumerable dreams, these have ranged from a dream about when precisely he would die, to his assertion that God had told him in a dream to expel the Asians from Uganda and launch a national economic war.

David Martin, a westerner, regards Amin's beliefs in occult powers as 'ridiculous'. It would be illuminating, were it possible, to find out how many of the less educated and less westernized of Uganda's masses would share David Martin's views on the matter. It is conceivable that every time Amin has proclaimed a major dream, it has at best been Ugandan intellectuals that have laughed secretly. Some of the other Ugandans might dispute the validity or authenticity of this or that particular dream claimed by Amin, but perhaps the great majority would not dispute the proposition that some dreams are intended to be guides for action, and that supernatural forces might at times be in communion with a leader.[10] But is it good for African political culture to have such beliefs resurrected? Would it add to the viability of African political systems to invoke occult powers as a basis for policy-making?

This writer, as a westernized or semi-westernized African intellectual, has strong reservations about some of General Amin's political 'superstitions'. It is arguable that such beliefs from Africa's indigenous heritage deserve to die quietly, just as they died previously in most parts of Europe. And yet the very 'ridiculous' nature of such beliefs to westernized African intellectuals provides a challenge to their own cultural self-contempt, and may at least increase their sympathy and understanding for many of their rural compatriots.

The Oxford philosopher, John Plamenatz, once asserted: 'The vices of the strong acquire some of the prestige of strength.'[11] As the rustic soldiers have acquired power, and demonstrated their political strength, perhaps some of the prestige of that strength might rub off on the peasant warriors' cultural 'weaknesses'.

The current generation of adult westernized African intellectuals might never be able to transcend fully their cultural self-contempt, but the next generation of educated Africans might have learnt from their military rulers the capacity to understand and sympathize with certain aspects of the culture of the villages. Some of these beliefs in occult powers might die a natural death before long, but when African intellectuals can respect these they will learn to respect other aspects of African culture as well.

These are only a few of the basic themes that we hope to explore. Destiny has condemned the African educated class to a special role in the twentieth century. This book is, in a sense, a collective biography of the African intelligentsia. It is about the rise and decline of a class, its strengths and weaknesses. It is also about its prospects for a new lease of life.

References and notes

1. James S. Coleman, 'The politics of sub-Sahara Africa', Case No. 3 in Gabriel A. Almond and James S. Coleman, *The Politics of the Developing Areas*, Princeton University, Princeton, New Jersey, 1960, p. 278.
2. Kwame Nkrumah, *Ghana, the Autobiography of Kwame Nkrumah*, Nelson, Edinburgh, 1957.
3. Georges Balandier, *Ambiguous Africa: Cultures in Collision*, Chatto & Windus, 1966.
4. J. H. Price, 'The Gold Coast Legislators', *West Africa*, 26 May 1956, p. 325.
5. Coleman, op. cit., pp. 341-2.
6. *Uganda Gazette*, **LIV**, 6 (1961), pp. 185-304; **LV**, 9 (1962), 325-44. The percentages were 47 per cent in the case of DP candidates drawn from the teaching profession; and 33 per cent of UPC candidates drawn from the same professional pool.
7. An alternative rendering in English is to be found in Constance Farrington's translation of Frantz Fanon's *The Wretched of the Earth*, Grove Press, New York, 1963 edn.
8. Lucian W. Pye, 'Armies in the process of political modernization', in *The Role of the Military in Underdeveloped Countries*, ed. John J. Johnson, Princeton University Press, Princeton, New Jersey, 1962, pp. 81-3.
9. Aristide R. Zolberg, 'The military decade in Africa', a review article in *World Politics*, **XXV**, 2 (1973), 319.
10. Consult David Martin, *General Amin*, Faber, 1974, p. 16.
11. John Plamenatz, *On Alien Rule and Self-Government*, Longmans, 1960.

PART ONE

A STUDY OF ORIGINS

1 Education and the Quest for Salvation*

Colonialism was not simply a political experience for Africa; it was even more fundamentally a *cultural* experience. The values of the African world were profoundly disturbed by what would otherwise have been a brief episode in African history.

We accept for our purposes in this book the definition of acculturation which views it as the process by which an individual or a group acquires the cultural characteristics of another through direct contact and interaction.

> From an individual point of view this is a process of social learning similar to that of adult socialization in which linguistic communication plays an essential role. From a social point of view *acculturation* implies the diffusion of particular values, techniques and institutions and their modification under different conditions.[1]

It is indeed worth accepting this distinction between values, techniques and institutions when we are exploring what Africa has borrowed from the West. The modern school itself is an institution so borrowed. The style of instruction, the general ethos of the school, and the curriculum help to determine what values and techniques are transmitted within those walls. Techniques require an infrastructure of supportive values. This is particularly clear in economic behaviour. Certain commercial techniques from the West can only be transferred to an African society if there are supportive entrepreneurial values in the host society to sustain the techniques. Britain did not try to transmit either all its values or all its techniques to the colonies even if this were possible. Only some British values and some British skills were promoted in African schools. But did these partial values match with the partial skills? Given the skills which were being sought, were

---

* This chapter is based on a paper jointly written by Dent Ocaya-Lakidi and Ali A. Mazrui, 'Secular skills and sacred values in Uganda schools', presented at a conference, 'Conflict and Harmony between African and Western Education', organized by the Institute of Education and the School of Oriental and African Studies, University of London, October 1972. I am indebted to my co-author and to the University of London for permission to use the paper as a basis for this chapter.

the African schools fostering the right normative orientations?

The Techno-cultural Gap

It is a contention of this chapter that a profound incongruence lay at the heart of the imported educational system in Africa. The wrong western values were being provided as an infrastructure for the set of western skills introduced in the country. We might call this gap between norms and techniques the *techno-cultural gap* of the western heritage in Africa.

A major reason for the gap in the field of education lies in the paradoxical role of the missionary school in Africa. On the one hand, the missionary school was supposed to be the principal medium for the promotion of 'modern civilization' in Africa. On the other hand, western civilization on its home ground in Europe had been going increasingly secular. In the colonies the missionaries were propagating a concept of Christian religiosity which was already anachronistic in the West.

The missionary school as a principal medium for helping Africa towards a secular civilization was thus also the central medium for the propagation of a new concept of the devout society. The best schools in colonial Africa were often religious schools. The missionaries were bringing into Africa a religious feature of western civilization, the Christian values, in a form which most westerners had already rejected in the course of their own modernization. Sacred, sometimes fanatical and prudish values were central to African educational systems — and yet the ultimate imperial aim was at the same time to produce from the schools African men and women with modern secular skills necessary for the new society of the twentieth century. A heritage based on a techno-cultural gap was thus bequeathed to Africa, formulated in a new kind of clash between the City of God and the City of Man.

There is at least a symbolic parallel between the Christian vision of the world, of life, of death and, finally, of heaven, and the modern western conception of formal education which has also tended to be Christian in outlook.

According to one well-known Christian thinker, St Augustine, man is a fallen angel, which is why he now finds himself on earth. What he must do now is to prepare himself as well as possible in order to be taken back into heaven. Life on earth is therefore, according to him, a pilgrimage; a long journey for reunion with God. But this reunion, according to Christian thinking generally, can occur only at that moment when the soul or spirit separates from the body. But it must be a soul which has been correctly prepared for the company of God by those chosen by God himself.

There are at least three things in this vision which are reflected clearly in the kind of education the British introduced into Africa. There is, first of all, the idea of the *Christians* leading *pagans* into the *light*. In the educational system we see the *teachers* leading the *ignorant* into *knowledge*. There is, secondly, the idea of a pilgrimage, of a long journey from sin to virtue; from earth to heaven; from the way of Satan to that of God. More important, in this connexion, there is here the idea of the final *arrival*. One's soul finally arrives at its destination. Our school system reflects this scheme exactly. It is a series of ladders, of ordeals, with a destination. And here, too, one finally arrives. Thirdly, there is an important emphasis, in the Christian vision of the world, on the need for separating things of the body from those of the spirit or the soul; that is, separating the material from the spiritual. This emphasis, too, is to be found in our schools, although in a greatly modified form today.

Let us take these three things in turn beginning with the last one. It is not accidental that Augustine in his adolescence — when he was not yet a saint — joined for a short period a certain religious sect which flourished during his time. This sect, called the Manicheans, explained the world in a most interesting way. There were, they claimed, two guiding principles on earth. There was, first of all, the principle of light, of Goodness, of God. This they called *Ormuzd*. Then there was the opposite principle, the principle of darkness or Satan, which they termed *Ahriman*. The virtuous man, according to the Manicheans, was the man who had as little dealings as possible with *Ahriman*, concentrating only on *Ormuzd*. In practical terms the good Manichean used his body barely, and only to keep alive. He did not eat meat, he avoided sex, he did not drink nor did he smoke. He tried as much as possible not to enjoy any part of his body. He concentrated all his attention on things of the spirit. To live was to live spiritually and, moreover, it was the only way to finally 'arrive'.

At best this is a Weberian ideal type. One will look in vain in any of the hundreds of schools in Uganda; none of them practise this kind of life. Perhaps if you were to go to certain special educational institutions you might indeed find people who are 'Manichean' in their way of life. In the convents and seminaries they try as much as possible to steer clear of worldly affairs; concentrating instead on things of the spirit. But these are highly specialized schools and as such have very little relevance for us here. When we talk here of the separation of body and soul in our educational institutions we should try as much as possible to relate it to the ordinary school, not the specialized.

In fact, of course, it would not be accurate to talk of most of our schools, till relatively recently, as 'ordinary'. Being mostly missionary in origin and missionary run, they could not possibly be ordinary; and were not. But these missionaries were not, in their way of life, exactly or absolutely Manicheans. They were concerned not to exclude totally the body from the soul, the things of the world from those of heaven;

but rather to de-emphasize one as against another. One reason for this was that Christianity itself naturally emphasized the spiritual at the expense of the bodily; but the other was that the early British missionaries were hoping to win a moral battle in Africa which the industrial revolution in England had helped to make them lose at home, in spite of all the self-righteous rhetoric of the Victorians — the struggle for a more righteous outlook on life.

The Victorian age lasting perhaps till about the turn of the century, an age from which most of our early English missionaries were drawn, was characterized by exaggerated morality. The best symbol of it is, of course, the joyless Victorian Sunday. The Sabbath was to remain sober and free from any kind of entertainment. There were other things as well. There was the puritans' rigorous standard of sexual behaviour, 'with its intense concern for female innocence — or, as its opponents contended, for female ignorance.'[2] It was a society where the novel was read in family gathering; where, therefore, the novelist was expected to avoid topics which might cause embarrassment to the young, especially young girls.

This is why the early missionaries, who were also the founders of Africa's early schools, were somewhat shocked at what they considered a rather loose sexual morality among the Africans. The headmistress of Gayaza High School in Uganda, for example, right at the outset regarded her vocation as going beyond the confines of the boarding-school compound to the lives of the people beyond. 'The missions regarded the home environment as the greatest drawback, sufficiently bad in the estimation of one missionary to describe the school as an attempt "to save the girls of Uganda".'[3] It is not surprising, then, that one of the first things the missionaries sought to bring under control both in schools and in the villages as a whole was sex in all its manifestations. And they sought to do this by proceeding to discourage 'important areas of African cultural life, on the assumption that these contributed to moral laxity and sinful appetite.'[4]

To enjoy one's body, especially to enjoy sex was the supreme sin and crime in almost all the missionary schools and all other crimes were made relative to this. To steal, to insult the teacher, to miss classes or to fight a fellow student were one kind of crime punishable by a few strokes of the cane or two hours hard labour in the teacher's potato field. To be caught writing a letter to a girl or, even more unthinkable, to be caught with a girl was to face immediate automatic expulsion from school.

This is why at Gayaza, and most girls' schools, the school became 'a fortress' the only entrance to which was 'via the porter's lodge, through which no girl was allowed to pass unless accompanied by a matron.'[5] Boys' boarding schools were guided by a similar philosophy. This was succinctly stated by the Reverend A. L. Kitching who was emphatic in recommending the system for the daughters and sons of chiefs. He had served in Toro, Acholi and Teso, and saw the need for a uniform system in most of Uganda.

For the successful presentation of lofty motives a new atmosphere is essential. Though they may learn to make such motives a matter of habit, while pursuing their old course of daily life, yet if they are to be woven into character, isolation from degrading influences, so far as is possible, is essential during the early years. For this purpose the boarding schools are the most efficient instruments and from our schools we hope to see emerge a generation of chiefs and teachers in whose hearts the child is developed and the devil crushed . . . [6]

The destruction of the 'pagan' African culture was naturally accompanied by attempts to replace it with *some* aspects of the English way of life. Next to making the boys and girls upright Christians, this was an important aim of the Christian educators. Accordingly student boarders were, among other things, initiated into table manners, including the use of knives and forks. Acculturation into these aspects of the English way of life was to prove a much more successful project than the attempt to produce consistent Christians.

The Origins of Cultural Schizophrenia

The paradox of the missionary school has had long-term consequences for Africa. It may even lie at the heart of widespread *cultural schizophrenia* in Africa as a whole. Christianity soon showed itself unable to withstand adequately these pressures. First, the Christian ideal had to compete with vast opportunities for material advancement that were beginning to open up, for the young men especially. Secondly, once a man became literate, a whole new world became accessible to him. If he was naturally curious, he could find out answers to puzzles by reading literature other than the Bible. These often tended to undermine the faith. Christianity is still taken more seriously in Africa than in Europe, but it has had problems even in Africa. It is not surprising that by the early 1920s complaints about 'the demon of materialism' operating among the school population were already becoming widespread among the missionary educators. It was increasingly hope of material gains which had taken over as any schoolboy's basic motivation. Thus in 1919 a missionary, writing about Uganda, observed: 'It is the dream of each budding schoolboy ultimately to go to Budo, for it is the pathway leading to some of the most important positions in Uganda.' [7] A breakdown of the kind of jobs taken by the graduates of Budo would show most of them joining government and the teaching profession, but hardly anyone becoming ordained a priest. In spite of this evidence that Africans went to school in pursuit of secular skills, the accompanying values of education were still religious.

Outside the schools not only did the Christians destroy African cultures in the name of the new religion; but their manner of introducing the new faith could only lead to its own decline without adequate alternative values. The cultural schizophrenia was aggravated when attempts were made to Christianize even African deities. As Okot p'Bitek put it:

> Somehow, the Christian missionaries managed to convince themselves that the central Luo really believe in a high god called Lubanga, who after creating the world withdrew from it, and though still supreme, takes no interest in his creations. As Russell put it, 'The essence of the Christian message as presented in Uganda has, I would say, been something like this. You believe in a high god, but you believe that that god, having made the world, had no further interest in it and is not concerned with your troubles and joys . . .' Rev. John Taylor, Secretary of the Church Missionary Society wrote, 'undoubtedly, it was the influence of the mission and their adoption of this or that name to designate the God of the Bible, which helped to crystallise the concept of the supreme creator even among those who did not become Christians', and he warns, 'If God remains "outside" much longer, Africa's this-worldliness will turn to materialism.'[8]

There have been attempts, in recent years, to interpret the Bible and religion in a more realistic style that does not make God turn his back on the world. But in many cases this has come too late to effectively avert either the tensions of cultural schizophrenia or the triumph of unmitigated materialism among the new Africans.

In the schools this ambivalence finds expression in such phrases as 'suffering without bitterness', 'arriving', 'falling into things'; phrases which are applicable to the larger society as well. The school system is seen as a pilgrimage involving ordeals by stages; therefore involving intense suffering which one must bear to the end. For to reach the end of the educational ladder is to finally arrive and to be able to 'fall' into a comfortable job — exhausted, but fortunately not having to work any more. In this regard the student and his father are mutually supportive. Education becomes a secular pilgrimage towards a paradise of leisure. The father 'invests' in the son by putting him through school in the hope of a bigger financial return when the former finally arrives: certain aspects of African traditional societies are relevant here.

In much of East Africa, as in many other African societies, the idea of having many children is connected both to the risk of infant mortality and the hope of parental immortality. The period after one's death was often divided between the earlier period of 'death within living memory' and a later period concerning 'death beyond living memory'. But how else did one remain remembered for long except through one's children and one's children's children? The more the children, the better the chances of some surviving to carry one's name down, given the high rate of infant mortality.[9]

Though the idea of insuring for the future (through insurance policies) is recent in Africa, the idea of what happens to the dead after death is primordial. With the destruction of basic aspects of African cultures, however, the basic link between the living and the dead waned and weakened. But the link between the parents (soon dying) and their sons strengthened in a materialistic-expectation sense. Now the concern was not more sons for immortality, but better-educated sons for old age in this world.

The techno-cultural gap has continued to haunt Africa's educational system. Secular skills were given a religious infrastructure. And when the infrastructure was rejected, there were no alternative supportive values for the new secular ambitions. Many schools taught the virtues of obedience instead of the ethos of initiative; they taught fear of God instead of love of country; they taught the evils of acquisition instead of the strategy of reconciling personal ambition with social obligation. Religious indoctrination was paramount; political education was anathema. Yet the schools were also intended to help create modern viable societies.

Even those tribal communities that responded well to the western stimulus discovered the constraints of the techno-cultural gap. In this regard it is worth looking at the case of the Baganda in historical perspective, and then go on briefly to compare the Baganda with the Japanese. Both the Baganda and the Japanese were particularly successful in responding to the West while remaining for a while deeply loyal to a tradionalist self. Yet, as we shall later briefly indicate, there were important differences in their response to the western cultural impact.

The Desocialization of African Education

In the case of Buganda, the palace was both the central political institution and the central educational institution. A system of social mobility hinged, in part, on this dual role of the court. The system of education was profoundly socially-oriented, at least to the extent of being inter-linked with the survival of the social system.

Because the Kabaka's court was the pinnacle of both the political and the educational systems of traditional Buganda, social commitment and service to the king and nation were embedded in the educational system. Personal ambition and patriotic performance were inextricably intertwined. The Ganda traditional educational system was indeed elitist, but there were strong expectations of honourable service from the elite.

The Royal family alone was regarded as superior to and separate from other classes in virtue of their birth. With this single exception, any member of a clan could rise to the highest position in the land, if he succeeded in making himself conversant with state affairs, was brave in warfare and shrewd in council. As a rule either the sons of the chiefs . . . or those who had been brought up as pages, became chiefs, and took the lead among the people partly owing to their birth and surrounding, but partly owing to their superior training which as pages they had received.[10]

It was the king's and to a lesser extent the chiefs' courts which were thus the most important school for those interested in important public positions. Consequently almost every chief of Buganda who had children chose some for service in the palace 'that they might learn good behaviour. And . . . when there were chieftainships to be distributed, the Kabaka thought first of his pages, and not of others, because . . . the palace was the school.'[11]

What the British colonial administration did in Uganda was to replace the palace as the educational institution with formal schools. They also introduced the art of reading and command of English language as critical qualifications for attaining high official positions in the land. It is in this sense that Governor Johnston's assurance to the country in 1900 marks a turning point in the development of education in Uganda. The governor said then:

So far from wishing to shut the Baganda out of the Government of their own country, I want to encourage them to enter into that Government. I want their boys to learn English so that they may take the place of the Indian clerks in the Government offices.[12]

The road to offices and the key to advancement was thus to be through the English language. The process of desocializing the educational system, or separating it from ancestral social structure, was under way. Soon there was a passion for learning how to read and write, especially how to read and write English, among all those who could have contact with the schools—to the detriment of any other subjects. Those who would have been pages, and from there advanced to become leaders, now saw that within the context of the new 'palace' the English language replaced court etiquette and the need to please the Kabaka as means of advancing in life. This led to a number of important developments. Among the most important was that the educational system remained elitist but lost its original patriotic commitment and practical orientation.

It became extremely difficult for a long time to introduce technical subjects in schools. The experiences of the first two leading high schools in Uganda—Mengo and King's College, Budo—bear this out. Pious statements in favour of practical training were made from very early on. Winston Churchill as an Under-Secretary in the British Government spoke strongly in favour of technical education when he visited Uganda in 1907. At Mengo he said:

I hope the boys educated here will . . . acquire not merely the education of letters and words, but also the education of practical things and useful and technical acquirements, or at any rate will acquire that facility for comprehending those strong principles of character which will make them straightforward and trustworthy persons, fit to be the props and pillars of the people of Uganda.[13]

The new elitism was literary and intellectual. At Mengo matters were not made easier by a restrictive hill site which did not encourage school agricultural work. Nor was the school's first headmaster as interested in technical or agricultural activities as he was in teaching the Bible as part of the school curriculum. And at both Mengo and Budo it was so much easier to promote the arts than the sciences, let alone the technical, because of the great expense required for the latter. Given a very deep religious commitment by the headmasters and teachers of both schools and the natural closeness of Bible reading to literary pursuits, no one was going to go out of his way to promote the less related, more difficult studies in the sciences and technology. It is, however, noteworthy that the founder headmaster of Budo and his brother managed to establish a school tradition whereby each top form tried very hard to leave behind at Budo a permanent physical remembrance when they left. This might be a levelled football pitch, or a sports shade. Nevertheless technical subjects remained very much peripheral to the school curriculum.

Subjects other than English-oriented literary ones became merely tolerated by the students because they were a means to be able to remain in school and so be able to learn English. Watson has pointed out, in this connexion, that

> The intelligent pages in the Lubiri were quick to link education with religion and their interest in Mackay's technical and agricultural schemes were only means to this end. The ability to read the written words became the overwhelming passion of the quick Baganda.[14]

If for technical training this attitude spelled failure from the start, for sacred acculturation it was to lead to something more ambivalent. The Christian religion as well as the Muslim religion were successful in undermining the Ganda indigenous religious beliefs. But because access to the written word was through at least lip service to the new religions, especially Christianity, religion ran the risk of being dropped as soon as it had served its purpose as a passport to certain schools or had ceased to be a pre-condition for acquiring a literary education. This phenomenon is at the root of the problem of sacred value acculturation today. With the erosion of both traditional and imported sacred values, a spiritual void had sometimes been created.

What happened in Buganda affected other parts of Uganda. Literary as opposed to technical or agricultural education was ennobled and in this form it spread throughout Uganda. Within Buganda itself the new palace and court life following colonization was the life-style the common person ultimately measured himself against—to such an extent that the chief's court was the Kabaka's palace on a small scale, while the commoner (*mukopi*) was a 'chief in his own house'. It was only natural, of course, that the sons of chiefs and those of other nobility should look down upon manual, technical, agricultural, and industrial work as being the work of the *mukopi* and therefore below their dignity. Unfortunately for the history of educational development in Uganda, it was these very sons of chiefs who first had the advantage of going to school. By establishing that the proper education fit for the nobility was literary education, they conditioned the great masses of Buganda to think in like manner.

This thinking was to spread throughout Uganda for two reasons. First, the success of Mengo and Budo convinced the educational authorities that other schools up-country would benefit from the same or similar educational patterns as in Buganda. The literary emphasis and the boarding system thus both became irremovable parts of all the missionary-run schools in the country. But, secondly, Buganda now assumed leadership over the other parts of Uganda in almost all aspects of modern development; including leadership in the number of Ganda recruited into the Colonial Civil Service. It became clear to the rest that the key to Ganda success was education. And the nature of education involved had long been decided. So Uganda schools proceeded to lay emphasis on education for the purpose of a decent job, which meant office job. This in turn reinforced the emphasis on reading and writing English.

The Ganda and the Japanese

A comparison between the Ganda and Japanese versions of westernization reveals significance differences in levels of acculturation. It may well be that the Ganda borrowed more of the *values* from the West than the Japanese and fewer of the *techniques* from the West than the Japanese. A number of factors may go towards explaining the difference between the responses of the two peoples. One was direct colonization of Buganda as against a looser, far more informal external threat experienced by Japan.

Japan, after the Second World War became similar in experience to Buganda. The American occupation had an impact more nearly comparable to what Buganda experienced under British colonization. Japanese assimilation of western values following the American occupation was therefore at least as rapid as anything that the Ganda underwent under the British. But until that actual occupation by the Americans, the Japanese borrowed more techniques than values from the West, while the Ganda borrowed more values than techniques from the West.

Another major differentiating characteristic which may account for the different levels of acculturation concerns precisely the issue of language. The fact that the Japanese undertook their modernization primarily through the Japanese language, and did not become linguistic converts to an alien idiom, accounted for the slower pace of value acculturation as distinct from technical acculturation. The prestige of the English language in Buganda and the extent to which it was used as a medium of instruction and education for the elite, as well as for the aspiring elite, profoundly conditioned the orientation of the leaders. In the words of one observer, Lloyd A. Fallers:

A good many of the elite have, for half a century been educated in the very type of institution best calculated to produce the maximum socialisation impact — the English 'public school' type of boarding school, after which the Baganda schools were modelled. The leading Buganda government officials and the leaders of the most important political parties are overwhelmingly 'old boys' of the two elite boarding schools — one Anglican and the other Roman Catholic.[15]

Fallers has also referred to 'most subtle levels of cultural change at which it is possible here only to hint'. He refers to mode of clothing as a manifestation of acculturation:[16]

One of the striking characteristics of Buganda is the ability to wear Western clothing with a real feeling for style. Over much of Africa, Western clothing is worn like an uncomfortable, ill-fitting uniform, but Baganda men and women have penetrated sufficiently into the inner recesses of Western style that many of them can wear Western clothes with real taste.[16]

At the level of clothing there may be little difference between the Japanese and the Ganda, if anything. Since the American occupation, the Japanese have assimilated western clothing styles with more thoroughness and completeness than anything achieved anywhere else in the non-western world. The multitudes in Tokyo are overwhelmingly attired in a western style and basically according to western tastes. But the retention of the Japanese language as the primary medium of intellectual discourse, and transmission of values, remains a major difference between the Japanese and Buganda.

Another factor which accounts for the greater value-acculturation of the Ganda as compared with the Japanese brings us back to religion. Christianity has had a greater impact in Buganda than in Japan. The Ganda have embraced the western version of the Christian religion with a deep sense of inner response. So important has religion been in Uganda that it seems to have played a greater role in the politics of the nation than it has done in most other countries of Africa. The Christianization of Buganda must therefore be counted as a critical additional level of difference in acculturation between the Ganda and the Japanese.

But the achievements of the Japanese in technical acculturation have been far more impressive than anything in Uganda. It is not quite clear what the ultimate explanation for this particular differential is. But several factors no doubt have a bearing. Questions concerning relative size between Japan and Buganda could themselves explain both why Buganda was conquered faster by the values of the West than Japan and why she could make less impressive use of western techniques than Japan. In terms of value assimilation small size facilitates the process of assimilation, giving the whole operation the rapidity of diffusion which a small area and population can afford. But a successful adoption of techniques in such massive areas as industrialization and economic reorganization requires a greater scale of operation. Japan had a bigger base on which to build a modernized economy, and more impressive resources to mobilize for the endeavour. Size might therefore be important in explaining both the rapid value-assimilation in Buganda and the less impressive technical assimilation as contrasted with the Japanese experience.

The difference in colonial control was also relevant. The direction of change in Buganda was far less in the hands of the Ganda than the direction of change was in the hands of the Japanese in Japan. The Japanese educational system did remain elitist, but social commitment and patriotic obligation survived the modernization of the educational system. Indeed, patriotic obligations in Japan were even deepened by modernization. But the precise modes of the economic response by the Ganda had to be related to the high dictates of policy of the imperial power. The range of activities engaged in by the populace had also to be subject to broader aims of British overrule.

But this latter brings us back to the techno-cultural lag. The Japanese were in a position to transform the educational system themselves, and to choose the relevant forms of indoctrination to accompany the transmission of the new skills. They were in a position to innovate educationally, and experiment with new forms of technical and vocational training. They were spared too painful a clash between the pursuit of modernity and the pursuit of piety. Even after independence, Buganda cannot have quite the flexibility and educational choice enjoyed by Japan. After all, Buganda is part of a country, rather than a country by itself.

But independence has opened up new opportunities for re-appraising the educational system of Uganda as a whole. Yet in that very reappraisal we have come full circle. Some of the questions which independent Uganda has to ask herself are exactly the same questions which colonial policy-makers asked for Uganda at the beginning of the century. The ultimate differences may not lie in the questions asked but in the answers given.

Towards Closing the Techno-cultural Gap

It is quite clear then that dissatisfaction over the inadequacy of modern education in the country has tended to bear in two opposing directions at once. On the one hand westernization is being sought, virtually without limits, in the area of techniques and technology. On the other, there is opposition to certain aspects of the western way of life, a way of life which, however, may well be crucial in the successful application of western technical and technological skills. One old question for the educator to answer anew is this: to what extent is it possible to import western technical and technological skills without at the same time importing also such aspects of the western way of life as are relevant and necessary for the use of such skills? Furthermore, to what extent might such skills, devoid of their relevant western cultural accompaniments, succeed in the African cultural context? Can there be a return to traditional African values without sacrificing any possibility of a scientific or technological revolution?

The sentiment to return to and promote African traditional values is itself natural enough. It is born out of pride in what is one's own; fortified by nostalgic memories of a past in which there was much more harmony than now prevails. For traditional African societies succeeded admirably in being able to teach skills which were compatible with their own sacred values. It is this harmonious relationship between the two arms of education which is now largely lost.

The voice of an eighteenth-century French thinker sometimes seems to taunt contemporary Africa:

> We see, on every side, huge institutions, where our youth are educated at great expense, and instructed in everything but their duty. Your children will be ignorant of their own language, when they can talk others which are not spoken anywhere. They will be able to compose verses which they can hardly understand; and, without being capable of distinguishing truth from error, they will possess the art of making them unrecognisable by specious arguments. But magnanimity, equity, temperance, humanity, and courage will be words of which they know not the meaning. The dear name of the country will never strike their ears; and if they ever hear of God, it will be less to fear than to be frightened of him.[17]

Rousseau went on to insist that education should teach the young 'what they are to practise when they come to be men;'[18] thereby anticipating what has become an important feature of today's world: the emergence of *relevance* as a moral imperative, a supposed lack of which, in African education, has quickly assumed the proportion of a crisis. Modern education in Africa has been charged, again and again, with being irrelevant to African conditions and incapable of preparing the young for 'what they are to practise when they come to be men.' In

Africa it is generally agreed that the educational system leaves much to be desired in what ought to be its cardinal aim: to impart technical skills in a relationship of harmony with socially committed values. *The answer may lie in the dual strategy of Africanizing humanistic studies, on the one hand, and increasing technical and vocational training on the other.*

Acculturation in technical skills itself has two dimensions. For society as a whole, government has for a long time been concerned about the fact that very few indigenous technicians are being produced by the educational system. This concern is, in the final analysis, the specific manifestation of something bigger, of the urge and the imperative for rapid development. A commentator has pointed out in this connexion:

> As the East African countries have attained independence one after another, they have dedicated themselves to the struggle against the triumvirate evils of 'poverty, ignorance and disease'. Each country has charted ambitious schemes of economic development to implement this fight. But another way of looking at East Africa's problems is to regard them as different facets of the same evil of scientific under-development with which emergent countries are faced. [19]

A scientific-technological revolution is one strategy for winning the struggle; but the educational system has done little to bring this revolution about.

The other aspect of acculturation in technical skills concerns, not economic development as such, but the idea of individual self-reliance. The days when government took it upon itself to *give* jobs to all of its educated and skilled citizens are now about over. Increasingly individuals will have to become privately employed. They are unlikely to succeed in this without basic training in technical skills or training in modern economic operations. Perhaps this is what one parliamentarian was arguing, soon after independence:

> The whole thing boils down to this simple fact that our educational system should aim at providing the country with productive labour and we have to accelerate the growth of local co-operation between businessmen and the schools . . . I am completely convinced that most of our employment problems are going to be solved if we have technical education. [20]

This acculturation in technical skills for self-reliance is going to become more relevant as the active population continues to outstrip job opportunities which is reflected, above all, in the 'school leavers' who fail to get jobs or who get jobs for which they are overqualified.

But in addition to expanding vocational training, a major thrust should be undertaken towards Africanizing more systematically the academic and humanistic side of the African curricula. This latter endeavour might need to be accompanied by more research into traditional modes of African education and how these handled the relationship between values and skills. Too much harmony between values and skills may conceivably be dysfunctional. Was that one reason why Africa lagged behind technologically for so long?

At this stage we can only guess. But we do have some factual clues already. Technological and material advancements did occur in traditional Africa, but under the apparently firm control of social values, these in turn being derivatives of religious norms. Innovations in technical skills were not often allowed to stand in opposition to, or attempt to improve on, the existing way of life.

This can only mean two things. Innovations in traditional Africa were mostly improvements rather than transformations. People tried new methods of doing the same thing better; rather than of doing new things. Secondly, qualitative change was imperceptibly slow. This means that the sociology of technical skills was conservative rather than revolutionary. It was also a part of life in the sense that everyone was taught virtually the same skills as everyone else. The question of preparing other means of advancement over one's fellow men thus did not arise. The road to fame did not lie in specialization; it was through being able to do better than most *all* the things an average man was expected to perform. This always had two components: the successful doing of things, impinging on technical skills, one's resourcefulness and determination, and correct behaviour, having to do with society's sacred values. All of these aspects of socialization occurred in the context of one's family; and they occurred together. But, even more important, to be 'in the process of being educated' and to be living a life were inseparable.

It is not easy to think of any activity in the old societies where the mind was being exercised while the body was lax — unless it be a man lying in his bed at night worrying about something; or old men whose times were now past smoking and deliberating under a tree. Life generally was at once active, fun and creative. One did not first prepare for life and then — when the time came — live it. One lived from birth to grave. Turnbull is correct when he says:

> The young child in any African society is treated with a great deal of love and care, and for his first few years . . . he has an easy life, full of pleasure and fun. If he misbehaves in any way, he is nearly always excused since, being a child, he does not know any better. . . . Once they can walk, or even crawl, they are left much more on their own till real education starts around the age of seven. Older brothers and sisters and grandparents, keep a watchful eye on them, and sometimes join their games.

He goes on to say of Pygmies in particular (but we may take it as illustrative for African societies generally) that:

Almost everything a young child does is teaching him about adult life, or preparing him in other ways. Some games, such as gymnastics on vine swings, develop muscles and good sense of balance. Games like this are particularly popular among the Congo Pygmies, where the men are continually climbing trees and need to be strong and alert and able to jump about without losing balance. All these games, then, are education for the children, though the children think of them as sheer fun.[21]

Here then we have an example of the kind of education that is three things at once. First, it is relevant to the society in which the child will spend his entire life. Second, it is fun, not agony. Finally, the child does not postpone the process of life till later when he is grown up. He is living fully now and enjoying it. This is in marked contrast to our modern education where learning is work and often dull work at that; where life is suspended till final arrival; and where what is taught is often just barely relevant to the society in which the school is situated. African education was characterized by those three things and it was far more successful than modern education in accomplishing what modern education has failed to do in Africa: the production of a fully integrated personality who lives as part of a relatively moral society; a society that lives fully *now*, not one that constantly prepares for salvation in the future. We therefore have much to learn from the past. They were able to impart knowledge and techniques—be it in hunting, fighting, digging or art (for boys), or cooking, baby-caring, household management, etc. (for girls)—at the same time as they built into these youngsters character, respect for labour, and a sense of full life.

What emerges so clearly from the experience of the past is the importance of sacred values as the umbrella under which all other things, including training in technical skills, ought to occur. It is the question of what these values ought to be, more than anything else, that is troubling African educators today. Literary education triumphed, riding upon an undercurrent of materialism. The next phase of African education may well see technical education succeeding for the same reason. This would simply not be acceptable.

On Africa's eastern seaboard Tanzania's Julius Nyerere has consistently addressed himself to just this problem. Nyerere has fallen back on African traditional values themselves as a guide for modern Tanzanian society. He sees such principles as 'love', 'sharing and hard work', 'freedom within unity', 'rights combined with obligation' as values which should guide the new society. They must remain the sacred values for modern Tanzania.

If these principles are to be preserved and adopted to serve the larger societies which have now grown up, the whole of the new modern educational system must also be directed towards inculcating them. They must underlie all the things taught in the schools, all the things broadcast on radio, all the things written in the press. And if they are to form the basis on which society operates, then *no advocacy of opposition to these principles can be allowed.* [Italics added]. [22]

Uganda, too, has been fully aware of the need to solve the question of sacred values. Edward Rugumayo, when he was Minister of Education, was one of those who have been seriously grappling with the question of the proper values which schools should inculcate into the young. In a speech at King's College, Budo, in Uganda in June 1972 he said:

> The big question is: What components of character should we educate for as teachers and parents? Our guide is usually based on what we as individuals regard as important. Some of us regard proper table manners, others type of dress, other manner of speech, others what kind of religion, as being important indicators of a person's character. [23]

The minister went on to list the following desirable qualities with which few would disagree. The positive educational qualities which he regarded as being of paramount importance which should form part of the character of our youth and citizens, he said, were:

> An independent mind capable of judging and analysing problems objectively; the ability to live in a collective society with the major aim of serving it; one's loyalty to his motherland in a patriotic and nationalist way; hard work, industry and scholarship; a democratic spirit in conducting day to day affairs with one's friends and work-mates, and the ability to see and emphasize the strong qualities in individuals under our charge or in charge of us. [24]

In his opinion the start for all these things 'must be made in schools. The teachers and the parents are all responsible for the overall character training of their children.' [25]

It is our contention, in slight disagreement with the minister, that parents, more than teachers, are going to be the ones to bring about the new Africa — if they really try. Schools can indeed train for democracy by emphasizing the school council system. They can train for objective decision-making by imparting to students a wide knowledge of things and phenomena and the techniques of their analysis. They might even make an attempt towards making work dignified. But they would not have touched on the root cause of the problem of today. First, they would not have tackled the crucial question of the kind of attitude which looks on life as divided into two parts: a hard, unpleasant, dull and painful earlier period when one must tolerate everything; followed by a soft, enjoyable, leisurely period after one has arrived.

Secondly, those who have 'arrived' often display an unrestrained spirit of acquisitiveness precisely because they think that, having now arrived, they are entitled to get more for their sons and daughters who are in turn seen as investments which must later realize profits in material terms. This situation will continue. It will stop only when African societies have closed effectively the techno-cultural lag inherited from colonialism, and created instead a healthy balance between education as a process of socialization and education as a process of releasing the individual.

Expanding technical training and accelerated indigenization of the content of education may prove indispensable if Africa is to find a harmony between values and techniques as she undergoes the agonies of developmental transformation. We shall return to some of these issues as we look more closely at the interaction between education, society and politics in subsequent chapters.

References and Notes

1. See G. Duncan Mitchell, *A Dictionary of Sociology*, Routledge & Kegan Paul, 1968.
2. Introduction to *The Norton Anthology of English Literature*, Vol. 2, W. W. Norton, New York, 1962, p. 643.
3. Tom Watson, 'History of Christian Missionary Society High Schools in Uganda, 1900-1925: the Education of a Protestant Elite', unpublished PhD thesis, Department of History, Makerere University, Kampala, 1962.
4. Ali A. Mazrui, 'Moral puritanism under a military theocracy: the sacred origins of Uganda's Second Republic', Lecture delivered at Makerere Main Hall, 20 July 1972, mimeo.
5. Watson, op. cit.
6. A. L. Kitching, *On the Black Waters of the Nile*, T. Fisher Unwin, 1912, p. 276, cited in Watson, op. cit.
7. *Uganda Notes* (May 1919), 55. Cited in Watson, op. cit.
8. Okot p'Bitek, *Religion of the Central Luo*, East African Literature Bureau, 1971, pp. 49-50.
9. For a full discussion of these see Ali A. Mazrui, 'Public opinion and the politics of family planning', *Rural Africana* (Michigan) (Spring 1971), 38-44
10. John Roscoe, *The Baganda: an Account of their Native Customs and Beliefs*, Macmillan, 1911, p. 246; F. Cass, 1965.
11. P. M. Lwanga, *Obulamu Bw'Omutaka, J. K. Miti, Kabazzi* (Life of the Clan Head, J. K. Miti, Kabazzi), Kampala, 1954, p. 3. Cited by Watson, op. cit.
12. Johnston to Jackson, 24 January 1900. In Watson, op. cit.
13. Ibid.
14. Ibid.
15. Lloyd A. Fallers, 'Ideology and culture in Uganda nationalism', *American Anthropologist*, **63** (1961), 677-86.
16. Ibid.
17. Jean-Jacques Rousseau, 'A discourse on the arts and sciences', in *Rousseau: the Social Contract and Other Discourses*, translated with an introduction by G. D. H. Cole, revised and augmented by J. H. Brumfitt and John C. Hall, Everyman's Library, Dent, 1955, pp. 136-7.
18. Ibid., p. 137.
19. Professor W. B. Banage, 'East Africa's scientific revolution', *East Africa Journal* (July 1964), 7.
20. Uganda, *Parliamentary Debates*, 21 November 1962, p. 563.

21. Colin M. Turnbull, *Tradition and Change in African Tribal Life*, World Publishing Company, New York, 1966, pp. 60-2.
22. Julius K. Nyerere, *Freedom and Unity: a Selection from Writings and Speeches, 1952-1965*, Oxford University Press, 1966, p. 14.
23. The Hon. E. B. Rugamayo, Minister of Education: 'Education for character training', *Mawazo*, 3, 3 (June 1972), 11. (From a text of a speech given at King's College, Budo, 21 June 1972.)
24. Ibid.
25. Ibid.

2 Education and the Quest for Sovereignty

While education in the African colonies was indeed often intended to save souls and consolidate colonial control, it was later called upon to serve a paradoxical additional role—preparation for African sovereignty. In this chapter we turn to this dialectic between colonial education and the pursuit of ultimate African sovereignty.

In the last chapter we focused especially on Uganda, partly because Uganda offers a particularly revealing illustration of the interplay between cultural, political and religious variables in an African society. On the sectarian front, Uganda has sometimes been called 'the Ireland of Africa', with all the tensions between religion and politics. On the cultural front, we referred to the description of the Ganda as 'the Japanese of Africa'. These are comparative epithets which emphasize the unique combination of social processes in the Ugandan situation, partly initiated by the contact between Christian missionaries and the African peoples.

In the earlier parts of this chapter we again focus on a single country to illustrate wider themes, but our choice this time is Zaire. We shall later look at the broader problem of cultural sovereignty with a wider African focus. On the issue of whether education is indispensable for effective political self-government, Zaire on attainment of independence was again a particularly illuminating example. The armed forces mutinied almost as soon as the Belgians departed from the country in 1960, and the country was soon faced with a variety of political crises, from Katanga's secession to armed anarchy elsewhere. Ethnic tensions took an ugly turn, Belgian paratroopers intervened, the major powers faced the risk of a new conflict similar to the war in Korea, and the United Nations was then compelled to raise its own forces for the pacification of what was then the Congo. Were the Congolese not yet ready for independence? And how was their standard of education related to the question of capacity for self-government? These are the issues discussed in this chapter. We shall focus on that moment of Zaire's independence in 1960, but we shall use the name under which the country was then known, the Republic of the Congo (Leopoldville).

Towards Alternatives to Colonial Tutelage

As political consciousness spread in colonial Africa, and the legitimacy of colonialism itself was increasingly in question all over the world. The case for continued colonial rule in turn increasingly came to rest on the concept of 'preparing' the dependent peoples for the 'responsibilities of self-rule'. And the central element in this preparation was considered to be education. As the Director-general of UNESCO once put it in a speech on a United Nations' Day, 'Amongst all the factors of independence, responsibility, progress, stability, education in the widest sense of the word occupies a central place.'[1] That being the case, one could take education as a case study of the implications of legitimizing colonial rule in terms of what the colonial power did to prepare the colonial peoples for self-rule. And perhaps there is no better point of departure for an analysis of those implications than the historic Afro-Asian resolution before the United Nations General Assembly in November 1960 which, in urging a 'speedy' end to colonialism, was careful to add that 'inadequacy of political, economic, social and cultural preparedness' should not serve as a pretext for delaying independence.

At the time it was stipulated, this provision received considerable criticism from some sections of opinion. The *New York Times*, for example, found it 'dubious' in view of the Congo experience on her independence.[2] The Catholic journal, *America*, put the objection in clearer terms when it observed, 'The whole world knows the tragedy that overtook the Congo. . . . The Congolese people were not "politically, economically, socially and culturally" prepared to assume the responsibilities of self-rule.'[3]

One assumption behind this kind of argument was that colonial rule accomplished this preparation at a faster rate than what might be achieved by the territory itself without colonial tutelage. This was not always true with regard to that aspect of preparation directly related to building schools and colleges and raising the standards of literacy of the country as a whole. Colonial Kenya was one case in point. In 1945 Jomo Kenyatta, then Kenya's nationalist 'agitator', complained:

> Although the Africans pay so much in taxes, the education of their children is poor. . . . The Government spends eight shillings per head on the education of African children while it spends £49,255 for the education of less than 2,000 European children.[4]

Nearly fifteen years later Kenyatta's young successor, as the most prominent leading African nationalist of Kenya, Tom Mboya, could observe to his American hosts at the time:

> Often my questioners [in the United States] assumed that the colonial powers were primarily concerned with the education of our people and that there were deliberate training programs looking forward to the day of independence. . . . In Kenya the per capita

expenditure on the education of a European child amounts to £35 a year while that for an African child is £5.[5]

The conclusion which Mboya drew from this and other factors was that—from the point of view of the Africans themselves—colonial rule, far from being an argument for rapid educational development, was indeed an agent of retardation. He cited the example of Ghana in these terms:

> When the All-African Cabinet took over the government, about 20% of the country's children were in school. In five years this government has raised the figure to 85% and continues to open a new school every other day.[6]

We know that, in spite of the almost complete initial collapse of educational development in Zaire on independence, the country was soon to make greater progress in this field than it had done under continued Belgian rule. In almost every case on the continent an independent African government has invested more in education than did its colonial predecessor.

In addition independence tends usually to diversify a country's educational benefactors. This is borne out by developments in bilateral cultural relations between Africa and the major powers, and illustrated also by the activities of the United Nations agencies, with particular reference to UNESCO. The rapid emergence of African countries into independence introduced a sense of urgency and a determination to meet the problem of educational deficiency quickly and effectively. Towards the end of 1960, the year when seventeen states became independent, the Director-general of UNESCO described the problem of education as 'far and away the biggest single task facing UNESCO.'[7] And he drew particular attention to tropical Africa as an area which bore 'its own distinguishing features'—among which he cited first of all its 'sense of great urgency due to the rapid emergence of so many countries into independence'.[8] The result is that UNESCO's new budget from that year on gave priority to this area. It started by allocating to newly independent Congo (Zaire) the largest single amount ever devoted in a single year to a single country.[9]

What all this meant at the time to the people of the colonial territories was that the choice did not need to be '*either* you accept colonial tutelage *or* your educational progress will be retarded.' Partly because of the priorities of African governments and of the implications of cultural diplomacy by the great powers, and partly because of a growing international sensitivity to educational needs everywhere on the globe, the end of colonial rule could widen, rather than narrow, the sources of assistance for needy areas. Because there was no longer a single power to be accounted responsible for its dependencies, other powers—for a variety of reasons—helped to fill the gap in support of the efforts of the African government. External help ranged from providing dozens of teachers and volunteers to scholarships for African students.

It was significant that the United States government, for example, offered the Republic of the Congo three hundred scholarships as what was described as an 'independence present'.[10] And to underline the significance of this, one American observer asked the following questions:

> Why was the offer not made a year and a half ago, when Belgium announced its intention to grant eventual independence to the Congo? What are we doing today to provide educational opportunities for those African countries remaining under colonial rule in which college graduates are as scarce — i.e., virtually nonexistent — as in the Congo?[11]

The American journal which made this observation, *Africa Today*, went on to note that the 'standard answer' to these questions was that the United States could not grant scholarships 'to governments unwilling to accept them' — meaning, at the time, the colonial governments. However, the journal felt that greater effort should be made to persuade colonial governments to take this issue more seriously in the remaining colonies. And then, as if to emphasize the cold war implications of all this, *Africa Today* not only suggested the alternative of giving scholarships to students who had escaped from the colonial areas but apparently sought to make this suggestion more persuasive by drawing attention to the fact that 'There is no dearth of such students in the Universities of Eastern Europe.'[12]

To African nationalists it was becoming increasingly clear that by pressing for independence a territory need not be biting off the hand which educationally feeds it. Indeed, by its acquisition of sovereignty, the needy territory might well stand to widen its choice of sources of help. Further, the United Nations and the major powers, quite apart from the traditional humitarian concern of such specialized agencies as UNESCO, were learning fast that unstable governments in isolated areas of the world could be a threat to general stability in the region as a whole. The world organization was therefore seeking with greater vigour than ever to mitigate instability by rapid assistance in education and training. As Secretary-general Dag Hammarskjöld indicated in his last annual report before his death, there is a growing recognition that education and training 'hold the key not only to the material welfare of the newly independent countries but also to the very stability of the new states.'[13]

Arising from this recognition of the urgent issues involved, the United Nations, among other things, began to feel the need for co-ordinating its efforts. For example, UNESCO's action in Tropical Africa was partially integrated into a *general* action involving some co-ordination of the United Nations' specialized agencies in this field. And while the Security Council was discussing the problem of getting

Belgian troops out of the Congo in July 1960, and UNESCO was discussing the problem of replacing the missing Belgian teachers in that country, the Economic and Social Council was seeking ways and means for linking together into some sort of coherence the 'opportunities for international co-operation on behalf of newly independent countries.'[14]

The question which began to arise was whether, given this considerable dependence on the international community at large, the new states really did achieve meaningful independence when the colonial ruler withdrew. By biting off the imperial hand that had fed them, were they not in danger of substituting the collective strong arm of the international community as a whole?

One factor which may restrain that collective arm is the very fact that its collectivity includes an increasing number of states in a similar predicament of need and just as jealous of their newly won sovereignty. Certainly within the activities of the United Nations, this is a restraining influence of considerable efficacy. As the Director-general of UNESCO once put it:

> There is no question whatever of taking over the responsibilities of these [needy] states but of supporting states engaged in their own effort to mobilize their resources and make their full contribution to international exchanges. The impulse comes from the African governments; the objectives are their own. [15]

It must, however, be remembered that this sort of policy by organs of the United Nations postulates a government sufficiently organized to have fairly coherent objectives. On attainment of independence the Congo lacked this. The result was that, although the Organisation des Nations Unies au Congo (ONUC) did a great deal to assist what civil administration there was, it was considerably handicapped pending the achievement of 'some measure of stability in the Central Government'.[16]

As regards work connected more specifically with UNESCO, fifty-four 'technical assistance experts' were dispatched to this newly independent country to reinforce both the Central and the Provincial Ministries of Education. This was done because it was vital for 'the effectiveness of all other forms of assistance which UNESCO may be called upon to afford the Congo in the sphere of education'.[17] That being the case, it was at best a dubious claim that those 'technical assistance experts' were there just to respond to the Congo's own 'impulse' and to objectives formulated by the Congolese Government itself. It seemed more likely it was the experts who provided the impulse. At any rate, in the *formulation* of Congolese objectives, the United Nations' organs played a substantial role. Part of the problem was indeed a dearth of educated expertise at the local level.

Nevertheless, the mere fact that efforts were made to draw the

Congolese themselves into the formulation of those objectives was an improvement over the colonial era. Throughout Africa dependence on others there may still remain, but the difference in kind is important. Instead of being gradually 'prepared' for a sovereign status yet to be attained, African countries are now rapidly assisted to consolidate at least some aspects of a sovereign status already being realized. One may not go the whole way with the opinion of UNESCO's Director-general at the time that 'the interests of the international community here coincide with the most urgent national aspirations'.[18] Certainly in the Congo this coincidence was not easy to discern with any clarity. There was considerable obscurity and a confusion of flux and conflict as to what constituted the 'urgent national aspirations' of the Congolese. Nevertheless, it is safe to say that for the sake of mitigating tensions in the world at large, if not for specifically Congolese interests, it had become a matter of international concern that the Congolese be given urgent 'international assistance to help them in their endeavours to reap the benefits and assume the responsibilities of independence'.[19] And as it has been noted that 'amongst all the factors of independence, responsibility, progress, stability, education in the widest sense of the word occupies a central place'[20] it was in that field that priority was given in the *long-term* assistance to that new state.

Colonial Education and the Problem of Relevance

But why was the need so great in the Congo? Was this central factor of 'responsibility, progress, stability' entirely ignored in Belgian colonial policy in that country? What had made it possible to speculate that, in spite of all the chaos of that first year of independence, the Congolese could emerge better educated in a shorter time than they might have done under continued Belgian rule?

One popular answer sometimes given soon after the disaster overtook the Congo was that the Belgians, unlike the British, did not pay enough attention to the education of their dependent peoples. This may be true, but it raises the further question as to what constitutes 'enough' attention to education. After all, education by the missionaries in the Congo went back more than half a century. This was a significant time-span in the colonial history of Africa. By 1906 the educational arrangements of the Congo were, in fact, put on an official basis under the Concordat between Leopold II and the Vatican.[21]It is true that the colonial government itself did not start schools of its own until 1954 when it was felt that such schools — apart from educating more Congolese — could serve as models to which the private schools might approximate and thus help to bring about 'an improvement in the general quality of education for the Africans'. [22] Nevertheless, the missions had accomplished a good deal by that date — with some help from schools operated by the big commercial and industrial companies and mining corporations.

By 1957 it could be estimated that there were approximately 30 000 schools in the Belgian Congo and Ruanda Urundi — with more than 1 645 000 students in primary and pre-primary schools and more than 50 000 in post-primary schools of one kind or another.[23] The number of children receiving some kind of formal education would appear to have been between one-third and two-fifths of the total number of school-age children in the country. As one observer put it,

> At the rate at which schools were then being provided and teachers being produced, almost the entire school-age population, girl and boy alike, were expected either to be in primary school or to have had some such schooling by the early 1960's. Post-primary facilities were expected to be available then for those living in more accessible areas and capable of profiting by them.[24]

By January 1960 — six months before independence — there seemed to be enough grounds for at least hazarding the claim that the rate of literacy in the Congo was 'the highest in sub-Saharan Africa'.[25]

What then made the Congo, following independence, in the eyes of so many a people not 'politically, economically, socially or culturally' prepared to assume self-rule? One answer is, of course, that literacy can be a necessary condition for capacity for self-rule without being a sufficient condition. And if the Congo had fared worse than other areas of Africa less literate than the Congo, the reason might well have been that the other constituent variables of such capacity were more lacking in the Congo than elsewhere. To pursue these other variables in detail would carry us beyond the scope of this chapter. What could be done here is to glance at what correlation there is between education and some of these other variables.

It may be significant that after spending considerable time on the wording of their historic 1960 resolution calling for a 'speedy' end to colonialism, the Afro-Asian sponsors of the resolution did not include 'educational' in their series of epithets qualifying preparedness for self-government. They spoke of 'political, economic, social or cultural preparedness' but made no mention of the argument that a territory may not be prepared *educationally*. It is possible that the notion of being sufficiently educated to assume self-rule is implied in the very concept of 'preparedness' — and if the preparedness is for economic functions, it would be understood that a sort of *economic* education is the very basis of that preparedness. This then would seem to shift the criterion of evaluating Belgian rule in the Congo from the issue of how *much* education it brought about to the issue of what *type* of education accrued from that rule.

This aspect of the problem does not seem to have been sufficiently considered by critics of that provision of the Afro-Asian resolution which insisted that 'preparedness' for self-rule was not to be used as a pretext for delaying independence for the remaining colonial territories. And yet it was a vital element in any attempt to evaluate the degree to which a prolonged colonial rule was 'legitimate' from this point of view. The person who argued that self-government should not be granted until literacy in a colonial territory was achieved not only started from the hypothesis that colonial rule sought to bring literacy about, but probably also from the postulate that the *kind* of literacy emphasized by the colonial regime constituted preparation for the problems which a native government in a given area would be called upon to deal with on attainment of self-rule.

And yet, could this new postulate really be taken for granted? In a passage which brings home the absurdity of some of the educational policies which were followed in the colonies at one stage or another, Sir Ivor Jennings once drew attention to the time when the Ceylon system of education under British rule was determined by syllabuses drafted in London for the benefit of English students. He said he had no doubt that in 'English Literature' the following colloquy was common:

Teacher: 'O daffodil we weep to see you fade away so soon.'
Pupil: What is a daffodil?
Teacher: Just an English flower, but the examiners will not ask questions on that. Take this note: The imagery in this poem . . . [26]

Sir Ivor went on to observe that this sort of thing was extended even to mathematics. The pupil was not asked to work out the profit on a transaction in copra at so many rupees a candy, but the profit on a transaction in cotton at so many pence a pound. As for history, it was

of course, English history, and Ethelred the Unready was more important than Panakrama Bahu the Great. The student knew all about the English coalfields and had not the least notion where plumbago was found in Ceylon, still less why. [27]

Sir Ivor himself saw as one consequence of this the fact that English education consisted in 'acquiring irrelevant knowledge'. [28] And perhaps the irrelevance he refers to can be applied at least as much to the problems of self-rule as to anything else.

In this respect, a curious phenomenon was that the missions in Central Africa as a whole tended to be more awake to the need for directing education towards relevant *worldly* needs than were colonial governments. As long ago as 1933 a Commission of Inquiry was set up by the Department of Social and Industrial Research of the International Missionary Council, and its terms of reference at the narrowest were the 'effects of the coppermines of Central Africa upon Native Society and the work of the Christian Missions'. Among the Commission's recommendations was that 'educational emphasis of Missions should be directed towards preparing Bantu youth to serve the needs of Bantu rather than European society'. To this end the Commission recommended that

> the mission societies of the Territory study together the goal towards which their education is directed, define its purpose and visualize the results which they are aiming to achieve. If such study is to be of ultimate value the co-operation of the Government must be secure.[29]

No less significant, but easier to overlook as an important factor, were the Commission's recommendations that for the sake of rural stabilization 'the syllabuses for the mission schools should be drawn to dignify farming as a vocation'.[30]

At least in some of the colonies the missionaries did attempt to narrow the techno-cultural gap. Certainly, the importance of dignifying a vocation was not to be underestimated. In the British territories neighbouring the Congo, for example, it had proved difficult to attract young people to be trained as artisans — and when they were so trained, it had often proved almost as difficult to persuade them to *work* as artisans. The author was himself involved in the public relations section of a new technical institute in Mombasa, Kenya, in the late 1940s and early 1950s, and knows from experience the difficulties involved in trying to project at that time the work of, say, a motor mechanic as an adequately dignified job in the teeth of a prejudice strongly in favour of white collar work — which, in this instance, often meant working as a clerk.

Kai von Hassel when he was premier of the Government of Schleswig-Holstein (he was himself born in East Africa) once put the problem in these terms: 'A mere vocational training is not enough; it has to be supplemented by truly educational efforts designed to develop a sense of occupational dignity and pride.'[31] Von Hassel confessed that when he lived in Africa he had himself been 'sceptical to a certain degree towards the Christian missionaries'. But on a closer comparison with the results of the government schools in the continent as a whole, he had had second thoughts about mission schools: 'They seem to be better able to form independent artisans who want to be artisans. They give their pupils not only occupational training but also ethical values and professional standards.'[32]

If that is the case (and the evidence is contradictory), then we have here an instance of another correlation — this one being between the type and prestige of the education given, on the one hand, and the agencies for education, on the other. And since, as Lord Hailey put it, the Belgian Government relied 'to a greater extent than either the British or the French Governments upon the work of religious bodies as agencies of education',[33] there may well be a connexion between this and such pre-independence observations about the Congo as the following:

the encouragement given in the Congo to African skilled workers is turning an African proletariat into a lower middle class . . . [The gulf between 'trade' and 'profession'] will inevitably narrow; meanwhile, given the opportunity to develop their skill and intelligence, the Africans of the Congo show none of that surly discontent that is becoming so marked a feature of cities such as Johannesburg and Nairobi. [34]

However, even if the original impetus behind the vocational ends of education in the Congo was to be attributed to the initiative of the missions, it must be remembered that this was to become the official policy of Belgium as a colonial power. The emphasis came to be solidly on vocational training and for improving the material well-being of the Congolese. The rationale was that the 'pursuit of moral and social well-being is closely linked with the development of material well-being, the one being the mainstay of the other'. [35]

Here again then, it would seem, the Belgians exhibited greater realism than the other colonial powers with whom they were later to be unfavourably contrasted. There was little in the Congo of that British emphasis on Wordsworth and his 'dancing daffodils'. In theory, of course, even the British policy emphasized that 'the educational program should be designed for the majority and should follow a course which would give due consideration to the cultural peculiarities of the various regions'. [36] But in practice it was more the Belgians than the British who tried to live up to this and seemed pledged to the policy of seeking to produce 'better Africans, and not copies of Europeans who could never be more than humans of a third category'. [37]

Of course, it is possible to interpret all this as no more than an attempt to rationalize something undertaken for other considerations. It is, for example, arguable that Belgian policy merely amounted to a recognition that it *paid* to have workers who were not afflicted by any of that 'surly discontent that was becoming so marked a feature of cities like Johannesburg and Nairobi'. Whatever the motivation behind Belgian policy, however, there was no denying the practical results. As Negley Farson put it twenty years before Zaire's independence:

> This implacable determination on the part of Brussels that the Congo native must progress in spite of himself is tinctured with a practicalness that leads to cynicism and not infrequent acts of petty brutality. But under it you find the astonishing growth of a native middle class, composed of clerks, railway employees, locomotive drivers, native chauffeurs driving the big motor lorries of the Vici-Congo transports into all parts of the Congo, and an amazing number of first class mechanics. [38]

Such seemed to be the result of purposeful vocational training. What must not be overlooked is that it was in turn the *cause* of the further spread of such training to other sections of the populace. It has been well observed that in peasant agricultural countries, literacy begins to diffuse when a society starts to change in its occupational structure, and parents find a strong incentive to send their children to school or arrange somehow that children acquire some of the new skills. Since urban-industrial occupations often require some reading and writing, education begins to be regarded as a passport that leads the individual 'from the hard and primitive life of the subsistence farmer to the haven of non-agricultural employment'.[39]

This, however, is not to be taken to mean that Belgian policy in the Congo was of the type that led to a heavy concentration in wage employment and a correspondingly small percentage in the category of small producers of cash crops—as in areas such as, say, Southern Rhodesia or the Union of South Africa. In fact, James S. Coleman, for one, sees the uniqueness of the Congo in this connexion in the following terms:

> As in the white oligarchic states there has been a heavy recruitment into wage employment, but unlike those societies the Congolese Government [before independence] has played an active role in fostering the development of the indigenous agricultural economy and in ensuring a wider distribution of the benefits of commercialization and industrialization.[40]

Mass Literacy versus Elite Formation

What then was wrong with Belgian educational policy considering it had this kind of relationship with the other variables which together might constitute capacity to run a modern state?

On the criterion of how much education the Belgians provided for the Congo, it would seem that it compared more than just favourably with what, say, the British achieved. On the criterion of what *type* of education—with all the relevance to practical needs on which Sir Ivor Jennings seemed, in the passage quoted, to be insisting—the Belgians also emerge triumphant in this analysis so far. What, then, were the grounds on which rested the case of those who applauded French and British results when they compared these with Belgian?

The answer seems to lie in the fact that there is another sense of 'how *much*' education apart from the sense of the widest possible distribution, just as there is another sense of 'what *type*' of education apart from that of relevance to practical everyday utility. These distinctions in turn amounted to the whole dilemma between mass education and elite-formation.

On the other sense of 'how much' education one could do no better than to juxtapose two observations which were made within months of one another. The first is by Homer Bigart in January 1960—that the rate of literacy in the Congo was 'the highest in sub-Saharan Africa'.[41]

This, it will be remembered, was before the Congo became independent. Some nine months later, Ambassador Dayal of India, working for the United Nations, found it more relevant to the problems of Congolese self-government that there was 'an almost complete lack of trained personnel'. Specifically, Dayal noted that at the time of independence there were 'only seventeen Congolese university graduates, not one doctor, no engineers, professors, architects, etc., and few, if any, qualified lawyers'.[42] The difference between Bigart's observation about the 'high rate of literacy' and Dayal's comment on 'only' seventeen university graduates constitutes the difference between the two senses of how much education the Belgians left behind in the Congo. In spite of his understandable use of the word 'high' to describe literacy in the Congo, Bigart was, in fact, referring to a *wide* distribution of a *low* level of literacy. In Dayal's assessment, however, the measure of education was tending to be vertical (up to what level of attainment particular individuals reach) rather than horizontal (how widely distributed among the population). Dayal was worried about an elite void at a time of independence.

The link between this other sense of how much education and the other sense of what type of education should be obvious — not least because in education, perhaps more so than in other matters, the distinction between a qualitative criterion and a quantitative one is fine indeed. It is, in fact, so fine that although in this analysis it has so far appeared that the Belgians related their educational policy to the practical needs of the Congolese, it still made sense to Ambassador Dayal to observe in his first report to the secretary-general of the United Nations that under Belgian colonial rule in the Congo 'an elaborate economic structure and a Western society of a high material standard was superimposed on the African inhabitants, with almost no social or economic connection with the life of the average Congolese'.[43] Perhaps Ambassador Dayal, in this instance, was overstating his case. But there was no getting away from his next observation that by September 1960 this 'superstructure' had, 'to a large extent, almost been abandoned'.[44] Nor can one fail to detect an element of irony when a publication of the United Nations could sum up the speech of a Belgian representative on a United Nations Committee in a single, telling paragraph: 'Belgium pointed out its role in the expansion of the economy of the former Belgian Congo. Among other things, it was pointed out that the Congo had the best transport facilities in Africa'.[45]

This was the complete summation of the Belgian speech by the publication. Clearly building transport facilities and producing semi-skilled artisans is not the all-in-all of attending to the practical needs of a people. It falls short of that because in the very process of providing such answers to a people's needs, other needs were created *as*

a consequence. What was said about France by the French Report of
the Langevin Commission can — with due modifications as to degree
and data — be said about the changes which occurred in the Congo
and the new needs arising from those changes:

> Mechanization, the use of new sources of energy, the development
> of means of transport and communication, the intensification of
> industry, increased production, the participation of large numbers
> of women in economic life for the first time, the extension of
> elementary education — all these factors have brought about a
> marked change in living conditions and in the organization of
> society. In 1880, because of the rate and scope of economic
> progress, elementary education had to be extended to the working
> classes. Now, for the same reason, we are faced with the problem of
> recruiting more and more trained staff and technicians.[46]

The conclusion which the French Commission drew from these new
demands of modern economic life was that the educational system
needed complete remodelling — 'since its present form is no longer
suited to economic and social conditions'.

Applied to the Congo by the 1950s on the eve of independence, the
conclusion needed little modification. The need for what the French
Commission called 'more and more trained staff and technicians' was
the need which Dayal linked with his observation about the 'almost
complete lack of trained personnel' in the Congo. So immediate did
the Ambassador consider the need that he felt it had to be filled 'for a
long time to come, by large numbers of technicians from abroad'.[47]

And in this lies the major weakness of Belgian colonial policy in the
Congo. By giving the Congolese vocational training, Belgium may
have raised their standard of living to a higher level than that of
neighbouring Africans. She may have gone quite far in meeting the
material needs of *individual* Congolese. But collectively those
individual Congolese now formed a new society — with a wider span of
necessary leadership roles than that entailed by the less complex
standards of their neighbours. To revert again to a French
observation, Roger Gal, Adviser to the French Ministry of National
Education, may just as well have included the Congo in his generalized
statement that 'society needs social leaders in far greater numbers than
hitherto, as well as more leaders in science and technology'.[48]

It is this side of educational preparation for self-government that
Belgium failed to provide. As the late Premier Lumumba said to a
United Nations Press Conference on 25 July 1960: 'I do recognize . . .
that there was progress in the economic and social fields . . . [But]
everything, absolutely everything, was operated by the officials of
Belgium. Discontent was not slow to come'.[49] Lumumba himself
contrasted this with what had been going on in British and French
dependencies where 'every effort to speed up the political emancipation of the territories' had, in his opinion, been made.[50] In the British

case, one explanation for the contrast may well be that, unlike the Belgians, the British were pledged to eventual political emancipation relatively early in their imperial history in Africa. This factor would not, however, explain the contrast between the French and the Belgians since neither envisaged, when they formulated their respective policies, a very radical separation of their territories from the metropole. However, since what Lumumba described as political emancipation need not mean a separation as radical as independence but could conceivably be realized in what the General Assembly of the United Nations once called 'other separate systems of self-government',[51] perhaps the justification for the contrast between the French and the Belgian results may well be found in different concepts of what would constitute self-government for their territories. Perhaps the same explanation can be added to the other point of contrast already mentioned in regard to the British.

From Educational Policy to Political Experience

The late Tom Mboya of Kenya, on one of his visits to the United States, once referred to some of the most persistent questions he had to face abroad on the eve of Africa's independence:

> Are Africans ready for self-government? I was often reminded [at meetings with Americans] of the lack of adequate numbers of educated personnel to run the new governments which we in Africa have been demanding. I was told that the high illiteracy rate would make it impossible for Africans to operate a democracy successfully.[52]

It is not certain whether Mr Mboya was thinking of the problem in terms similar to our analysis in this chapter. If he was not, then the juxtaposition of the two elements of vertical and horizontal spread of education in this fashion is a happy accident. For the purpose of building up a democracy, it may well be, as Seymour Martin Lipset argues,[53] that widespread literacy is a necessary if not a sufficient condition. And if we accept the rationale put forward in defence of Belgian colonial policy before the Congo's independence became a pressing issue, it would seem that Belgium's horizontal educational preparation was a more logical base for a democracy than the production of a ruling elite inherent in vertical preparation. According to at least one observer nearly a decade ago, Belgium had embarked on a programme 'to lift gradually the status and living standards of the black population until, in the course of time, blacks and whites can be integrated on an equal basis in a common society'.[54]

Having this in mind, it would appear that those who, following the Congo's disaster, unfavourably contrasted Belgian rule with, say, the 'British experience in nation building',[55] were using the word 'nation' in a different sense. This is particularly so if one accepts the observation made by John Plamenatz of Oxford University at that time:

> The loudest enemies of the West [in colonial territories yet to be 'moulded' into nations] are often among the most Westernized, though not always Westernized in the best sense. . . . European withdrawal from a non-European country can lead to misgovernment . . . by the standards of the people living under it, partly no doubt because it does not accord with ancestral folkways still only in the process of dying, but partly also (and perhaps even more) because it belies principles and expectations which the people have acquired from the West.[56]

This consideration should make Belgium's historic role in Africa a more effective approach to nation-building than the British role. This is assuming we concede that bringing up the masses slowly but *evenly* is a sounder way of achieving political integration — and hence a base for democracy — than producing a highly articulate intellectual elite with the rest of the population still engaged in 'ancestral folkways.' In terms of achieving that sense of self-government in which the 'self' is to be interpreted in the Lincolnian sense of 'the people' as a whole governing '*themselves*', it would thus appear that it is to the Belgians that the laurels of logical preparation belong, rather than to the British. In actual fact, neither Belgium nor Britain committed themselves in advance to a mutually exclusive either/or proposition between vertical and horizontal educational preparation. Just as Britain looked forward to achieving widespread literacy before handing over power, Belgium looked forward to producing highly qualified personnel before 'granting political rights'. The difference was one of *initial* emphasis.

In some aspects there was, as it has been intimated earlier, little difference between Belgian and British educational policies in the colonies — in theory both were supposed to be distinguishable from the elite-producing policy of the French. It is, however, clear that in spite of this

> official declaration that British rule aims at a broad educational basis for the masses of the dependencies, it must be stated that the end result thus far has been, like that of the French, the creation of a small educated intelligentsia.[57]

The British were less doctrinaire in their colonial policies anyhow than either the Belgians or the French. British eclecticism therefore inevitably included divergent trends. When the author completed his undergraduate studies in England on a Kenya Government scholarship, and was then recommended by his university for an extension of that scholarship to enable him to do graduate work, the colonial Government of Kenya declined, partly on the grounds that the money which would be spent on enabling the author to proceed to the PhD was needed to produce another BA for the country. Kenya's choice in this instance was conceived as being between producing one Kenyan with the PhD and producing two with the BA.[58]

It is, of course, arguable that at the level of the BA the vertical educational preparation can afford to give way to the horizontal. But when — as it was partly implied in a general sense in Belgian policy — the choice is brought to the level of choosing between two Congolese with primary education and one with secondary, and then between two with secondary education and one with a degree, the soundness of the policy of choosing the two becomes more dubious.

Perhaps it would have worked if Belgium had had the time for preparation initially envisaged for the policy. But, in the words of the late Adlai Stevenson, 'the pressure of nationalism rapidly overtook the preparation for the necessary foundation essential to the peaceful and effective exercise of sovereign self-government'.[59] And when such pressures force a choice between, on the one hand, a highly qualified intelligentsia ready to realize self-government in terms of effectiveness and, on the other hand, an evenly widespread but vertically limited literacy as a prerequisite for realizing self-government in terms of popular participation, it is the former that has a stronger claim to priority. After all, even liberal democratic self-government presupposes a certain degree of effectiveness if there is not to be too much 'self' and not enough 'government'.

On balance then, the British genius for 'muddling through' did for a while yield happer results in former British colonies like Ghana and Nigeria than the 'logic' of the Belgians had done in the Congo. Yet even this was only a temporary advantage. Nigeria ended up with an agonizing civil war; Ghana with chronic economic instability; Uganda, Kenya and Sierra Leone with fluctuating ethnic tensions. Producing an educated elite might still have been a better preparation for political sovereignty than spreading bare literacy among the masses — but clearly more was needed than just an elite.

Perhaps, in the ultimate analysis, the best school for self-government is self-government itself. Preparation for it could never have been completed under colonial conditions. The harsh classroom of sovereign experience itself had to supplement the lessons taught by missionary and colonial institutions.

From Political to Cultural Sovereignty

But educational and other colonial policies had cultural as well as more narrowly political consequences. It may well turn out that the quest for *cultural sovereignty* in Africa after attaining independence will be slower and more drawn-out than the original fight for political independence.

Zaire under General Mobutu Sese-Seko has now added the pursuit of *authenticity* to the nation's concerns. The general abandoned his own Christian name of Joseph in rebellion against the western assumption that no indigenous African name could properly be 'Christian'. President Mobutu then insisted that all indigenous citizens of Zaire should have African instead of Euro-Hebraic names. Passports were recalled and reissued with new indigenous names. The country's name was also changed from the Congo to Zaire in a controversial bid to attain greater authenticity. Western dress and cosmetics were strongly discouraged. A new relationship between the government and the Catholic hierarchy was insisted upon; and educational reforms involving more emphasis on Africa's own cultural heritage were modestly initiated. Zaire's quest for cultural sovereignty was under way.

But clearly this issue is much wider than Zaire and has involved more leaders than just Mobutu. Indeed, three very different African personalities could be grouped together as the vanguard of the African quest for cultural sovereignty – Jomo Kenyatta of Kenya who wrote an early anthropological work in defence of Kikuyu values; Léopold Senghor of Senegal, who wrote poetry in honour of negritude; and Mobutu of Zaire, who initiated reforms in his country in pursuit of African authenticity.

If we adopted Senghor's concept of negritude to apply to the philosophies of all three personalities, it would follow that there were elements of negritudist response to white domination not only among those once ruled by France but also those ruled by Britain and Belgium. An inner longing for cultural sovereignty was restless in the bosoms of all colonized black people, but this longing did not always conquer the simultaneous sense of cultural inadequacy and dependency.

Jomo Kenyatta was a cultural nationalist before he became a nationalist of any other kind. He was preoccupied with the defence of the traditional culture of his people before he became interested in the cause of African political participation as such.

In a sense most nationalists of his generation started by being primarily culture-oriented in their preoccupations. And political parties themselves sometimes grew out of semi-cultural associations. In Nigeria Chief Obafemi Awolowo's party, the Action Group, was to some extent an offspring of a 'pan-Yoruba cultural society', *Egbe Omo Oduduwa* ('society of the descendants of Oduduwa', the culture hero and legendary ancestor of the Yorubas).[60] And the Northern People's Congress, as led by the late Sardauna of Sokoto, 'was simply a Moslem, predominantly Hausa, cultural society – the *Jami'a* – renamed and adapted'.[61]

Yet Jomo Kenyatta was a cultural nationalist in a more profound sense than was normal in much of British Africa at that time. A major reason for this is that Kenyatta was a nationally-conscious member of the Kikuyu tribe at a time when important aspects of Kikuyu culture were under threat. It is partly because of this historical accident that Jomo Kenyatta needs to be placed decisively within the stream of the philosophy of negritude.

As we indicated, it is with French-speaking Africa that the word 'negritude' is normally associated. And it is among French-speaking blacks at large that negritude as a movement has found its *literary* proponents. The term itself was, as we know, virtually coined by Aimé Césaire, the poet of Martinique, as he affirmed:

> My negritude is no tower and no cathedral
> It dives into the red flesh of the soil.[62]

Césaire's poem was first published in a Parisian review in 1939. As we mentioned, in Africa itself the movement's most distinguished literary proponent came to be Léopold Senghor, the poet-President of Senegal. And it has been Senghor who has helped to give shape and definition to negritude as a general philosophical outlook. In his own words:

> Negritude is the whole complex of civilized values — cultural, economic, social and political — which characterize the black peoples or, more precisely, the Negro-African world. All these values are essentially informed by intuitive reason. . . . The sense of communion, the gift of myth-making, the gift of rhythm, such are the essential elements of negritude, which you will find indelibly stamped on all the works and activities of the black man.[63]

Senghor's definition as given here, though illuminating, is not in fact complete. Negritude is not merely a description of the norms of traditional Africa; it is also a capacity to be proud of those values even in the very process of abandoning them. Sometimes it is a determination to prevent too rapid an erosion of the traditional structure.

Whether we take Senghor's own definition, or give it greater precision, it is clear that a believer in negritude need not, of course, be a French-speaking literary figure. 'Negritude is the awareness, defence and development of African cultural values', Senghor has said elsewhere.[64] Such awareness, defence and development need not, of course, take the form of a poem in French. To limit the notion of negritude to a literary movement is to miss what the literary outburst has in common with other forms of cultural revivalism. The name negritude might indeed owe its origin to a literary figure, but the phenomenon which it purports to describe has more diverse manifestations. In any case the term negritude is too useful to be allowed to die with a literary movement. In the post-colonial era, negritude can encompass the whole restless urge for cultural authenticity in Africa.

Not that a romantic literary preoccupation with an idealized Africa is likely to come to an end all that soon. There will be black poems of such a romantic bias for at least another generation. What need to be defined now with a wider vision are the boundaries of the phenomenon as a whole. If negritude is indeed 'the awareness, defence and development of African values', we could usefully divide it into three broad categories. We might distinguish between artistic negritude, anthropological negritude, and political negritude. Senghor is primarily an exponent of the artistic stream, Kenyatta of the anthropological, and Mobutu of the political.

The artistic wing concentrates on defending or enriching the black aesthetic heritage — from dance to poetry, from drama to folktales. Sometimes artistic negritude affects even the study of African history. An African historian who succumbs to literary romanticism in his study of ancient African empires like Songhai and Mali is, in this sense, within the stream of the literary aspect of artistic negritude.

Anthropological negritude is on the whole more directly related to concrete cultural behaviour than literary negritude normally is. In its most literal form anthropological negritude is an empathetic study of an African tribal community by an African ethnologist. The book *Facing Mount Kenya* even on its own would have been enough to make the younger Kenyatta a proponent of anthropological negritude. But our use of 'anthropological negritude' goes beyond the academic discipline of anthropology. There is more to this side of negritude than a formal study of a tribe. As we shall argue later, there is a link between, say, Elijah Masinde, the prophet of *Dini ya Misambwa* in East Africa, and Aimé Césaire, the sophisticated poet of Martinique. At any rate literary negritude and certain African messianic movements are different responses to one interrelated cultural phenomenon. Both the Greco-Roman aspect of European civilization, and the Judeo-Christian side of it, have sometimes forced the African into a position of cultural defensiveness. As we shall show later, these two mystiques have come into Africa wrapped, to some extent, in Europe's cultural arrogance. The Greco-Roman mystique contributed to the birth of literary negritude as a reaction; the Judeo-Christian sense of sacred superiority contributed to the birth of Ethiopianism and African syncretic churches at large. The latter phenomena have intimate links with, or are themselves manifestations of, anthropological negritude.[65]

Jomo Kenyatta's career has, in a sense, been a combination of the religious and the academic aspects of this kind of negritude. The theme of primeval values has been recurrent in the evolution of his thought, ranging from the defence of female circumcision in the 1920s to the events surrounding the Mau Mau insurrection a generation later. The central thesis proposed here concerning Kenyatta is that the controversy over female circumcision in Kikuyuland, coupled with related forms of cultural threat, had psychological repercussions in Kikuyuland similar to those we normally associate with the French assimilationist policy at large. And in no single person was this phenomenon more effectively embodied than in the personality and political career of Jomo Kenyatta.

As for political negritude, we intend this to mean centrally directed policy reforms involving not only cultural festivals but also questions of power. Mobutu's confrontation with the Catholic hierarchy on the limits of the Vatican's power in independent Zaire is a case in point.

We have discussed in the introduction related aspects of Mobutu's version of political negritude. What should be noted here is that although Mobutu is one of the most dramatic exponents of this approach to authenticity, less dramatic experiments in political negritude have been attempted elsewhere. Political negritude could, after all, concern itself with the revival of certain indigenous methods of handling political problems or certain indigenous ideological formulations. To the extent to which Julius Nyerere's *ujamaa* in Tanzania is an attempt to relate modern socialism to traditional African collectivism, his experiments include aspects of political negritude. Those forms of socialism in modern Africa which insist that Marx and Lenin are at best only partly relevant to Africa, and that Africans should seek some of their answers to modern problems from their own cultural heritage, are indeed affected by at least the mood of political negritude.

Behind Mobutu's preoccupation with authentic names and dress, behind Kenyatta's defence of the circumcision rites of the Kikuyu and their ceremonies of oath-taking, even after independence, behind Senghor's philosophy and poetry and his patronage of Negro-African arts, as well as behind Nyerere's insistence on residual ideological authenticity, lies the historic if still incoherent urge of black Africa to move from the political sovereignty of the flag to the cultural sovereignty of the soul.

References and Notes

1. *UNESCO Chronicle* (Paris), **VI**, 12 (1960), 436.
2. Editorial, *New York Times*, 29 November 1960, p. 36.
3. Editorial, *America* (New York), **104**, 12 (1960), 392.
4. *Kenya: Land of Conflict*, International African Service Bureau publication, No. 3, Manchester, England, 1945, p. 5.
5. *New York Times Magazine*, 28 January 1959. Of course, virtually all European schoolchildren go to school whereas only a fraction of African children do so. For a comparison of government expenditure on children *in* school, a UN publication gives for 1957-58, £954 000 on 11 446 European children and £2 292 000 on 609 991 African children. See UN publication 'Reports on non-self-governing territories' (East Africa), No. ST/TRI/B.1959/2, pp. 22-3.
6. *New York Times Magazine*, 28 January 1959.
7. Assessment by the Director-general based on a parallel analytical summary of the reports of member states and of his own reports from 1958-1959. UNESCO Document 11/C9(II), 14 November-13 December 1960, p. 13.
8. Ibid.

9. For an account of the measures taken by UNESCO to meet the collapse of the educational structure in the Congo following independence, see 'UNESCO action in the Congo', *UNESCO Chronicle*, **VI**, 12 (1960), 439-46.
10. Editorial, 'Scholarships and statesmanship', *Africa Today*, **VII**, 5 (1960), 4.
11. Ibid.
12. Editorial, *Africa Today*, **VII**, 5 (1960), 4.
13. Report of the Secretary-general, United Nations, 1960, E/3387, para 7(e).
14. See *UNESCO Chronicle* (Paris), **VI**, 12 (1960), 436.
15. The Director-general of UNESCO said this on the occasion of the United Nations Day, 24 October 1960. See *UNESCO Chronicle* (Paris), ibid.
16. See Ambassador Dayal's First Report on the Congo (covering the period up to 20 September 1960), United Nations, S/453 and Corr. 1, 2. Dayal from India headed the UN investigation.
17. 'UNESCO's action in the Congo', *UNESCO Chronicle* (Paris), **VI**, 12 (1960), 445.
18. *UNESCO Chronicle* (Paris), **VI**, 12 (1960), 436.
19. Proceedings of the UN Economic Commission for Africa—see 'Editorial by the Director General', *UNESCO Chronicle* (Paris), ibid.
20. From speech on United Nations Day, 24 October 1960, by UNESCO's Director-general. See *UNESCO Chronicle* (Paris), ibid.
21. The Concordat gave the Catholic Missions a virtual control of African education as well as some subsidies from the government. Permission was also granted to Protestant Missions to run schools, though these had to wait until the 1920s before receiving any government grants.
22. The phrase is that of A. Buisseret, then Minister of Colonies in the Belgian Government, quoted in *New York Times*, 4 January 1955.
23. Acknowledgement for these 1957 figures is due to George H. T. Kimble, *Tropical Africa*, Vol. II, Twentieth Century Fund, New York, 1960, pp. 115-16. For the Congo alone, an estimate for 1956 puts the number of children in school at 1 282 645—see Rupert Emerson, *From Empire to Nation*, Harvard University Press, Cambridge, Mass., 1960, p. 66. Annually, the figure was rising.
24. Kimble, op. cit., p. 166.
25. This assessment was made by Homer Bigart, the *New York Times* correspondent, on 3 January 1960.
26. Chapter on 'Universities in the colonies', in Lyle W. Shannon's *Underdeveloped Areas*, Harper, New York, 1957, p. 117.
27. Ibid.
28. Ibid., p. 118.
29. *Modern Industry and the African* (Report of Commission of Inquiry set up by Department of Social and Industrial Research of International Missionary Council, under chairmanship of J. Merle Davis), Macmillan, 1933, pp. 338-9.
30. Ibid.
31. 'East Africa: a test-case for development assistance', *Mombasa Times* (Kenya), 9 March 1961, p. 2.
32. Ibid.
33. Lord Hailey, *An African Survey*, Oxford University Press, 1957, p. 1206.
34. Vernon Bartkett, *Struggle for Africa,* Praeger, New York, 1953, p. 98.
35. M. A. de Vleeschauwer (Belgian Minister of Colonies at the time), 'Belgian colonial policy', *The Crown Colonist*, **XIII** (August 1943), 549. See also *West African Review*, **XIV** (November 1943), 26-30.
36. H. A. Wieschhoff, *Colonial Policies in Africa*, African Handbook 5, Committee on African Studies, University of Pennsylvania, Philadelphia, 1944, p. 87.
37. L. Frank, *Etudes de colonisation comparée*, 1924, p. 123. This particular English rendering occurs in Lord Hailey's *An African Survey*, op. cit., p. 1209.
38. Negley Farson, *Behind God's Back*, Harcourt, Brace, New York, 1941, pp. 417-18.
39. Hilda Hertz Golden argues this out in her 'Literary and social change in underdeveloped countries', first published in *Rural Sociology*, **20**, 1 (1955), 1-6. A discussion of this phenomenon in the African setting is to be seen in Nuffield

Foundation and Colonial Office, *African Education: a study of Educational Policy and Practice in Tropical Africa*, Oxford University Press, 1953.

40. James S. Coleman, 'The politics of sub-Saharan Africa' in *The Politics of Developing Areas*, ed. Gabriel A. Almond and James S. Coleman, Princeton University Press, Princeton, New Jersey, 1960, p. 277.

41. 'News of the week in review', *New York Times*, 3 January 1960.

42. Report for week ending 11 November 1960, *The Chronicle of United Nations Activities* (New York), VI, 45, column no. 2699.

43. Ibid.

44. Ibid.

45. Ibid., column no. 2705.

46. Quoted in *UNESCO Chronicle* (Paris), V, 12 (1959), 395.

47. Report for week ending 11 November 1960, *The Chronicle of United Nations Activities* (New York), VI, 45, column no. 2699.

48. 'Secondary education and the modern world', *UNESCO Chronicle* (Paris), V, 12 (1959), 394.

49. *Africa Today* (New York), VIII, 5 (1960), 13.

50. Ibid.

51. General Assembly resolution 742 (VII), 7 November 1953, Annex.

52. *New York Times* magazine section, 28 January 1959.

53. Seymour Martin Lipset, *Political Man*, Doubleday, New York, 1960, pp. 56-7.

54. A. T. Steele, *New York Herald Tribune*, 27 December 1952.

55. The phrase occurs, among other places, in a leader in the *East African Standard*, Nairobi, 7 September 1960.

56. John Plamenatz (Fellow of Nuffield College, Oxford), *On Alien Rule and Self-Government*, Longmans, 1960, pp. 90-1.

57. H. A. Wieschhoff, *Colonial Policies in Africa*, op. cit., p. 88.

58. For what interest it may have, it may be pointed out that in this particular case Kenya was not forced, after all, into such an 'either/or', thanks to a Rockefeller scholarship taking the author to a Columbia MA and a Nuffield College studentship which took him to an Oxford D.Phil.

59. See *Department of State Bulletin* (official weekly record of US foreign policy), XLIV, 1136 (1961), 498.

60. See Richard L. Sklar, *Nigerian Political Parties*, Princeton University Press, Princeton, New Jersey, 1963, pp. 67-72.

61. Thomas Hodgkin, *Nationalism in Colonial Africa* (1956), Muller, 1962 reprint, pp. 154-5.

62. This rendering is from Gerald Moore, ed., *Seven African Writers*, Oxford University Press, 1962, p. 8.

63. Léopold Senghor, 'Negritude and African Socialism', in *St Antony's Papers on African Affairs*, Vol. 2, ed. Kenneth Kirkwood, Chatto & Windus, 1963, p. 11.

64. *Chants pour Naëtt* Senghers, Paris, 1950. This English rendering is from Léopold Senghor, *Prose and Poetry*, ed. John Reed and Clive Wake, Oxford University Press, 1965, p. 97.

65. The connexion between literary negritude and separatist religious movements is discussed in a related context in Chapter 4, 'Ancient Greece in African thought'.

3 The Emergence of Modern Orators

We have indicated that modern education not only created tensions between sacred and secular elements in Africa's social experiences, but also began to politicize ambitions in new ways. But ambitions in this respect are political *ends*. What we need to examine also is the impact of education on political *means*. This latter area includes techniques and styles used in the pursuit of political objectives.

Politics itself is partly a process of purposeful communication for public ends. Messages are transmitted, interests are articulated, grievances expressed, and preferences are defined and promoted. The styles of articulation are varied, ranging from whispers in the corridors of power to loud demonstrations in the market place. The technology of articulation is also of a wide range, encompassing on one side societies with a television set in every room to, at the other end, societies with isolated tribes untouched by modern communications except for the annual arrival of a government representative in a mobile cloud of dust sometimes called a jeep.

In this chapter we are addressing ourselves to a particular style of political articulation – the manipulation of words, with special reference to oratory. We define oratory as skilful and sometimes eloquent use of oral, verbal symbols for public or collective effect. The societies considered here are those of Africa south of the Sahara in recent times. From the point of view of oratory, an important factor about Africa to bear in mind concerns the recent attainment of literacy in many societies. These societies had previously evolved styles of politics which did not need the written word. It is to this historical background that we should first turn, before we examine the difference which imperialism and modern education made.

Oratory in a Pre-literate Polity

A pre-literate society tends to be functionally diffuse and structurally undifferentiated. The policy in such a society is not autonomous; politics is fundamentally inseparable from agriculture, religion, kinship, law, and other aspects of custom. It is arguable that in no society is the polity easily separable from these other dimensions of

64

social behaviour. That may indeed be so. Even the most modernized states have not fully separated religion from politics or distinguished the judicial from the political process. Indeed, the latter two processes are deliberately fused in those modernized societies which put a special premium on constitutionalism as a foundation for determining the boundaries of legitimate political behaviour.

All that we want to suggest with regard to the pre-literate society is that it has the kind of accompanying characteristics which make functional and structural diffuseness even greater than in more modernized entities. We accept as a premise that the capacity to read and write is an aspect of modernization as understood in our century; and therefore the absence of that capacity is in some sense pre-modern.

A major platform for oratory in a pre-literate society is indeed the judicial process itself. Where laws are not written, but are based on immemorial tradition, the oral articulation of the principles in dispute assumes extra relevance. To some extent poetry and the law become intertwined. The capacity to make a case in moving poetic terms becomes a skill for defending one's rights in the judicial process. In a pre-literate judicial process proverbs become functional equivalents of precedents in law. A major legal principle could be captured in a long-established proverbial formulation. Legal proverbs are of course part of the heritage of the English language, as well as of African languages. Proverbial principles like 'ignorance of the law is no excuse' have been profoundly influential in defining the boundaries of legitimate behaviour. And a proverb like 'an Englishman's house is his castle' has been significant in assuring rights of privacy.

The survival of trial by jury has maintained a link between Anglo-Saxon law and judicial process, on the one hand, and the traditions of pre-literate societies on the other. Because the jury is recruited from ordinary people, the clever manipulation of popular wisdom by the lawyers in the case can be important in influencing the perspectives of the jurors. Certainly rhetoric concerning the privacy of the home, or the sanctity of family life, is usually guaranteed to strike a positive response in the average juror. 'Yes, indeed, an Englishman's house is his castle' — the average juror might reason in silence as he listens to the rhetoric of counsel.

In pre-literate societies proverbs have an even higher premium. They are part of the oral tradition of the society as a whole, and do not have the competition of a written tradition which both enriches the oral flow and provides an alternative fund of wisdom. Proverbs in a pre-literate society do not lose their power by being commonplace. Cliches are not despised for being repetitive. On the contrary, tradition itself is definable in terms of repetition. The effective use of proverbial wisdom becomes good law itself.

Oratory then in a pre-literate society need not rest on the orator's verbal originality, but might be even more dependent on styles of using familiar formulations in a new way. Oratory can be verbal ritual, sharpening the boundaries of familiar conceptual territory. In this particular domain originality consists not in the freshness of the expressions used, but in the aptness of the context.

But there is room also for individual originality and individual wit. The domain of metaphor and simile offers particularly great potentialities for the skilled orator. The orator may be standing before a chief, making a case of a judicial kind concerning land rights. He may then use the simile of his rights as a husband, and play on the shared metaphor of planting seed, the shared imagery of sexual and agrarian fertility. An effective use of comparative imagery could help decide a case. The chief sits there, perhaps the elders sit with him depending upon the society and the case in question. The chief and the elders listen to the wit of the defendant, or of the defendant's spokesman, as imagery from agriculture becomes interspersed with imagery from family life. Cultivation and impregnation, seed and semen, become indistinguishable. The chief nods, the elders smile, and the case makes some progress.

Next to proverbs are riddles as raw material for oratorical stimulation. Some have even argued that riddles are prior to all other forms of oral literature. In the words of Charles Francis Potter:

> Contrary to the common assumption that they are mere word puzzles proposed by punsters at evening parties, riddles rank with myths, fables, folktales, and proverbs as one of the earliest and most widespread types of formulated thought. A good case could probably be made for their priority to all other forms of literature or even to all other oral lore, for riddles are essentially metaphors, and metaphors are the result of the primary mental process of association, comparison, and the perception of likenesses and differences.[1]

Potter refers to the definition of a riddle as given in *Everyman's Encyclopedia* – 'A paraphrastic presentation of an unmentioned subject, the design of which is to excite the reader or hearer to the discovery of the meaning hidden under a studied obscurity of expression'. But Potter had a functional definition of riddle: 'A real folk riddle, represents a group effort of some humble but intelligent people to find or create a little humour or beauty or both in the rather bleak and often difficult world in which they find themselves'.[2] In Swahili a riddle is called *Kitandawili*. The man who is about to spin the riddle is in the functional role of someone throwing the gauntlet. In fact he proclaims the word '*Kitandawili*' – and the person who is prepared to take him on answers '*Tega!*'. The latter literally means 'set the trap!'. The challenger then proceeds to set the verbal trap – and the person who has accepted the challenge attempts to fathom the inner meaning of the verbal snare.

The tradition of riddles has continued in the modern age in televised quiz games. But the modern quiz is more a demonstration of one's *factual* knowledge than a demonstration of capacity to interpret verbal artistry. To use a Semitic example:

A woman said to her son,
'Thy father is my father,
And thy grandfather my husband;
Thou art my son, and I am thy sister.'

The answer to this riddle is 'it was the daughter of Lot who spake thus to her son'. (Genesis xix. 30-8.)

Riddles in the English language include:

What flies forever
And rests never?

The answer to this one is the wind. Also primordial as a phenomenon is fire:

The more you feed it
The more it'll grow high,
But if you give it water,
Then it'll go and die.

In many African societies imagery connected with hunting also carries earthy domestic implications. The song of the bwola dance among the Acholi of Eastern Africa has a number of references to the warrior and the hunter; but while some of these references carry their literal meanings to one audience, they acquire a different meaning to another.

The spear I used to trust
The spear sleeps in the cold oh
The great lone hunter
The warrior I used to trust
He has speared me with the end of the broom.

Okot p'Bitek tells us about the double meaning to different audiences.

Whereas the old men [present at a dance] took the spear to represent the might of the clan and the hunting prowess of their hunters, the young women were joking with the young men about sex. The spear was taken as the symbol of manhood, representing the penis. . . . And the song the women sang particularly stressed the words: 'he has speared me with the end of the broom,' singing it with amused pleasure and sarcasm . . . [referring to the] 'cooling' the virility of the men, so that their penis would become soft like the end of the grass broom.[3]

The thrill of riddles is a thrill of double meanings. Studied ambiguity is often a major aspect of oratory.

The skills of ambiguity which Jomo Kenyatta had used before he was tried for managing Mau Mau in Kenya came to bewilder the prosecution when the day of the trial came. Kenyatta was skilled in using Kikuyu proverbs and Kikuyu riddles with tremendous effect at the beginning of the 1950s in Kenya. Had Kenyatta been denouncing Mau Mau or encouraging it? Had he been denouncing the use of violence for the promotion of nationalist ends in Kenya or was he a champion of violent revolution? Was he urging the Kikuyu to turn against the white man and against Christianity or was he preoccupied with more 'legitimate' African ambitions?

> Kenyatta was reported to say one thing openly and then to take his tribesmen off by themselves where he spoke in that allusive Kikuyu idiom which defies translation into language comprehensible to western political tradition. A favourite metaphor he used was between religious sects and weevils. 'The many Kikuyu religions (or sects), are weevils which spoil the food in the granaries. We are the food, and the religions (or sects) are weevils.' The missionaries understood him to refer to Christianity, and one of their informants at these meetings may have reported his words in this sense, which the written record conceals.[4]

Many a European did complain at the time about the 'diabolical cleverness' of Kenyatta's oratorical ambiguities.

> A panga [long knife] is meant to be used. If you put it on a table and leave it there, it is useless. Similarly, if we don't help ourselves God isn't going to come down from above and help us. But if we exert ourselves, He will be on our side.[5]

At first sight the use of the image of panga might seem obvious as a weapon. And yet the panga is used much more as an agricultural implement than as a military weapon. It serves some of the functions of an axe in large parts of rural Kenya. Why then should this implement necessary for agricultural cultivation be left idle on a table? Was Kenyatta urging more hard work from his people? Or was he bursting forth with a war cry? Again the ambiguity seemed to be studied. Kenyatta was using a style suited to a pre-literate society, though at a period when literacy had already entered the scene.

Many of the techniques of pre-literate oratory assumed the existence of a face-to-face society. There were times when the hidden meaning required considerable specific knowledge to interpret. And the level of specificity might at times be drawn from the intimacy of kinship itself. Oratory in a pre-literate polity also operates within a substantial area of *consensus*. The art of persuasion generally consists of exploiting effectively shared values and predispositions. But to the extent that most pre-literate societies are also profoundly traditionalist societies, the arts of persuasion in that kind of context operate even more deeply in consensual surroundings. Oratory becomes substantially a skill in the manipulation of ancestral symbols through the medium of words.

Some of the more developed traditional African polities even had special court orators, called upon to use verbal skills to remind the king himself of his ancestral duties. Among the Thonga of Southern Africa there were two court personages who played this kind of role. One was a praise singer and the other the rough equivalent of a court jester. The praise singer was a herald, and the jester a grand critic of the king himself.

> Every morning, before sunrise, the chief was awakened by the herald's loud song, which praised the deeds of departed rulers and disparaged the incumbent. In the light of predecessors, the singer cried, the present chief was a coward and a child, not to be compared with his father, his grandfather, and their glorious ancestors. The court jester, in addition, acted as a public censor, freely insulting everyone and enjoying perfect immunity when he loudly criticized the chief.[6]

Such court personages had to excel in the arts of proverbs and riddles, wit and humour. They had to command admiration as they served the functions of censure on behalf of the ancestors themselves. The power of custom, consensus, and ritualistic verbal symbols, all found an embodiment in those royal jokers in the court of Thonga.

The Colonization of Oratory

With the consolidation of European rule in Africa, both the nature and the functions of oratory began to change. The old forms of verbal behaviour in public did not all disappear by any means, but significant alterations occurred. There were also whole new areas for oratorical endeavours as European hegemony introduced new ambitions for the local people, new rewards and new punishments.

Particularly important from the point of view of verbal behaviour was the coming of the new European languages, with special reference to English and French, and these were acquired primarily through the educational process. The impact of English and French on political behaviour in Africa has been not only deep but also varied. These metropolitan languages helped to establish new criteria of social and political stratification, new motivations for economic endeavour, as well as new styles of political communication. Africans who acquired literary and oral skills drawn from these metropolitan languages enhanced their capacity for social mobility. Almost everywhere in Africa the economic value of English or French was greater than the economic value of mastering several African languages together. There were more jobs and occupations which 'required' a knowledge of English or French than there were occupations which demanded the mastery of several indigenous languages together.[7]

From the point of view of the history of oratory in Africa, the colonial experience added three important new dimensions. We have already referred to the first of these — the coming of French and English, and the gradual politicization of those languages in African conditions. The second colonial change of great relevance to the history of oratory in Africa was the enlargement of political scale. New territorial entities were created, bringing together a variety of what would otherwise have been separate political entities. The majority of African states may indeed be small states by world standards in terms of population, but even those are significantly larger than most of the pre-colonial political units of Africa.

Evidently verbal behaviour for public purposes is transformed in situations of enlarged political scale. Oratory becomes necessary not just for making a case before a chief in a village, but also for making an impact on populations geographically distant and culturally divergent from one's own. Verbal skills which were adequate at a tribal *baraza* in Tabora were no longer adequate if the effort was directed towards influencing events in Tanganyika as a whole.

The new technology also helped in enlarging the political scale. The coming of the motor car and jeep, and later the increasing political use of aviation, all helped to widen the functional boundaries of the polity. The transistor radio was a major technological factor behind the enlargement of political scale in Africa. Verbal skills against a background of these technological innovations underwent the kind of changes necessary for the larger political market place.

In addition to the coming of new metropolitan languages and the enlargement of political scale was the new arrival of the written word. Literacy began to affect styles of oratory. The majority of people were indeed still illiterate, but increasingly those who were capturing leadership and influence were the literate. These leaders in turn evolved oratorical skills, partly drawn from their literate skills, but also influenced by the wider oratorical culture of their societies.

One important transformation which took place was the move from the use of indigenous proverbs to the use of quotations from towering European authors. The great orators of African anti-colonial movements from the 1930s to the end of the 1950s were often people whose greatest speeches were in either English or French, and some of these speeches quoted generously from British, French and American writers. The writers that were quoted often included imperial poets. The audiences that the African orators had in mind included metropolitan audiences in Europe.

A claim can be made for the proposition that the most imperialist of all British poets was Rudyard Kipling. After all, he gave imperialism the poem 'The White Man's Burden', and provided poetic and rhetorical legitimation for the white man's efforts to dominate the world. And yet, in spite of Kipling's stature as the imperialist versifier par excellence, the man has featured favourably in many an African speech. On the eve of an election in Nairobi, before a massive crowd waiting to hear his last speech before the great day, Kenya's Tom Mboya stood there and recited to the African audience the whole of Rudyard Kipling's poem 'If'. The whole concept of leadership unflappable in the face of adversity, unwilling to pass the buck, ('The buck stops here!'), unwilling to collapse under the weight of pressures, and characterized by the supreme British virtue of the 'stiff upper lip', seemed captured in those lines from that militant British patriot:

> If you can keep your head when all about you
> Are losing theirs and blaming it on you;
>
> .   .   .
>
> If you can meet with Triumph and Disaster
> And treat those two impostors just the same;
>
> .   .   .
>
> If you can talk with crowds and keep your virtue,
> Or walk with Kings — nor lose the common touch,
>
> .   .   .
>
> If you can fill the unforgiving minute
> With sixty seconds' worth of distance run,
>
> .   .   .
>
> Yours is the Earth and everything that's in it,
> And — which is more — you'll be a Man, my son!

There in Nairobi was Mboya, that immortal son of Kenya, worn out by the exertions of campaigning, nervous about the election the next day, confronting an eager audience of fellow black people listening to his words of wisdom. Mboya was later to communicate to posterity the following paragraph:

> I read out to the great crowd the whole of Rudyard Kipling's poem *If*. When facing the challenge of nation-building, nobody can claim to have played a manly part if he has not '. . . filled the unforgiving minute/With sixty seconds of worth of distance run'.[8]

Across the border in Uganda, Rudyard Kipling had had a similar impact. Mr J. W. Lwamafa, Minister and Member of Parliament, commemorated President A. Milton Obote's ten years in Parliament with the observation:

> He is essentially a man of crisis — he has a unique flair for solving them, but once solved, he will never wait for applause, he simply moves on to the next problem as if nothing had happened. No one reminds me more than President Obote of Rudyard Kipling's poem (which, by the way, I have got framed and hanged in my office) and more particularly the verse, 'if you can keep your head when all about you are losing theirs'.[9]

Kipling, the poet of the white man's burden, had turned out to be the poet of the black man's leader. The man who had contributed significantly to the phraseological heritage of the English language was also serving inspirational purposes for African politicians within their own domestic systems. The poem 'If' became a functional equivalent both of an indigenous proverb and a lesson in the Catechism. The impact of British values on colonized Africans was interacting with residual ancestral ways.[10]

Audiences varied. Some audiences could be expected to understand the general direction of anglicized or gallicized African oratory. In West Africa it was already possible for an audience with very little education to understand a good deal of English. But in East Africa command of the English language was still heavily correlated with formal education. Sometimes it did not even matter whether a large or even a substantial section of the audience had no idea what the speaker was talking about. A good many members of the audience sometimes enthused over what sounded like long words. Words ending with *-ization* or *-ism* could send an audience into ecstasy if enough of them were used near together to create an impression of massive verbal power. It might even be said that while literary quotations were the functional equivalent of proverbs, the real functional equivalents of riddles were long English words. The audience might know just enough to recognize not only that the language was English but also that long words were being used.

What can so easily be overlooked is that oratory itself was to some extent a functional alternative to political patronage. The colonial period was a period when the new African leaders, emerging with new metropolitan oratorical skills, did not as yet command the economic and political resources to use as adequate patronage for the consolidation of political support. In a situation where candidates for leadership already have economic resources, allegiance can be established and alliances co-ordinated through the manipulation of tangible economic rewards. But anti-colonial agitators in pre-independent Africa were seldom in control of a scale of economic and political resources which could compete with what the authorities had at their disposal. Most of the carrots, as well as most of the sticks, were under the control of the colonial authorities. What the local agitators could do to tilt the balance of political support and enthusiasm of the population depended a good deal on verbal skills. Tangible rewards constitute a more direct manipulation of political appetites; but in the absence of those rewards, the political imagination has to be manipulated instead. The promise of bigger things in the future, as against smaller rewards more immediately, has to be formulated in terms which appeal to the popular imagination. The new anti-colonial agitators therefore needed all the verbal power at their disposal to help their prospective followers transcend immediate appetites and engage in ultimate dreams. It was Kipling himself who said in 1923 'Words are of course the most powerful drug used by mankind'.[11]

From Kipling to Lenin

The enlargement of political scale, literacy and the use of metropolitan languages together constituted mutually reinforcing media of political centralization. As independence approached, both centralization and the enlargement of scale entered a new phase. Particularly important from the point of view of the sociology of verbal behaviour were the extension of the franchise and the growth of political parties. Mounting demands by anti-colonial activists led to piecemeal concessions from the imperial authorities, including significant electoral liberalization. This was especially striking in the British colonies. The emergence of the Legislative Council as the focus of African political ambitions on the national level had a profound effect on political recruitment and the sociology of oratory. The metropolitan languages assumed extra importance in situations where votes were being courted across tribal boundaries. Political parties needed to have a national following whenever possible, and the majority of African countries did not have indigenous languages which were nationally understood. Qualifications for recruitment into the national arena of politics normally included competence in the metropolitan language. This was institutionalized when candidates wishing to stand for elections to the Legislative Council were required to show evidence of competence in the imperial language. Africa emerged into independence with legislatures which insisted on knowledge of either English or French before candidates could claim the right to represent their people.

As candidates scrambled for a chance to a national political career, and as political parties sought to establish support in different regions, both organizational and communicative skills assumed a new premium. Oratory as a political resource sometimes lay across both organization and communication. The content and devices of oratory also underwent a change in this period. There were new symbols to be invoked. Among the changes which took place was the radicalization of rhetoric. This might be formulated in terms of a transition from Kipling to Lenin, from quotations drawn from western creative literature to vocabulary drawn from leftist rhetoric.

A leader like Kwame Nkrumah started with a style which included quotations from such literary figures as Alfred Tennyson and William Wordsworth. But Nkrumah's last book while he was still in office was entitled *Neo-colonialism, the Last Stage of Imperialism* echoing Lenin's *Imperialism, the Highest Stage of Capitalism*. And when Nkrumah fell from power, and spent his last years in exile in Guinea, his vocabulary got even more radicalized. He kept on producing books from Conakry, each more saturated with Marxist rhetoric than the one before. The Nkrumah who had prided himself on having been inspired by Alfred Tennyson was not quite the Nkrumah who sought treatment for his last fatal illness in a hospital in Bucharest, Rumania. The radicalization of the rhetoric was also a radicalization of general orientation.

On the east coast of Africa Julius Nyerere of Tanzania appeared to be caught up between Shakespeare and Marx. The younger Nyerere in the 1950s did not hesitate to use Shakespearean lines in his public pronouncements—'Men at some times are masters of their fates!' Later on Julius Nyerere translated *Julius Caesar* into Swahili, the play whose lines he had often borrowed for political purposes. Yet by the time he was translating his second Shakespearean play, *The Merchant of Venice*, Nyerere no longer used Shakespearean lines in his speeches. What he did use was a vocabulary partly drawn from European socialism. Terms like class privilege, monopoly, class exploitation, as well as the longer-standing concepts of imperialism and capitalism, entered the mainstream of oratorical phraseology in Tanzania. From the point of view of raw rhetoric for speech-making, a transition had taken place from Kipling to Lenin.[12]

But, paradoxically enough, the rise of radical rhetoric coincided with the decline of oratory both in Ghana and Tanzania. The heyday of oratory in modern African countries was the period when the legislature remained a major arena of political articulation. The Legislative Council which had been created during the colonial period evolved into the National Assembly of independence. The nature of parliamentary life put a special premium once again on oratorical skills. Politicians carefully prepared their speeches, or commissioned speech writers to prepare them for important moments in the National Assembly. At that time one did not have to be a minister in order to get publicity for one's speech. A good speech could command the attention of newspapers, and gained the speaker a moment of glory at breakfast when the morning paper was consulted.

But the radicalization of rhetoric in Africa coincided with the decline of political openness. The old days of debate and verbal confrontations, the great moments of oral duels, began to recede into history in one African polity after another. With the decline of free speech, and the rise of one-party systems, and the expansion of patronage, came the decline of oratory itself. Fewer and fewer politicians were allowed the freedom to make major speeches. Fewer politicians prepared their own speeches. Indeed, the mass media were now dominated by ministerial pronouncements and presidential decrees. In some countries ministers virtually claimed a monopoly of space in local newspapers, and certainly on the radio. The days when a good back-bencher's speech could capture the imagination of a reporter, and result in a sensational morning edition, have in a number of African countries decisively retreated into historical oblivion.

Of course not all great orators are necessarily great debaters. Even among the founding fathers of modern African polities there are striking differences in orientation. Milton Obote of Uganda was a more accomplished debater than Jomo Kenyatta of Kenya, and yet Kenyatta was at the same time a greater orator at mass rallies than Obote ever managed to be. Until the eve of independence Kenyatta did not succeed in becoming a member of the Legislative Council. But in some ways it was just as well that he did not. In the words of his biographer, Murray-Brown, 'Kenyatta was never at ease in English debating circles and he would have been at a disadvantage among the hostile settlers in that chamber'.[13] But give Kenyatta a whole stadium and a platform, with an audience that understands either Swahili or Kikuyu, and the oratorical skills of the man become activated. He can use both humour and invective with devastating impact. He can use earthy, sexual language with impressive and varied effects on a mass audience. But in the legislative chamber Kenyatta would shrink into verbal ineffectualness. Indeed, he has never regarded Parliament as a place for his own political performances. In this respect, he is in sharp contrast to Milton Obote. Obote was clearly a supremely gifted parliamentarian. Within the chambers of the National Assembly he knew how to manipulate verbal symbols and verbal messages. He knew how to create an atmosphere in the chamber, and arouse collective parliamentary response. The radicalization of his own rhetoric in the direction of neo-Marxist formulations coincided once again with a groping for a one-party system and a decline of open debate. Even when Uganda was fully an open society Milton Obote was a great parliamentary performer. Certainly by his last year in office he was the only man independent enough to capture not only the attention but also the imagination of the National Assembly. But faced with a mass audience in the outer political world, Obote was competent but not outstanding. If he shared a platform with Jomo Kenyatta there was no doubt who would be overshadowed and verbally outwitted.

It was in personalities like Tom Mboya that the role of debater and orator were most convincingly fused. The late Tom Mboya perhaps still remains in memory the greatest political debater that East Africa has so far produced, and one of the greatest orators. Julius Nyerere also fuses debating with oratorical skills. But while as an orator he may be at least as good as Mboya was, as a debater he is a little less dazzling. But both debating and solo-oratory were important political resources for these figures in their rise to prominence and power.

We started this chapter from a premise that much of politics was a process of communication and transmission of messages. Because of this basic element in politics, verbal behaviour is an important dimension. Verbal behaviour can be private as well as public. Politics as intrigue in the corridors of power relies on different styles of verbal behaviour from politics as a process of public confrontations.

In Africa's experience we traced oratory in pre-literate societies, and saw it at work in a range of activities, from the judicial process to the functions of a court jester.

In colonialism we witnessed the enlargement of political scale, the arrival of the new metropolitan languages, the impact of literacy on political rhetoric, and the centralization of political recruitment. These processes had consequences for the nature of politics in Africa after independence, and later provided an infrastructure for a general transition from a rhetoric influenced by Kipling and other literary figures to a rhetoric shaped by Lenin and other leftist thinkers.

We drew attention to the decline of oratory arising from a decline of free speech and consolidation of one-party states. But we should also note in conclusion the negative impact of military power on oratory as a political resource in parts of contemporary Africa. We shall return to this theme later. Military coups rely more on the gun than the gift of the gab. Political centralization persists after the coup; and the soldiers reaffirm a commitment to the enlarged political scale even if they have to fight a civil war to maintain it. But competence in a metropolitical language is not a precondition for a military coup in Africa; nor are the skills of the pen necessarily required to supplement the power of the sword in the short run.

But under the soldiers — as under the old westernized politicians — the battle between Kipling and Lenin continues. A profound cultural schizophrenia continues to influence the behaviour of post-colonial Africans, be they in western-type military uniforms or western-style lounge suits. The content of their rhetoric and oratory provides one indicator of that schizophrenia — as a struggle continues between a western jingo, an African juju, and a Marxist giant. The changing nature of African oratory provides important clues concerning a wider cultural struggle in which the black races are engaged.

References and Notes

1. Consult 'Riddles', *Dictionary of Folklore, Mythology and Legend*, Vol. 2, Funk & Wagnalls, New York, 1950, p. 938.
2. Ibid., p. 944.
3. Okot p'Bitek, *Religion of the Central Luo*, East African Literature Bureau, Nairobi and Kampala, 1971, pp. 100-1.
4. Jeremy Murray-Brown, *Kenyatta*, Allen & Unwin, 1972, p. 238.
5. *East African Standard* (Nairobi), 18 August 1948.
6. Eugene Victor Walter, *Terror and Resistance: a Study of Political Violence*, Oxford University Press, London and New York, 1969, p. 71. Consult also Henri A. Gunod, *The Life of a South African Tribe*, 2 vols, Neuchatel, Switzerland, 1912, Vol. 1., pp. 397, 402.
7. The impact of the English language on social and political stratification is discussed more fully in Ali A. Mazrui, *Cultural Engineering and Nation-Building in East*

Africa, Northwestern University Press, Evanston, Illinois, 1972, especially chapters 6, 7, and 16. Consult also Mazrui, *The Political Sociology of the English Language: an African Perspective*, Mouton. The Hague, 1975.

8. Tom Mboya, *Freedom and After*, André Deutsch, 1963, p. 114.

9. *Thoughts of an African Leader*, compiled by the editorial department of the *Uganda Argus*, Longman Uganda, Kampala, 1970, p. 68.

10. See Ali A. Mazrui, 'Towards the decolonization of Rudyard Kipling', *Quadrant* (Sydney, Australia), **XVI**, (September-October 1972), 12-17. This theme of the decolonization of Rudyard Kipling anticipated my book *A World Federation of Cultures* (Free Press, New York, 1976), the research for which was funded by the Carnegie Endowment for International Peace and the Institute for World Order, New York. The book was completed when I was a Fellow of the Center for Advanced Study in the Behavioral Sciences, Stanford.

11. Speech, 14 February 1923. See *The Times* (London), 16 February 1923.

12. In 1934 Nkrumah applied to the Dean of Lincoln University in the United States for admission as a student. In his application he quoted from Tennyson's *In Memoriam*: 'So many worlds, so much to do, So little done, such things to be.' In his autobiography, Nkrumah says this verse was to him then, as it still was when he wrote the autobiography, 'an inspiration and a spur'. 'It fired within me a determination to equip myself for the service of my country.' See Nkrumah, *Ghana: the Autobiography of Kwame Nkrumah* (1957), Nelson, paperback ed., 1960, p.v. For an illustration of Nyerere's use of lines from Julius Caesar in a political pamphlet see Nyerere's *Barriers to Democracy*, Dar es Salaam.

13. Murray-Brown, *Kenyatta*, op. cit., p. 252.

PART TWO

EXPANDING INTELLECTUAL HORIZONS

4 Ancient Greece in African Thought

Western education in Africa came with new intellectual horizons, as well as the seeds of intellectual dependency. The new intellectual horizons were a form of liberation, a new capacity to transcend ancestral ways. But there was also the risk of imitation and blind deference, a tendency to adore western civilization and all that it was supposed to stand for. However, there was in addition a safety valve of potentially decisive implications. This was Africa's cultural nationalism. Concurrent with expanding horizons and reduced indigenous self-confidence was the confused emergence of African cultural nationalism.

These three factors could start a process which could culminate in the rewriting of the world's intellectual history. What was ancient Egypt's impact on the miracle of ancient Greece? How African was ancient Egypt? How European was ancient Greece? How relevant are such questions not only as a basis of interpreting the past but also as a basis of structuring Africa's intellectual future? We are not yet in a position to give definitive answers to such questions. Indeed, the answers may lie in the womb of history. But in this chapter let us at least explore the implications of ancient Greece for modern Africa.

The Greeks are credited with having started many things. In his first important publication in 1947 Kwame Nkrumah suggested that the very idea of European expansionism went back to the Greeks and their immediate successors. The phenomenon of Europeans conquering each other might have been older than the Greeks. But the phenomenon of a major European intrusion into another continent had its grand precedent in what Nkrumah called 'the idea of Alexander the Great with his Graeco-Asiatic empire'.[1]

If Nkrumah was exaggerating, his exaggeration was academically respectable. It is a respectable academic tradition to be able to discover the Greek root of almost every important phenomenon of the modern world. It is almost always safe to say, 'It all goes back to ancient Greece'. This is often a myth — but it is a myth with a capacity to fulfil itself. A thinker starts suspecting that his thoughts have their roots in ancient Greece. He turns to the Greeks to find antecedents of his own thoughts. And before long his thinking is indeed affected and stimulated by what he reads of Greek ideas. The ideas of African nationalists have at times been influenced by the tendency to refer themselves back to the Greeks. It is all bound up with the place of Greece in the total mythology of 'European civilization', and the influence of this mythology on the course of African history.

The ambition of this chapter is therefore threefold. First, it aspires to throw some light on the nature of this classical mystique in Africa and the response of African nationalism to it. Secondly, we intend to discuss briefly how East Africa relates to the mystique and to the wider African reaction, and thirdly to pose the question whether ancient Greece was, in any meaningful sense, a European civilization.

My own interest in these matters is not, of course, that of a historian. It is the interest of a student of social thought and political behaviour. But social thought itself must often reflect on the findings of historians for new insights into man's image of himself. What we are reflecting upon here are matters which do indeed have a bearing on the crisis of identity facing African nationalists. What must not be forgotten is that there is also a crisis of identity confronting every modern African university — and the mystique of ancient Greece is at the heart of it.

Let us then first try to fathom the political meaning that this classical mystique has had in contemporary Africa. The first thing which needs to be noted is that in an important sense the mystique of ancient Greece contributed to the total cultural arrogance of Europe in relation to the rest of the world. At his inaugural lecture as Regius Professor of History at Oxford in December 1841 Thomas Arnold gave a new lease of life to the ancient idea of a moving centre of civilization. Arnold argued that the history of civilization was the history of a series of creative races, each of which made its impact and then sank into oblivion, leaving the heritage of civilization to a greater successor. What the Greeks passed on to the Romans, the Romans bequeathed in turn to the Germanic race. And of that race the greatest civilizing nation was England.[2]

Lord Lugard also came to share the vision of Britain as a successor to Rome. In his book *The Dual Mandate* Lugard asserted that Roman imperialism helped to transform the inhabitants of the British Isles into a civilized nation. Those islands then became a *civilizing* nation in their own right. To use Lugard's own words:

As Roman imperialism . . . led the wild barbarians of these islands of Britain along the path of progress, so in Africa today we are repaying the debt, and bringing to the dark places of the earth . . . the torch of culture and progress.[3]

In more extremist hands than Lugard's the Graeco-Roman heritage of the West was used for worse purposes. Biological explanations were sometimes advanced to show that it was right that the whites should have produced a Greek intellectual miracle and that the blacks should not. The ultimate proof of the higher biological intellectuality of the European stock was that they had to their credit the most intellectual of all ancient civilizations. It was inconceivable that the Negroes could ever have produced an Aristotle. The Negro stock could not even produce a language to compare with that evolved by the Greeks. Nor was that the furthest that cultural arrogance could go. In his address to the Congress of Africanists in Accra in December 1962, Nkrumah cited the case of John C. Calhoun, 'the most philosophical of all the slave-holders' of the southern states of America. Calhoun had apparently once said that if he could find a black man who could understand the Greek syntax, he would then consider their race human, and his attitude towards enslaving them would therefore change. Nkrumah agreed with the reaction of a Zulu student at Columbia university who, commenting on Calhoun's criterion of what is human, said in an oration in 1906:

> What might have been the sensation kindled by the Greek syntax in the mind of the famous Southerner, I have so far been unable to discover; but . . . I could show him among black men of pure African blood those who could repeat the Koran from memory, skilled in Latin, Greek and Hebrew, Arabic and Chaldaic.[4]

It is evident that Calhoun's charge against the blacks was more severe than the simpler accusation that the blacks were incapable of producing a language to compare with ancient Greek. Calhoun was asserting that the black man was not only incapable of inventing such a language; he was also incapable of understanding it when invented by someone else. Nkrumah was too modest to remind the International Congress of Africanists that when he himself obtained his Master of Science degree in education from the University of Pennsylvania many years before, he became a full instructor in philosophy and first-year Greek. And Nkrumah was not even the best African specialist in either of these subjects. He had countrymen better versed in those subjects than he.[5]

Negritude and the Greek Heritage

In a book he published two years after the International Congress of Africanists Nkrumah discussed the influence of the Graeco-Roman mystique on the kind of education which colonialism bequeathed to Africa. Not only the study of philosophy but also of history in Africa was to him distorted by that mystique. As Nkrumah put it:

> The colonized African student, whose roots in his own society are systematically starved of sustenance, is introduced to Greek and Roman history, the cradle history of modern Europe, and he is encouraged to treat this portion of the story of man together

with the subsequent history of Europe as the only worthwhile portion.[6]

It was partly because of such elements of European cultural pride that movements like that of negritude came into being. Negritude is an idealization of the traditional culture of the black man. In a profound sense negritude is therefore the black man's response to the Graeco-Roman mystique. That mystique had psychological implications for black people which were not shared by other colonized peoples in Asia. As Thomas Hodgkin once pointed out, no western European seriously questioned the fact that there had been periods in the past when Arab and Indian civilizations, owing little to European stimulus, flowered. But, in the words of Hodgkin, 'the case of the peoples of Africa is different'.[7] For them it was not a simple case of recovering a dignity which everyone concedes they once had. It may indeed be an attempt to recover their own respect for themselves, but it is also an endeavour to exact for the first time an adequate respect from others. As I have said elsewhere, self-respect and respect by others, difficult to separate as they usually are, are in the Africans' case even more so. And in regard to negritude there prevails a deep conviction that there is dignity in cultural defiance itself.

Jean-Paul Sartre was right when he described negritude as evangelical.[8] Perhaps there might even be a mystical link between, say, Elijah Masinde, the prophet of *Dini ya Msambwa* in East Africa and Aimé Césaire, the sophisticated poet of negritude in Martinique. At any rate literary negritude and certain African messianic and separatist movements are, as we noted earlier, different responses to one interrelated cultural phenomenon. We should remind ourselves here that the sources of European civilization were not exclusively Graeco-Roman. It would perhaps be more correct to regard the ultimate fountains of European culture as being the old Israel as well as Greece. The achievement of imperial Rome was to fuse the two traditions and bequeath to Europe a civilization which was both Graeco-Roman and Judeo-Christian.

But as these two traditions entered the lives of black people they often came wrapped in Europe's cultural arrogance. The Graeco-Roman aspects of that arrogance contributed to the birth of negritude; the Judeo-Christian sense of sacred superiority contributed to the birth of Ethiopianism and African syncretic churches at large. B. G. Sundkler, in his contemplation of the Black Christ movements of South Africa, was suddenly reminded of a verse as old as Xenophanes:

The Ethiop's Gods have dusky cheeks,
    Thick lips and woolly hair;
The Grecian Gods are like the Greeks,
    As tall, bright-eyed, and fair.[9]

Sometimes that old intellectual arrogance of Europe which underestimated the mind of the black man was extended to the religious sphere. Calhoun might have doubted if a black man could ever understand the Greek syntax; others have sometimes doubted if the black man could ever comprehend the trinity. And whenever the black man has turned away from European Christianity and embraced a separatist version, some of his judges have felt vindicated. In her book *New Nations* Lucy Mair refers to the theory held by some people that 'the assimilation of Christian doctrine is an intellectual exercise too difficult for some "primitive minds".' She pointed out that those who held this theory used it to explain Ethiopianism and similar separatist movements. They argued that such 'primitive minds' had not only misunderstood Christian doctrine and reproduced it in a garbled form but, in the effort, had sometimes become mentally deranged and abandoned themselves to the new cults. Professor Mair herself rejected the theory.[10] But for our purposes here what matters is that such a theory does exist and is obviously akin to Calhoun's prejudices about the Greek syntax. It is this which leads us to the conclusion that both the Graeco-Roman and the Judeo-Christian elements of European civilization have sometimes forced the African into a position of cultural defensiveness. Ethiopianism emerged as a form of poetic protest in action. And negritude became, in Sartre's word, 'evangelical'.

One particularly sophisticated type of African response to the Graeco-Roman mystique of the West is the response of Léopold Senghor. Senghor acknowledges that Greek civilization is pre-eminently an intellectual civilization. Does this make Greeks and Westerners at large more intellectual as a group of human beings than black people are? For Senghor the answer is yes. He has argued that the genius of Africa is not in the realm of intellectual abstraction; it is in the domain of emotive sensibility. As he once put it in his own inimitable way, 'Emotion is black . . . reason is Greek.'[11]

When under attack Senghor reformulates his views to some extent. His interpretation of original Africa has sometimes exposed him to the charge of having deprived the traditional African of the gift of rationality. Senghor defends himself with his usual ingenuity. But ultimately he still insists on regarding the African as being basically intuitive, rather than analytical. He has said: 'Young people have criticized me for reducing Negro-African knowledge to pure emotion, for denying that there is an African "reason" . . . I should like to explain myself once again . . . European reasoning is analytical, discursive by utilization; Negro-African reasoning is intuitive by participation.'[12]

Elsewhere Senghor emphasizes that this 'analytic and discursive reason' was part of the Graeco-Roman heritage of Europe at large. 'One could even trace the descent of Marxism from Aristotle!' Senghor asserts.

Descartes had asserted that the ultimate proof that I exist is that I think: in his famous words, 'I think, therefore I am.' But according to Senghor, African epistemology starts from a different basic postulate. For the African Negro the world exists by the fact of his reflection upon his emotive self. 'He does not realise that he thinks; he feels that he feels, he feels his *existence*, he feels himself.'[13]

In short, Negro-African epistemology starts from the premise, 'I *feel*, therefore I am.'

Kwame Nkrumah, in his book *Consciencism*, also discusses Descartes' postulate. Nkrumah argues that the fact that 'Monsieur Descartes' is thinking is no proof that his body exists. It is certainly no proof that the totality of his person is in being. Nkrumah is out to deny that matter owes its existence either to thought or to perception. In a sense he would disagree both with the reasoning which says, 'I think, therefore I am', and with the reasoning which argues, 'I feel, therefore I am.' But to the extent that feeling is a more 'physical' experience than thought, it is a greater concession to the autonomy of matter. The kind of philosophical idealism which puts our bodies in our minds instead of our minds in our bodies was to Nkrumah no more than an indulgence in 'the ecstasy of intellectualism'.[14]

But Nkrumah would certainly not go to the extent of denying the African the gift of 'analytical and discursive reason'. As he himself put it at the inauguration of the University of Ghana in November 1961, 'We have never had any doubt about the intellectual capacity of the African.'[15] Yet the measure of that African capacity has sometimes been deemed to be the extent to which the African could grapple with Greek thought. Calhoun might have used the ability to understand the Greek syntax as a criterion of whether the African was human. But Africans themselves have sometimes invoked the ability to grapple with Greek concepts as a criterion that the African was indeed an intellectual being. Cheikh Anta Diop of Senegal, in trying to establish the academic calibre of the ancient African university in Timbuktu, found it pertinent to assert that at that university, 'Aristotle was commented upon regularly, and the trivium and quadrivium were known as one does not go without the other. Almost all the scholars were completely experienced in the Aristotelian Dialects and the commentaries of formal logic.'[16] Nkrumah also used to talk proudly of Anthony William Amoo, the Ghanaian, who in the eighteenth century taught philosophy at the University of Wittenberg in Germany and 'wrote dissertations in Latin and Greek'.[17]

The most intellectual of all Nkrumah's own works is *Consciencism*. To some extent, the book is a collaborative effort. Nkrumah himself acknowledges the assistance of his Philosophy Club, of which Professor William Abraham, the Ghanaian philosopher, was presumably a member. In spite of its many and serious imperfections, there is no doubt that the book is the work of the intellect. Diallo Telli, later secretary-general of the Organization of African Unity, took part in a ceremony to launch the book, and he asserted that the book deprived of all validity 'the accumulated lies about the so-called congenital inability of African man to raise himself to the highest levels on the plane of thought'.[18] Telli was substantially right in seeing the book in those terms.

Yet *Consciencism* is also the least Africa-oriented of all Nkrumah's books. Descartes is by no means the only western philosopher discussed in it. Much of the book is in the tradition of Greek 'analytic and discursive reason'. The dilemma of African cultural nationalism is implicit in Diallo Telli's evaluation. In order to establish her intellectual equality with the West, Africa has to master western versions of intellectual skills. Africa has to establish that she can be as 'Greek' as the next person.

But sometimes African nationalists have wanted to go further than this. They have wanted to assert an African role in the growth of Greek culture itself. A crucial link in the chain of this reasoning is another mystique that we must now look at — the mystique of the Nile. And it is this mystique which brings in not only northern Africa but also eastern.

East Africa, the Nile and the Middle East

A Ghanaian intellectual, Michael Dei-Anang, once wrote the following poem:

> Dark Africa?
> Who nursed the doubtful child
> Of civilization
> On the wand'ring banks
> Of life-giving Nile,
> And gave to the teeming nations
> Of the West
> A Grecian gift![19]

Few would today seriously dispute that there was an Egyptian influence on at least the earlier phases of the Hellenic civilization. In the words of Henry Bamford Parkes, 'The Euphrates and the Nile valleys were the original sources of the civilization of Western man.'[20] This consideration affects eastern Africa in two ways. First, because the precise nature of ancient Egypt's links with countries south of her might be important in determining whether Egypt's civilization was, in any meaningful sense, an African achievement. The second consideration which makes eastern Africa relevant is at once simpler and of more permanent repercussions. If the Nile was a source of civilization, East Africa was the source of the Nile. The latter fact was not fully grasped until centuries later, but the mystery of the source of the Nile came to have important historical consequences for this part of the continent.

To the Greeks much of Europe was as dark a continent as much of Africa. But the question of where the Nile originated had compelling symbolism. It was at once a symbol of Greek ignorance about eastern Africa and a symbol of Greek curiosity about it. It was a symbol of Greek ignorance because the ancients did not as yet know for certain that the great river had its birth in these parts. But the mysterious floods of the Nile, as well as the river's mysterious source, were more a part of Greek scientific interest than anything that ever happened in the remoter parts of Western Europe. The Greeks even looked at the birds disappearing into the African horizon and speculated about their destination. If Nkrumah is right, then 'Eratosthenes and Aristotle knew that the cranes migrated as far as lakes where the Nile had its source.'[21]

Even if it were true that this part of Africa was as dark a continent to the Greeks as much of Europe was, there was one difference. The darkness of eastern Africa was one of scientific fascination. The darkness of parts of Western Europe was, to the Greeks, devoid of intellectual compensation. But it might not even be true that eastern Africa was as dark to the ancient Greeks as north-western Europe was at that time. In a meaningful sense, East Africa was a subordinate sector of the classical world. It had this status partly through its connexion with the Nile Valley as a whole and partly through its links with the Middle East proper. It is therefore just conceivable that ancient East Africa might have been more a part of the classical world known by the Greeks than some parts of Europe could ever claim to be. Of course, since much more archaeological work has been done in Western Europe than in Africa, the volume of evidence is seriously uneven. But L. S. B. Leakey, for one, has hazarded the generalization that, because of isolation, sub-Saharan Africa as a whole was, for a while, 'in a cultural state very similar to that of Britain at the time of the coming of the Romans'.[22]

Yet if the isolation of Africa south of the Sahara as a unit was comparable to that of Britain, the isolation of eastern Africa on its own might have been less severe. There is evidence of trade down the Red Sea, as well as from the Persian Gulf, from very early times. As Gervase Mathew has pointed out, the list of imports into East Africa mentioned by the *Periplus of the Erythrean Sea* as a historical source 'suggests the existence of a fairly evolved culture'. One could go on to add that it also suggests a significant commercial intercourse much older than the *Periplus* itself.[23]

Sir Mortimer Wheeler has put East Africa alongside Mediterranean Africa as the two parts of the continent which, on present evidence, have had the longest intercourse with the outside world. To use Sir Mortimer's own words:

Two regions of Africa . . . have long looked outwards to worlds across the seas. The first of these is the Mediterranean coastland which has always been inclined to share its ideas with Europe. The second is the East African coastline, the coastline of what we know as Somalia, Kenya and Tanganyika, which has long shared its life with Arabia and India and continues to do so today.[24]

Later on the Middle East exerted a different kind of cultural influence on eastern Africa, particularly with the coming of Islam in coastal settlements. And even late in the Christian era there were areas of Europe which were no more closely integrated with Mediterranean Europe than the East African coastline was integrated with the Middle East. In the nature of the relationship between these areas, Roland Oliver might be exaggerating when he says: 'Certainly Islam's African fringe can bear comparison with Christendom's northern European fringe at any time up to the late sixteenth century.'[25] The exaggeration lies in the dateline he chooses. Well before the sixteenth century Europe had already become more closely integrated as part of Christendom than the East African coast was integrated with the southern sector of the Middle East. But Oliver is at least right in asserting that the integration of Europe was completed well after Islam had come to East Africa.[26]

What we should not overlook is that the Islamization of the East African coast was only a new manifestation of an older phenomenon — the phenomenon of East Africa's contacts with certain parts of the classical world. Later developments had their genesis in the general cultural interrelationship within the classical world as a whole. As Marshall G. S. Hodgson has pointed out in a stimulating article on 'The interrelations of societies in history':

> The Mediterranean Basin formed a historical whole not only under the Roman Empire but before and since. . . . The core of the Middle East was the Fertile Crescent and the Iranian Plateau, to which lands north and south from Central Eurasia to Yemen and East Africa looked for leadership, as did increasingly even Egypt, despite its distinct roots in its own past.[27]

But, as we mentioned, East Africa's links with this world were not merely through its historical intercourse with the Middle East proper. They were also through its primeval relationship with the Nile valley as a distinct sub-section of the classical world. This relationship, though as yet only vaguely understood, is giving rise to challenging hypotheses. Fifty years ago a towering British scholar and archaeologist, Sir Ernest Wallis Budge, put forward a hypothesis which, by 1954, was getting incorporated into the movement of historical negritude. In his book on Negro civilizations, Dr J. C. DeGraft-Johnson of Ghana cited the testimony of Sir Ernest Budge that ancient Egyptians might have been, in part, Ugandans. DeGraft-Johnson quotes the following passage from Budge:

There are many things in the manners and customs and religions of the historic Egyptians, that is to say, of the workers on the land, that suggest that the original home of the prehistoric ancestors was a country in the neighbourhood of Uganda and Punt.[28]

Elsewhere Budge argues that Egyptian tradition of the Dynastic Period held that the aboriginal home of the Egyptians was Punt. But where was Punt? Budge answers in the following terms:

Though our information about the boundaries of this land is of the vaguest character, it is quite certain that a very large proportion of it was in Central Africa, and it probably was near the country called in our times 'Uganda'.[29]

Our information about the boundaries of Punt is still vague and controversial. And Budge was sometimes rash. But whatever the accuracy of speculations such as his, there is enough evidence to indicate significant primeval contacts down the Nile Valley, and movements of peoples in both directions. 'It is to the Nile Valley that we look for the original link between Egypt and all south of it', one historian once asserted.[30] And two other historians traced back to Egypt an ancient ceremony in western Uganda on the accession of an Omukama of Bunyoro.[31] Perhaps less scientific was the conviction of a Bishop of Uganda earlier in the century — Bishop Alfred Tucker of the Church Missionary Society — that there were aspects of the Kiganda culture which 'must' have been of Egyptian origin.[32]

The distribution of the Nilotes along the Nile Valley is another aspect of interest in trying to determine the degree of contact along the valley. An essay on ancient Egypt in the 1953 edition of the *Encyclopaedia Britannica* claims that there was a significant Nilotic element in the ethnic composition of early Egypt. The evidence for such claims is confused. But the speculations arise partly out of the apparent cultural diffusion along the Nile Valley as a whole, and among populations descended from or affected by the Nilotes and Nilo-Hamites. One line of interpretation is to see Egypt as a recipient of certain influences from the south. The other is to see Egypt as the ultimate source of certain cultural elements discerned in the lives of people elsewhere in the continent. 'That certain ritual practices and beliefs found in Equatorial Africa are of Egyptian origin need not reasonably be doubted,' G. W. B. Huntingford has asserted. And he too turns to the Banyoro of Uganda to illustrate his thesis.[33]

There is much in the history of the Nile Valley that we have yet to discover. And in any case some of the cultural influences were carried up or down the valley long after the glories of classical times. But the evidence of primeval contacts down the Nile Valley, and of significant movements of populations, is already persuasive enough. It is these contacts along the Nile, *plus* the intercourse through the Indian Ocean and the Red Sea, which converted at least some ancient East

Africans into more meaningful members of the classical world than, say, ancient Britons could claim to be.[34]

How African Was Ancient Egypt?

What this whole question is related to is, of course, the general problem of how far the ancient Egyptian civilization can, in a significant sense, be regarded as an African civilization. This latter problem is at the heart of African cultural nationalism at large. And it is to this that we must now address ourselves more specifically.

In the final analysis, there are at least two basic ways in which a culture might be alien to Africa. One is when the culture itself comes from outside Africa. The second is when the people who develop that culture within Africa are themselves of recent alien extraction. In the latter case the new civilization would be one which the alien group did not bring with them from outside; they cultivated it as something new *after* arrival in Africa. So the culture in its new peculiarities is in that sense native-born. But partly because the particular group which develops that culture is itself of alien origin, the culture falls short of having full indigenous status.

The nearest example in modern Africa is perhaps the Afrikaner ethos of South Africa. In an important sense the political thought of Afrikaner nationalists is nearer to being native-born than the political thought of a black African Marxist or a western liberal. For better or for worse, the ideology of apartheid is an outgrowth of a particular sociological situation in Africa itself. It is a poisonous plant which has grown out of the soil of Africa. To that extent it is more native to Africa than Marxism. In other words, Verwoerd was more peculiarly Africa-oriented in his ideological responses than some of his Marxist and western liberal critics can claim to be.

But apartheid is a poisonous growth that the rest of Africa would rather weed out. And the plant falls short of full indigenous status partly because those who are cultivating it with such care and affection are of recent alien extraction as a group. Their alien nature would have become less pronounced if they had allowed themselves to mix more with the natives and to be influenced by them. But their exclusiveness preserves their alienness in Africa as well as their alienation from those with whom they live. The question begins to be asked: Is the Afrikaner culture really a plant of the African soil? The calculated foreignness of the cultivator arouses the suspicion that although the plant might have grown in Africa, the seed might be as foreign as the cultivator. Apartheid as an ethos might therefore be deemed to be a *product* of Africa without being elevated to the status of being *native* to Africa.

A similar kind of reasoning has tended to affect the status of the ancient Egyptian civilization. Even if that civilization flourished on African soil, its status as an African civilization would partly depend on whether the Egyptians themselves were African. Were the ancient Egyptians immigrants from Eurasia? Or were they really native to the African continent? Cultural nationalism in modern Africa has wanted to emphasize that ancient Egyptians were indeed African. But how can you establish this point? Logically there is no reason why a people should not be natives of Africa without being *black*. The idea that all the people of each continent ought to be one colour is a dogma which has completely ignored the example of multi-coloured Asia. The yellow peoples of Japan and China, the dark Tamils of Ceylon, the brown Gujerati in India, are today all part of the Asian continent. The ancient Egyptians need not therefore have been black in order to qualify as natives of Africa. And yet, if they can be shown to have been black, their links with sub-Saharan Africa would be easier to take for granted. There is evidence that at least a section of ancient Egyptians were negroid. Basil Davidson, in his romanticism, sometimes over-argues the vision of a glorious African past. But he is probably well within the evidence available when he tells us the following:

> An analysis of some 800 skulls from pre-dynastic Egypt—from the lower valley of the Nile, that is, before 3000 B.C.—shows that at least a third of them were negroes or ancestors of the negroes whom we know; and this may well support the view, to which a study of language also brings some confirmation, that remote ancestors of the Africans today were an important and perhaps dominant element among populations which fathered the civilization of ancient Egypt.[35]

Whether the Negro element among ancient Egyptians was only a third, or more, or less, the fact that it was there has become a part of African cultural nationalism in our own day. As one such nationalist, Cheikh Anta Diop of Senegal, put it: 'It remains . . . true that the Egyptian experiment was essentially Negro, and that all Africans can draw the same moral advantage from it that Westerners draw from Graeco-Latin civilization.'[36] What makes Cheikh Anta Diop's position extreme is not his Africanization of the Pharaohs. It is not even the simple claim that ancient Egypt influenced the Hellenic civilization—a claim which few scholars would dispute. Diop's extremism is in the magnitude he assigns to that Egyptian influence. At his most reckless, he virtually credits ancient Egypt with all the major achievements of the Greeks. But even when he does not go quite so far, he at least claims that Egypt was to the Greeks what the western impact has been to Africa in our times. To use his own words:

> From Thales to Pythagoras and Democritus, Plato and Eudoxe, it is most evident that all those who created the Greek philosophical and scientific school and who pass for universal inventors of mathematics . . . were disciples educated at the school of the Egyptian priests.[37]

Diop goes on to assert that if Plato, Eudoxe and Pythagoras had remained in Egypt for thirteen to twenty years, 'it was not only to learn recipes'. He then draws the telling analogy in the following terms:

The situation is similar to that of under-developed countries in relation to their ancient metropolises. It does not occur to a national of those countries, whatever his nationalism, to dispute the fact that modern technique has been spread from Europe to the whole world. The rooms of the African students at the *cités universitaires* in Paris, London, etc., are comparable from all points of view to those of Eudoxe and Plato at Heliopolis, and they may well be shown to African tourists in the year 2000.[38]

But here again a dilemma faces Africa as she seeks to demonstrate that she has a past as glorious as that of other nations and people. She needs the testimony of those other nations for that purpose. Even in the attempt to establish that ancient Egyptians were at least partly Negro, contemporary black nationalists sometimes turn to the Greeks for evidence. Cheikh Anta Diop himself cites from Graeco-Roman sources at large. And the late W. E. B. Du Bois, the distinguished American Negro, used to cite the testimony of Herodotus that ancient Egyptians were 'curly-haired' in the African sense.[39] All this is understandable. Since Africans were often trying to combat western disparaging assertions, it made sense that they should on occasion have to turn to authorities regarded as respectable by Westerners themselves. The appeal to the Greeks, to Aristotle and Herodotus, was inevitably one respectable source of authority.

The question of whether or not ancient Egypt was African was only an acute form of a broader confrontation between African cultural nationalism on the one hand and certain assumptions of orthodox western scholarship on the other. There was one compound western assumption in particular which could not but clash with African pride. This compound assumption took one of two main forms. One form was the belief that whatever was worthwhile in ancient and medieval Africa was of alien origin. Professor C. G. Seligman belonged substantially to this school. He regarded the Hamites as 'the great civilizing force of black Africa from a relatively early period'. And he considered the Hamites to be Asiatic in origin, with ties of kinship with what he called 'the European representatives of the Mediterranean race'.[40]

Seligman might have overestimated the amount of Hamite blood in Africa, or the prevalence of alien influence behind old African civilizations. In any case the conception of Hamites as related to what Seligman called 'the Mediterranean race' could be one extra piece of evidence that eastern Africa was part of the classical world in a sense in which much of ancient Europe was not. In short, Seligman was granting more to Africa than would be granted by some of his contemporaries in Europe. We referred at the beginning of this chapter to the inaugural lecture of a Regius Professor of History at Oxford in December 1841. Professor Thomas Arnold had, as we indicated, talked about a moving centre of civilization which had travelled from classical Greece to England. More than 120 years later another Regius Professor of History at Oxford, Professor Hugh Trevor-Roper, put forward the other side of this particular coin of ethnocentrism. In 1963 Trevor-Roper went on record as saying, 'Perhaps in the future there will be some African history to teach. But at present there is none; there is only the history of Europeans in Africa. The rest is darkness . . . and darkness is not a subject of history.'[41] Both the Seligman and the Trevor-Roper theses were manifestations of a somewhat arrogant historiography, but the Seligman version had compensating factors which were absent from the version of Trevor-Roper.

In any case, a revolution has already started in western scholarship on Africa. In August 1966 Ethiopia expressed Africa's appreciation of the work of Roland Oliver, Professor of African History at the University of London. Professor Oliver was awarded a prize by the Haile Selassie I Trust for what the citation described as a 'very considerable contribution to the development of African historical studies'. Partly on the success of this revolution in western scholarship depends the transformation of Africa's response to the Graeco-Roman mystique. Negritude is an essential part of that response. For too long Africans had been too blatantly denied a creative capacity. They had been too often denied moments of civilization in their past. In an important sense, the black man became the most deprived of all colonized peoples — and his reaction became peculiarly his own. As Melville J. Herskovits once exclaimed, 'But there isn't the Indian equivalent of *negritude*.'[42] The Indians had after all been allowed to keep their Ashokas in full regal splendour.

As Africans begin to be given credit for some of their own civilizations, African cultural defensiveness will gradually wane. Not everyone need have the confidence of Leopold Senghor as he asserts that 'Negro blood circulated in the veins of the Egyptians.'[43] But it is at any rate time that it was more openly conceded not only that ancient Egypt made a contribution to the Greek miracle, but also that she in turn had been influenced by the Africa which was to the south of her. To grant all this is, in a sense, to universalize the Greek heritage. It is to break the European monopoly of identification with ancient Greece.

How European Was Ancient Greece?

And yet this is by no means the only way of breaking Europe's monopoly. In order to cope with the cultural offensive of the Graeco-Roman mystique, African cultural defenders have so far emphasized the Africanness of Egypt's civilization. But a possible counter-offensive is to demonstrate that ancient Greece was not European. It is not often remembered how recent the concept of 'Europe' is. In a sense, it is easier to prove that ancient Egypt was African than to prove that ancient Greece was European. In the words of R. R. Palmer and Joel Colton:

> There was really no Europe in ancient times. In the Roman Empire we may see a Mediterranean world, or even a West and an East in the Latin- and Greek-speaking portions. But the West included parts of Africa as well as of Europe, and Europe as we know it was divided by the Rhine-Danube frontier, south and west of which lay the civilized provinces of the Empire, and north and east the 'barbarians' of whom the civilized world knew almost nothing.[44]

The two historians go on to say that the word 'Europe', since it meant little, was scarcely used by the Romans at all.[45] Even as late as the seventeenth century the notion that the land mass south of the Mediterranean was something distinct from the land mass north of it was something yet to be fully accepted. Melville Herskovits has pointed out how the Geographer Royal of France, writing in 1656, described Africa as 'a peninsula so large that it comprises the third part, and this the most southerly, of our continent'.[46]

Nevertheless, it was perhaps the Romans who laid the foundation for the incorporation of Greece into Europe as we know it today. A crucial part of the process was the spread of culture. William H. McNeill reminds us that 'under the Roman Empire, an increasingly cosmopolitan, though still basically Hellenic, civilization extended tentacles even to remotest Britain'.[47] And so north-western and northern Europe gradually became, in a sense, Greek in culture. And yet there was no logical necessity why Greece herself should in turn become European in physical context. The fact that the rest of Europe was Hellenized did not in itself make Greece European — any more than the fact that Jamaicans are anglicized need today convert England into a West Indian island.

The *logic* of this point might be incontrovertible, but European map-makers had other ideas. By the eighteenth century they had made fairly sure that the seat of the most intellectual of all civilizations was placed firmly within the arbitrary boundaries of what they increasingly called 'the continent of Europe'. Greek philosophers might have conquered the minds of Europeans; but European map-makers had their own back when, in their projections, they quietly captured the territory of Greece on the battlefield of the atlas. In his article, 'The interrelations of societies in history', Marshall Hodgson discussed some ethnocentric elements of his analysis and made the following assertion: 'We must begin with the map. A concern with maps may seem trivial; but it offers a paradigm of more fundamental cases. For even in maps we have found ways of expressing our feelings.'[48] Hodgson goes on to ask why Europe was classified as one of the continents while India was not. He asserts that it is not because of any geographical features, nor even because of any marked cultural breach of the limits chosen. 'The two sides of the Aegean Sea have almost always had practically the same culture, and usually the same language or languages and even the same government.' Why then did Europe become classified as a continent? In making it a continent, Hodgson points out, it was given a rank disproportionate to its natural size. In spite of that, Hodgson asserts, 'Europe is still ranked as one of the "continents" because our cultural ancestors lived there.'[49]

And yet, for an Anglo-Saxon or a Frenchman to talk confidently of 'our ancestors, the Greeks' is, in some sense, no less absurd than a reference by a Senegalese schoolboy to 'our ancestors, the Gauls'. Imperial ideologues had legitimized their expansion into Asia and Africa partly on their being heirs to the only valid civilization, the Graeco-Roman one. But in fact the first act of cultural imperialism that Europe committed was that act of incorporating Greece into the map of Europe. So successful has Europe been in this that today even the Greeks themselves would, if forced to choose, perhaps regard themselves as European first and Mediterranean only second. The only mitigating factor in this blatant act of cultural impersonation is that Europeans did become the great carriers of the Graeco-Roman heritage in these later periods of world history. In an act of cultural piracy Europe has stolen classical Greece. But later, in an act of territorial annexation, 'Europe stole the world'. And in the colonies which she annexed she passed on the message of Greece.

In eastern Africa that old mystique of the Nile was to have a new relevance. The quest for the elusive source of the Nile helped to prepare the way for a new European penetration into the region. In the olden days eastern Africa might indeed have been more a part of the classical world than ancient Britain was. But by the end of the nineteenth century the brightest jewel of Britain's African crown was perhaps Egypt itself. The British Foreign Office inherited from history the doctrine of the Unity of the Nile, and converted it into a new imperial postulate. Historians differ as to the practical significance of the doctrine in British policy. But the balance of the evidence is probably on the side of those who regard it as an important conditioning factor in British attitudes. Ronald Robinson and John Gallagher remind us that 'the idea that the security of Egypt depended upon the defence of the Upper Nile was as old as the pyramids'. They point out its effect on Salisbury who in 1889 to 1890 decided that if Britain was to hold on to Egypt, she could not afford to let any other European power obtain a hold over any part of the Nile Valley. The two historians assert that in so doing, Salisbury took what was perhaps the critical decision of the Partition of Africa: 'Henceforward almost everything in Africa north of the Zambesi River was to hinge upon it.'[50]

Under Salisbury's successors the doctrine of the Unity of the Nile Valley helped to seal the fate of Uganda. As Robinson and Gallagher put it with reference to Rosebery's vision, 'the Cabinet quarrels over Uganda were really quarrels over Egypt'.[51]

And so the snowball of imperial annexation proceeded. Egypt was important for Britain's whole Middle Eastern strategy, and so Egypt had to remain occupied. But Egypt depended so much on the Nile, and the Nile passed through the Sudan. So the loose Egyptian suzerainty over the Sudan had to be converted into a strong British sovereignty. But the unity of the Nile valley was not complete unless its very source was controlled by the same power. So Uganda had to be under British control. But the way to the Lakes from the important port of Mombasa was through what came to be known as Kenya. So Kenya had to be annexed too. The forceful torrent of British expansionism shared a valley with the River Nile — and overflowed into other areas of the East African land surface.

Towards Africanizing Ancient Greece

With that imperialism eastern Africa has also sensed a strong cultural impact. She has felt herself in communion with a civilization which is at once new and strangely reminiscent of ancient ties. The gift of Greece has come with a new bearer, acquiring a new lustre on the way. Ancient Britons might have been less immediately connected with the Hellenic miracle than were the inhabitants of the Nile Valley. But the modern Britons brought the spirit of Greece back to the banks of the river.

But can we concede to Europe the role of bearer of Greek culture without conceding her the right to Greece itself? The answer is, indeed we can. The point which needs to be grasped is that Europe's title to the Greek heritage is fundamentally no different from Europe's title to Christianity. In these later phases of world history Europe has been the most effective bearer of both the Christian message and the Greek heritage. But just as it would be a mistake to let Europe nationalize Christianity, it would be a mistake to let her confiscate the Hellenic inheritance. The Greeks must at last be allowed to emerge as what they really are — the fathers not of a European civilization but of a universal modernity.

The distinction is a matter of importance to a modern university in Africa, where medical graduates might take the Hippocratic oath, historians trace their origins to Herodotus, and political scientists study the *Politics* of Aristotle. In his own inaugural address the first principal of the University College of the Gold Coast, D. M. Balme, complained about the careless use of the term 'European civilization' as the central preoccupation of a university. He said:

It may be justifiable that the things which are studied at universities . . . are themselves the instruments of civilization. It happens to have started in Greece . . . and it spread first through Europe. But it is high time we stopped calling it European.[52]

Traces of ethnocentrism are still very evident in the address of this European classicist. He seems to insist that the Graeco-Roman heritage is the only profitable preoccupation for a modern university. But at least he no longer insists that the heritage is European. This is a step forward.

In the meantime the classics could increasingly be made to serve the purposes even of African nationalism itself without offending the ultimate postulates of that nationalism. One area of possible service is the area of language. It was Aristotle who once remarked, 'Nature, as we often say, makes nothing in vain, and man is the only animal whom she has endowed with the gift of speech.'[53] And it was Léopold Senghor many centuries later who proclaimed, 'Language is a power in Negro Africa. Spoken language, the word, is the supreme expression of vital force, of the being in his fulfilment.'[54] Yet Aristotle's own ancient language had by now a different kind of power within Africa itself, and was not even primarily a spoken language. On the eve of Ghana's independence Nkrumah lamented the following situation: 'At present such is the influence of Europe in our affairs, that far more students in our University are studying Latin and Greek than are studying the languages of Africa.'[55]

Yet what Nkrumah might have overlooked was the potential value of Greek and Latin as allies of African languages in their war against modern European languages. In a paper, 'Swahili in the technical age', Dr Mohamed Hyder, then lecturer in Zoology at the University College, Nairobi, posed the problem in stark terms. He asked whether it was possible to write a serious scientific paper in Swahili on the subject of 'The effect of thyroid stimulating hormone on the radio-active iodine uptake beef thyroid tissue *in vitro*'. His answer was that if a serious attempt was made to develop a 'technical limb' to Swahili, this was indeed possible. The title of the paper would, it is true, include terms like *thairodi, homoni, ayodini, redioaktivu na invitro*. However, Dr Hyder goes on to assert that

> there is no good reason why this development of a 'technical limb' . . . of Swahili through the Swahilization of such terms should weigh heavily on our consciences. Examination of any technical or scientific journal in English, French, German, Russian or Chinese shows clearly that such technical terms are really international in usage. Look up the word 'thyroid' or 'radioactive' in any of these languages and you would find that apart from the token digestive processes exerted on them, they are practically the same the world over.[56]

In a *Présence Africaine* lecture delivered in November 1961 Pierre Alexandre, the French linguist and Africanist, linked this issue more specifically to the scientific utility of the classics:

It would be wrong to say that African languages are a barrier to the teaching of science and technical subjects. The syntactical structure of those known to me would not provide any major obstacle to the pursuit of logical reasoning. The absence of technical terminology in the vocabulary is all the more easy to remedy since, in fact, the international technical terminology is based on an artificial assembly of Greek and Latin roots. The Parisian who speaks of a 'telegram' rather than 'far-off writing' is expressing himself in Greek, in the same way as a Duala who speaks of 'telefun'.[57]

In no other field is the international neutrality of the classical languages better illustrated than in the sciences. In their war against the deadly encroachment of English and French, the African languages must therefore seek an alliance with Latin and Greek. For some African languages such an alliance might indeed be a matter of life and death. Sometimes the classics are not only neutral as between modern European languages and modern African. The classical languages are sometimes called upon to be neutral between one African language and another. Margaret Macpherson has reminded us how, late in the 1940s, Makerere decided that its motto should no longer be in Luganda and so representative of only a fraction of the academic population of the college. The motto became the Latin one of *Pro Futuro Aedificamus*. Mrs Macpherson said: 'It may be protested that Latin represents no section of the community at all, but its use is hallowed by academic and heraldic custom and many may feel it is better to represent none than only some.'[58] In this case then Latin was called upon to help the cause of Pan-Africanism at Makerere and spare Luganda the envy of others. But when called upon to build up Swahili and Luganda to the level of scientific respectability, Greek and Latin would be serving the cause of linguistic negritude as well. 'There are more things in heaven and earth, O John Calhoun, than are dreamt of in your philosophy.'

Perhaps that is the road towards the universalization of the Graeco-Roman heritage. There is already evidence that even the most radical of African nationalists are beginning to assert a claim to that heritage without being culturally defensive at the same time. In June 1964 *The People*, the militant newspaper of the ruling party in Uganda, carried an article entitled 'The formative years of Dr Milton Obote' (then Ugandan premier). According to the article, Dr Obote's headmaster at the college in Mwiri 'made it a practice to read the "Republic of Plato" with the top form every Tuesday'. The article then asked: 'Had this reading of Plato anything to do with the moulding of Obote's thoughts?' The question was left tantalizingly in the air.[59]

When Kwame Nkrumah returned to Achimota as a famous man

twenty years after his student days there, he gave a talk, 'The political philosophy of Plato'. Afterwards his old teacher, Lord Hemingford, went to congratulate him — and added humorously that although he had to admit that he had taught Nkrumah, he wanted to make it quite clear that he was in no way responsible for the political ideas he had just heard.[60]

But perhaps one of the most important speeches of Nkrumah's career was the speech with which he moved what came to be known as 'The Motion of Destiny', a motion on fundamental constitutional reform prior to independence. It was in that speech that Nkrumah referred to Aristotle as 'the master'.[61] At that mature stage of African nationalism such an acknowledgement was not a submission but a conquest; not a retreat into subservience but a move to transcend.

References and Notes

1. Kwame Nkrumah, *Towards Colonial Freedom*, Heinemann, 1962 reprint, p. 1. This chapter is based on my inaugural lecture as Professor of Political Science at Makerere University College, Kampala, Uganda, given on 25 August 1966.

2. See T. Arnold, *Introductory Lectures on Modern History*, New York, 1842, esp. pp. 46-7. Consult also Philip D. Curtin, *The Image of Africa, British Ideas and Action, 1780-1850*, University of Wisconsin Press, Madison, 1964, pp. 375-7. See also Arthur Penrhyn Stanley, *Life and Correspondence of Thomas Arnold*, Ward, Lock, 1845, esp. pp. 435-8.

3. F. D. Lugard, *The Dual Mandate in British Tropical Africa*, William Blackwood, Edinburgh, 1926, p. 618.

4. See Nkrumah's address opening the Congress, *Proceedings of the First International Congress of Africanists* (11-18 December 1962), ed. Lalage Bown and Michael Crowder, published for the Congress by Longmans, 1964, p. 12.

5. See Kwame Nkrumah, *Ghana: the Autobiography of Kwame Nkrumah*, Nelson, 1957, p. 27.

6. Nkrumah, *Consciencism*, Heinemann Educational Books, 1964, p. 5.

7. Thomas Hodgkin, *Nationalism in Colonial Africa*, Frederick Muller, 1956, p. 172. See also Ali A. Mazrui, 'On the concept of "We are all Africans"', *The American Political Science Review*, LVII, 1 (1963), 97.

8. See Jean-Paul Sartre, *Orphée Noir*, Preface to *Anthologie de la Nouvelle Poésie Négre et Malgache*, ed. L. S. Senghor, Presses Universitaires de France, 1948.

9. B. G. Sundkler, *Bantu Prophets in South Africa*, Oxford University Press, 1961 ed., p. 279. Consult also F. B. Welbourn, *East African Rebels: a Study of Some Independent Churches*, SCM Press, 1961, and Sylvia L. Thrupp, ed., *Millennial Dreams in Action*, Mouton, The Hague, 1962.

10. Lucy Mair, *New Nations*, Weidenfeld & Nicolson, 1963, pp. 172-3.

11. L. S. Senghor, *Négritude et Humanisme*, Seuil, Paris, 1964, p. 24.

12. Senghor, *On African Socialism*, Pall Mall, 1964, p. 74.

13. Senghor, 'The spirit of civilization, or the laws of African Negro culture', Proceedings of the First International Conference of Negro Writers and Artists, *Présence Africaine*, special issue (June-November 1956), 64, 71. Elsewhere, Senghor describes Descartes as 'The European *par excellence*'. See his 'De la négritude. Psychologie du Négro-Africain', *Diogène*, No. 37 (1962), parts of which are available in English under the title of 'The African apprehension of reality' in *Léopold Senghor Prose and Poetry*, ed. and trans. John Reed and Clive Wake, Oxford University Press, 1965, pp. 29-35.

14. Nkrumah, *Consciencism*, op. cit., pp. 16-19.

15. See 'Ghana's cultural history', extracts from his speech at the Inauguration, *Présence Africaine*, 13, 41 (Second Quarter 1962).

16. Cited by Erica Simon, 'Negritude and cultural problems of contemporary Africa', *Présence Africaine*, 18, 47 (Third Quarter 1963), 135.

17. Nkrumah, 'Ghana's cultural history', op. cit., 9.

18. See *Ghana Today*, 8, 4 (1964).

19. From Michael Dei-Anang's poem 'Africa speaks'. Immanuel Wallerstein uses these as opening lines for his book *Africa: the Politics of Independence*, Vintage Books, New York, 1961.

20. Henry Bamford Parkes, *Gods and Men: the Origins of Western Culture*, Alfred A. Knopf, New York, 1959, p. 52.

21 See Nkrumah's Address to the First International Congress of Africanists, 12 December 1962, op. cit. For a short but comprehensive account of the Nile as a question of scientific speculation see B. W. Langlands, 'Concepts of the Nile', *Uganda Journal* (Speke Centenary Number), 26, 1 (March 1962), 1-22.

22. See L. S. B. Leakey, *The Progress and Evolution of Man in Africa*, Oxford University Press, 1961, p. 16.

23. See Gervase Mathew, 'The East African Coast until the coming of the Portuguese', in Roland Oliver and Gervase Mathew, eds., *History of East Africa*, Vol. 1, Clarendon Press, Oxford, 1963, pp. 94-5, 97-9. See also the *Periplus of the Erythrean Sea*, trans. W. H. Schoff, Longmans Green, New York, 1912.

24. See the chapter by Sir Mortimer Wheeler in *The Dawn of African History*, ed. Roland Oliver, Oxford University Press, 1961, p. 2.

25. See Roland Oliver's concluding chapter in *The Dawn of African History*, ibid., p. 97.

26. See also Roland Oliver and J. D. Fage, *A Short History of Africa*, Penguin Books, 1962, especially Chapter 8.

27. *Comparative Studies in Society and History*, V, 2 (January 1963), 232, 233.

28. Dr J. C. de Graft-Johnson, *African Glory: the Story of Vanished Negro Civilizations*, Watts, 1954, p. 8.

29. Sir Ernest Wallis Budge, *A Short History of the Egyptian People*, Dent, 1914, p. 10.

30. A. J. Arkell, 'The Valley of the Nile', in *The Dawn of African History*, op. cit., p. 12.

31. The ceremony was that of 'shooting the nations' by firing arrows to the four points of the compass. Roland Oliver and J. D. Fage link this with the concept of divine kingship, 'Egypt's eventual legacy to so much of the rest of Africa'. See their book *A Short History of Africa*, op. cit., p. 37. For a different interpretation of the concept of divine kingship in Uganda, see Merrick Posnansky, 'Kingship, archaeology and historical myth', *Uganda Journal*, 30, 1 (1966), 1-12.

32. Alfred R. Tucker, *Eighteen Years in Uganda and East Africa*, Vol. 1, Edward Arnold, 1908, pp. 86ff.

33. See G. W. B. Huntingford, 'The peopling of the interior of East Africa by its modern inhabitants', in *History of East Africa*, Vol. 1, op. cit., pp. 88-9.

34. The situation was, of course, changed when Rome expanded more significantly westward in Europe.

35. Basil Davidson, *Old Africa Rediscovered*, Gollancz, 1961, p. 28.

36. For a brief version of his views on this, see Cheikh Anta Diop, 'The cultural contributions and prospects of Africa', Proceedings of the First International Conference of Negro Writers and Artists, *Présence Africaine*, special issue (June-November 1956), 347-54.

37. Cited by Erica Simon, 'Negritude and cultural problems of contemporary Africa', *Présence Africaine*, 18, 47 (Third Quarter 1963), 140.

38. Ibid.

39. See, for example, W. E. B. Du Bois, *The World and Africa* (1946), International Publishers, New York, enlarged ed., 1965, p. 121.

40. See, for example, C. G. Seligman's *Races of Africa*, Oxford University Press, 1957 ed., pp. 10, 87.

41. For a brief account of Hugh Trevor-Roper's views see *West Africa* (London) no. 2433 (1964), p. 58. See also Basil Davidson's article on the following page of the same issue. For a more complete account of Trevor-Roper's views on this matter see his lecture in *The Listener*, 28 November 1963.

42. See Wellesley College, *Symposium on Africa*, Wellesley College, Mass., 1960, p. 37.

43. See Léopold Senghor's 'Negritude and the concept of universal civilization', *Présence Africaine*, **18**, 46 (Second Quarter 1963), 12.

44. See R. R. Palmer in collaboration with Joel Colton, *A History of the Modern World*, Knopf, New York, 1962, 2nd edn., p. 13.

45. Ibid.

46. See Wellesley College, *Symposium on Africa*, op. cit., p. 16.

47. William H. McNeill, *The Rise of the West*, University of Chicago Press, Chicago and London, 1963, p. 250.

48. Marshall Hodgson, 'The interrelations of societies in history', *Comparative Studies in Society and History*, op. cit., 227-8.

49. Ibid., 228.

50. Ronald Robinson and John Gallagher with Alice Denny, *Africa and the Victorians*, St Martins Press, New York, 1961, p. 283.

51. Ibid., p. 320

52. D. M. Balme, 'Inaugural address to first ordinary convocation, 2nd December 1950', *University College of the Gold Coast Notices*, 1950-51, No. 5.

53. See *Aristotle's Politics* trans. Benjamin Jowett, Clarendon Press, Oxford, 1953 reprint, pp. 28-9.

54. Senghor, 'The spirit of civilisation', First International Conference of Negro Writers and Artists, *Présence Africaine*, op. cit., p. 58.

55. Nkrumah, *I Speak of Freedom*, Mercury Books, 1962 ed., p. 103.

56. 'Swahili in the technical age', *East Africa Journal*, **II**, 9 (1966), 6.

57. 'Linguistic problems of contemporary Africa', *Présence Africaine*, **13**, 41 (Second Quarter 1962). 21.

58. *They Built for the Future: a Chronicle of Makerere University College*, Cambridge University Press, 1964, p. *ix*.

59. *The People* (Kampala), 13 June 1964, p. 5.

60. *Ghana, the Autobiography of Kwame Nkrumah*, Nelson, 1957, p. 16.

61. Ibid., p. 157.

5 Mahatma Gandhi and Black Nationalism

This chapter* is about a faith which faltered—perhaps a god that failed. The beginnings of modern nationalism in Africa coincided with a profound belief in the power of non-violence. The new generation of African intellectuals growing up in the interwar years responded for a while to the message of Mohandas Gandhi. Gandhi and the Christian missionaries helped to delay for at least three decades the emergence of guerrilla movements in much of black Africa. The Mau Mau movement in Kenya was one outstanding exception. Since then Mau Mau has had many successors and imitators in Africa. African countries which have produced guerrilla movements in the last ten to fifteen years include South Africa, Namibia, Zimbabwe (Rhodesia), Angola, Guinea (Bissau) and the Cape Verde Islands, Mozambique, the principality of São Tomé, the countries of the Afars and Issas (formerly French Somaliland, now Djibouti), the Comoro Islands and the Canaries. In addition there have been violent movements against African regimes. These have included movements in Cameroun, Chad, Eritrea, and Uganda.

Not all these movements have shown the same combative determination as that demonstrated by Mau Mau. Some of them have been a symbolic and collective affirmation that violence is the only route to liberation. Yet the very proliferation of these guerrilla movements, and their legitimacy in the eyes of most Africans all over the continent, signifies an important transformation in the norms of resistance among African nationalists. What is the history of this transformation? Is it the sociology of transition from Mahatma Gandhi to Frantz Fanon? Indeed, how did Gandhism come to be Africanized in the first place?

Gandhi in Black History

India was the first non-white British dependency to emerge from colonial rule. This fact alone was bound to influence anti-colonial

*An earlier version was presented as a paper at the annual conference of the International Association for Peace Research, held at Bad Neuheim in the German Federal Republic in November 1972.

103

movements elsewhere in the Empire. One area which felt the impact of the Indian example was West Africa. J. S. Coleman has reminded us that a few educated West Africans were inspired quite early by the Indian example into forming the National Congress of British West Africa.[1] The West African Congress was established in 1920, following a conference at Accra which was called by Caseley Hayford, the distinguished Gold Coast barrister and a founding father of Ghanaian nationalism.

For a while the most admired aspect of the Indian National Movement was its apparent success in unifying diverse groups. In that same year of 1920 the *Lagos Weekly Record*, a pioneer nationalist paper in Nigeria, had the following observations to make:

> West Africans have discovered today what the Indians . . . discovered thirty-five years ago, that placed as they were under the controlling influence of the foreign power, it was essential to their wellbeing that they should make a common cause and develop national unity. . . . We hope the day will soon come when . . . Hausas, Yorubas, and Ibos will make a common stand and work hand in hand for their common fatherland.[2]

Sixteen years later the most admired feature of the Indian National Movement was still its apparent unity. Chief H. O. Davies of Nigeria affirmed in 1936: 'Africans should follow India – the only way is for Africans to co-operate and make sacrifices in the struggle for freedom.'[3]

But the emergence of the Muslim League in India as a serious secessionist movement soon shattered the myth of unity in the Indian model. A new word entered the vocabulary of West African nationalism – the word was 'Pakistanism'. The fear of such a bid for secession became more pronounced in Africa as India approached its goal. In 1947 Obafemi Awolowo, the leader of Nigerian nationalism in the Western Region, and still a major figure in Nigerian politics, made the following observation: 'With regard to the effect of religious differences on political unity, India is an outstanding example. Her experience is well worth bearing in mind in tackling the Constitutional problems of Nigeria.'[4]

More than ten years later Nigeria was still worried about the danger of secessionism based on religion. Independence was only two years away, as it turned out. But Nnamdi Azikiwe, the father of modern Nigerian nationalism and later first president of the Republic of Nigeria, was all too conscious of the risks of dissension. He said:

> It is essential that ill-will be not created in order to encourage a Pakistan in this country. The North and the South are one, whether we wish it or not. The forces of history have made it so. We have a common destiny.[5]

Azikiwe was an Ibo and a Christian. The tragedy of Nigeria had yet to be explored in all its devastation. The Nigerian Civil War was in effect basically ethnic rather than religious, but the Biafran propaganda machine was very effective in exploiting the Christian sensibilities of the western world and portraying the war in a manner reminiscent of the tactics of the Muslim League in British India.

But well before the Nigerian tragedy, the experience of the Indian sub-continent had indeed ceased to be the model of national unity for which it had been admired in the 1920s. On the contrary, the Indian sub-continent became a lesson to Africa on the dangers of dissension. Nigeria, because of its rough division between a Muslim North and a Christian South, was particularly haunted by the danger of partition — and that later tragedy which engulfed the country made those forebodings all the more poignant. But Nigeria was not the only African country that had drawn this kind of lesson from India's experience. The Convention People's Party of the Gold Coast included in its 1954 Election Manifesto the following battle cry: 'We have seen the tragedy of religious communalism in India and elsewhere. Don't let us give it a chance to take root and flourish in Ghana. *Down with Pakistanism!*'[6] What was growing was a deep sensitivity to the great link between violence and primordial identity. The hazards of a plural society had already been dramatically illustrated in the Indian experience. The incredible slaughter of Indian by Indian upon the partition of the sub-continent deeply affected many politically conscious Africans in the colonies at that time.

Much later there was to be a second partition of the Indian continent — the break-up of Pakistan and the emergence of Bangladesh. In a curious manner while the first partition which created Pakistan was a triumph of religion, the second partition which created Bangladesh was a failure of religion. In 1947 religion emerged as a potentially viable foundation for nationality, and Mohammed Ali Jinnah became the founding father of a new Islamic state. But by 1972 the Indian sub-continent was experiencing an alliance between a Hindu woman, Indira Gandhi, and a Bengali Muslim nationalist, Mujibur Rahman. Both the triumph of religion in British India in 1947, and the collapse of religion in 1972, were accompanied by carnage and horrifying violence.

It is against this background that the legacy of Mahatma Gandhi assumes pertinence both for the Indian sub-continent itself and for the status of India as a potential model for the Third World. India's loss of stature upon losing the unity of her nationalist movement by no means meant the end of India's potentiality as a model in other ways, nor of India's influence on the positive aspirations of Third World nationalists elsewhere. The Indian model in the 1930s had already been acquiring other qualities which came to compel admiration at the same time as it was losing the old quality of national cohesion. Pre-eminent among those new qualities were those which were brought out and sharpened by Gandhi's movement of passive resistance.

Quite early in his life Gandhi himself saw non-violence as a method which could be well suited to the black man as well as the Indian. He regarded the method as promising for both black Americans and Africans. In 1924 Gandhi said that if the black people 'caught the spirit of the Indian movement, their progress must be rapid'.[7] By 1936 Gandhi was wondering whether the black people, as perhaps among the most oppressed of all peoples, might not be the best bearers of the banner of passive resistance. To use Gandhi's own words: 'It may be through the Negroes that the unadulterated message of non-violence will be delivered to the world.'[8]

In the United States the Gandhian torch came to be passed to Martin Luther King—who kept on affirming Gandhian principles as reciprocal race violence caught up with the slow pace of ethnic liberalization in his country. King, a devout Christian, tells us how he once despaired of love as a solution to social problems. He had read Nietzsche and his idea of the Will to Power, and this shook his faith in mere love. Then one Sunday afternoon he travelled to Philadelphia to hear a sermon by Dr Mordecai Johnson, President of Howard University. Dr Johnson had just returned from a trip to India. In his address in Philadelphia he spoke on the life and teachings of Mahatma Gandhi. Martin Luther King was so moved that upon leaving the meeting he went to look for books on Gandhi's life and works. Prior to reading Gandhi, King had been driven to the view that the Christian ethic could only cope with a crisis of relations between *individuals*. The 'turn the other cheek' philosophy and the 'love your enemies' precept were only valid when individuals were in conflict with other individuals.

> Gandhi was probably the first person in history to lift the love ethic of Jesus above mere interaction between individuals to a powerful and effective social force on a large scale. . . . I came to feel that this was the only morally and practically sound method open to oppressed people in their struggle for freedom.[9]

In a sense, if Jesus was Marx, Gandhi was Lenin. Just as Lenin had operationalized in institutional and organizational terms the revolutionary ideas which Marx had thrown out to the world, so Gandhi had operationalized in organizational and collective terms the love ethic bequeathed by Jesus to situations of man's confrontation with man.

In Africa the Gandhian torch passed to Kwame Nkrumah, the leader at that time of Gold Coast nationalism. In June 1949, Nkrumah launched the strategy of 'Positive Action' as a form of harassing British authorities to grant one concession after another to the nationalist movement. Some of his fellow Africans in the country were apprehensive about the implications of the strategy. In his autobiography Nkrumah tells us how he explained the strategy to a critical traditional local council.

I described Positive Action as the adoption of all legitimate and constitutional means by which we could attack the forces of imperialism in the country. The weapons were legitimate political agitation, newspaper and educational campaigns and, as a last resort, the constitutional application of strikes, boycotts and non-co-operation based on the principle of absolute non-violence, as used by Gandhi in India.[10]

With the launching of 'Positive Action', Nkrumah earned the name not only of 'Apostle of Freedom' but also of 'Gandhi of Ghana'. Years later Nkrumah was to say: 'We salute Mahatma Gandhi and we remember, in tribute to him, that it was in South Africa that his method of non-violence and non-co-operation was first practised.'[11]

But was it really a tribute to Gandhism to refer to a country where passive resistance had still *not* paid? Would it not have been more polite to be silent about South Africa as the first testing ground of Gandhian methods? Yet Nkrumah was not being sarcastic. He was genuinely saluting the Mahatma as the intellectual influence behind his own method of Positive Action. The truth of the matter is that it took African nationalism quite a while to realize that Gandhism was not always successful. At the 1958 All Africa People's Conference in Accra one of the major debating points became the issue of whether violence was, or could be, a legitimate instrument of the African nationalist. The Algerians were then at war against the French for their own independence, and they put up a spirited case in defence of armed insurrection, supported by speakers from other Arab African states. But black Africa was still not yet convinced of the wisdom of armed insurrection, and certainly not convinced of the wisdom of public acclaim for such means from the conference in Accra.

Two years later Kenneth Kaunda in Central Africa was still almost fanatical in his attachment to Gandhism. In a discussion with Colin Morris published in 1960, Kaunda conceded that where people were denied access to a democratic system of government, there was a great temptation to resort to what he called 'non-democratic means'. He cited for illustration the experience of Cyprus and Malaya at the time. But Kaunda then went on to emphasize: 'I could not lend myself to take part in any such campaigns. *I reject absolutely violence in any of its forms as a solution to our problem.*'[12]

Although Kaunda is not basically a philosopher at all, he did place his attachment to non-violence in the context of a broader philosophical view of the world. Curiously enough, Kaunda seemed to believe that there was something unnatural in being non-violent. He did not share the romanticism which saw man as being essentially peaceful. On the contrary, Kaunda felt that 'man, just like any other animal, is violent'.[13] Yet the distinctive thing about man is that he could conquer certain aspects of his own nature. An alternative way of putting it is to argue that the nature of man includes the capacity to modify his own nature by cultivating certain aspects of it and partially repressing others. Morally, man was capable of moving upward to a higher nature. In Kaunda's words:

> First of all we must understand that non-violence is, as Mahatma Gandhi described it, a 'big experiment in man's development towards a higher realization of himself.' This is obviously a slow process as all recorded history shows. Man . . . is violent. But he has so many finer qualities than other animals that we should entertain this Gandhian thought.[14]

The Sociology of Black Gandhism

Evidently significant processes of pacific socialization had been under way in the black world to produce such adherence to Gandhian techniques. It is one of the curious things of history that, outside India itself, Gandhism passed not to fellow Asians, but to black people in the New World and in Africa. It was not without significance that the first non-white winners of the Nobel Prize for Peace were Ralph Bunche, Chief Albert Luthuli and Martin Luther King. Martin Luther King later came also, upon his death, to be the first winner of the Nehru Prize for Peace. The process of pacific socialization was in part based on western Christianity as transmitted in the black world. Kenneth Kaunda, Albert Luthuli, Martin Luther King were all products of a devout upbringing in Christian terms. Even Nkrumah had many of his earlier sensibilities fundamentally affected by the impact of Catholicism.

The success of Gandhism in Africa while it lasted was a measure both of the success and failure of Christianity. In some ways Mahatma Gandhi became a political antidote to Jesus Christ. Just as Saint Augustine had once allied Christianity with the concept of *Pax Romana*, so Christianity later came to be linked to the whole vision of *Pax Britannica*. In Africa Christianity came to be associated particularly with colonization. In one of his early speeches of the 1940s, Jomo Kenyatta is said to have compressed into a witticism a feeling of disaffection shared by many other nationalists: 'The white men came and asked us to shut our eyes and pray. When we opened our eyes it was too late—our land was gone.' Much later Albert Luthuli, himself a devout Christian, came to feel keenly the handicap which his religion was experiencing in the age of nationalism in Africa. Luthuli lamented: 'The average African says the white man is the cause of all his troubles. He does not discriminate between white men and see that some come here for material gain and others come with the message of God.'[15]

It was in contexts of this kind of reasoning that Mahatma Gandhi sometimes became a nationalist antidote to Jesus Christ. The message of Jesus had been used to encourage submission from the natives. The message had not been presented as a call for 'non-violent *resistance*' but at best for 'non-violence'. Christianity could even be interpreted to mean 'non-resistance' — a coming to terms with those in authority, whoever they might be. 'My kingdom is not of this earth' — this declaration came to imply what E. H. Carr called 'a boycott of politics'. But Carr was wrong in bracketing Gandhism and Christianity together as '*doctrines of non-resistance*'. What Gandhi offered to black nationalism was the element of resistance, added to the passivity of imperial Christianity. Carr was wrong in extending the description, 'boycott of politics', to Gandhism as well as to Christianity. On the contrary, as Martin Luther King discovered, Gandhism was for the black man a politicization of Christian doctrine.[16] What we have had then in the black world is pacific socialization which was partly Christian derived, but which was also to some extent in rebellion against certain aspects of Christianity.

The South African origins of Gandhism continued to affect the destiny of the movement for a while. It was between 1906 and 1908 that a civil disobedience campaign was launched in South Africa under the leadership of Gandhi, directed against laws in the Transvaal which required Indians to carry registration certificates. The movement did have an impact on African opinion in South Africa.

Leo Kuper has reminded us of a series of Gandhian protest experiments in South Africa in those early years. African women in Bloemfontein used the technique of civil disobedience in 1913 in their protests against the extension of pass laws to them by municipalities in the Orange Free State. The women's movement spread to other towns, and continued for a few years. In 1919 the African National Congress started experimenting with these techniques in Johannesburg. The Communist Party in Durban in 1930 also went 'Gandhian'. The Indians in South Africa resisted in 1946 in a similar way in protest against the Asiatic Land Tenure and Indian Representation Act. Meanwhile the struggle in India itself was helping to give Gandhian tactics global visibility and capturing the imagination of politically conscious blacks in South Africa, as well as elsewhere. Then came the South African Campaign for the Defiance of Unjust Laws of 1952, again using Gandhian techniques of civil disobedience. But in the very wake of such tactics, the system in South Africa was closing up and getting more intolerant.

The Gandhian resistance in South Africa in the early 1950s was an alliance between blacks and Indians in the Union. It was in July 1951 that the African and Indian Congresses and the Franchise Action Council of the Coloureds appointed a Joint Planning Council. The aim was to co-ordinate the efforts of Africans, Indians, and Coloured peoples in a mass campaign for the repeal of the pass laws, the Group Areas Act on racial segregation, the Separate Representation of Voters Act which was moving in the direction of further curtailment of the political rights of Coloureds, and the Bantu Authorities Act seeking to ensure a retribalization of Africans. The campaign was successful in terms of the degree of involvement of the three groups, but a failure in terms of its aims. The failure was even more significant as an indicator of the limits of Gandhism, and the implications of this for pacific socialization in Africa at large.[17]

Strategies of resistance to racial domination in South Africa were then more regional than national. In September 1958 there had come into being further north a movement called the Pan-African Freedom Movement of East and Central Africa (PAFMECA). The aim of the organization was to co-ordinate nationalist movements mainly in British East and Central Africa and ensure periodic consultations on strategy and methods of agitation for self-government. At that time nationalism in British Africa was still significantly under the influence of Gandhism. But black nationalists in South Africa and Southern Rhodesia were becoming disenchanted with the principle of non-violence. Such militant nationalist movements from further south became more directly affiliated to the nationalist movements elsewhere in Central and in East Africa when PAFMECA finally became PAFMECSA — the Pan-African Freedom Movement of East, Central, and Southern Africa. This was a major change. Before long neo-military liberation movements from further south assumed greater influence within the organization. In the words of Richard Cox:

> The Liberation Movements in addition to swelling PAFMECSA, changed its policy fundamentally. The use of violence was a recurrent theme. . . . Nelson Mandela . . . of South Africa made an unexpected appearance and, to great applause, spoke of sabotage, of people turning their faces from the paths of peace and non-violence.[18]

Nor was Mandela among the extremists, although he was later to be imprisoned in South Africa after a grand trial alleging treason and sabotage. There were other voices from the southern part of the continent which were even more militant. But at least as significant was the report that Kenneth Kaunda, later to become president of Zambia, was the only delegate at that conference who did not applaud the new mood of violent militancy.

Something was happening in black Africa, partly under the influence of the very country where Gandhi had first practised passive resistance. South Africa was the cradle of African Gandhism — was it also going to be its grave?

The Limits of Gandhism

As a strategy of agitation, Gandhi's *satyagraha* depended for its success on three clusters of factors. Firstly, it depended on the qualities of the agitator himself; secondly, on the qualities of the regime at whom the agitation was directed; and thirdly, on the nature of the cause behind the whole crusade.

In 1963 Kenya's Tom Mboya—who had been Chairman of the Accra Conference five years previously where non-violence had been debated so keenly by Africans—made a remark which echoed much of the general African disenchantment with Gandhian techniques. Mboya observed in his autobiography: 'Even those African leaders who accept Gandhi's philosophy find there are limitations to its use in Africa.'[19] What limitations? Again some of the limitations may lie in the African himself; some may lie in the regime that the African is struggling against; and some may lie in the changing objectives for which Africans are striving, and within these clusters of factors lie the boundaries of effective pacific socialization. Socialization in the direction of a preference for peaceful methods of resistance may itself hinge on a variety of other pre-conditions. One important pre-condition concerns the general political culture of the groups in question.

Did the African share those aspects of India's political culture which had made Gandhism such a success in India? Such a question was raised with Nkrumah soon after he threatened Positive Action in the Gold Coast a few years after the end of the Second World War. Nkrumah was summoned before the Colonial Secretary of the Gold Coast, Mr R. H. Saloway, According to Nkrumah, Mr Saloway warned him in the following terms:

> But don't you see that this Positive Action that you are planning will bring chaos and ultimate disorder into the country? . . . now India was a very different matter. The Indian was used to suffering pains and deprivations, but the African has not that spirit of endurance.[20]

If this was a claim that the African was more prone to violence than the Indian, the claim is dubious. In the history of de-colonization there have been few slaughters more appalling than the carnage between Hindus and Muslims when the sub-continent was partitioned. We have also had the remarkable experience of the agony of Bangladesh, again involving people of Indian extraction. And the history of India herself since independence has been characterized by recurrent outbursts of linguistic, religious, and other forms of riots.

In fact Positive Action in Ghana was by no means the chaotic failure that Saloway thought it would be. Strategic strikes and demonstrations were managed with effect. Nkrumah had been haunted by the fear that Saloway might be vindicated. As Nkrumah put it, 'Mr Saloway's words hammered in my brain in mockery—"Now, had this been

India!"' But Positive Action in the Gold Coast contributed its share to the country's progress towards self-government. And the failure of civil disobedience in South Africa was due less to the violent propensities of the African than to the extra repressiveness of the regime.

Yet, on at least one major point, Saloway was right. It was true that the Indian was used to certain forms of suffering and deprivation the like of which was virtually unknown to most Africans. For one thing, poverty in India can become more severe than it hardly ever becomes in Africa. But from the point of view of pacific socialization, an even more important consideration is that Hinduism sometimes makes a virtue of suffering and hardship. As E. W. F. Tomlin put it in a somewhat dramatic form:

> If a half-naked or wholly naked Hindu . . . deliberately starves himself to within an ace of death or nearly buries himself alive — or actually does so — we tend to dismiss these acts as mere wanton aberrations, the product of ascetic high spirits. Such a judgement is superficial. . . . The Yogi is simply a man who takes the Hindu philosophy to its logical conclusion.[21]

This Hindu philosophy was probably an important contributory factor to pacific socialization as an aspect of Hindu political culture. And this in turn was a fact behind the success of Gandhi himself in Indian politics, and the viability of Gandhism for a while in Indian political conditions. Gandhi became acceptable as a spiritual leader because the society valued the qualities of asceticism and self-discipline which he exemplified. And Gandhism worked in India both because Gandhi himself had become a spiritual hero and because the qualities of martyrdom and physical endurance which he demanded for passive resistance were far from alien to the Hindu temperament.

This is in contrast to the political culture of most African societies. As I have had occasion to say elsewhere, Africa has no ascetic tradition of the Hindu kind. The idea of lying across a railway line as a form of passive resistance would fire few imaginations on the African continent. As for the idea of 'fasting unto death', this became almost uniquely Indian. There are indeed instances where the spirit of non-violent resistance needs a certain suicidal resignation to work effectively. This temperament of suicidal resignation, complete with a philosophical tradition behind it, is more evident in India than in Africa. As an aspect of the political culture of the country, Indian asceticism has been profoundly relevant in the whole process of pacific socialization in that country.

Sometimes the qualities needed in the agitator for the success of such techniques of resistance become indistinguishable from the purposes and ends of that resistance. Certainly the particular role taken by a leader could determine whether or not *satyagraha* was meaningful.

As we indicated, Kenneth Kaunda was an almost fanatical Gandhian for as long as he was a nationalist agitating against British rule in Northern Rhodesia. Then finally independence came. Kaunda became head of state. Could a head of state in Africa, or indeed anywhere else in the world, ever regard it as meaningful to assert, as Kaunda had once done, 'I reject absolutely violence in any of its forms as a solution to our problems'?

There was certainly an element of tragedy in what Kaunda was driven to do almost as soon as he assumed the reins of state on attainment of independence in 1964. Followers of Alice Lenshina, the Prophetess of the Lumpa Church, exploded into acts of brutality. Kaunda, an essentially peaceful man, was driven to make ruthless decisions — like the remarkable order he gave for the capture of Alice 'dead or alive!' Kaunda as head of government was now embarking on a drive against violent fanatics — and Kaunda the man became almost guiltily defensive as he said, 'Let them call me a savage!' [22]

Had Kaunda completely renounced his old Gandhian principles of 'rejecting absolutely violence in any of its forms'? In his defence it must indeed be argued that the doctrine of 'absolute non-violence', which was never even espoused by Gandhi himself, would in any case only make sense if one were struggling *against* a government. It could not make sense as a policy to be pursued by a government in power. One could say to a government: 'Do not use more force than is necessary.' But it would not be meaningful to say to a government: '*Never* use violent methods of law enforcement!' What if the government was up against a gang of armed lawbreakers? What if one group of citizens was using violence against another? What if there was an armed insurrection by an extremist minority? In order to cope with such crises no government can afford to renounce the use of armed force. Indeed, political analysts since Max Weber have sometimes defined the state in terms of its 'monopoly of the legitimate use of physical force within a given territory'.[23]

Kaunda in 1960 was a man struggling against a government. He was in a position to say: 'I reject absolutely violence in any of its forms as a solution to our problems.' What he must have meant was that he rejected the use of violence by his fellow citizens against the government of the country. But Kaunda by August 1964 *was* the government of the country. And the Lumpa Church could only be subdued by counter-violence from government forces.

As for the degree of Kaunda's anger against the Lumpa Church, it might have been due less to the use of violence as such by members of the church than to the apparent pointlessness of it all. In an impassioned speech to Parliament in Lusaka, President Kaunda attributed to the Lumpa Church 'a queer teaching that men must kill before they die'. In response to people with such a belief, Kaunda assured the house: 'My Government will spare no efforts to bring them down as quickly as possible. Even if it means other people calling me a savage then I am going to be one.'[24]

Fortunately it was not long before the Prophetess Alice appealed to her followers to desist from their acts and uphold the law. Peace was restored in Zambia. Yet the Lenshina outbreak remains a major landmark in the evolution of Kaunda's attitude to violence. With a rude shock he was forced to face the ultimate responsibilities of governing. Perhaps he even suddenly remembered that Gandhi himself never had to form and head a government. Satyagraha worked in India as a strategy for winning self-government, but its relevance was limited in the *exercise* of self-government. Zambia in turn was now self-governing. But the strategy which enabled it to win this status was not operational as a method of ruling a country.

The ideological shock which Kaunda sustained as a result of the Lenshina outbreak was an important preparation for his attitude when Ian Smith unilaterally declared Rhodesia's independence the following year. Kenneth Kaunda was among the most vocal advocates of the use of military force against the Smith regime. Kaunda not only asked Britain to send troops into Rhodesia in order to safeguard the Kariba Dam, his government even claimed a secret understanding with Britain that physical force would be used against Smith by a certain date if economic sanctions failed to work. The British government denied there had been any such understanding. But even if the 'understanding' was wishful thinking on the part of Kaunda's government, it was a measure of a new attitude towards the legitimacy of violence.

What we have in the role of Kaunda as president and his need to use physical force is, as we indicated, a merger between the agent of *satyagraha*, and the cause against which the *satyagraha* is used. What we have in addition, symbolized by Ian Smith, is the kind of regime against which *satyagraha* would in any case not work. It may have been George Orwell who argued that the world would never have heard of Mohandas Gandhi had he been born in Stalin's Russia. The argument here was that the regime would not have tolerated a continuing defiance of this kind. Gandhi would have ended up in Siberia, or been quietly liquidated.

There were moments when Gandhi announced in advance the kind of lawbreaking he intended to perpetrate — and while the limelight of the world was focused on him, he would proceed to engage in that exercise. His famous march to the sea to make salt was a case in point. The march worked because it was permitted to take place and because the limelight of the world was focused on this thin little man walking with earnest determination towards a symbolic moment of law-breaking.

What the experience of British India indicates is that Gandhism works against oppressors who have retained some residual liberalism.

The British officials in India might not have been liberal had they been left to themselves. But they were accountable to a society in England which was subject to liberal constraints. To that extent there were limits to the brutality which could be used to suppress civil disobedience without causing a serious political uproar at home in England. Gandhism worked against oppressors who would refrain from giving the order that the train move when agitators had placed themselves along the railway line to stop it moving.

That being the case, Gandhism could have worked in Rhodesia for as long as Rhodesia was ultimately accountable to London. This would have involved British pressure exercised on the local Rhodesian regime to restrain it from a brutal suppression of civil disobedience, and to encourage it towards concessions. But once Ian Smith successfully carried out a unilateral declaration of independence, and the British restraining influence was severed, Gandhian techniques could no longer be trusted to work within Rhodesia. There is for the time being no precedent of a beleaguered white community, isolated in power in a former colony, being willing to give up that power without violence. What we have is the experience of colonial regimes withdrawing to their metropole without violence. A number of the former British colonies and the former French colonies attained their independence without using methods which were contrary to the spirit of *satyagraha*.

Even in the case of Algeria and Kenya, it was not an illustration of white settlers surrendering their power to Africans. It was a case of the colonial government in Europe being no longer willing to support the white settlers in maintaining themselves in power. The Algerians won their independence when de Gaulle withdrew the French commitment to the status quo, and gradually recalled the army back to France. The local white Algerians were themselves furious and felt betrayed. They would never have given Algeria to Algerians if they had had the power to refuse. Similarly, the Kenya settlers would not themselves have agreed to independence under black Africans but for the fact that the British government in London was no longer prepared to maintain a white settler regime in Nairobi.

We can therefore say that de-colonialization in the sense of the withdrawal of a distant colonialism back to the metropole is quite feasible under the impact of non-violent protest. But de-racialization in the sense of ending a minority white government, in a situation where the white government does not rely on the metropole, has so far not been accomplished non-violently. The only question which remains is whether it ever can be accomplished violently. An internal revolution in South Africa, or an internal violent insurrection in Rhodesia, remain as almost the only potential techniques of ending white dominance.

But is there such a thing as international Gandhism? Is there such a thing as international *satyagraha*? There may indeed be. After all, an essential aspect of passive resistance is, quite simply, *non-co-operation*. attempts in Africa at boycotting South African goods, or refusing to recognize South African passports, are all forms of non-co-operation. When a number of African states decided to stop trading with South Africa, that was international Gandhism. It was certainly the internationalization of the concept of *satyagraha* in its non-co-operative dimensions.

But the question still remains whether even international *satyagraha* can work in a situation like that of South Africa. Are sanctions as a form of internationalized Gandhism likely to have the necessary effect on an entrenched racial hegemonic minority? Some experiments in this direction have already been attempted, but the outcome so far does not warrant excessive optimism about the efficacy of this kind of strategy given the regimes against which it is directed.

Yet in another racial situation, that of the United States, *satyagraha* did work to some extent. Martin Luther King did symbolize a movement that was not entirely a failure. White Americans, like the British in India, had in their political culture a residual liberalism. That political culture was not willing to allow too much brutality against those who were protesting extra-constitutionally. Given that regime, Martin Luther King's tactics stood a chance. Yet even in the United States we have to look not merely at the residual liberalism of the regime, but also at the particular aims and purposes of the resistance. The American experience reveals that while Gandhism might work in increasing political and social equality, it is less effective in the task of achieving *economic* equality. The right to vote has been extended to more black Americans, partly as a result of Gandhian tactics. This de facto extension of the franchise has increased political equality in the United States. The integration of restaurants, communications and schools has increased social equality. But the right not only to a decent income but to an income commensurate with American prosperity has proved more difficult to achieve without resort to urban rioting and violence.

Economic equality for blacks in the United States could either be attained through the triumph of socialism or through the full participation of black people in the central stream of American capitalism. There seems to be no adequate intermediate method of achieving black economic equality. Either the blacks must become fully a part of American capitalism, and have their fair share of millionaires, tycoons, and ownership of the means of production as private investors; or the blacks and the whites should become subject to a socialist mode of distribution. Property in a liberal political culture is too well protected to be easily given away without pressures which go beyond peaceful and Gandhian methods. Black people in Africa could win independence through Gandhi; black people in

America could win the vote through Gandhi; black people in the world could win a seat in a white restaurant through Gandhi. But Gandhi was too ascetic, too frugal, too anti-materialist to be of much help in the fight for a bigger share in a capitalist cake. The black resort to rioting and violence in American cities, painful as it is while it lasts, may be an inescapable precondition for the economic restructuring of American civilization. Here then once again we have outlined the limitations of passive resistance in relation to the ends and purposes which are being pursued.

Conclusion

On 20 October 1972, Kenya should have been celebrating the twentieth anniversary of the 'official' outbreak of the Mau Mau insurrection. It was on 20 October 1952, that the colonial authorities in Kenya realized the seriousness of the movement and declared a state of emergency. And yet there was no such celebration in Kenya. The day passed virtually unnoticed.

Kenya was presided over by Jomo Kenyatta, a man whom the colonial authorities had convicted on charges of helping to found and manage Mau Mau. At the head of affairs across the border in Uganda was Idi Amin, a man who served on the side of the colonial forces within Kenya and participated in the attempt to suppress the movement. At the helm in Tanzania was Julius K. Nyerere, a man who shrank in horror from the violence of both sides in the 1950s, and who decided to encourage a nationalist movement based on non-violence and moderation in contrast to the rebellion in Kenya. In other words, by the time Mau Mau was due for celebrating its twentieth anniversary, three important perspectives on the movement were symbolized by the three presidents who together presided over the East African community.

But also captured in the picture of twenty years later were other dimensions of the total African experience. Amin, who had been a loyal soldier of the colonial authorities and had participated in the violent pursuit of Mau Mau fighters, was by 1972 actively engaged in drastically reducing British influence and power in independent Uganda. Kenyatta was, by October 1972, much closer to the British in sympathy than the man across the border who had once helped to chase, on behalf of the British, desperate Kikuyu fighters. East Africa had changed since those Kikuyu warriors turned their backs on both Christianity and *satyagraha*.

Yet Mau Mau was in a sense being celebrated elsewhere in Africa. After all, the movement was the first great black African liberation movement of the modern period. It was in the jungles of Southern Africa and the deserts of former French Somaliland that Mau Mau was truly being commemorated. All these efforts which were now being made in Southern Africa to consolidate resistance, organize sabotage, and dispel white power and privilege, had for their heroic ancestry that band of fighters in the Aberdare forests of Kenya. However, underlying all these new revolutionary activities and liberation commitments must remain the question of whether there are any real alternatives. Is violence the only route to African liberation from now on? Is Gandhi well and truly dead? Is *satyagraha* a thing of the past? The evidence is on the side of those who say, 'There seems little rational basis for further illusions about peaceful change'.

Apart from Ethiopia and Liberia, black Africa was once divided into three types of white-dominated territories. First, there were colonies recognized as colonies and not as provinces of the metropolitan power in Europe; secondly, there were colonies that were regarded as overseas provincial extensions of the metropole; and thirdly, there was the category designated as 'white man's country'. This last was the category with a significant white settler presence. The most successful from the point of view of consolidating white control right into sovereign status was South Africa. Rhodesia regarded herself as being on the way towards becoming another South Africa; and so did the Kenya settlers until the outbreak of the Mau Mau insurrection.

Of the three categories of white-dominated territories, the easiest to liberate was the first one — those countries which were not regarded as extensions of the metropole and did not have a large settler presence. The fact that Ghana was the first black African country to attain independence illustrated this phenomenon. But if an African country was either regarded by the metropolitan power as an overseas province or had a large white settler presence, violence has so far always been a precondition for liberation. Violence was necessary in Algeria both because Algeria was regarded as an extension of France and because of the large white presence in the country. Violence was necessary in Kenya mainly because of the settler presence. There is no precedent so far in Africa's experience for liberation to take place where white settlers are in effective control locally in Africa, or where the colony in Africa is designated as a legal extension of the mother country.

The remaining countries still under white rule in Africa fall into either or both of those obstinate categories that have so far necessitated violence in order to break white control. The phenomenon of these liberation movements therefore has the logic of history behind it, though a sharp distinction has to be drawn between liberation movements in exile (in Dar es Salaam or Lusaka) and liberation movements effectively operative among the peasants of their own countries. The latter stand a chance of gradually transforming the political situation. But guerrillas in exile are often reduced to being symbols of resistance rather than effective instruments of revolution.

What both types of movements illustrate is the triumph of Frantz Fanon over Mohandas Gandhi, the triumph of the stengun over *satyagraha*. Sociology and history have helped to radicalize African strategies of resistance, and the Gandhian chapter in the annals of black nationalism has come irresistibly to a close.

References and Notes

1. J. S. Coleman, *Nigeria: Background to Nationalism*, University of California Press, Berkeley, 1958, p. 191.
2. See *Lagos Weekly Record*, 20 April 1920.
3. Cited by Coleman, op. cit., p. 203.
4. Obafemi Awolowo, *Path to Nigerian Freedom*, Faber, 1947, pp. 50-3.
5. Nnamdi Azikiwe, *Zik: A Selection from the Speeches of Nnamdi Azikiwe*, Cambridge University Press, 1961, p. 102.
6. The Manifesto is partly reproduced in *The Political Awakening in Africa*, eds. Rupert Emerson and Martin Kilson, Prentice Hall, New Jersey, pp. 110-17.
7. See *Young India*, 21 August 1924.
8. *Harijan*, 4 March 1936.
9. Martin Luther King, *Stride Toward Freedom*, Ballantine Books, New York, 1958, pp. 76-7.
10. Kwame Nkrumah, *Ghana, the Autobiography of Kwame Nkrumah*, Nelson, 1957, p. 92.
11. Nkrumah, 'Positive Action in Africa' in *Africa Speaks*, eds. J. Duffy and R. A. Manners, Van Nostrand, New York, 1961, p. 50.
12. Kenneth Kaunda and Colin Morris, *Black Government*, Christian Literature, Lusaka, 1960.
13. See *New Africa*, 5, 1 (January 1963), 14.
14. Ibid.
15. Quoted in the *New York Times*, 19 March 1961.
16. See E. H. Carr, *The Twenty Years' Crisis*, Macmillan, 1939. Consult also Ali A. Mazrui, *Towards a Pax Africana*, Weidenfeld and Nicolson and University of Chicago Press 1967, Chapter XII, and Mazrui, *The Anglo-African Commonwealth*, Pergamon Press, Oxford, 1967, Chapter 1. I have borrowed from my earlier works and attempted to elaborate and clarify further some of those early propositions.
17. For a fuller discussion of civil disobedience in South Africa in the first half of this century, consult Leo Kuper, *Passive Resistance in South Africa*, Cape, London, 1956, and Kuper's more recent essay 'Non-violence revisited', in *Protest and Power in Black Africa*, eds. Robert I. Rotberg and Ali A. Mazrui, Oxford University Press, New York, 1970, pp. 788-804.
18. Richard Cox, *Pan-Africanism in Practice, PAFMECSA 1958 to 1964*, Oxford University Press, 1964, p. 54.
19. Tom Mboya, *Freedom and After*, André Deutsch, 1963, pp. 50-2.
20. Kwame Nkrumah, *Ghana: Autobiography*, op. cit., p. 96.
21. E. W. F. Tomlin, *The Oriental Philosophers*, Harper & Row, New York, 1963, p. 231.
22. Reported in *Uganda Argus* (Kampala), 7 August 1964.
23. Max Weber, 'Politics as a vocation', in *From Max Weber: Essays in Sociology*, trans. Hans H. Gerth and C. Wright Mills, Oxford University Press, New York, 1958, pp. 77-8.
24. *Uganda Argus* (Kampala), 7 August 1964.

6 Rousseau and the African Legacy of the French Revolution

It has naturally been more in French-speaking than in English-speaking Africa that the French Revolution has influenced black intellectuals. The influence originally took three forms. One was the impact of the revolutionary tradition in France on French colonial policy itself. Secondly, there was the legacy of the French Revolution among those Frenchmen who opposed colonialism. And thirdly, there was the intellectual influence exerted by those high-sounding ideas of 1789 upon the minds of young Africans in French schools in the twentieth century.

It is odd to think of colonial policy as having been influenced by the French Revolution, but many of the assumptions of the French assimilationist policy could be traced to the idea that the cultural past of a people could indeed be wiped out. Edmund Burke, the Anglo-Irish contemporary critic of the French Revolution, captured this underlying revolutionary assumption well when he took the revolutionaries to task for 'acting as if they had never been moulded into civil society and had everything to start anew'.

A century-and-a-half later the heirs of revolutionary France were now established in bourgeois power and were framing policies for African societies which had fallen under their rule. That old assumption of 1789 that the past could be wiped out, and a higher culture implanted, was now applied to African societies. The French assimilationist policy in Africa was born, committed to the Gallicization of black Africa in the grand revolutionary style.

Another level of influence exerted by 1789 on the fortunes of twentieth-century Africa came through French radicals and dissenters. The French Communist Party itself — though paying homage more to the Russian Revolution than to the French — has nevertheless also often seen itself as a higher incarnation of revolutionary France. Many of the rebellious students in 1968 — as France hovered on the edge of widespread civil strife — conceptualized their challenge to authority within a self-conscious national revolutionary tradition which went back to the eighteeenth century and beyond.

French radicals and dissenters, including the Communist Party, were once very influential among Francophone African nationalists. The Rassemblement Démocratique Africaine (RDA), the nationalist movement in the French colonies in the 1940s and early 1950s, received direct organizational, financial and moral support from the Communist Party in metropolitan France. Again, the ideas of the Russian Revolution of 1917 were the most immediate, but these were in any case deemed to be a continuation and elevation of 1789 and 1848. The class struggle continued from the ancien régime to the Fourth Republic.

In addition to the impact of the French Revolution on both French colonialism and the French critics of colonialism, there was the direct intellectual influence of 1789 on young Africans who read about the revolution or who studied the history of political ideas in Europe. In this third area of influence, the recipients were by no means limited to French-speaking Africans. Many of the more philosophically oriented of Anglophone Africans found inspiration at least from Jean-Jacques Rousseau, if not directly from the revolution of 1789. Indeed, philosophically in Africa it has been Rousseau who has provided a connecting intellectual link between the French Revolution and some of the ideas of African nationalism. Let us now take a closer look at this interplay of ideas. [2]

Rousseau and African Populism

At a state dinner to mark Ghana's independence in March, 1957, Kwame Nkrumah first invoked the dramatic device of asking the band to play Ghana's new national anthem. He then made his point, saying:

> Here today the work of Rousseau, the work of Marcus Garvey, the work of Aggrey, the work of Caseley Hayford, the work of these illustrious men who have gone before us, has come to reality at this present moment. [3]

Of these figures mentioned only Rousseau was non-Negro. Nkrumah was suggesting that a triumph of nationalism on that great day of the Gold Coast liberation was a triumph for the revolutionary spirit of Rousseau, as well as of the Negro heroes. Thomas Hodgkin has also claimed that 'the spiritual ancestor' of the kind of popular nationalism which inspired movements for independence in some African countries was indeed Jean-Jacques Rousseau. [4]

In African situations where there was more than one party, Rousseau's notions tended to be the favourite of the dominant party, seeking a monopoly of authority in dealing with the colonial power. After independence Rousseau was still more a favourite of a ruling party than of dissident groups. But there were occasions when some of his ideas were put to alternative uses. Not long after the crisis in Uganda in the middle of 1966, a letter by a Mr Kiryankusa appeared in a local newspaper suggesting that the victory of the central government over the regional government of the king of Buganda was a vindication of the contractual sovereignty vested in the ruling Uganda People's Congress (UPC) by the people. A brave letter by a Mr Musoke came in reply from a small place in Uganda. The opposing letter had the following to say:

> I would suggest that the traditional distinction between a contract of government and a contract of society in political theory is quite relevant to the politics of state formation in Africa today. The society, the people of Uganda, is one thing; the government of Uganda is another. . . . What Kiryankusa is telling us is that Uganda made a contract with the UPC! That is of course nonsense.

The correspondent of the village of Mpigi went on to say:

> I would go as far as Rousseau and deny that there is any fixed contractual obligation between society and government. Society is free to *change government any time, or even to abolish government and live in anarchy.*[5]

But what is the relationship of all this to populism in Africa? The relevance of Rousseau in Africa is partly direct, partly derivative, and partly by analogy. When it is direct it is, of course, the impact of Rousseau's own ideas that we are looking at. When it is derivative we might be looking at the impact of, say, an aspect of French revolutionary tradition. When Rousseau's relevance is by analogy, we are in fact asserting the meaningfulness of comparative political ideology even where no interplay of ideas between two ideological universes is immediately discernible.

Mass populism in Africa has taken a variety of forms, ranging from messianic movements and separatist popular churches in South Africa and Zambia to general rural discontent in, say, the Congo. What we are concerned with here is not mass populism as an outburst of activity, but intellectualized populism as a relationship of ideas. It is the populist elements of African political thought that we are here examining, rather than the behaviour of, say, Alice Lenshina or Elijah Masinde as leaders of popular religious movements.

Many of the leaders of thought in Africa are also decision-makers in government. Their ideas are sometimes in danger of being underestimated simply because they are not themselves putting them into practice. An African leader may propound populist ideas and yet pursue different policies. And yet we are not being fair to the ideas when our judgement of them is based on the accident that the thinker is also a head of state. There might indeed lie a fundamental insincerity between the man's behaviour and the ideas he propounds. Yet insincerity of this kind is a moral rather than an intellectual fault. The man's ideas may have intellectual worth even if his behaviour is morally dubious. Rousseau himself was the prime example of intellectual greatness combined with what was at times nothing less than moral depravity.

In fact, there is more sincerity in African leaders than their critics sometimes suggest. And one or two of the leaders are perhaps among the most politically conscientious men on the world scene. All we would like to stress here is that African ideologies can have important populist components even if African policies are not always in accord with them. It is on these components when intellectually refined that Rousseau has a bearing and, with him, the broader impact of the French Revolution.

Populism and the Individual

It is not merely with the masses that populism concerns itself. It also makes assumptions about the worth of the individual, attaching a special value to him. This is not to be confused with the kind of glorification of the individual which we normally associate with liberalism. What the populist ethic tends to glorify is the *ordinary* individual. Indeed populism is often a romanticization of the ordinary. This is a different frame of reference from that of the liberal ethic. What the liberal ethic has tended to value has not been the ordinariness of an individual; it has more often been his *individuality*. And the concept of individuality is more intimately connected with the notion of distinctiveness than with that of ordinariness. That is one reason why that great champion of individualism, John Stuart Mill, was always fearful of the 'mediocrity' of ordinary people. It was not the ordinary person that Mill wanted to protect and cultivate; it was the extraordinary one. And it was often *against the ordinariness* of others that Mill sought to protect his intellectually exceptional citizen. In short, the paramount value for Mill was not the concrete individual. It was more the quality of individuality, with all its suggestions of uniqueness. We can, therefore, say that opposition to mediocrity is quite consistent with the liberal ethic, but such an opposition cannot easily be reconciled with the values of populism.

If we now turn to Rousseau's thought, a different picture presents itself from what we get in Mill. Many of the assumptions of Rousseau's thought amount to a glorification of the ordinary. There is first his view that every individual ought to participate directly in government. To Rousseau, government by consent is a poor substitute for real self-government. The former principle allows for the possibility of being ruled by others. That is what representative government is all about. But real self-government for each individual demands direct participation by him in decision-making.

Rousseau realizes that if you get the exceptional few and the ordinary multitudes to participate together in ascertaining the general will, there is a danger that simple-mindedness might prevail. When he idealizes the ordinary people he does not necessarily go to the extent of attributing to them an infallible collective wisdom. What he finds in them is a purity of intention rather than a clarity of judgement. 'Of itself the people wills always the good, but of itself it by no means always sees it'. [6] Unlike Mill, Rousseau is not repelled by 'collective mediocrity'. For Rousseau the intellectually gullible can still be morally glorious, 'The general will is always in the right, but the judgement which guides it is not always enlightened'.

In the *Discourse on the Origin of Inequality* Rousseau has a similar theme, but here more individualized. He says: 'Above all, let us not conclude, with Hobbes, that because man has no idea of goodness, he must naturally be wicked'. [7] Again he insists that ignorance is not ignominy. His defence of the simple-minded sometimes attains lyrical dimensions.

But it is easy to move from a romanticization of what is average to an idealization of what is *below* average. The cult of the ordinary moves a step further back and becomes a cult of the sub-ordinary. It is the latter concept which leads to the pedestal of the 'noble savage'. According to this new frame of reference, ultimate heroism lies not with the lower classes of civilized society, for these have already been partially corrupted. The real heroes are those who are yet untouched by the full rigours of technical and rational complexity.

This concept of the 'noble savage' was to constitute an intellectual tradition which, for the black man, culminated in negritude. As indicated earlier, it was Aimé Césaire, the West Indian poet, who eulogized his black brothers, describing them as:

Those who have invented neither powder nor the compass;
Those who have tamed neither gas nor electricity;
Those who have explored neither the seas nor the skies.

Jean-Paul Sartre describes this as 'a proud claim of non-technicalness'. [8] It is certainly a revelling in simplicity which echoes aspects of Rousseau's romantic primitivism. In both negritude and Rousseau's primitivism one characteristic particularly stands out. It is a pervasive distrust of rationality and a faith in emotive sensibilities. The great exponent of negritude in Africa itself is, as we have already mentioned, Léopold Senghor. He contrasts negritude with Cartesian coldness: '"I think therefore I am", wrote Descartes, the European *par excellence*. The African might say, "I smell, I dance . . . I am".' Senghor goes on to assert: 'It is this gift of emotion which explains negritude'. [9]

To some extent this return to the emotions is a quest for authenticity; and such a quest amounts to a rebellion against imitation. Rousseau rejected the eighteenth-century theory of aesthetics in which imitation was the real purpose of art. He substituted for it the view that the act of creation was not to copy but to fill the art form with an emotional and passionate content. To create then becomes an act of emotional liberation.

Sartre traces the issue of black authenticity to the very basis of prejudice against the Negro. Prejudice against Jews can be cultural or religious prejudice. And culture and religion are artificial to the extent of being the outgrowth of man-made institutions in historical perspective. But prejudice against blackness is a prejudice against bare nature itself. In Sartre's words,

> A Jew, white among white men, can deny that he is a Jew, can declare himself a man among men. The Negro cannot deny that he is a Negro nor claim for himself this abstract uncoloured humanity. He is black. Thus he is held to authenticity.[10]

Prejudice against the black man is, therefore, based on one of his indissoluble bonds with nature. It is sometimes argued by white liberals that colour should not matter as it is 'only skin-deep'. Black is a characteristic of the African's appearance — and appearance is equated with superficiality. But the African's appearance is not a superficial irrelevance — it is part of his essential authenticity. If there must be prejudice, let it by all means be based on the essential uniqueness of the Negro — his blackness.

This romanticization of what is natural is also what leads to a glorification of intuition over reflection, emotion over rationality. Senghor never approaches Rousseau's denunciation of the thinking man as 'a depraved animal'.[11] But he does share Rousseau's conviction that 'the human understanding is greatly indebted to the passions'.[12] And it is the African rather than his white conqueror that had the good sense to permit the human passions to yield their maximum wisdom. Thus the central feature of the cultural values of Africans is what Senghor calls 'their *emotive attitude* towards the world'.[13]

There is a danger in romanticizing simple emotions too much, if one is at the same time eager to demonstrate the essential ordinariness of the African. Negritude is apt to drift into an exaggerated portrayal of traditional precolonial Africa as a Garden of Eden. Perhaps this is part of a larger African phenomenon. Perhaps it is a curious aspect of the planting of Christianity itself in Africa that there is an absence of conviction that man before the invention of colonialism was ever evil. Yet there are occasions when African nationalism itself rebels against the myth of eternal innocence. To be inherently innocent is to cease to be ordinary. And so nationalists like Julius Nyerere of Tanzania have been known to protest in terms like these:

> It would be absurd to imply that . . . precolonial Africa was an ideal place in which the 'noble savage' of Rousseau lived his idyllic existence. The members of this social unit were no more 'noble' than other human beings.[14]

Ezekiel Mphahlele, the South African writer, is more specifically rebellious against the pristine assumptions of negritude. At a conference in Dakar, Mphahlele once exploded into saying:

> I do not accept . . . the way in which too much of the poetry inspired by negritude romanticizes Africa — as a symbol of innocence, purity and artless primitiveness. I feel insulted when some people imply that Africa is not also a violent Continent. I am a violent person, and proud of it because it is often a healthy state of mind.[15]

In Mphahlele the cult of African ordinariness triumphs over the myth of African innocence.

As an inspiration for populist enthusiasm either the myth of innocence or the cult of ordinariness could be effective. Indeed, in Rousseau and in African nationalist thought the two concepts are often dificult to disentangle. Yet they can be logically contradictory — and still not lose their inspirational function.

Populism and Society

But for analytical purposes it is possible to argue that the myth of innocence is exclusively a feature of the nationalist component of African thought, while the cult of ordinariness retains crucial relevance for problems of resource allocation and the quest for a classless society after independence.

All African political leaders are self-consciously engaged in the activity of nation-building. In broad terms, this activity expresses itself in the search for the appropriate institutional arrangements, the appropriate economic structure, and the appropriate emotional involvement by the masses. The cult of ordinariness now interacts with other aspects reminiscent of Rousseau. It interacts with an ethos of antipluralism and a desire for mass participation in national affairs.

The supremacy of the general will in Rousseau is a denial of the validity of pluralistic interests. The wills of competing interest groups can only encumber the discovery of the composite will. Bonapartism in France often invoked this argument. This thesis is one which, in various ways, has also been embraced by a number of African leaders. Before independence the idea of a general will was translated into a concept of popular sovereignty to be embodied in a united movement against colonial rule. As Thomas Hodgkin pointed out once, a congress-type political party in the colonies was apt to claim that it embodied the national will and represented all the people. According to Hodgkin, the party's 'dominant concept is "popular sovereignty", and its spiritual ancestor is Jean-Jacques Rousseau'.[16]

After independence the idea of 'popular sovereignty' has sometimes been even more insistently argued. Immanuel Wallerstein has argued that the political ideology of Sékou Touré's political party, Parti Démocratique de Guinée (PDG) has been a combination of Hobbes,

Rousseau, and Lenin. Wallerstein himself tends to think that there is more of Hobbes than of Rousseau in the intellectualized ethos of the PDG. But he does concede that there is much in the tone of Guinean ideology which favours a community of sentiment and a reverence for citizenship similar to that found in Rousseau.[17]

The anti-pluralistic implications of the general will take the form of an opposition both to tribalism and to the formation of competing social classes. Here again the myth of a previous age of innocence is often invoked. Certain social characteristics of the past, notably communalism and co-operation, are mobilized to strengthen a new antipluralistic ethos. In using certain aspects of the past as building blocks for the future, African thinkers are perhaps departing radically from one aspect of Rousseau's thought in the *Social Contract*. The new social order created by the contract was supposed to be an autonomous entity, rather than a stage in a process of evolution going back to the age of innocence. What Rousseau's social contract created was a communal entity with no historical antecedents, but having instead an absolute validity of its own from the moment of its creation.

In a sense, the achievement of the African version of antipluralism is to bridge the gulf between two otherwise contradictory aspects of Rousseau's thought. The age of primitive innocence is, in some of its aspects, converted by Africans into a model for the new form of popular order. The new order should avoid conditions for class conflict. For its inspiration it should look to the essential classlessness of African traditional arrangements. Intellectualized African populism is, in this way, apt to go on denying the previous existence of classes in Africa. But if the existence of classes is ever admitted, then 'historically' it is regarded as having no attribution of social distance and no accompanying feeling of social deprivation or social injustice.

In the modern African doctrine of antipluralism, drawn from the tribal past to glorify community and co-operation, there is a tendency to ignore the relative lack of *trans-tribal* co-operation in the traditional model. Though wedded to the ideal of authenticity, African leaders are now obliged to invoke an artificial identification of interests in the hope of raising enthusiasm and transcending ethnic differences.

Here again the cult of ordinariness comes into play. This cult now becomes a weapon against social pluralism. To glorify ordinariness is to assert a form of egalitarianism. And the latter in turn is a commitment against the growth of privileged groups in conflict with each other and with the underprivileged. In practice the new political class in most African countries is itself creating a mode of living often marked by a certain amount of affluence, and probably out of gear with the national ideology that some of the leaders are propagating. The leaders themselves are a living and agonizing example of the problem of reconciling the will of the individual with the general will. But the cult of ordinariness can sometimes ease the process of reconciliation by encouraging demonstrative identification. And so President Nyerere digs with the people. The leaders of Tanzania assert their ordinariness by the ritual of using a shovel or pushing a wheelbarrow. Indeed, the presidential shovel becomes one more symbol of a general ethos of antipluralism; Rousseau's concept of popular sovereignty becomes wedded to the Marxist concept of proletarian solidarity.

From this position there is an easy transition to the ethic of mass involvement, which also has antecedents in Rousseau: no political system is legitimate unless it rests on the active participation of all its citizens. This in turn involves the suppression of selfish impulses and the emergence of the secular reign of the common good. Out of a personal maladjustment is therefore supposed to spring a moral activism, marked by a rejection of hedonism. And so the Arusha Declaration of the Tanzania African National Union demands hard work and self-reliance from all citizens in a shared involvement in nation-building.[18] To some extent this is a departure from Rousseau. According to the ideology of the PDG in Guinea and TANU in Tanzania, the route to personal and national regeneration is explicitly through sacrifice and hard work. Yet under Rousseau's scheme there appears to be no incompatibility between moral activism and physical laziness.[19] Nevertheless, Rousseau's notion of individual participation in fulfilling the general will does have logical connexions with those African policies which put a premium on mass involvement in nation-building.

Is this the path by which the masses become virtuous? To be virtuous in the eighteenth-century sense did not require the accidental influence of climate or geography. The total involvement of the masses in an appropriate political structure provided both a path to virtue and an escape from a pre-moral society. But in contemporary Africa mass involvement in 'human investment' or in 'self-help' schemes is regarded as a return to an older moral order. As Nyerere once put it:

> In traditional African society everybody was a worker . . . as opposed to 'loiterer' or idler . . . it was taken for granted that every member of society—barring only the children and the infirm—contributed his fair share of effort towards the production of wealth. . . . A society which fails to give its individuals the means to work, or, having given them the means to work, prevents them from getting a fair share of the products of their own sweat and toil, needs putting right. Similarly, an individual who can work—and is provided by society with the means to work—but does not do so, is equally wrong.[20]

Thus an intricate interplay between the cult of ordinariness, the ethos of antipluralism, and the ethic of mass involvement has in this case led to the emergence of ideological toil. For a country like

Tanzania this is one more step away from the colonial legacy. There had been something rather unfeeling about the 'law and order' administrative ethos of the colonial period. The whole apparatus of this colonial legacy came to be something of an impediment to the emotional engagement of the people at large. The political neutrality of the Civil Service — supposedly linked to the notion of a two-party or multiparty system — had all the coldness of bureaucratic rationality. Further, the political neutrality of the Civil Service was inconsistent both with the ethos of antipluralism and with the ethic of mass involvement. In the words of Nyerere again:

> Once you begin to think in terms of a single national movement instead of a number of rival factional parties, it becomes absurd to exclude a whole group of the most intelligent and able members of the community from participation in the discussion of policy simply because they happen to be civil servants. In a political movement which is identified with the nation, participation in political affairs must be recognized as the right of every citizen, in no matter what capacity he may have chosen to serve his country.[21]

And to this wisdom Rousseau might perhaps give a nod of approval.

Populism and International Relations

But it is not merely domestic policy which is affected by populist notions. Recent events would seem to indicate a growing impact on some ideological postulates of international relations also. It is to this phenomenon that we must now turn.

Early in 1965 Léopold Senghor had occasion to say: 'For my part, I think Afro-Asianism has been superseded, for this form of solidarity should be extended to Latin America and to *tiers monde* in general'.[22] A few months later an unusual conference took place in Havana. Cuba was host to an Asian-African-Latin American conference of solidarity sponsored by the Afro-Asian People's Solidarity Organization. The conference was held from 5 to 15 January, 1966. The outcome was the creation of a Tricontinental People's Solidarity Organization, with an executive committee provisionally in Havana. This conference was primarily of leftist radicals. It had been preceded in the spring of 1964 by the United Nations Conference on Trade and Development held in Geneva. At Geneva, Africa, Asia, and Latin America had confronted the developed countries of the world, and demanded a transformation of the international trade system in the direction of better terms for producers of primary products and more concern for the needs of the underdeveloped world at large.[23] The whole concept of the Third World perhaps signified the emergence of a new form of populism — global populism. Both the Havana conference of radical leftists and the Geneva conference of government representatives of all ideological persuasions were symptoms of a new movement just emerging. It was perhaps the bare beginning of global protest of the indigent against the affluence of the developed world — heralding later demands for a 'New International Economic Order'. For African intellectuals, the concept of the Third World is an attempt to transcend their old nationalist bonds of colour and emphasize instead the bonds of shared poverty. Perhaps that is what Senghor meant by 'Afro-Asianism has been superseded, for this form of solidarity should be extended to Latin America and to *tiers monde* in general'.

Global populism as conceived in Africa is particularly drawn towards using Marxist tools of analysis. Nyerere, for example, used them in the following way:

> Karl Marx felt there was an inevitable clash between the rich of one society and the poor of that society. In that, I believe, Karl Marx was right. But today it is the international scene which is going to have a greater impact on the lives of individuals. . . . And when you look at the international scene, you must admit that the world is divided between the 'Haves' and the 'Havenots'. . . . And don't forget the rich countries of the world today may be found on both sides of the division between 'Capitalist' and 'Socialist' countries.[24]

If we accept this analysis, the Soviet Union is itself a bourgeois country — a member of the middle and upper classes of the global society. But within this global society there is no global *state* which Africa, Asia, and Latin America could capture in their global proletarian revolution against the rich. The Africans and Asians on their own may have captured the votes in the United Nations General Assembly — but that is an instrument which is hardly strong enough to 'oppress' the rich countries with. Indeed, the United Nations would almost certainly collapse tomorrow, if American support were withdrawn. The utopia of this international class system cannot therefore be the withering away of a global state already existing. At its most ambitious it can only be the creation of a world state or world government. For the time being there is no world state to wither away. Perhaps a world government is not possible either. The best which can be conceived is an equitable global *authority* which would administer things, even if it never governed men.

Of this whole line of reasoning, however, Rousseau would be suspicious. The idea of a world government tends to be a brainchild of what Rousseau called 'cosmopolitans'. And it is these people whom Rousseau accused of trying to 'justify their love of their country by their love of the human race and make a boast of loving all the world in order to enjoy the privilege of loving no one'.[25] For Rousseau the *patrie* or fatherland is the widest loyalty that the human heart can *authentically* be capable of. But now a few African intellectuals were going beyond the bonds of nationality, or even of blackness. Indeed, the concept of the Third World signifies a shift of emphasis from *pan-pigmentationalism*, or the affinity of colour, to *pan-proletarianism*, the affinity of being economically underprivileged. Mamadou Dia, the former Prime Minister of Senegal, called the first section of his book 'The revolt of the proletarian nations'. He quoted Gabriel Ardant's powerful line that 'the geography of hunger is also the geography of death'.[26] Sékou Touré describes Africa itself as a 'continent of the proletarian peoples'.[27] This view of Touré's is different from the view which sees Africa as a 'classless continent'. A proletarian Africa is, after all, a class in itself—one class within a global class system.

Like the French Communist Party, African populism in its global dimension owes much more to Marx than to Rousseau. Yet the distinction might not perhaps be all that rigid. To save the ancient age of innocence Rousseau had wished someone had cried out to his fellow men: 'You are undone if you once forget that the fruits of the earth belong to us all, and the earth itself to nobody'.[28] The movement of pan-proletarianism as captured in the concept of the Third World is perhaps a new version of that cry which alas was never uttered to save Rousseau's age of innocence. Global populism is a new form of antipluralism. 'It is one of the most important functions of government to prevent extreme inequality of fortunes', Rousseau had asserted.[29] The mitigation of inequalities is a mitigation of antagonistic pluralism. This is as true internationally as it is true intranationally. In the ultimate analysis then, populism at the international level is a dream which seeks to globalize the general will—and turn it from being the will of society to being the will of man.

Conclusion

John Plamenatz once reminded us of the towering importance of Rousseau even when placed alongside a figure like Marx:

> Rousseau's influence on social and political thought has been immense. We invoke his name less often than Marx's because the revolution which he helped to inspire happened so much longer ago and because there are no powerful bodies who profess adherence to his doctrines, but we use his ideas just as much. . . . Equality, democracy, and freedom: to these three words Rousseau gave new meanings, and meanings which are important because they express aspirations more and more widely shared since his time. He used old words to say new things and was more original than he knew.[30]

Rousseau's countrymen later participated in the colonization of Africa, and helped to popularize further some of Rousseau's principles in the very process of breaking them in practice. In the wake of this colonization and of western education, Africa has heard moral echoes

from eighteenth-century France. And man has made one more
attempt to force himself to be free.

References and Notes

1. Edmund Burke, *Reflections on the Revolution in France* (1791).
2. Much of what follows is based on Ali A. Mazrui and G. F. Engholm, 'Rousseau and intellectualized populism in Africa', *The Review of Politics*, **30**, 1 (January 1968) 19-32.
3. Kwame Nkrumah, *I Speak of Freedom*, Heinemann, 1961, p. 107. Marcus Garvey was, of course, the Jamaican who fired the imagination of American Negroes and started a 'Back to Africa' movement in the United States earlier this century. Aggrey was a Ghanaian philosopher, and Caseley Hayford, a barrister, was one of the founding fathers of Gold Coast nationalism.
4. Thomas Hodgkin, *Nationalism in Colonial Africa*, Muller, 1956, 1962 reprint p. 144.
5. Letter in *The People* (Kampala), 20 August 1966, p. 3. The emphasis is original.
6. This rendering is from the Everyman's Library edition of *The Social Contract and Other Discourses*, translated and with an introduction by G. D. H. Cole, revised and augmented by J. H. Brumfitt and John C. Hall, Dent, 1955, p. 31.
7. Ibid., p. 181.
8. Jean-Paul Sartre, *Black Orpheus*, trans. S. A. Allen, Paris, n.d., pp. 42-3.
9. *De la Négritude, Psychologie du Negro-Africain*, 1962. The rendering in English is from Léopold Senghor, *Prose and Poetry*, ed. and trans. John Reed and Clive Wake, Oxford University Press, 1965, pp. 32, 35.
10. Jean-Paul Sartre, op. cit., p. 15.
11. Jean-Jacques Rousseau, *A Discourse on the Origin of Inequality*.
12. Ibid.
13. Léopold Senghor, *Prose and Poetry*, ed. and trans. Reed and Wake, op. cit., p. 35. The emphasis is original.
14. See Julius Nyerere, *Freedom and Unity: a Selection from Writings and Speeches, 1952-1965*, Oxford University Press, Dar es Salaam, 1966, p. 12.
15. 'Negritude and its enemies: a reply', *African Literature and the Universities*, ed. Gerald Moore, Ibadan University Press for the Congress for Cultural Freedom, Ibadan, 1965, p. 23.
16. Thomas Hodgkin, op. cit., p. 144.
17. Immanuel Wallerstein, 'The political ideology of the P.D.G.', *Présence Africain*, 12, 40 (First Quarter 1962), 38-9.
18. *The Arusha Declaration and Tanu's Policy on Socialism and Self Reliance*, Publicity Section, TANU, Dar es Salaam, 1967.
19. In *A Discourse on the Origin of Inequality* Rousseau satirizes the excessive preoccupation with work which civilized society tends to promote. He mentions that in the northern temperate countries this work mania is aggravated by climate.
20. Julius Nyerere, 'Ujamaa: the Basis of African Socialism', TANU pamphlet, April 1962. Reprinted in the collection of Nyerere's works, *Freedom and Unity: a Selection from Writings and Speeches, 1965-1967*, Oxford University Press, Dar es Salaam, 1968, pp. 165-6.
21. Nyerere, 'Democracy and the party system' (1963). See *Freedom and Unity*, op. cit., p. 203.
22. See *Africa Diary*, 19-25 June 1965.
23. See Ali A. Mazrui, 'Africa and the Third World', *On Heroes and Uhuru-Worship: Essays on Independent Africa*, Longmans, 1967, pp. 209-10.
24. Nyerere, 'The second scramble' (1961). For a later version of the same theme, see *Freedom and Unity*, op. cit., pp. 207-208.

25. Jean-Jacques Rousseau, *Le Contrat Social* (1762). See C. E. Vaughan, *The Political Writings of J-J Rousseau*, Cambridge University Press, 1915, Vol. I, p. 453.
26. See Mamadou Dia, *The African Nations and World Solidarity*, trans. Mercer Cook, Thames & Hudson, 1960. Ardant is quoted on p. 19. See also Ali A. Mazrui, 'Africa and the Third World', op. cit., p. 211.
27. See Sékou Touré, 'Africa's destiny', in *Africa Speaks*, eds. James Duffy and Robert A. Manners, Van Nostrand, New York, 1961.
28. Jean-Jacques Rousseau, *A Discourse on the Origin of Inequality*, p. 192.
29. Ibid., p. 250.
30. John Plamenatz, *Man and Society*, Vol. I, Longman, 1972, pp. 440, 442.

7 Islam and Radicalism in African Politics

In the first full decade of African independence the fall of three black political figures was a matter of profound concern to the radical school of African thought. These three black men bore the names of Patrice Lumumba, who was killed in his own country in February 1961, Kwame Nkrumah, who was overthrown by a military regime in February 1966, and Apolo Milton Obote, who was overthrown in a military coup in Uganda in January 1971. Almost exactly ten years separated the fall of the first, Lumumba, from the fall of the last, Obote. These three names constituted the triumvirate of radical martydom in recent African history.

When Patrice Lumumba was assassinated, his children needed a refuge. They needed security and education. Of all the countries in the African continent, the Lumumba children found this security and education in Egypt. Egypt was a Muslim country. Was this purely a coincidence? Kwame Nkrumah was overthrown in a rather embarrassing situation. He was overthrown when he was on an official visit to Peking as President of Ghana. Midway through the formalities of that official visit he had ceased to be President of Ghana. Where was he to go next? Of all the countries of the world, and of the continent which he loved so much, Nkrumah chose to go to Guinea. Guinea was a Muslim country. Was that purely a coincidence? When Milton Obote was overthrown in January 1971, he lobbied for support in African capitals. The five countries which gave him support in those initial days were Tanzania, Somalia, Zambia, the Sudan, and Guinea. The voices of Guinea, Somalia, and the Sudan were clearly Muslim voices. Tanzania had a Catholic president, but two Muslim vice-presidents—Abeid Karume and Rashidi Kawawa. And the population of the country had a preponderance of Muslims. Of all the countries of the African continent, over forty of them, Obote's support, in his moment of political need, came disproportionately from Muslim countries. Was this purely a coincidence? Is it really a coincidence that the three greatest martyrs of the African revolution, at least as seen by the radical wing of African political thought, should have found their most immediate solace from countries associated with the Islamic religion? Nor must it be forgotten that when the new military regime offered a prize of a million shillings for the arrest and delivery of Obote to Uganda, and people started speculating where Obote would go on leaving Tanzania, the three favourite candidates among journalists and theorists consisted of one communist country and two Muslim countries. Speculation was that either Obote had gone to Yugoslavia, which the Yugoslav Embassy in Kampala vigorously denied, or he had gone to the Sudan, or he had gone to Algeria. The fact that two out of the three most popular countries among journalists and theorists were Muslim countries again raises the issue of whether there is indeed a special relationship between Islam and political radicalism in Africa.

But what is a 'Muslim country' anyway? The first thing which needs to be noted is that a Muslim country need not be an Islamic 'state'. An Islamic state is a country which proclaims Islam as a state religion. An African example of such a state is Mauritania. A Muslim country, on the other hand, need not have a state religion. It is Muslim only by reference to census figures.

But need a country have a majority of Muslims before we can describe it as a Muslim country? This would be our normal criterion. Yet African conditions are such that we should perhaps look not for an overall majority of Muslims, but for a clear preponderance of Muslims over Christians. The largest single group may still consist of animists or followers of African traditional religions. But if we are sure that there are many more Muslims than Christians in a particular country, and that there is a diffuse neo-Islamic culture generally, we might for certain purposes regard that country as primarily Muslim.

The curious thing with regard to the fall of the third radical hero, Milton Obote, was the simple fact that Obote had been succeeded by a Muslim in Uganda. Uganda had for the first time in its existence as a state a Muslim head of state. Yet it was precisely at such a moment that Obote, a Protestant, managed to rally diplomatic support from several Muslim countries in his favour and against Amin, at least in those initial phases following the coup. What does this indicate? If this indicates that Muslim radicals are radicals first and Muslims second, does that state of affairs dictate a re-evaluation about the relationship of religion and politics in Islam? Amin's own radicalization and nationalist militancy were still two years away in the future.

The first approximation to a Marxist revolution in East Africa took place on the Muslim island of Zanzibar. Both the so-called Arab 'oppressors' of old Zanzibar and the African masses in whose name the revolution was carried out were overwhelmingly Muslim. How much of a coincidence was this? At first glance the fact that the most successful carriers of Marxist ideas in Africa have so often been of Muslim upbringing might seem to be merely a bizarre accident. The image of Islam in parts of Africa would seem to be that of a conservative force. And the experience of Northern Nigeria would indeed seem to confirm that Islam is basically conservative. And yet, if that is the case, it is not Zanzibar alone which needs to be explained away, a further examples will indicate. When a few years ago Africa was divided into the Casablanca and the Monrovia groups, the radicals were the Casablanca states. Yet of the six countries which constituted the Casablanca group, five were Muslim countries. The five were Guinea, Mali, the United Arab Republic, Morocco, and Algeria (then represented by a government-in-exile). Nkrumah of Ghana was the odd man out at Casablanca.

A few years later, when Ian Smith unilaterally declared Rhodesia' independence, nine African countries broke off diplomatic relations with Britain in compliance with the ultimatum of the Organization of African Unity demanding firm British action. Six of these nine were clearly Muslim countries — Mali, the United Arab Republic, Algeria, Mauritania, Guinea, and the Sudan. The seventh country was Tanzania, a country which now includes revolutionary Zanzibar which has a preponderance of Muslims over Christians and with a neo-Islamic Swahili culture. Of those who carried out the OAU resolution on breaking off diplomatic relations with Britain, many resumed relations quite early. By 1968 only the Congo (Brazzaville) then represented the non-Muslim sector of Africa. Of the first nine to break off relations Nkrumah's Ghana was the only other clearly non-Muslim country to honour the OAU resolution on Rhodesia. The rest were primarily Muslim. How much of an accident was this?[1]

Today we continue to find that, in relative terms, the most radical countries in the African continent are Tanzania (including semi-autonomous Zanzibar), Somalia, Guinea, Congo (Brazzaville), the Sudan, Burundi, Algeria, Egypt, and, in a special sense, Libya. Two-thirds of the relatively radical and militant African governments are of Muslim countries and evidently enjoying considerable Muslim support. How much of a coincidence is this?

A student of Islam in Africa, Dr Ibrahim Abu-Lughod of Northwestern University, USA, has pointed out the tendency of many political analysts to pay lip service to 'the indigenous forces at work in African societies' — and then proceed to ignore those forces. He estimates that one out of every three people in the African continent today is a Muslim. He therefore concludes that 'a serious investigation of political trends will have to take into account the role of Islam'.[2] Yet to take full account of the impact of belief-systems on political behaviour in Africa would need systematic study of the local societies from country to country. Such a comprehensive study has yet to be undertaken. What this chapter is attempting to do is merely to formulate broad hypotheses about Islam in Africa and its relation to the impact of Marxist and related radical ideas and of westernism at large.

Islam and Marxism

An assumption taken for granted in this chapter is that every leftist regime in Africa — indeed in the modern world — owes something to Marxism. Indeed, 'leftism' here means partial responsiveness, conscious or unconscious, to Marxist postulates. A regime which is completely Marxist is atheist. But a regime can be leftist in system of government internally, or in adopting a socialist economy, or in pursuing a militant leftist foreign policy, and still allow itself a place for God. Marxism itself can, in other words, be adopted at different levels. One cannot adopt the whole baggage of Marxist metaphysics without rejecting God. But one can certainly be attracted by the Marxist critique of capitalism, or Marxist interpretation of the function of the state, and still belong to a religion. And yet in this chapter we must begin with the Marxist view of religion. And we must remember that by the very fact of being a West European, Karl Marx was in closer contact with Christianity than with Islam in his own personal experience. We must therefore relate his view briefly to Christianity before we relate it to Islam.

A useful starting point is Marx's famous formulation of what he regarded as the psycho-sociological function of religion. Marx asserted that 'Religion is the sigh of the oppressed creature, the sentiment of a heartless world, and the soul of soulless conditions. It is the opium of the people'.[3] The poor come to terms with their lot because of the promise of better things to come. The poor therefore tend to be the more religious. And the privileged classes rely on religion to promote social cohesion, and therefore give their privileged status greater security. Religion thus becomes a diversionary tactic that distracts the attention of the poor away from the injustices of this world and makes them concentrate instead on the blissful state of the hereafter. God at least is just, even if the present social system is not.

Many of the more radical African nationalists have accepted this Marxist view of religion and made it part of their theory of colonization. They have argued that the Bible was used as a diversionary tactic by the colonizers in order to avert the danger of African resistance. When Kenya's Oginga Odinga was a radical, he said as much at a number of different meetings. Addressing the University College, Dar es Salaam, for example, Mr Odinga once said: One of the reasons why the African was poor was because the White man used the Bible to soften our hearts, telling Africans not to worry about earthly wealth as there would be plenty in heaven'.[4] Many years previously Jomo Kenyatta had reportedly said similar things.[5] This kind of statement was either a modification of the Marxist conception of religion as a strategy of diversion or an interpretation which happened to coincide with the Marxist conception.

Friedrich Engels, Marx's collaborator, once even conceded that there was a socialist content in Christianity from the start. 'Only thi Christianity, as was bound to be the case in the historic conditions o its birth, did not want to accomplish the social transformation in thi world, but beyond it, in heaven, in eternal life after death, in the impending "millennium".'[6] By this interpretation, the Christian heaven was a socialist state, the classless society which lies beyond the grave.

But Engels himself then goes on to say in passing that 'the religious risings of the Mohammedan world' presented what he called 'a peculiar antithesis' to this Christian remoteness. In a footnote Engels suggests that Islam is, in fact, a more materialist religion than Christianity. In this he is not entirely wrong. And in that might lie Islam's strength in revolutionary terms. For Muhammad it did not make sense to say 'my kingdom is not of this earth'. On the contrary, Muhammad carried out a specific act of political revolution and overthrew the Meccan oligarchy by physical force. Unlike Jesus, Muhammad lived to form a political community himself—and that was the genesis of all future Muslim states.

Nor did Islam encourage excessive asceticism or too radical a retreat from wordly preoccupations. Vows of poverty and celibacy, and glorification of physical suffering, were on the whole all alien to the ethos of Islam. And even the Islamic paradise is more concrete, earthy, and even sensuous in the pleasures it describes than the Christian heaven. By this very quality of being more materialist, Islam was a little more secular. At least when you judge the two creeds in their original forms before the death of their founders, there is no doubt that Islam was nearer to being a secular religion than Christianity. Of course, neither was completely secular since both were ultimately based on God as the ultimate cause and explanation. Islam was more secular only in relative terms—especially in the concessions it granted to the here and now.

This paradox of relative secularity within orthodox Islam could bring Islam a little closer to Marxist materialism. And yet even if both Islam and Marxism were secular religions to the same extent, this need not mean that they have the same universe of ethics and ideals. In fact, at least at first glance, they seem to have divergent conceptions of what constitutes legitimate economic behaviour.

Muhammad might well be the only founder of a major religion who was once a man of commerce. He attended to some of the trading interests of his wealthy wife. Mecca itself was at that time, and before Muhammad's time, almost as much a centre of trade as a religious focus for Arabs from distant parts of the peninsula. And a verse from the Koran assures Muslims that it is not wrong to seek a livelihood in trade and exchange in the course of the pilgrimage. (Verse 198, *Sura Al-Baqarah*.) Moreover, the Prophet himself is credited with the saying: 'Nine portions of God's bounty are in commercial activity'.

In Africa, too, the spread of Islam came to be associated with trade. The Nigerian historian, K. O. Dike, put it in the following terms in his major work on the Niger Delta:

> The buying and selling of commodities is almost always accompanied by the contact of cultures, the exchange of ideas, the mingling of peoples and has led not infrequently to political complications and wars. Trade with the Arabs, by way of Saharan caravans, brought medieval West Africa into touch with the world of Islam, and with Islam came Arab culture and civilization.[7]

Trans-Saharan commerce was, in a sense, an earlier and rudimentary form of economic transformation in West Africa.

Many centuries after its birth Christianity became even more concerned with worldly affairs than this. But the Protestant ethic, or the spirit of capitalism, had to some extent to await the Reformation. Max Weber was probably right in regarding the 'moral justification of worldly activity' as among the most important results of the Reformation. John Calvin's conception of the *calling* would seem to have elevated commercial activity even higher than it was elevated in Islam. In its extreme form, the conception did perhaps come near to Weber's description of it as a belief that

> the fulfilment of worldly duties is under all circumstances the only way to live acceptably to God. It and it alone is the will of God, and hence every legitimate calling has exactly the same worth in the sight of God.[8]

In short, the capitalist revolution in the West occurred only when Christian doctrine was reinterpreted to allow more room for worldly materialism. Yet a comparable materialism seems to have been present in Islam from the outset. Islam asked believers to punctuate their lives with prayer and good work — and then go back to legitimate worldly activities. In *Sura Al-Jumuah* the Koran says to the believers:

> O Ye who believe! when the call is made for Prayer on Friday, hasten to the remembrance of Allah, and leave off all business. That is better for you if you only knew.

> And when the Prayer is finished, then disperse in the land and seek Allah's grace, and remember Allah much, that you may prosper. [Verses 10 and 11.]

Anti-cumulative aspects of Islam

This Islamic equivalent of the Protestant ethic fell short of developing into capitalism because of other factors in Islam which inhibited it. One factor was the collectivist nature of Islamic loyalties. It is true that commerce was encouraged in Islam. But so were a host of responsibilities towards relatives and co-religionists. These responsibilities hampered accumulation. As for the Islamic laws of inheritance, they are almost calculated to thwart intergenerational capital formation. There is a built-in distributive device in the Islamic code of inheritance. The wealth of a man is inherited by too many relatives — and a man cannot cheat his way out of this distribution by writing a special will to leave his thriving business to only one relative. Such a will can be challenged in a Kathi's court, and if what the man is trying to give away is more than a third of his total estate, the challenge would probably be successful.

Karl Marx was under the impression that among Islam's more important influences in Asia was the discouragement of private property in land. In a letter to Engels in 1853 Marx discussed land in India and in Java, and then said: 'It seems to have been the Mohammedans who first established the principle of "no property in land" throughout the whole of Asia'.[9] A more common influence of Islam is not to discourage private property in land altogether but to inhibit the growth of large estates, because of the built-in distributive device that we have attributed to the Islamic law of inheritance.

In East Africa early in the century the Islamic law of inheritance was a major obstacle to the introduction of some of the legal aspects of western economic individualism. In Kenya in 1908 the colonial authorities enacted the Lands Titles Ordinance. For some parts of the country this was a major landmark in the story of British attempts to introduce their own ideas of land tenure and title, with survey and registration. In Tanganyika a similar policy was pursued soon after the British takeover from the Germans. There were areas designated as tribal land to which such rules of individual tenure and title were not intended to apply. But it was assumed that since Islamic law did recognize individual ownership the rest of the postulates of the western system of ownership could be easily introduced. And so a system was evolved by which, in the words of Sir Philip Mitchell, 'no title to real estate could be registered, nor ownership or tenancy proved, without survey, conveyance and all the paraphernalia so dearly loved by English lawyers'. Mitchell goes on to recount how unsatisfactory the whole system was as applied to the Muslim populations of the Protectorate of Kenya and the coast belt of Tanganyika. A Recorder of Titles was appointed, and people with previously unregistered titles, surveyed or unsurveyed, were given a chance to prove their claims under the new law. But by 1922 'it was realized that the Mohammedan law of inheritance was making the new titles obsolete almost as fast as they could be issued'.[10]

In fact, the actual physical partitioning of land was not common. What was common was a rapid change in the list of beneficiaries of the income derived from the land. Years before becoming Governor of Kenya, Mitchell had dealt with issues involving the Islamic law of inheritance. In fact, he once translated from Swahili into English a handbook on the subject by Sheikh Ali bin Hemedi, the Kathi (Muslim magistrate) of Tanga.

> Briefly, on the death of a free man or woman . . . the property must be divided in fixed shares between the heirs in varying degrees; they may include parents and uncles, aunts and cousins, as well as brothers and sisters, children and grandchildren . . . I wrested with minute divisions of houses, coconut palms, rice fields, orchards and much else . . . estates worth a few thousand shillings and divided into many hundreds of shares were common.[11]

In short, the encouragement of commerce in Islam did not in East Africa go with the kind of economic individualism which made the Protestant ethic in the West so accumulative. Such considerations should help to make Islam in several African countries compatible with the socialist version of modernity.

But did all this apply to Zanzibar? Surely before the revolution large Arab-owned estates in land were the rule rather than the exception? This is substantially true. And yet, in a curious way, the Muslim law of inheritance in Zanzibar did help to prepare the way for the Marxist revolution of 1964. The most knowledgeable academician so far about the background of the Zanzibar revolution is Professor Michael Lofchie of the University of California. In his book on the revolution Dr Lofchie had the following to say:

> Despite the persistence of considerable economic advantage, the political viability of the Arab oligarchy [in Zanzibar] had been critically impaired during the seventy-three years of British protection. . . . This decline was the result of several factors: the indebtedness crisis, recurrent depression in the clove industry, and the Islamic system of inheritance which divided property among all eligible heirs. Partitive inheritance was especially harmful economically, as in two or three generations many of the larger estates often became fragmented into tiny units no larger than peasant farms. . . . Whereas the Arabs' position in the past rested upon their superior force as a caste of colonial invaders and upon an ability to use this force to dominate the economy, their security now depended upon the intrinsic stability of a parliamentary system.[12]

Although Islam and Marxism had been, to an extent, antagonistic forces within the Sultanate, certain features of Zanzibar's Islam contributed to the triumph of certain aspects of Zanzibari neo-Marxism.

If we go back to the very origins of Islam in Arabia we find that there too the Muslim state under the early Caliphate was almost excessively distributive in its attitude to its own resources. Tradition has it that the Caliph Omar clothed himself in course linen and wore sandals of fibre in which he walked the streets, refusing to ride. In a sense, he saw himself as the state and wanted to ensure that little was spent on the state. There developed also a kind of military socialism as a principle of sharing the spoils of conquest. Omar was once accused by one of his own subjects of having taken more than his fair share of the spoils. Omar considered it a matter of fundamental importance to prove the man wrong.

The distributive aspect of Islam is, of course, intimately related to the egalitarian. The Prophet Muhammad himself was, in a sense, the paradox of a 'proletarian aristocrat'. He was born of the noble tribe of the Quraish but he came from a poor family and had worked in humble jobs. At first his modest upbringing, in spite of noble blood, was an impediment to his religious mission. As Reuben Levy has put it,

> when the Prophet Muhammad first proclaimed his new dispensation, even though he was a full member of his tribe of the Quraish, his lowly origin, coupled with his humble occupation as a camel-driver, put a serious obstacle in the way of his success.[13]

But his very marginality as a poor, camel-driving aristocrat later became his strength. The poor were captivated and the noblemen eventually capitulated. A relative egalitarianism, based on common faith in Islam, emerged quite early as a basic precept of the religion. Modern socialists in the Muslim world sometimes exaggerate the egalitarian aspect of early Islam. Islam was more egalitarian in intention than in achievement. But there were enough levelling tendencies within it to make the capitalist spirit of creative individual accumulation difficult to sustain.

In his *Sociology of Religion*, Max Weber draws our attention to yet another aspect of Islam which is basically anti-cumulative. This is the Islamic attitude towards certain forms of risk-taking. In Weber's words: 'The restriction against gambling [in Islam] obviously had important consequences for the religion's attitude toward speculative business enterprises'.[14]

Islam's disapproval of interest on loans and savings is also anti-cumulative in its implications. Islam in East Africa continues to frown on the whole idea of receiving interest on one's savings account in a bank. Inhibitions today about accepting interest from one's bank are much less developed than they used to be thirty years ago. But there endures among more orthodox Muslims in parts of Tanzania and Kenya a certain uneasiness about accepting interest from one's bank. This is an inhibition which is withering away. But that it has ever existed is a matter of some pertinence in the economic history of Muslim communities in such areas.

Islam and Modernity

All these factors in Islam which were, from the outset, at once communalistic and anti-cumulative come to look 'anti-modern' by the nineteenth century. Modernity had come to be conceptualized in vigorous individualist terms. The 'dead weight of Islam' seemed to be stifling the individual initiative of its followers.

But if the radicalism of the nineteenth century was the ethic of individualism, that of the twentieth century has, on the whole, tended to be the ethic of social fellowship and welfare. Modernity has retreated a little from rugged liberalism back to some form of communalistic fervour. The welfare state in western countries, as well as the communist revolutions elsewhere, are part of the same retreat of modernity.

Islam in Africa is finding it easier to come to terms with this new form of modernism. What is making a reconciliation even more probable is that twentieth-century modernism, unlike that of the nineteenth century, need no longer be identified with Christendom. The division of the world between western and communist countries is partly a division between modernized Christian nations and modernized atheist nations. To Muslim nationalists and militants, this makes modernism itself religiously neutral. Islam can thus remain collectivist and anti-western without being incompatible with modern trends.

Separation of Religion and Politics

A related political factor is the role of the state in Islam. It has often been argued that Islam is specially congenial to totalitarianism. The assertion here is that Islam claims total control over the life of the believer. The idea of separating the political self and the spiritual self is untenable, so it is claimed. Those who attribute such a characteristic to Islam can marshal considerable historical and theological evidence. They can even cite remarks by eminent Muslims themselves, such as the following:

> You are able to say, and no one will censure you, that the Muslim Brotherhood is a Salaphite movement, a Sunnite way, a Sufi truth, a political organization, an athletic club, a cultural and scientific society, a company, and a social doctrine.[15]

It is indeed true that from its very beginning as a religion, Islam has concerned itself with state issues and political affairs as well as with issues of salvation of the soul. But the difficulty arises when out of this premise is drawn the conclusion that while Muslims are incapable of separating religion from politics, Christians are. Part of the difficulty hinges on a major philosophical confusion in the West. It is too often taken for granted that to separate Church and State is also to separate religion from politics. In practice this conclusion is seldom sustained. With the First Amendment of the Constitution of the United States, the United States attempted to establish the doctrine of separating Church from State. There were no institutional links between religious establishments and any of the governments. But although Church and State were thus institutionally separated, religion and politics have refused to be kept apart to the present day. That is why the election of John F. Kennedy as the first Roman Catholic President of the United States was so significant. A Catholic President was a major step forward towards realizing the underlying spirit of the First Amendment. The Protestant monopoly of the White House was beginning to crack. And yet even now what we do not know is how long it will take before either of the major American political parties will feel brave enough politically to put forward a non-Christian as a presidential candidate. Perhaps only when a follower of Judaism enters the White House will the United States have effected a separation of religion from politics convincing enough to be comparable to their older achievement of separating Church from State.

Another way of illustrating this dual distinction is by comparing India with Great Britain. India is a secular state by the provisions of her constitution — yet she has religious riots every so often; Britain, on the other hand, is *not* a secular state in the sense of trying to separate Church from State. On the contrary, the Queen is both head of State and head of the Church of England. The Archbishop of Canterbury is appointed by the Prime Minister, and major doctrinal changes in the Church of England need approval of the British Parliament, either directly, or by derivation of authority.[16] Yet, although Great Britain has not separated Church from State, she has succeeded to a remarkable extent in keeping religion out of politics. The state subsidizes virtually all interdenominational schools — something which might be unconstitutional in the United States. Yet passions on religious matters or debates on religious issues are a rarer phenomenon in British politics than in either American or Indian politics.

In the wake of the crisis in Northern Ireland, the question which arises is whether sectarian passions in England itself might be reactivated if the period of violence in Northern Ireland continues for too long. The Irish Republican Army has on occasion carried violence and sabotage into the heart of the United Kingdom itself. John Kelly, former Chairman of the Belfast Citizens Committee and a leading member of the Militant wing of the IRA, said in an interview with the Dublin *Evening Herald* as early as 1971 that the IRA was planning a major sabotage campaign in Britain. Targets — commercial and government and local authority installations — had already been selected, according to Mr Kelly. Kelly asserted that the IRA was 'ready to take the fight to the cities of London, Birmingham, Coventry, Liverpool, Manchester, and indeed all the major British cities'.[17] The IRA has indeed done just that on occasion.

What this situation in Ireland raises, particularly when examined in relation to the danger of escalation of violence between Catholics and

Protestants and its spillover effects into Great Britain itself, is the simple question of whether the British capacity to separate religion from politics as has been evolved over the years will sustain a serious setback in the immediate future. Will English Catholics and English Protestants begin to look at each other with a rediscovered sense of difference and hostility if the Irish Catholics and the Irish Protestants continue to spill each other's blood, and if militant Irish Catholics effectively carry the war into the heartland of the United Kingdom? What this situation raises is the possibility of reversing a fairly successful achievement in national integration at the level of inter-denominational relations in England itself. But until that happens we continue to have a situation where a country which has so far refused to disestablish the Church of England and has therefore refused to declare England a secular state has nevertheless one of the most remarkable records of religious toleration and separation of religion from politics in the history of the world.

But what does this issue of separation of Church from State look like within the African continent itself? How far does the experience within Africa bear out the suggestion that Islam is incapable of separating religion from politics while Christianity is more nearly able to achieve that insulation? The African evidence certainly belies that proposition. While the American electorate was wondering in 1960 whether to elect its first Catholic President, the Senegalese Muslims had already elected Léopold Senghor as their own Catholic President. And the preponderant Muslims of Tanzania had been following enthusiastically the leadership of Julius Nyerere, another Roman Catholic. It might rhetorically have been asked: 'Who was demonstrating a capacity to insulate religion from politics? Was it the country which had had a First Amendment separating Church from State for almost two hundred years before electing a Catholic head of state? Or was it African followers of a religion which was supposed to assign everything to God, and leave nothing for Caesar?' These are questions that Muslims in Senegal and Tanzania, both countries with a preponderance of Muslims over Christians, might, in a mood of self-congratulation, well have asked.

African Muslims have already demonstrated in two very influential African countries a readiness to accept a Catholic leadership. General Amin is the first Muslim head of state in a predominantly Christian country within Africa. And General Amin came into power through a military coup. In other words, even within Africa itself, while there has been a readiness on the part of a Muslim country to accept through the ballot box the leadership of a Christian, there has been less readiness on the part of a Christian country to accept in free elections a Muslim head of state.

The Nigerian experience was evidently different. Muslim political dominance at the federal level arose out of an assumed numerical superiority. The North was assumed, at least by cultural derivation and influence, to be Islamic. The head of state was Azikiwe, a Christian nationalist. The head of government in Nigeria before the coup was Tafawa Balewa, a Muslim. But even then Southern Nigerians never fully accepted Northern leadership at that time; they merely acquiesced in it for the time being. And when Biafra decided to make a bid for secession from Nigeria, one of the platforms Biafra was using was to accuse Muslims of religious genocide. So successfully was Biafra's religious propaganda carried out that a large number of Christian religious institutions went all out to extend considerable religious support to the separatist movement, not merely in terms of tending the sick, helping the injured and educating the orphaned, but also in lending concrete financial and moral support to a separatist movement. So successful was the Biafran propaganda machine in convincing even the Vatican that the Ibo were about to be slaughtered by Northern Muslims that the Pope, in one of his less cautious statements as the civil war was coming to an end, made a declaration based on a belief that such a slaughter was imminent and appealed for mercy and equanimity for the Ibo, a largely Catholic group.

But what sort of factors in the texture of society would make possible an effective isolation of religion from politics? The requisite social climate for such a separation would need to combine at least two of four variables. The variables are, quite simply, religious toleration, religious apathy, tolerance in politics and political apathy. Religious toleration and tolerance in politics overlap but they are not identical. A society might extend respectful toleration to all religious denominations — and yet be intolerant towards this or that political party or political movement. In that case you would have full religious toleration, but fail to have a general spirit of tolerance in politics. On the other hand, a country might pass certain laws against specific Mormon practices — and yet allow the Mormons full freedom to speak out against those laws, or form a political party committed to their repeal, or put pressure on existing parties as a lobby of voters. In such a case the country would have restricted the religious freedom of the Mormons but not their political freedom — it would have denied them full religious toleration while letting them enjoy tolerance in political protest. As for the other two variables of religious apathy and political apathy, one could be measured by how many people go to church and the other by how many people come out to vote. Neither of these measurements is particularly accurate but at least they help to illustrate the two types of apathy.

What made Muslims in Senegal and Tanzania ready to accept the leadership of a Catholic for so long? A number of factors helped this situation to come about. Some of those factors might no longer apply to Senegal. There is a danger in the days ahead of Senghor remaining in power in Senegal by means other than those of general popularity.

Yet there is no escaping the fact that a Catholic president did manage to rule, with a substantial popular base, a country that was over eighty per cent Muslim. Of the four variables we mentioned as possible conditions of a social climate which divorces politics from religion, the two which have tended to operate both in Senegal and Tanzania are probably a relative religious toleration and a relative political apathy. Michael Crowder has written about the spirit of tolerance of contemporary Senegalese Islam: 'Islam in Senegal is peculiarly tolerant, not only in its concessions to traditional beliefs among more recently converted groups, but also towards Christians'.[18] I would argue that a similar tolerance is characteristic of Islam in Tanzania. But, as we indicated earlier, a mere toleration of the religious prerogatives of other faiths is not by itself enough to keep religion out of politics. It needs to be reinforced either by a spirit of tolerance in politics or by a general political apathy. For a long time Tanzania was the most politically apathetic of the three mainland territories of East Africa. While political consciousness and nationalist organizations were emerging in Kenya and Uganda, the people of Tanzania seemed to be supremely indifferent to it all. Tanzania's Islamic culture — even if not Islamic affiliation as such — might well have been a contributory factor. Muslims in Africa south of the Sahara have often tended to be among the least politically conscious of their countrymen.

What must not be forgotten is that apathy is often a fertile ground for a united revolutionary commitment should the right leadership emerge. Because people have been generally apathetic, there are fewer fervent political ideals to compete with each other or to resist a new political programme which comes with a new leader. The propensity to produce rebellious leaders and submissive followers finds a new outlet. And so, from being the least politically conscious, Tanzania gradually becomes the most dynamic state in Eastern Africa. Perhaps Senegal, too, might have become more dynamic had the leadership allowed itself to be — or had the army remained neutral as between Léopold Senghor and Mamadou Dia. For the moment the country at large might still remain substantially apathetic. But, as Martin Klein ominously points out, 'in Dakar's Medina one tends to find varying mixtures of French Marxism and Islamic modernism'.[19]

Islam and Political Structure

From ideology we move to political structure. There might be factors in Islam which favour a one-party structure. Bernard Lewis once denied that Islam was democratic in the liberal sense:

> There are of course elements, even important elements in Islam, especially in the early period, which we not unjustly call demo-cratic, but on the whole the tendency which is usually adduced in support of this thesis is equalitarian rather than democratic.[20]

He emphasizes that egalitarianism is 'a very different thing' from democracy — and goes on to argue that the egalitarian ethic goes with authoritarian institutions at least as well as with democratic ones.[21]

From Bernard Lewis's account of Islam let us extract the two concepts of *egalitarianism* and *authoritarianism* as a point of departure. A combination of these two precepts could so easily give you the Leninist principle of 'democratic centralism'. In the Soviet Union the principle of democratic centralism implied what a commentator has called 'a combination between the principle of mass participation at the bottom and the concentration of leadership at the top'.[22]

Sékou Touré in Guinea adopted this Leninist principle. Guinea under him became an example both of authoritarianism and egalitarianism. To use Touré's own words:

Democracy and the freedom of all party workers [in Guinea] are expressed in the framing of problems, in their discussion, and in the choice of solutions for them. On the other hand, the leadership of the party has complete liberty in the execution of assigned responsibilities and in the evaluation of the forms of action appropriate for the objective conditions of their execution. . . . The choice of tactics to be employed was up to the leadership of the party. This required that the authority of the leadership be complete.[23]

Touré's friend, Kwame Nkrumah, was a great believer in the idea of 'mobilizing the masses'. When he broke away from the United Gold Coast Convention in June 1949 it was partly because the UGCC was a little too aristocratic for him. And yet it was Nkrumah himself who said: 'Mass movements are well and good, but they cannot act with purpose unless they are led and guided by a vanguard political party'.[24] So he conceived his own new party, the Convention People's Party, as one which was of mass involvement but with strong and fairly centralized leadership. It worked for a while in Ghana — without any help from Islam. Would it have worked for a longer period if Ghanaians were overwhelmingly Muslim? That would indeed be a rash claim. All one can say with confidence is that Christianity, particularly the Protestant version, tends to promote a growing sense of individualism. And an African society which is getting too individualized cannot easily be democratically centralized at the same time. If Ghana had been overwhelmingly Muslim, or even overwhelmingly Catholic, it might have been a little more hospitable to centralizing tendencies than it actually was.[25] A tutor at Makerere in the early 1950s said that if he received a report about the character of a prospective student from his former headmaster saying 'excellent', the meaning varied according to whether the headmaster was Catholic or a Protestant. To paraphrase it a little, the term 'excellent' from a Catholic headmaster meant 'responsible and obedient'. The term 'excellent' from a Protestant headmaster meant 'responsible and shows initiative'.[26] It is the Catholic meaning of 'excellent' — the combination of responsibility and obedience — which is the nearer to the Islamic ethos.

Radicalism and a Tradition of Rebellion

But why should this kind of ethos ever lead to radicalism in the politics of Muslim countries? Partly because Islam has not only a tradition of submissive following but also, paradoxically, a tradition of rebellious leadership. This is an important difference from Catholicism. Since Catholicism has an institutionalized source of authority in the form of the Church, Catholic orthodoxy is easier to define. It is easier to establish what the correct line of religious behaviour is. But Islam has no institutionalized priesthood. It has no Vatican or papal authority. It has no special procedures for modifying theological interpretations. And so although Islam and Catholicism both value the quality of obedience, in Islam it is not always clear who or what is to be obeyed. Hence the tradition of Mahdism in Islam — a new leader emerges and sounds the call to revolt. Friedrich Engels, the intimate collaborator of Karl Marx, saw this phenomenon, but his explanation of it was too cynical. Engels refers to 'religious risings in the Mohammedan world, particularly in Africa' and interprets them naïvely as being essentially revolts of the Bedouin underprivileged against the prosperous trading Muslims in the towns. Thus yesterday's underprivileged become tomorrow's privileged class — and a new wave of rebellion comes from the desert. To use Engels' own words:

> The Bedouins, poor and hence of strict morals . . . unite under a prophet, a Mahdi, to chastise the apostates and restore the observation of the ritual and the true faith, and to appropriate in recompense the treasures of the renegades. In a hundred years they are naturally in the same position as the renegades were: a new purge of the faith is required, a new Mahdi arises, and the game starts again from the beginning. That is what happened from the conquest campaigns of the African Almoravids and Almohads in Spain to the last Mahdi of Khartoum, who so successfully thwarted the English.[27]

Engels' attempts to explain Mahdist movements in terms of pure class war are a little too simple. If the class element was present in the movements, it was certainly not in the naïve form which Engels describes. What the Mahdist movements illustrated was this propensity in Islam to produce rebellious leaders and submissive followers. The rebelliousness of the leaders and the enthusiastic submissiveness of the followers go back to Muhammad himself and his own original following. Of all the major religions of the world, perhaps none was born with a greater outburst of militancy than

Islam. Engels himself describes the original assertion of Muhammad as a 'religious revolution'. But he is wrong in his claim that the new religion was nevertheless eager to portray itself as a 'return to the old, the simple'. [28]

Jesus might have been a gentle and cautious reformer, Buddha a meditative teacher, but Muhammad was an outright rebel against the ways of his ancestors. To a certain extent Islam did claim to be a return to the purer message of Jesus. But while Muhammad placed himself in the same tradition as Moses and Jesus, he did not place himself directly in the tradition of the Arabian idol-worship. Some room was given in Islam for some religious figures in the history of the Arabs themselves. But on the whole *the antecedents of Islam were not Arab but Hebrew.*

Of course the Arabs and the Jews were themselves closely related at that time. In fact, Engels even argued once in a letter to Marx that 'the Jews themselves were nothing more than a small Bedouin tribe, just like the rest, which local conditions, agriculture, and so forth, placed in opposition to the other Bedouins'. [29] But there is no doubt that by Muhammad's time the Jews and the Arabs had, linguistically and culturally, become distinct sub-groups of the Semitic whole. The beginning of Islamic universalism lay in Muhammad's transcendence over subracial differences. Whatever else Muhammad was, he was not an Arab nationalist. That is what made him a revolutionary — he could transcend his own Arab sub-group. He was, as we indicated, a rebel against the ways of his immediate ancestors. And in that rebellion he captured the loyalty of a growing number of followers. That was the genesis of the militant tradition of rebellious leadership and submissive following in Islam, a tradition which, in varying forms, has recurrently broken out in Islamic history since Muhammad himself set the momentous precedent.

In this or that part of the Muslim world, this is a tradition which can lie dormant for generations. But it is susceptible to outbursts of new life under a certain type of stimulation. Europe's impact on the Islamic world in the nineteenth and twentieth centuries has often provided this kind of stimulation. The aggressive modernity of Christian Europe gave some Muslim countries a sense of insecurity and sometimes an inferiority complex. This Islamic defensiveness in relation to European Christianity, interacting more recently with nationalist opposition to western imperialism, has been a major reason why there is a disproportionate number of Muslim countries among Africa's radical states. The radicalism often manifests itself in diplomatic postures, rather than directly in socio-economic terms. With some notable exceptions, the most militant countries in Africa have so far continued to be disproportionately Muslim countries — though sometimes under non-Muslim leadership. But even their diplomatic postures in the post-independence era have an enduring economic theme — the fear of economic dependence and a pervasive suspicion of neo-colonialism. Much of radicalism in the new countries is still, in some sense, economically based in many of its central assumptions. The impact of Lenin, and of Marxism generally, is part of the explanation. In fact Lenin's most distinctive contribution to African political thought is perhaps his theory about the economic causes of imperialism. What is fascinating is that his theory has sometimes interacted with Islamic defensiveness against the West, and given rise to a new kind of rebellious leadership and submissive following in parts of the Muslim world. The rebellion is sometimes against the West, sometimes against Islamic orthodoxy, and often against both. From Indonesia to Algeria, from Syria to Mali, a certain responsiveness to defiant radicalism continues to be a feature of the total political climate. It is a mixture of intellectual dependence on radical socialism as derived from European militancy, on one side, and a groping for genuine intellectual and cultural autonomy, on the other side.

What is also happening in parts of the Muslim world is the phenomenon of a secular Mahdism. Of course, more orthodox forms of Islam still persist and, as might be expected, clashes do sometimes occur between the old and the new. But in a profound sense it still remains true that militant Muslim leaders like Nasser in the early days of the Egyptian revolution, Sukarno in his more successful days in Indonesia, Abeid Karume when he ruled Zanzibar, and Sékou Touré in Guinea are all semi-secular equivalents of militant Mahdist leaders. The fusion of egalitarianism with authoritarianism, the deep-seated cultural defensiveness against the Christian West, the self-conscious and defiant sense of community, the congruence with the anti-cumulative aspects of the Marxist version of modernity, have all contributed to give a significant number of Muslim countries a leftist orientation.

Let it again be emphasized that Islam does not adequately explain this phenomenon. But let it also be stressed that no explanation is adequate without it.

References and Notes

1. These issues were first discussed in a similar context in Ali A. Mazrui, 'Islam, political leadership and economic radicalism in Africa', *Comparative Studies in Society and History*, **IX**, 3 (1967), pp. 274-91.
2. 'The Islamic factor in African politics', *Orbis*, **VIII**, 2 (1964), 425-6.
3. See Lewis S. Feuer, ed., *Marx and Engels: Basic Writings on Politics and Philosophy*, Doubleday, New York, 1959.
4. See *Uganda Argus*, 5 September 1966, p. 3.
5. See Montagu Slater, *The Trial of Jomo Kenyatta* (1955), Mercury Books, 1965 edn., p. 76.
6. See Engels, 'On the history of early Christianity', in Lewis S. Feuer, ed., *Marx and Engels: Basic Writings on Politics and Philosophy*, op. cit., p. 169.

7. K. O. Dike, *Trade in the Niger Delta, 1830-1885*, Clarendon Press, Oxford, 1956, p. 5.

8. Max Weber, *The Protestant Ethic and the Spirit of Capitalism*, trans. Talcott Parsons, Scribner's, New York, 1958, p. 81.

9. See Karl Marx and Friedrich Engels, *On Colonialism*, Foreign Languages Publishing House, Moscow, p. 313.

10. Sir Philip Mitchell, *African Afterthoughts*, Hutchinson, 1954, p. 144.

11. Ibid., p. 142.

12. Michael Lofchie, *Zanzibar: Background to Revolution*, Princeton University Press, Princeton, New Jersey, 1965, pp. 270-1.

13. Reuben Levy, *The Social Structure of Islam*, Cambridge University Press, 1962, p. 54.

14. Max Weber, *Sociology of Religion*, trans. Ephraim Fischoffs, Beacon Press, Boston, 1964.

15. This is a statement from Hasan Al-Banna, in *Al-Ikhuwan al-Muslimun*, p. 79, cited by Nabih Amin Faris, 'The Islamic community and Communism', in *The Middle East in Transition*, ed. Walter Z. Laqueur, Praeger, New York, 1958, p. 356.

16. For an analysis of some of the implications of this last point, see J. H. Heubel, 'Church and State in England: the price of establishment', *The Western Political Quarterly*, XVIII, 3 (1965), 646-55. Consult also the Free Church Federal Council, Commission on Church and State, *The Free Churches and the State*, Carey Kingsgate Press, 1953, and S. Garbett, *Church and State in England*, Hodder & Stoughton, 1950. These issues are also discussed in my paper 'Islam, political leadership, and economic radicalism in Africa', *Comparative Studies in Society and History*, op. cit. The paper is reprinted as Chapter XI in Mazrui, *On Heroes and Uhuru Worship, Essays on Independent Africa*, Longmans, 1967, pp. 157-82.

17. 'IRA threatens gun war in UK', *The Observer*, 15 August 1971, p. 1.

18. Michael Crowder, *French Assimilation Policy in Senegal*, Oxford University Press, 1962, p. 86.

19. Martin Klein, 'The relevance of African history: a case study from Senegal', annual meeting of the African Studies Association, Philadelphia, October 1965. Mimeo.

20. Bernard Lewis, 'Communism and Islam', in Walter Z. Laquer, ed., *The Middle East in Transition*, Praeger, New York, 1958, p. 318.

21. Ibid.

22. Consult, for example, Robert V. Daniels, ed., *A Documentary History of Communism*, Random House, Vintage Books, New York, 1960, Vol. I, pp. 47-8.

23. See Paul E. Sigmund, Jr., ed., *The Ideologies of the Developing Nations*, Praeger, New York, 1963, pp. 167-8.

24. Ibid., p. 184.

25. Although the Protestants were the largest single group among non-animists in Ghana, Nkrumah himself was of Catholic upbringing. However, by the time he returned from studying abroad he was 'a Marxist socialist and a non-denominational Christian.'

26. For a somewhat different version see F. B. Welbourn, *Religion and Politics in Uganda, 1952-62*, East African Publishing House, Nairobi, 1965, p. 10.

27. Friedrich Engels, 'On the history of early Christianity', in Lewis S. Feuer, ed., *Marx and Engels: Basic Writings on Politics and Philosophy*, Doubleday Anchor Books, New York, 1959, p. 169.

28. Engels' letter to Marx from Manchester, approximately 24 May 1853. See *Marx and Engels: Basic Writings on Politics and Philosophy*, op. cit., p. 453.

29. Ibid.

8 Christianity and Humanitarianism in African Diplomacy

Christianity is partly based on the concept of sacrifice. The son of God gave his life on the cross for the atonement of man. Out of this idea emerged the twin principles of love and altruism. How far have these principles been upheld by Christianity in Africa? And what have the consequences been for African diplomacy after independence?

A distinction needs to be made here between the Christian message and the European *messengers* who brought it. Reservations have been expressed by a number of African nationalists about the role of the European missionaries in Africa. During the colonial period most Christian institutions were, as indicated in Chapter 1, supportive of the imperial order. There were times when European churchmen spoke up against some of the excesses of colonial rule, but on balance the right of Europeans to rule Africans was seldom questioned by the churches. On the contrary many reaffirmed that imperial 'right', and warned the subject peoples against 'the sin of disobedience'. The Christian message was thus often reinterpreted by the European messengers so that it could more effectively serve Europe's imperial order in Africa.

Yet, by bringing modern education to parts of Africa, the churches and missionaries participated in creating both the beginnings of modern nationalism and the beginnings of global awareness. Modern political consciousness grew among the educated Africans as they discovered more fully the gap between European moral precepts and European political practice. The moral precepts included the message of Christianity and its compassion; the political practice included the activities of the missionaries and their support for the imperial order. The gap between preaching and performance created disaffection. This intermingled with modern ideas of national self-determination, and gave rise to African nationalism.

Global awareness could be the first step towards genuine capacity for humanitarian commitment. Missionary education helped to globalize African perspectives partly through the logic of Christianity itself, partly through the logic of the imperial order, and partly through the content of modern education.

The logic of Christianity implied universalism. While traditional

African religions tended to be—like Judaism itself—tribal or communal religions, Christianity asserted universal validity. The Christian community was world-wide, and the God of Christianity recognized no 'chosen people'. The mere realization that Ibo Christians or Kikuyu Christians were part of a community scattered over the entire surface of the globe was itself a momentous experience for a village child. His horizons were widened by the very effort to identify with people he had never seen and would never see, and who were in any case many thousands of miles away from his rural school in equatorial Africa.

Like Christianity itself, the logic of the imperial order was also intellectually globalizing. Young Africans ruled by Britain learned before long that their lives were part of the History of the British Empire, which went back to the colonization of North America and the spread of *Pax Britannica* elsewhere. Names ranging from Boston (and its tea party) to Botany Bay (and its convicts), from Warren Hastings to William Wilberforce, were familiar to African school-children studying for Cambridge School Certificate in village schools. Once again African social horizons were made not only international but also intercontinental.

The third factor in this globalization is strongly related to the second. Modern education itself—whether or not it is Christian or imperial—cannot but reveal that the world is larger than any extended family, any tribe, any nation. Lessons in geography, history, literature (often English or French literature), physics and geometry were filled with names of either distant lands or distant heroes, made the more interesting by accompanying anecdotes. Newton looked at the falling apple and discovered the laws of gravity; and Archimedes looked at the water spilling from his bathtub before he stumbled upon the secrets of hydraulics and hydrostatics. With such foreign names around them the village children in Africa might also have exclaimed, '*Eureka, eureka!*—We have discovered the globe itself!'

It is because of these considerations that European missionaries in Africa deserve to be credited with having participated in fostering not only African nationalism but also the beginnings of African sensitivity to global issues. And yet for the time being humanitarianism in Africa remains profoundly suspect. African diplomacy is often at its most natural when it ignores the humanitarian pretensions of western policy-makers. We are back here to the question of origins. In spite of the globalizing tendencies of Christian activities in Africa, why does Africa continue to find it difficult to accept pure humanitarianism as a viable strategy in real life? Why does Africa remain suspicious when others claim to be humanitarian? Let us examine the roots of the phenomenon.

On Man and Kinsmen

Two aspects need to be examined. One is indigenous African tradition itself and how it related to questions of humanitarianism; the other is the Euro-Christian gap between principles and practice in the course of recent African history.

On the question of traditional factors, there is evidence to suggest that the concentrated loyalties of the kinship system are not easily compatible with the purely humanitarian impulse. It is almost as if there was a limit to how much responsibility man can accept for his fellow man. If he accepts a large area of responsibility within a system of extended kinship obligations, he reduces in the process his readiness to accept responsibility for more distant human beings.

Within the kinship system Africans know a level of human compassion and human obligation which is not even comprehensible to the western mind. The idea of a tribal welfare system, within which voluntary service and hospitality is extended to the indigent, the disabled and the aged, provides a striking model of the instinct of social fellowship in man. We all know of distant relatives we support, distant cousins who have a share in our salaries, distant kinsmen who call upon us as guests in our houses for days, sometimes for weeks. And yet it seems as if the very fact that we have a highly developed sense of responsibility towards our own kinsmen, a much more developed sense than is discernible in western society, has resulted in diluting our capacity to empathize with those that are much further from us.

The growth of individualism in the West has curiously enough resulted both in reduced collective responsibility within the immediate society and in increased capacity to empathize with man much further away, even in other lands altogether. The western individualist would be capable of rising to the occasion when news of a natural catastrophe in Pakistan or Chile reached him. With the African it is the reverse. He is much more moved by the day-to-day problems of a distant kinsman, than a dramatic upheaval in a remote part of the world.

And yet there are qualifications which need to be made here, especially in regard to the western response to humanitarian appeals. And these qualifications bring us to that Euro-Christian factor behind African suspicions of pure humanitarianism. The growth of individualism in Western Europe did indeed result in the rhetoric of humanitarianism, and sometimes even in the practice of humanitarianism. But these were the days when the humanitarian impulse in a liberal and Christian Europe took the form of imperial expansion and a racialist assumption of responsibility for the coloured races of the world. Kipling's concept of the white man's burden was, in the rhetoric in which it was formulated, a case of civilizing humanitarianism. The concept of spreading the gospel as enunciated by Christian missionaries was in turn a case of Christianizing humanitarianism. Both these themes in the history of Western Europe are inseparable from the history of imperial expansion. In other words, the whole phenomenon of colonial annexation, an imposition of white power over coloured races, was legitimated in history partly be reference to humanitarian and Christian principles. It may indeed have been significant, from the point of view of studying the relationship between individualism and humanitarianism, that the growth of liberalism in Europe coincided with the expansion of imperialism. Internal European renunciation of kinship and feudal obligations coincided with external European assumption of responsibility for people much farther away from their shores. Nevertheless, from Africa's point of view, it remains pertinent to measure European humanitarianism partly by the yardstick of the imperial experience.

More recently, there have been incidents since Africa's attainment of independence which have been defended on humanitarian grounds by the West, when in fact issues of racial solidarity on the part of the whites were discernible. A controversial example concerned the white hostages held by Congolese (Zairean) rebels in 1964 in their confrontation with their central government under Moise Tshombe. The hostages were later rescued by Belgian troops landing in what was then Stanleyville. But the Belgian troops used American planes in the process of this venture. Much of Africa was indignant. But the West justified the Stanleyville operation on the grounds that it was a humanitarian act. The whites were being saved from Congolese rebels. These whites were ordinary teachers, nurses, men, women and children, who happened to have been available in the Congo, often in professions of service and dedication to the Congolese. They were now being used as hostages and pawns in a civil war between the Congolese themselves. Was there not a case that the western powers should, on humanitarian grounds, rescue these hostages?

But were the Americans and the Belgians really putting their humanity first and their nationality and racial identity second in that actual operation? Conor Cruise O'Brien, the former United Nations representative in Katanga, pointed out the relative indifference of European and American opinion towards Congolese suffering as contrasted with the indignant compassion which was aroused on behalf of white prisoners. O'Brien suggested that the humanitarian sensitivity displayed in the West at the time of the Stanleyville rescue operation was, in fact, little more than an instance of racial solidarity. He indicated that Africa's own indignation against the operation had the same source as western self-righteousness in its regard — the main difference was that Africans lacked the power to send in paratroopers to rescue black victims from their oppressors in Dixie and South Africa.[1]

Catherine Hoskyns has also pointed to the role of the western press.

She first admits that the Congoleses did kill a number of Europeans and Africans. She goes on to add:

> Having said this, however, it is also clear that press and diplomatic reporting did to a considerable degree distort the extent, the circumstances, and the political implications of these deaths. . . . The main distortions [included] . . . the suppression of any evidence of violence on the other side; and the much greater coverage given to acts of brutality against Europeans than to those against Africans. The result was to tarnish the genuinely humanitarian reaction.[2]

African spokesmen themselves argued that the ultimate outcome of the rescue operation was the loss of many more lives than those actually saved. The paratroopers from Belgium fired their way to the hostages, killing a number of innocent Africans in the process. As the foreign minister of the Congo (Brazzaville) put it in somewhat dramatic terms at the time:

> What humanitarian principles are at stake, when, on the pretext of saving lives of an insignificant number of whites, tens of thousands of blacks are massacred . . . ? When we were younger, we learnt that in music one white note was worth two black ones. The famous humanitarian operation of Stanleyville has just proved to us that one white, particularly if his name is Carlson, if he is of American, Belgian, or British nationality, is worth thousands and thousands of blacks.[3]

Even if we made allowances for rhetorical exaggerations, it remains suspiciously true that no rescue operation of that scale would have been launched by the United States and Belgium if the hostages had not been white. The Belgians and the Americans were almost as susceptible to considerations of racial solidarity as the African nationalists who so bitterly resented their intervention in Stanleyville. The whole affair was, in a real sense, a conflict of racial sensitivities.

It is partly because of incidents of this kind, reinforced by the whole doctrine of the white man's burden in history, that the plea of humanitarianism is sometimes suspect in the eyes of the African nationalist. Even the Red Cross, as a movement ultimately predicated on the viability of the humanitarian impulse, has to grapple with this heritage of Africa's history.

Partly out of the problems emanating from the imperial past, two additional factors after independence have further hampered the realization of humanitarianism in Africa. One is the fact that Africa has become a highly politicized continent. The other is the fact that African politics are getting increasingly militarized.

The Politicization of Life

There seems to be little doubt that questions which, in other parts of the world, might be regarded as virtually non-political acquire in much of Africa political implications. Perhaps this is in the nature of the historical times in which we are placed, and the deep awareness of colossal political problems in most African countries.

Nkrumah in *I Speak of Freedom* prophetically pictured the doctrine of the primacy of politics in Africa: 'Seek ye first the political kingdom and all things will be added to it'. Political control was conceived by him as an inescapable precondition for economic and social fulfilment. It therefore made sense for Africa first to concentrate on winning political independence, and then to use the political power inherited through independence for other purposes of transformation.

But the tasks of transformation after independence inevitably entailed further political struggles. Very often the ambitions of African countries were large, encompassing the desire to forge numerous communities into cohesive nations within a lifetime, and transforming the borderline of poverty into a foundation for affluence within a generation. The new territorial entities created by the Euro-Christian impact have been maintained by the independent governments with ferocious possessiveness.

Although the ambitions of newly independent African countries are great, their institutions and capability for realizing these ambitions are weak. One of the persistent political problems in African conditions is simply the fluidity of institutions. Political parties arise and disappear, constitutions are passed and abandoned, political structures are set up and collapse. It is in the nature of political newness to experiment with new approaches in resolving conflict. But the very newness of African political systems gives them the quality of transience. What all this amounts to is a degree of instability in our countries. And our leaders are often forced to take precautions against the challenges to authority and dangers to fragile institutions. Christian schools might have helped to create modern African nationalism; but that is still a far cry from modern African *nations*.

It is partly because of this general atmosphere that many issues which could conceivably be non-political become, in Africa, politicized. Trade unions, intended at their inception for labour negotiations, begin to assume certain political functions. Schools and universities begin to feel the winds of external politics blowing into their very classrooms, and affecting the tone and spirit of their lectures. Religious denominations become conscious of the political implications of almost every move; and, sometimes, they even convert themselves into neo-political organizations. Even marriage, sometimes regarded as a profoundly private experience between two people, can become a matter of state—as the Zanzibari experience in 1970 in regard to mixed-marriages all too painfully illustrated.

Considering then that Africa is a highly politicized continent, humanitarian organizations which work best in conditions of political neutrality, are immediately faced with a major problem. The Red

Cross is a classic example. How can the work of the Red Cross, in a situation which involves deep political divisions, be adequately regarded as politically neutral? Is not the act of neutrality itself a political decision in certain situations? The International Red Cross is non-denominational in terms of those who benefit from it, but is Christian in origin and continues to draw much of its financial support from Christian sources. The 'cross' is a Christian cross.

Much of the work of the International Red Cross in the Nigerian civil war was disturbed by that simple factor of the high politicality of every major move. Positions taken which might be seemingly neutral inevitably revealed layers of politics underneath. The case of August Lindt, General Commissioner for West Africa of the International Committee of the Red Cross in 1969 was a case in point. At the end of May 1969 the Nigerian press launched a campaign against Mr Lindt. On 14 June, the Nigerian Government declared Mr Lindt 'persona non grata'. The International Committee of the Red Cross was indignant and issued a statement protesting against this action by the Nigerian Government in the following terms:

> The exclusion decreed against Mr Lindt by the Federal Government can but provoke profound surprise and deep regret within the I.C.R.C. and amongst all those who, so selflessly, assist the civilian populations, victims of the conflict now raging in Nigeria. Any government is, of course, free to maintain relations with whichever party it chooses and the International Committee will continue to respect today as it has done in the past, the sovereign rights of States. Nonetheless the members of International Committee cannot accept the accusations levelled against a man who has never spared either his health, or his efforts and who has performed magnificent work for which the International Committee wishes to express to him here its deepest gratitude. The I.C.R.C., whose teams in the field pursued their daily tasks unremittingly, hopes that the tensions engendered by this tragic conflict may diminish so that the innocent victims, who are the sole object of this concern, may continue to receive assistance.[4]

It may well be that some of the accusations levelled at Mr Lindt were inadequately appreciative of his dedication to the work in hand, and his desire to concentrate on alleviating the suffering of the civilian population in that war. Mr Lindt, perhaps more than most other people, was also profoundly aware that those who suffered were not simply the civilians on the Biafran side of the war. In Mr Lindt's own words: 'I have always endeavoured to draw public attention — directed too much in my opinion, towards Biafra — to the suffering among the population on the Nigerian side of the front.' Mr Lindt was also very much aware of the difficulty of appearing to be neutral. He seemed reconciled to being the target of attacks from either or both sides in the civil war because of the nature of the exercise.

My determination to remain objective was not always appreciated in this conflict where propaganda and psychological warfare play an important part. Our work was therefore the butt of attacks sometimes from one party, and sometimes from the other and even from both simultaneously.[5]

And yet of all the accusations which were levelled against Mr Lindt, the one which he particularly wanted to defend himself against in his letter to the President of the International Committee of the Red Cross exposed Mr Lindt's political naïveté in present-day conditions in Africa. For some reason Mr Lindt assumed that anyone who took the position that the conflict between Federal Government and Biafra could not be concluded militarily, but had to be done through peaceful negotiations, was not taking a political position. In other words: 'I would . . . reply to one approach. In private as in public I have said that the conflict should be resolved by peaceful means. I cannot consider this as a political attitude; it is merely, common sense.'[6]

The choice between a military victory by the Federal Government, giving the Federal Government greater flexibility in determining the terms of reconstruction after the war, and a negotiated peace falling short of victory by either side, giving Biafra more say in the terms of the settlement — this choice was evidently a political choice. If the Commissioner General for the West African International Committee of the Red Cross went about recommending a negotiated peace, and virtually asked the Federal Government to cease military operations so that such a peace could be negotiated, that commissioner was engaged in advocating a particular point of view. And as he himself put it in that letter to Mr Marcel Naville, he championed this peaceful approach to the Biafran problem 'in private as in public'. The public advocacy of such a position was even more explicitly political.

A related issue in the situation concerned the fragility of global perspectives both within Africa and among those seeking to influence the course of African history. The missionary schools might have helped to internationalize African horizons through the logic of Christianity, the imperial order and the content of western education in African schools, but such global awareness could only be a mere beginning towards the distant and elusive goal of human unity. The fate of Mr August Lindt of the International Committee of the Red Cross brought out echoes of the tragedy of Dag Hammarskjöld in relation to the Congo in 1960 and 1961. Could the United Nations remain neutral as between contending groups within the Congo once a United Nations presence had been established there? Patrice Lumumba took a step to immortality when he invited the world body to help in restoring order after the Congo's armed forces had mutinied and the country seemed to be falling apart so soon after the first independence celebrations. The disintegration of the Congo also appeared to be in danger of resulting in a conflagration of the world. There was a serious risk of a Soviet-American confrontation within the Congo if an alternative international presence in the country was not devised.

The Congo story at the beginning of the 1960s was a brief experiment in global police action. But, like the Red Cross, the United Nations came to be haunted by the fear of compromising her neutrality. When Moise Tshombe declared Katanga's secession from the Congo, was it the duty of the United Nations to help Prime Minister Lumumba in reasserting the authority of the Central Government? The Secretary-general Dag Hammarskjöld began to interpret the duty of the world body in neutralist terms. He reviewed the earlier precedent in Lebanon in the year 1958, and drew conclusions for the situation in the Congo in 1960. Hammarskjöld argued:

> It follows that the United Nations Forces cannot be used on behalf of the Central Government [of the Congo] to subdue or to force the Provincial Government to a specific line of action. . . . It finally follows that the United Nations, naturally, on the other side, has no right to refuse the Central Government to take any action which by their own means in accordance with the Purposes and Principles of the Charter, they can carry through in relation to Katanga.[7]

It was, in other words, no part of the United Nations functions to put down a rebellion on behalf of a central government which had sought its aid to restore order. As Argentina's representative, Mario Amadeo, put the argument at the time: 'To accept this sort of thesis would lead us to accepting or acquiescing in appeals from Members States' Governments every time a group of rebels rose within territories of those States.'[8] And yet for the United Nations to opt for neutrality between the central government (which had invited it in the first place) and a secessionist province was itself a decision of great political implications. That neutrality had long-term consequences for the Congo, the most dramatic of which were the events which led to the murder of Patrice Lumumba. A decision was made not to interfere when Lumumba was transported from the capital city into the hands of his enemy Moise Tshombe in Katanga. It was a supreme act of neutrality by the United Nations—and yet it was an act whose repercussions shook the African continent for at least another five years. Many Africans lost forever whatever belief in globalism and humanitarianism they might once have acquired at school. In the end, the United Nations did decide to take action against Katanga's secession, and Tshombe's bid to separate himself and Katanga from the Congo was frustrated. This was after a new interpretation of the legitimate role of the United Nations. And it was after the deaths of both Lumumba and Dag Hammarskjöld.

There are occasions when this African distrust of global humanitarian rhetoric merely reinforces the forces of intolerance in domestic politics within African countries. African regimes can be singularly inhumane in their treatment of political opponents. Does an organization like the Red Cross have a role to play in this? Visiting detainees is one issue which, in African conditions, it would be difficult to portray as an act of neutrality. Since 1958 about fifty governments of the world have authorized the International Committee of the Red Cross to visit about 100 000 detainees other than conventional prisoners of war. Of these fifty countries, about half were cases of internal tension but without disorder—and the detainees might therefore be regarded as purely political. The other twenty or more countries were indeed cases involving a domestic breakdown. The authorization given to the International Committee of the Red Cross by some of the governments has included limitations. The idea of systematic and repeated visits to political detainees, for example, was not normally approved of.

But could such visits, in any case, be politically neutral? What would be their purpose if they were? Of course, the Red Cross is not the same thing as Amnesty International. Amnesty International is a movement which questions political detention itself—whereas the Red Cross seeks to improve the conditions within the detention camps and prisons. Amnesty International is a movement of protest, concerned with human rights and civil rights. The Red Cross, on the other hand, seems more animated by the desire to reduce suffering than to fulfil rights. What kind of a prison-cell a detainee has, or what opportunities there are for him to see his wife, are much more important for the Red Cross than whether the detention was just in the first place. And yet it is precisely on questions such as these that the politicized nature of the African continent makes it difficult to draw distinctions. Can the act of detention itself be political, while the conditions under which it takes place remain purely neutral? There may be a strong case for visits by the International Committee of the Red Cross to the Zanzibari detention places. There has been a high degree of political arbitrariness in Zanzibar, and a sense of insecurity seems to prevail in some important sections of the population. Amnesty International would indeed be concerned about this aspect of the phenomenon. This could fall under the designation of conditions of detention rather than the reasons for detention. Still it is very hard to envisage an inquiry into conditions of detention in Zanzibar being conducted as something distant from politics.

Kenya, too, has had a number of detentions. Sometimes the casualness of presidential magnanimity is itself an indication of how wide is the area of discretion in determining who spends eighteen months as against who spends three years behind bars. Again, Amnesty International may be concerned about the reasons why a former member of an opposition party was in detention, or why any of his colleagues are still within prison walls. But can an inquiry into the actual conditions of detention be conducted without arousing political sensibilities?

In Uganda before Amin's coup five detainees were perhaps, in some sense, particularly controversial. These were the five ministers arrested at a cabinet meeting in 1966 by their colleague, Dr Milton Obote. They were detained from 1966 until Amin released them in 1971. Were the reasons for which they were detained legitimate? Amnesty International, as a movement of rights, should be concerned about that issue. The International Committee of the Red Cross might more meaningfully have addressed itself to the issue of whether the prisoners at Luzira were permitted to interact with each other, whether they were permitted access to radio or even to television, whether they were permitted reading material to pass long hours with, or whether toilet facilities were sufficiently humane. And yet what inquiry by the International Red Cross could be conducted into the degree of humanitarian comforts enjoyed by the five ministers in Uganda without arousing important issues of politics and security?

There are, of course, other areas of activity which humanitarian organizations could engage in which are much less politically sensitive than dealing with political detainees. Yet even in matters concerned with facilities for youth, community development, family planning, and others, humanitarian organizations in individual countries in Africa have to be greatly circumspect. One false step could lead to a serious political misunderstanding. The nature of the situation is such that political misunderstandings happen easily. The very principle of humanitarianism has yet to recover from the full consequences of the Euro-Christian order while it lasted in Africa. Dependency and fear have had a legacy of intolerance in Africa.

On Combat and Compassion

A related aspect of Red Cross difficulties in contemporary Africa is the partial militarization of politics in the continent. The militarization of politics in Africa has a number of levels. One level is the overt one when soldiers actually stage a coup and take over power. On 25 November 1965, the relatively long established regime of Joseph Kasavubu in the Congo (Kinshasa) was overthrown and General Joseph Mobutu assumed the presidency. On 22 December there followed the coup in Dahomey. The Central African Republic marked New Year's Day in 1966 with a coup, to be imitated two days later by Upper Volta. William F. Gutteridge might have been exaggerating, but there was certainly some evidence for his assertion that

> The effectiveness of Mobutu's employment of the restrained and reorganised Congolese Army to overthrow a disorganised political

regime provided a model and an example. To African soldiers aware of the French tradition in which they were trained, the lesson was easily assimilated from him and from one another.[9]

But the coup tradition was going to spill over into the English-speaking sector of Africa. On 15 January 1966 the regime of Sir Abubakar Tafawa Balewa in Nigeria was ousted in a military coup. A month later the world resounded to the news that Kwame Nkrumah, who had dominated pan-African politics for nearly a decade, had also been overthrown by his soldiers. The date was 24 February 1966. Since then there have been changes in some of these countries, including a temporary return to civilian rule in Ghana. But where those changes did not take place the soldiers remain in overt positions of political power.

Yet it is not merely in those countries which have soldiers actually holding political office that the military exerts some influence on the civilian authorities. Even in countries where the civilian authorities seem to be firmly in control there are undercurrents of interplay with military power. The need to reconcile the civilian with the military sectors of power in African countries is likely to remain one of the dominant themes of the first two decades of African independence. This is the second level of the militarization of politics of Africa.

But there is a third level of the militarization of politics in Africa. And this is the actual physical confrontations between political antagonists. The countries which have suffered most from this kind of experience so far have been the Sudan and Nigeria. In these cases, it became an instance of the central government poised against a particular region bidding to secede. Christian organizations were basically in sympathy with the separatists — the Southern Sudanese and the Biafrans. Because religious organizations became suspect to the central governments, humanitarian organizations were also suspect. Once again it is worth illustrating this with the fate of the International Red Cross.

Military factors are inevitably an important ingredient in the whole career of the Red Cross movement. The movement itself was conceived on the battlefield when Jean Henri Dunant was stimulated into imaginative planning by the agony of Solferino in 1859. Since then preoccupation with helping the wounded and looking after prisoners of war has been one of the more heroic aspects of the work of the Red Cross movement. There are, of course, more ordinary undertakings, not always celebrated in newspaper and magazine articles, but profoundly important nevertheless. The work of encouraging blood donors, and co-ordinating the availability of blood where needed in peacetime, can be as great a service to humanity as a visit to a camp of prisoners of war or political detainees. Nevertheless, some of the worst agonies sustained by man arise when man puts on his military uniform, proclaims his war-cry, arms himself, and gets ready to kill or injure his own kind. It is partly because of this that a major theme in Red Cross history has continued to be work in the sphere of dealing with victims of war, and of internal conflict.

The role which the national society of the Red Cross in a particular country may play in the case of internal conflict has preoccupied the movement on a number of occasions. One particularly significant occasion was the seminar which took place in August 1963 in Geneva addressing itself to the work of the Red Cross for the victims of armed conflicts. The International Committee of the Red Cross took up the question in a special report which the Committee presented to the 20th International Conference of the Red Cross at Vienna in 1965. The Conference adopted Resolution No. XXXI, urging the International Committee to continue its services to victims of *domestic* conflicts, and to aim for further strengthening of the humanitarian capability of the Red Cross in helping such victims.

Again the situation in Africa of militarized politics opens up whole new areas of internal wars. The political instability and institutional fragility which beset post-colonial Africa can all too easily precipitate armed confrontation. The Red Cross movement as a whole has begun to look at Africa as signifying almost a new era of potential activity.

Nigeria, as we have indicated, provided the agony of initiation into this kind of experience. We discussed earlier the action taken against August Lindt, partly in relation to his political position and his advocacy of a particular approach to the Nigerian crisis. But there was also an aspect of Dr Lindt's activity which was in reality more immediately military than political. He had threatened personally to lead five planes of the International Committee of the Red Cross from Fernando Po to the Biafra airstrip of Obilagu in defiance of the Federal Government of Nigeria. The Federal Government regarded the uncontrolled supply of relief to Biafra as being inevitably a matter with direct military repercussions. Proposals about opening up new routes, as recommended by the International Committee, often had military implications. Biafra on its part sought to define conditions for relief which were militarily of use to her. Biafra's insistence on night-flights for relief became the most critical issue in the tensions between the Federal Government, the International Committee of the Red Cross and Ojukwu. By July 1969, an official Biafran statement was accusing the International Committee of the Red Cross of 'openly supporting Anglo-Nigerian policies designed to starve the Biafran nation into submission'. On the other hand, officials on the Federal side in the war were complaining privately that some of the attitudes displayed by the Red Cross personnel were 'reminiscent of our colonial masters at their worst'.[10] A related complication were the unofficial contacts between the Red Cross and private religious organizations. When did humanitarianism become intervention?

Yet a further complicating factor was that it was not only the

International Committee of the Red Cross which was conducting the Red Cross activities in the war. Some other national committees, pre-eminently the National Red Cross Society of France, were also actively involved. And the Federal Government was firmly of the opinion that the French Red Cross had no inhibitions about including a supply of arms to Biafra in the relief it was providing. The French Red Cross certainly was much less interested in reaching a firm agreement with the Federal Government than the International Committee seemed to be. The national societies of the Red Cross of France and, seemingly, of the Scandinavian countries, bedevilled relations between the Federal Government and the Red Cross movement as a whole. Once again Euro-Christian humanitarianism appeared like rank interference. But what was even more significant was that Africa was testing afresh the viability of a movement of this kind, committed to political neutrality, yet seeking to operate precisely in those areas which are highly politicized and indeed often militarized. In the words of Colin Legum:

> The I.C.R.C.'s troubles in Nigeria brought to light how badly out of touch the organization was with the feelings of the Third World which was not inclined to accept uncritically the policies determined by a group of Europeans, however lofty their motives.[11]

The African experience was forcing the movement to re-evaluate itself. The Nigerian experience was critical in this. In the words of Jacques Freymond, the Vice-President of the International Committee: 'We have to adapt to meet changing situations and, in doing so, we must evolve or die'.[12]

A final area of militarization in Africa concerns the freedom fighters in Southern Africa and the Portuguese territories. Again the great African presence within the United Nations, on the one hand, and the lingering struggle in Southern Africa for black dignity, on the other, have opened new interpretations about the nature of war and the very definition of a prisoner of war. In December 1968, the General Assembly of the United Nations included in its Resolution on apartheid the declaration 'that Freedom Fighters should be treated as prisoners of war under International Law, particularly the Geneva Convention relative to the Treatment of Prisoners of War of 12th August 1949'. In the previous month the General Assembly in its Resolution on Portuguese Territories had called upon 'the Government of Portugal in view of the armed conflict prevailing in the Territories . . . to ensure the application to that situation of the Geneva Convention in relation to the Treatment of Prisoners of War of 12th August 1949'.[13] On the International Human Rights Year, the General Assembly 'further confirms the decision of the Teheran Conference to recognise the right of Freedom Fighters in Southern Africa, to be treated as Prisoners of War under the Geneva Conventions of 1949'.[14]

On this issue some of the church organizations have agreed with the United Nations and have turned out to be ahead of the more purely humanitarian institutions like the Red Cross. The World Council of Churches has even gone to the extent of providing financial support for liberation movements, to the indignation of many white South Africans. In short, there is a swing within some Christian movements in favour of greater commitment to African liberation.

By contrast, *The International Review of the Red Cross* took up some of these issues and, at times, appeared to be almost debating with the General Assembly about the status of African prisoners. The issue of broadening the definition of prisoners of war was evidently a matter of importance to the Red Cross movement. The *Review* asked:

> Is the General Assembly empowered to broaden, merely by a Resolution, a definition contained in an Article of a Convention which is now binding on more than 120 States?
> In any case, it would be highly desirable that liberation movements treat captured military personnel of the Governments concerned as prisoners of war and, consequently, authorize a neutral agency such as the I.C.R.C. to visit them. Negotiations with the other party would thereby be greatly facilitated.[15]

But some of the polemical response of the *Review* to these important issues did include constructive modifications of the General Assembly's recommendations.

> The question . . . arises whether it would not be better for the General Assembly that these persons be granted treatment as prisoners of war rather than prisoner of war status. Such a recommendation would be strictly humanitarian with no legal or political connotation and would probably more likely be followed by results beneficial to the persons requiring protection.[16]

These are ad hoc policy solutions. But in the final analysis, what the experience of the Red Cross in Africa illustrates is the profound relevance of local sensibilities in determining the performance of a humanitarian organization. And those local sensibilities remain inextricably linked to the legacy of both sacrifice and sacrilege, sincerity and cynicism, which have characterized the Euro-Christian impact on Africa in a historical perspective.

Conclusion

Any movement towards a more integrated world order has to try to understand the impediments to man's capacity for enlarged empathy. Again Africa's experience is distinctive, but has aspects which are illustrative of the kind of cultural and historical obstacles which humanitarian movements have to overcome in former colonial situations.

As we have indicated, a classic example of such a movement is the Red Cross. If one were to select three factors about contemporary Africa which are likely to bedevil the work of an organization like the Red Cross, one would be tempted to choose, first, the memory of the Euro-Christian historical gap between principles and practice; secondly, the fact that independent Africa has become a pre-eminently politicized continent; and thirdly, the fact that African politics have, in the last few years, become increasingly militarized.

In the background has been the legacy of the whole imperial experience. And central to that experience was western education, which has been partly fostered and strengthened by Christian missionaries. Missionary education in the majority of African countries helped to provide the first wave of modern African nationalists. What can all too easily be overlooked is the concurrent influence of missionary education in the direction of global awareness and the beginnings of *pax humana*.

What has remained operational for the time being is Africans' recollection of the emptiness of humanitarian rhetoric by Europeans in the past. It did not matter much whether these Europeans carried the religious banner of Christianity or the secular flag of western civilization. The two belonged to the same imperial order. Africa's historical memory of this Euro-Christian moral gap has remained a major impediment to the evolution of genuine humanitarianism in Africa. The continent's historical memory has reinforced an indigenous tendency to highlight the immediate obligations of kinship and underestimate the broader bonds of global empathy. 'Charity begins at home' is a dictum even more honoured in Africa than in the West, for better or worse. But the roots of globalism have already been planted in Africa's political culture. In spite of the perverse tendencies of the European messengers, the Christian message of sacrifice and universalism might one day find a new validation in the villages of equatorial Africa. And even the International Committee of the Red Cross might one day find in Africa the respect it has sought for its commitment to global ideals and humanitarian concern.

References and Notes

1. See Conor Cruise O'Brien, 'Mercy and mercenaries', *The Observer* (London), 6 December 1964.
2. See Catherine Hoskyns, 'Violence in the Congo', *Transition*, 5, 21 (1965). This incident is discussed in a related but wider context in 'External events and internal racial tension', Chapter 4 in Ali A. Mazrui, *On Heroes and Uhuru Worship*, Longmans, 1967, pp. 52-7.
3. South Ganeo, *United Nations Security Council Official Records*, 1170, 9 December 1964, pp. 14-16. Carlson was the American missionary who was killed by the insurgents.
4. Published in *International Review of the Red Cross* (Geneva), No. 100 (July 1969), 356.

5. Ibid.
6. Ibid., 361-2.
7. UN Document No. S/4417/Add. 6, 12, August 1960, pp. 3-4.
8. UN Document No. S/PV. 888, 21 August 1960, p. 74.
9. See Gutteridge's introduction to David Wood, *The Armed Forces of African States*, Adelphi Paper No. 27, Institute for Strategic Studies, London, April 1966, p. 2.
10. For some of the details of this triangular tension between Biafra, ICRC and the Federal Government of Nigeria, I am indebted to a manuscript on the Nigerian civil war by Colin Legum.
11. Ibid.
12. Ibid.
13. Resolution 2396 of 2 December 1968 and Resolution 2395 of 29 November 1968.
14. Resolution 2446 of 19 December 1968.
15. *International Review of the Red Cross* (Geneva), No. 100 (July 1969), 350.
16. Ibid.

9 The USSR and China as Models of Innovation*

Lenin bequeathed to the colonized peoples of the world a theory of imperialism but perhaps not a strategy of liberation. Lenin helped the Third World to understand the nature, motives and structural causes of imperial expansion—but he contributed little towards direct strategies for fighting imperialism. It is, of course, arguable that comprehending imperialism is itself a necessary part of the struggle against it. We are prepared to accept that proposition. But it is not the same thing as providing concrete methods of undermining imperialism at its foundations, or confronting it in a literal military sense.

In spite of some evidence to the contrary, Lenin on the whole believed that colonial liberation was linked to proletarian revolutions in the imperialist countries themselves. Marxist thought until lately tended to regard the proletariat of the industrialized countries as almost the inevitable catalyst for the liquidation of European empires. Two years after the Russian Revolution the manifesto of the Communist International at its first congress of 1919 put forward the doctrine that 'the workers not only of Annam, Algiers and Bengal but also of Persia and Armenia, will gain their opportunity of independent existence only when the workers of England and France have overthrown Lloyd George and Clemenceau'.[1]

Mao Tse-tung, on the other hand, appreciated early the distinctiveness of the predicament of colonized peoples, and the potential autonomous thrust that they were capable of launching for their own liberation even before the proletariat of the industrialized imperialist powers had captured control of the state. In the words of Kenneth W. Grundy:

> It is generally assumed that Mao Tse-tung contributed more to a general theory of guerrilla warfare than any single individual and that the impact of his thought upon guerrillas and counter-

*This chapter is based on a conference paper jointly written by Ali A. Mazrui and Roven G. Locke and originally entitled 'The Chinese Model and the Russian model in Eastern and Southern Africa: strategies of liberation and development'.

guerrillas is widespread. By and large this is a correct appraisal . . . Mao Tse-tung, by refining and systematizing thinking about guerrilla warfare, made guerrilla warfare both militarily and politically comprehensible and set it in the context of class struggle . . . to Mao, war (like revolution) must follow a 'scientifically ascertainable' course. Mao's skill was in his ability to pull together into a single operational theory a disparate body of ideas and data previously available and to abstract a set of principles with broader application than many at first realized.[2]

When we refer to the Chinese model in relation to Africa we are referring both to this theory and strategy of liberation and to the Chinese example in economic and technological development. On the other hand, when we are referring to the Russian model, this is primarily developmental. Lenin and Stalin between them built a new kind of state and initiated a new approach to development. Africa has been influenced both by Lenin's ideas on imperialism and 'monopoly capitalism' or 'the highest stage of capitalism' and by Russia's example of rapid economic technological transformation.

But let us first discuss models of liberation before we examine models of development. We shall then move on to models of international solidarity.

Marxist Revolution and Maoist Liberation

As indicated, Mao Tse-tung contributed less than Lenin to theories of imperialism but much more than Lenin to strategies of liberation, including tactics of armed resistance and guerrilla struggle. Two fundamental modifications to Marxism which Mao seemed to emphasize are, first, belief in the peasantry and, secondly, belief in the gun. Let us take each of these in turn.

Part of the core of Maoism is certainly reliance on the peasantry as the vanguard of the revolution. This is a significant modification and departure from European Marxism with its emphasis on the proletariat. As early as 1927, in his *Report on an Investigation of the Peasant Movement in Hunan*, Mao affirmed the leading role of the peasantry in the Chinese revolution.

The present upsurge of the peasant movement is a colossal event. In a very short time, in China's central, southern and northern provinces, several hundred million peasants will rise like a mighty storm, like a hurricane, a force so swift and violent that no power, however great, will be able to hold it back. They will smash all the trammels that bind them and rush forward along the road to liberation. They will sweep all the imperialists, war-lords, corrupt officials, local tyrants and evil gentry into their graves. Every revolutionary party and every revolutionary comrade will be put to the test, to be accepted or rejected as they decide. There are three alternatives. To march at their head and lead them? To trail behind them, gesticulating and criticizing? Or to stand in their way and oppose them? Every Chinese is free to choose, but events will force you to make the choice quickly.[3]

But Mao also, perhaps unlike early European Marxists, had a profound belief in the gun as well as in the peasantry. What the revolution needed was not just industrial action and a self-conscious proletariat. It needed the power which tends to reside in the gun. In Mao's words: 'Having guns, we can create Party organization. . . . We can also create cadres, create schools, create culture, create mass movement. Everything in Yenan has been created by having guns'.[4]

Mao saw the army not just as an instrument of war, but also as an instrument of revolutionary mobilization.

> When the Red Army fights, it fights not merely for the sake of fighting, but to agitate the masses, to organize them, to arm them, and to help establish revolutionary political power: apart from such objectives, fighting loses its meaning and the Red Army the reason for its existence.[5]

Among African liberation movements FRELIMO in Mozambique and PAGC in Guinea-Bissau came nearest to realizing this role of a revolutionary army at once as an instrument of war and as an instrument of mass-mobilization and rural organization.

Mao worked out ideas concerning when to advance in a guerrilla struggle and when to retreat; when to avoid the enemy and when to harass the enemy; when to go into hiding and when to start the chase.[6] He was sensitive to the difference between a situation in which the oppressed classes are fighting their own domestic masters and a situation in which all nationals are fighting an alien conqueror. China itself experienced both forms of struggle. The Chinese fought their own privileged classes, and organized to resist Japanese occupation; they fought to redistribute land in their own society as well as to thwart the machinations of western powers in China.

But has African experience entirely contradicted the older Marxist assumption that colonized peoples are most likely to attain their freedom when the proletariat in the imperialist metropolitan power themselves rise up against their own internal oppressors? In the case of the political liberation of much of French-speaking Africa, it certainly did not require a proletarian revolution in France to attain that result. Sékou Touré of Guinea acquired independence and radicalized his country in spite of the fact that the former colonial nation, France, was still far from a proletarian revolution. Also, in the case of the former British colonies at least some degree of independence in the political field, and considerable effort at self-reliance in countries such as Tanzania, have been achieved in spite of the fact that independence came to most of Africa while Britain was under the rule of the Tory Party.

The nearest vindication to the original Marxist and Leninist theory of colonial liberation seems to have come with the former Portuguese colonies in Africa. They attained independence after a major coup took place in Lisbon itself, and Portugal moved to the left. And yet, although this appears to be a vindication of the older Marxist version of the primacy of the proletariat in the imperialist countries, in effect the example of the Portuguese empire is a reversal of cause and effect. It was not a case of Guinea-Bissau, Mozambique and Angola owing their liberation to a coup in Portugal. On the contrary, it was a case of the Portuguese coup being substantially caused by the colonial wars waged by African liberation fighters. Once the coup took place it did, of course, facilitate early attainment of formal independence for Guinea-Bissau, Mozambique and Angola; but it is important to grasp the direction of causation.

The pattern may also have relevance for Zimbabwe (Rhodesia) and South Africa. Will the first signs of a cracking political system within Rhodesia or South Africa be a military challenge by the white military forces themselves against civilian authority in Salisbury or Pretoria? Is it now conceivable that the trend of events in Southern Africa will be in the direction first of increasing pressure from black liberation forces, secondly of frustrations among the so-called security forces fighting on behalf of the white regimes, and thirdly of new strains of civil-military relations within the white regimes themselves? Earlier in North Africa there was also an interplay of such factors between Algerian resisters and the French occupation. Indeed the first major case of a metropolitan coup leading to colonial liberation was the assumption of power by General Charles de Gaulle in 1958. The French army had become increasingly frustrated as a result of major setbacks, first in Indo-China and later in Algeria. By 1958 France herself was already weary of colonial war, and the politicians had not moved much further towards finding a solution for Algeria. The armed forces in the field in Algeria were getting increasingly restive. Finally a revolt on the part of the soldiers, challenging the very existence of the French Fourth Republic, created a national crisis of considerable proportions. The Fifth Republic came into being, a new status was offered to France's black African colonies. And in time Algeria itself became independent.

At a lower level of reality it was indeed true that a metropolitan coup in Paris was a major cause behind the acceleration of African liberation. What ought also to be remembered is that the metropolitan coup itself was substantially a response to a major military challenge from colonial liberation fighters. In this case, the initial challenge came from the Algerian insurrection under the National Liberation Front, and the strains which these fighters put on the French army finally snapped into a confrontation between the French army and the French Fourth Republic, leading to a collapse of that republic, the rise of de Gaulle, and the emergence of new possibilities for French colonies in the African continent.

On balance the evidence of armed liberation in Africa has been more in support of the Maoist than of the classical Marxist position. In the words of Mao's own dictum: 'The enemy advances, we retreat; the enemy holds, we harass; the enemy tires, we attack; the enemy retreats, we pursue'.[7]

The transmission of Maoist ideas was sometimes indirect. Maoism did influence Vietnamese, Cubans, and other Third World radical fighters. Ho Chi Minh and Che Guevara both show Maoist influence in this domain of liberation strategy. An armchair revolutionary guerrilla fighter was Kwame Nkrumah, who wrote about revolutionary warfare after he had been overthrown from power in a military coup in 1966. He was himself Mao's guest in Peking when the coup took place, and Nkrumah then retreated into exile in Guinea. He became increasingly radicalized in exile, but his thoughts on revolutionary warfare probably influenced African intellectuals, rather than African guerrilla fighters as such.[8]

But wherever guerrilla war is either discussed or implemented the Chinese example is at least remembered and at times has been used as an inspiration. On this issue Mao has certainly overshadowed not only Lenin but also to some extent Marx. But what of the developmental models in so far as they have been perceived in Africa? It is to these that we must now turn.

Building Nations and Building Socialism

Isaac Deutscher points out that the Chinese Communist revolution presents the paradox of 'the most archaic of nations avidly absorbing the most modern of revolutionary doctrines, the last word in revolution, and translating it into action, lacking any mature ancestry. Chinese communism descends straight from Bolshevism. Mao stands on Lenin's shoulders'.[9]

Mao was indeed profoundly influenced by Lenin, from the days when he first started studying Leninism in the 1920s. Mao also developed some respect for Stalin, in spite of Stalin's fluctuating loyalty to China. But it is very important to remember that Mao did not share many of the intellectual assumptions on which the organization and role of the Communist Party of the Soviet Union were based. Neither did Mao embrace the technocratic and industrial biases of the Soviet experience. Mao Tse-tung also tended to distrust the bureaucratic and elitist tendencies of the Stalinist heritage in Russia, again in spite of Mao's admiration of Stalin.[10]

The Chinese model of development as perceived in Africa might therefore be reduced to the following characteristics:

1. Distrust of technocratic and bureaucratic domination in the developmental process

2. Technological gradualism with a distrust of excessively rapid industrialization
3. Maximum economic self-reliance
4. Relative autarchy in trade relations, or at least substantial disengagement from the international capitalist system
5. Substantial rural decentralization to maximize rural development, but combined with local collective efforts.

The Russian model has tended to include at least the following:
1. Rapid industrialization
2. Large-scale collectivization of agriculture in spite of fluctuations in policy
3. Economic imperialism rather than economic autarchy
4. Faith in technocratic and bureaucratic foundations for the developmental process
5. Stabilized revolution rather than 'permanent revolution'
6. Democratic centralism, emphasizing central direction, rather than unified peasant initiative, implying ideological guidance but encouraging considerable local initiative.

In Africa as a whole the Soviet Union as a country has greater influence than the People's Republic of China, but there is probably greater African identification with and admiration for the Chinese experience than there is identification with the Soviet precedent.

Political models from one part of the world are transferred or diffused to other parts of the world by three different processes:
1. By imitation, implying a conscious attempt on the part of the receiving country to emulate the behaviour, style or techniques of the donor society
2. By imposition, whereby a dominant country with a model of its own proceeds to pass it on through imperialist means to another society
3. By acculturation, a slower process involving the internalization of aspects of the culture from which the alien model is drawn.

Western models of nation-building and of government in Africa were transferred mainly by imposition, at least in the sense of imperialist manipulation. The Westminster model as a system of government which many former British colonies received on attainment of independence, with due modifications, clearly implied institutional transfer by at least partial imposition. In this case what we have is a vertical transfer, from a highly industrialized dominant country to a technologically underdeveloped exploited country. The Westminster model and variations of the French system of bureaucracy transferred to the colonies were instances of *vertically imposed institutions*. On the other hand, approximations to the Soviet model (democratic centralism) in a place like Guinea (Conakry) constitute a *vertically imitative model*. The transfer is vertical because it is again from a northern industrialized source to a less developed recipient. But unlike the Westminster model democratic centralism in Guinea is a case of imitation or emulation of the Soviet Union rather than of actual imposition by the Soviet Union. Approximations to Chinese approaches to development in countries like Tanzania are instances of *horizontal model imitation*—borrowing from another member of the underdeveloped world, albeit a massive one.

The radicalization of Julius Nyerere in the last ten years has been due to a number of factors. But here let us satisfy ourselves with two such factors, one domestic and the other international—the domestic one was Tanganyika's union with Zanzibar; the international, the United Republic of Tanzania's co-operation with Communist China. It would of course be quite naïve to see Nyerere as someone under the spell of indoctrination by either Zanzibari revolutionaries or communist Chinese. On the contrary, domestic revolutionaries in mainland Tanzania have sometimes suffered under Julius Nyerere precisely because of their fervour. But there is little doubt that the impact of the union with Zanzibar has been radicalizing in its broader repercussions. There is also little doubt that Nyerere's discovery of China has had a major effect on his concept of development in relation to self-reliance, and on his view of international diplomacy at large.

At least in the initial period, Tanganyika's union with Zanzibar did bring to Dar es Salaam a significant radical pressure group from the island which strengthened those mainlanders who also wanted to see a sharp turn to the left. As indicated earlier, some of these radicals—both Zanzibari and Tanganyikan—have declined in direct personal influence on the government in Dar es Salaam. But this is not inconsistent with the proposition that union with Zanzibar has been an important radicalizing factor in the ideological evolution of mainland Tanzania.

As for the impact of China on Nyerere, it probably started with his anger at western criticism of his 'flirtation' with Peking. His disenchantment with the West over the railway line to Zambia, and Communist China's more positive response, inaugurated a new era in Nyerere's views of economic non-alignment. The diplomatic and economic collaboration with China must have increased Nyerere's own curiosity about the strategies of development of Mao Tse-tung's leadership. And Nyerere's political preference inclined him towards *Kujitegemea*, or spirit of self-reliance.[11]

Sometimes Nyerere simply discovered that there were similarities between his own thinking and his interpretation of the Chinese model. In this case there was no direct intellectual influence from China to Nyerere. There was instead a kind of intellectual congruence, a similarity of perspectives. But where Nyerere did discover such congruence, that very discovery sometimes reinforced his own faith and optimism about the utility of a particular line of thinking. This applies, among other things, to Nyerere's belief in technological gradualism. Tanzania under his leadership has been attempting a combination of ideological revolution and technological gradualism. In ideology the commitment is to the creation and maintenance of a revolutionary egalitarian ethic, seeking to create social accord and economic development without creating social and economic inequalities. Combined with this revolutionary egalitarian quest is a belief in technological pragmatism, a reluctance to undergo rapid technological change in spite of the commitment to rapid social transformation. To some extent, it is almost as if Nyerere was aware that the relationship between technology and egalitarianism is a tense one. The most egalitarian African societies have been the least technologically advanced.

Nyerere's distrust of a rapid application of sophisticated technology has been more an attitude of mind than a formal policy. But it has been an attitude of mind that is very conscious, influenced in part precisely by the desire to prevent a very rapid leap from the egalitarian simplicity of traditional Tanzania to a destabilizing mechanization of the countryside. In Nyerere's words when addressing an audience on the university campus in Dar es Salaam:

> Our future lies in the development of our agriculture and in the development of our rural areas. But because we are seeking to grow from our own roots and to preserve that which is valuable in our traditional past, we have also to stop thinking in terms of massive agricultural mechanization and the proletarianization of our rural population. We have, instead, to think in terms of development through the improvement of the tools we now use, and through the growth of cooperative systems of production. Instead of aiming at large farms using tractors and other modern equipment and employing agricultural laborers, we should be aiming at having ox-ploughs all over the country. The jembe [hoe] will have to be eliminated by the ox-plough before the latter can be eliminated by the tractor. We cannot hope to eliminate the jembe by the tractor.[12]

These ideas do provide a certain congruence with some elements of Maoist thought, especially since the economic break with the Soviet Union a decade and a half ago. Nevertheless, as between China and Tanzania some horizontal model imitation has taken place, reinforced by a certain basic similarity of outlook among the leaders of the two countries.

Africa does not as yet have a convincing case of model transfer by natural acculturation — in the sense of a slow and genuine assimilation of the political culture which underlies a particular foreign model. But models which are originally either imitative or imposed could in time become assimilated and culturally internalized. The chances of such internalization taking place partly depend upon the degree of prior *cultural congruence* between the society and the borrower, and not merely intellectual congruence between the respective leaders. Were there prior similarities between the cultural universe of rural China and the universe of rural Tanzania? Or—paradoxical as it may seem—are the prior cultural predispositions of Tanzanians nearer to those of the Russians than to those of the Chinese? Can we ever discover the answers to such questions? Or are the techniques of cross-cultural research too underdeveloped for such an enterprise?

Another condition for genuine assimilation of a borrowed model is the degree to which it allows itself to be modified by local circumstances and even local values. Marxism in China allowed itself to be modified by Chinese culture. By becoming partly localized, it became partly internalized. In his report to the Sixth Plenum of the Central Committee of the Chinese Communist Party as long ago as 1938, Mao Tse-tung entered into a discussion about the problem of relating Marxism to China's historical inheritance. Mao said:

> Today's China is an outgrowth of historic China. We must not mutilate history. . . . A Communist is a Marxist internationalist, but Marxism must take on a national form before it can be applied. There is no such thing as abstract Marxism, but only concrete Marxism. . . . If a Chinese Communist, who is a part of the great Chinese people and is bound to his people by his very flesh and blood, talks of Marxism apart from Chinese peculiarities, this Marxism is merely an empty obstruction. Consequently, the Sinification of Marxism—that is to say, making certain that in all of its manifestations it is imbued with Chinese peculiarities, using it according to the peculiarities of China—becomes a problem which must be understood and solved by the whole party without delay. . . . We must put an end to writing eight-legged essays on foreign models . . . we must cease our dogmatism, and replace it by a new and vital Chinese style and Chinese manner, pleasing to the eye and to the ear of the Chinese people.[13]

Although Nyerere is not a communist at all, there is some similarity between this old position of Mao Tse-tung's and Nyerere's own belief that socialism in Africa has to be Africanized, and that socialism in Tanzania must respond to Tanzanian realities. As Nyerere put it:

> We are groping our way forward towards socialism, and we are in danger of being bemused by this new theology, and therefore of trying to solve our problems according to what the priests of Marxism say is what Marx said or meant. If we do this we shall fail. Africa's conditions are very different from those of the Europe in which Marx and Lenin wrote and worked. To talk as if these thinkers provided all the answers to our problems, or as if Marx invented socialism, is to reject both the humanity of Africa and the universality of socialism. Marx did contribute a good deal to socialist thought. But socialism did not begin with him, nor can it end in constant reinterpretations of his writings.[14]

In Mozambique the Chinese are still important as advisers in the developmental process, just as they once influenced strategies of liberation. But the independence of Mozambique and Angola is too recent to give us an adequate clue of the degree to which any aspects of the Chinese model have been effectively transferred. Both Angola and Mozambique are experiencing severe stresses and teething troubles of independence, with significant areas of instability and institutional fluidity. In Angola, the Russians and the Cubans are by far the most important influences externally upon the policies and directions of the government of MPLA. The Chinese had backed MPLA's rivals, especially UNITA, but their support for their chosen allies in Angola was much more modest than the support that the Soviet Union and Cuba gave to MPLA. But even in the case of Angola it is feasible that some Maoist ideas of organization might influence policy-making in time. The Cuban model itself, to the extent to which it has Maoist echoes, might serve as a transmission belt for some degree of Maoist diffusion. But so early in the history of Angola all this is speculative.

In both eastern and southern Africa it would be true to say that it is sometimes difficult to determine where the influence of the Russian model ends and the impact of China's experience begins. As indicated, Tanzania's strategy of development has indeed been influenced by China but with major differences. Ethiopia, since the overthrow of Emperor Haile Selassie, was for a while led by students in a neo-Maoist direction. Many Ethiopian students have been inspired and exhilarated by China's experience and some of the thoughts of Mao Tse-tung. When the soldiers captured power in Addis Ababa they did not have an adequate sense of ideological direction, and the students turned out to be more influential in those critical months than might have seemed feasible. A model controlled by old men in China had generated youthful enthusiasm in eastern Africa. The gerontocratic tendencies of the People's Republic of China did not detract from China's capacity to arouse the admiration of young people in young nations in Africa. Ethiopia's neighbour, Somalia, was drawing lessons from both the Russian and the Chinese experiences. While other socialist countries have struggled to change the ways of settled peasants, Somalia has struggled to transform the life-style of nomads. Important social engineering is under way in Somalia, partly inspired by socialist experience elsewhere, but also conditioned by local innovation and determination.

Domestic Revolution and International Pragmatism

What is the link between model transfer and foreign policy? To some extent it is true that a major issue in the international competition between Moscow and Peking is over leadership among progressive countries in the world and influence on the direction of social revolution in the Third World. Both China and the Soviet Union have begun to take the developing countries quite seriously as a potentially decisive force in the last quarter of the twentieth century. Moscow sees itself as having the right credentials for leadership partly on ideological grounds of 'proletarian internationalism' and partly because of the Soviet Union's technological and military capacity to defend socialism at home and abroad. Peking has strongly opposed Moscow's claim to hegemony in the socialist world. Countries such as Angola might have discovered proletarian internationalism at just about the time that communist parties in western Europe were renouncing it and countries such as Yugoslavia, Rumania and China were feeling vindicated by the erosion of Soviet leadership.

On the whole both China and the Soviet Union, while pursuing revolution internally in their own countries, have chosen to be pragmatic in their foreign policies in more recent times. China has championed some of the most unlikely movements in Africa, including UNITA, while the Soviet Union has at times let regimes such as that of Nasser of Egypt lock up hundreds of Egyptian communists for the sake of wider considerations.

There is also little obvious link between influencing an African country's internal policy and influencing its external orientation, or vice versa. China has significantly influenced Julius Nyerere's domestic policy (*ujamaa* villages and all) but seems to have had little impact on Nyerere's foreign policy (as Nyerere's strong support of MPLA as against UNITA indicated). On the other hand, the Russians probably do have an influence on Idi Amin's foreign policy (in spite of occasional highly publicized differences), but they have had little impact on Uganda's system of government internally.

Ethiopia and Somalia have become closer ideologically since 1974 in terms of internal socialist measures—but are as deeply divided as ever in their relations with each other.

The Cuban factor in parts of Africa may lead to further horizontal model transfer by imitation. Since the Cuban model was itself influenced by both Russian and Chinese experiences, this Caribbean example may become a transmission belt for three alien models in Africa—Chinese and Russian as well as Cuban. A good deal depends upon the kind of institutional changes which will be made in places like Angola in the years ahead. Mozambique may also be responsive to all three models—alongside some genuine autonomous experimentation going back to the days of struggles against the Portuguese. In those days FRELIMO began to construct developmental and mobilization structures in liberated areas which may be important in the days ahead.

The Chinese have had both strong leadership and strong organization since their revolution. The Cubans have had strong leadership but probably less impressive organizational efficiency. The Tanzanians have had leadership which has been inspiring rather than strong in Castro's sense, and organizationally Tanzania is considerably more deficient than Cuba, let alone China. It is arguable that Ethiopia since the fall of the Emperor has lacked both leadership and organization. Mozambique is hazardously near the same condition. Angola may be building an organization, but does it have as yet nation-wide, effective and autonomous leadership? [15]

Perhaps whether the Chinese or the Russian models are transferable to Africa or not might ultimately hinge on whether Africa has the type of leadership, the level of organization, and the quality of cultural coherence which made Maoism for China and Leninism-Stalinism for Russia two of the most striking socio-economic experiments in human history.

Conclusion

Ever since Mao's death in September 1976 three basic questions have been hanging over the future of the Chinese model. These questions are not fully answered yet. Is China after Mao moving in the direction of reducing her self-reliance and increasing her interest in foreign technology? Is power within the Chinese system moving more firmly towards the bureaucratic elite and away from the ideologues? Are these processes influencing a rapprochement between the People's Republic and the Soviet Union?

The answers to these questions have wider diplomatic, economic and ideological implications. Importation of more foreign technology is almost bound to increase China's participation in the international capitalist system. It may profoundly alter China's relations with Japan, as Japanese offers of technological help begin to make headway. Japanese technology has been of interest to the Soviet Union as well, in spite of some setbacks in Russo-Japanese relations in recent times. In the years after Mao, China may well engage in considerable technological diplomacy and economic flirtation with both the Soviet Union and Japan. This is quite apart from the prospect of China's increasing contacts with the United States and western Europe. A change in China's policy concerning alien technology could also contribute towards solving the problem of Taiwan. A reabsorption of Taiwan into China seems inevitable in due course. Will this initially take the form of a quasi-federal relationship between Taiwan and the mainland? Taiwan's successful experimentation with western technology could give it a greater capacity to make a contribution to the economic vigour of a re-unified People's Republic. The shift of power to the bureaucrats in China could result in a modus vivendi with the Soviet Union over the border question. The Maoist struggle against the 'social imperialism' of the Soviet Union would thus be toned down.

All these ideological and diplomatic shifts could make China after Mao similar to Egypt after Nasser. A process of deradicalization would have got under way. In that event Chou En-lai — with his vision of an industrialized and stabilized China — might turn out to be of longer-term policy relevance for his country than the legacy of Mao himself as his memory recedes into history. But all this is speculative at this stage. The so-called 'mind of China' continues to be as 'inscrutable' as ever.

But in assessing the impact of the Chinese model on the Third World we have to bear in mind the simple proposition that Mao's body is now 'a-lying in the grave'. Can his 'soul keep marching on'? In Egypt, Nasser's 'soul' is temporarily subdued, but may find a new lease of life later. But what is more to the point in comparing Egypt with China is that Nasserism is by no means dead in other parts of the Arab world. It inspires Colonel Qaddafi of Libya; influences at least sections of the Baath party in both Iraq and Syria; played a part in the ideological tensions of the Lebanese civil war; and continues to capture the imagination of the youth all over the Arab world. Similarly, even if China after Mao deradicalizes domestically, and collaborates with both 'international capital' and 'social imperialism', the legacy of Mao could continue to play a significant role in some countries of Africa and in other parts of the Third World long after the Red Book of Mao's sayings has ceased to influence the political climate of Shanghai.

But in the final analysis, is there a single Russian or Maoist model of either development or liberation? Or are there several models, each reflecting *either* an aspect of a leader's response to a particular historical moment, *or* the varied and compound nature of the leader's own ideological personality, *or* some compromise worked out by the contending forces at work in China's or Russia's political process? The other question which arises is whether the effect of someone like Mao is inevitably 'in the eye of the beholder'. There may be as many Maoist, or indeed Russian, models of development as there are Third World observers to behold them. When therefore we talk about the influence of external paradigms on African behaviour, we may primarily be talking about African perceptions of those paradigms, however distorted those perceptions may be. In the words of Kenneth D. Boulding:

> It is what we think the world is like, not what it is really like, that determines our behavior. . . . We act according to the way the world appears to us, not necessarily according to the way it 'is'. . . . The 'image' then must be thought of as the total cognitive, affective, and evaluative structure of the behavior of the elite, or its internal view of itself and its universe. [16]

The beginnings of the Africanization of Marxism may lie in an African's *misinterpretation* of Marx. Precisely by getting Marx wrong an African could make the German revolutionary more relevant to the African condition. But this would only arise if the African's error was itself influenced by his own material and sociological predicament. In such a situation, reality affects the image and the image is the message. For better or for worse, the images of Lenin and Mao are beginning to be discerned in eastern and southern Africa. What should be remembered is that those images are often at their most creative when they are distorted by the mirror of Africa's own material experience and historical destiny.

References and Notes

1. Consult, for example, Robert V. Daniels, ed., *A Documentary History of Communism*, Vol. I, Vintage Books, Random House, New York, 1960.
2. Kenneth W. Grundy, *Guerrilla Struggle in Africa: an Analysis and Preview*, A World Order book, Grossman, New York, 1971, pp. 42-3.
3. *Quotations from Chairman Mao Tse-tung*, Foreign Languages Press, Peking, 1967, pp. 121-2.
4. Mao Tse-tung, *Selected Military Writings*, Foreign Languages Press, Peking, 1963, pp. 272-3.
5. Mao Tse-tung, 'On the rectification of incorrect ideas in the party', *Selected Works*, Vol. I, Lawrence and Wishart, 1954, p. 106.
6. Ibid., pp. 124, 222.
7. Ibid.
8. Kwame Nkrumah, *Handbook of Revolutionary Warfare*, Panaf Books, 1968. Consult also Ali A. Mazrui, 'Nkrumah: the Leninist czar', *Transition* (Kampala), VI, 26 (1966), reprinted in Mazrui, *On Heroes and Uhuru-Worship*, Longmans, 1967, pp. 113-34.
9. Isaac Deutscher, *Ironies of History—Essays on Contemporary Communism*, Ramparts Press, San Francisco, 1966, pp. 89-90.
10. Consult Maurice Meisner, 'Leninism and Maoism: some populist perspectives on Marxism-Leninism in China', *The China Quarterly*, 45 (January-March 1971), 4-19.
11. This part of the chapter was borrowed from William Tordoff and Ali A. Mazrui, 'The left and the super-left in Tanzania', *The Journal of Modern African Studies*, 10, 3 (1972), 427-45.
12. Julius Nyerere, 'The purpose is man', *Freedom and Socialism: a Selection from Writings and Speeches, 1965-1967*, Oxford University Press, Dar es Salaam and London, 1968, p. 320. See also Mazrui, *Cultural Engineering and Nation Building in East Africa*, Northwestern University Press, Evanston, Illinois, 1972, Chapter 15, pp. 247-62.
13 Mao, *Selected Works*, op. cit., Vol. II, pp. 258-61. A stimulating essay on the significance of Marxism is by Stuart R. Schram, 'Chinese and Leninist components in the personality of Mao Tse-tung', chapter in Gary K. Bertsch, *Comparative Communism: the Soviet, Chinese and Yugoslav Models*, W. H. Freeman, San Francisco, 1976, pp. 151-62.
14. Julius Nyerere, *Freedom and Socialism*, op. cit., p. 15.
15. We are grateful for stimulation on some of these issues to Professor Allen S. Whiting, Department of Political Science, University of Michigan. See Michel Oksenberg, *China's Developmental Experience*, Praeger, New York and London, 1973.
16. Kenneth D. Boulding, 'National images and international systems', *The Journal of Conflict Resolution*, III (1959), 121-2. For a fuller exposition of the theory, see Boulding, *The Image*, University of Michigan Press, Ann Arbor, 1956.

PART THREE

THE SEARCH FOR RELEVANCE

10 Education and Political Change

The first thing to be noted about national goals and political values in Africa after independence is their changeability. In the field of politics, we are living in a period of fluidity and impermanence. We are groping for new social directions, for new values, even for new cultures. Many peoples in Africa have had the experience of living together in one country for only a relatively few years. Some groups have still not interacted. They are separated by long distances within a given country, and are hardly aware that they are fellow citizens in the same country.

Then there is the diversity of cultural backgrounds confronting anyone who studies African countries and the composition of their societies. These different traditional cultures need never fully merge to form one national heritage, but some degree of integration needs to be encouraged so that the groups can gradually evolve a shared universe of ideas and values.

Nor can we ignore political instability in some African countries. It is not simply a question of how long a government stays in power. Some African governments have been known to stay in power longer than they would have done in some of the more developed societies of the world. A few governments have even been known to stay in power too long. Political stability, however, is not to be measured purely in terms of duration of office; it has to be measured by the yardstick of predictable duration of office. If a particular government stays in power for twenty years, we cannot say that those entire twenty years were really stable if throughout the period we expected the government to fall any time. In other words, a situation where the duration of office is subject to abrupt termination is a situation of relative instability, regardless of whether those who hold office succeed in averting their downfall or not. Of course, if governments change very quickly in any case, this would itself be a distinctive form of realized instability. We could, in fact, distinguish between immanent instability and active instability. Immanent instability is of the kind where one expects the government to fall any month, or any year, and yet the government remains in power year after year. But active instability is a situation where governments do fall in a relatively

187

unpredictable way from year to year. The termination of office could be by constitutional or by extra-constitutional means. In the French Third and Fourth Republics there was regime instability of a constitutional kind, and this was active rather than immanent. The governments did fall every so often as a result of particular votes in parliament, and the changing alignments of political parties. In Latin America and some African countries, there is active instability of an extra-constitutional kind, when governments are overthrown, usually with the intervention of the armed forces, occasionally as a result of popular agitation.

What is the duty of a teacher in the face of political instability which is either immanent or active? What national goals ought to be an important part of education, regardless of changes of regimes? Where should indoctrination come into the syllabus and in what form?

The Limits of Indoctrination

My own position has been that indoctrination in education is desirable in the primary schools; it is defensible in the secondary schools; but is quite demeaning beyond secondary education. It is desirable at the primary level because children need some guidance as they evolve a capacity for making choices, and the political world can seem mysterious and even frightening without some explanation. Transmission of political values to children at the primary level, provided the values are broad and rudimentary and basic to the task of living in society, is in my opinion an educational imperative. At the secondary-school level, the transmission of values should become more sophisticated, with a high degree of critical flexibility and individual choice permitted within the system. The higher levels of secondary education may begin to dispense with political education as a process of socialization, and embark on political analysis as a more detached and independent approach to the understanding of politics. By the time they complete the sixth form the students have to be treated as intellectual adults from the point of view of political values. In other words, the emphasis from then on ought to be in perfecting the critical faculties and sharpening individual reasoning, rather than transmitting social values. The period of indoctrination should be coming to a close by the end of secondary education, and preferably two years before the end of secondary education.

It is true that this conception of the role of socialization and indoctrination in education seems to be based on a contradiction. What we are saying is that at the level of the primary and secondary schools part of the aim of education is to inculcate in the children the values and norms of the society to which they belong. Such inculcation must be a form of moral and cultural indoctrination. And then the child, duly indoctrinated, may enter Makerere as an undergraduate.

What happens at that level? What I am suggesting seems to imply a sudden change. Instead of the child being taught what to value, the young person is now taught to be critical about almost every value. Instead of cultural indoctrination, there is now a partial cultural challenge and self-criticism. In certain disciplines, the university teaches the young to question the answers which they received at school. In extreme cases, university students pass through a stage of being atheists or agnostics in religion, and cynics in politics.

Should Africa really continue with this dichotomy, which has been partly inherited from a western frame of reasoning? Should not Africa abandon a system which teaches young people certain values in primary and secondary school and then encourages them to be cynical or critical about those values at university level? One possible answer is to say that indoctrination should not be taking place even below university level; another answer is to say that it ought to continue into university life. The latter kind of argument would assert that if nation-building is an inspiring lesson for children at school, why should it cease to be so in higher education? Why then should the inculcation of values end at the secondary-school level? The answer to this reservation lies in the simple observation that to teach a student in an institution of higher learning to be critical of the most cherished values is itself to inculcate a new value — the ultimate value of independent thought. Sometimes African leaders behave almost as if national political independence cannot be combined with individual intellectual independence — that freedom of thought is dangerous to the independence of a nation. But perhaps the truth lies nearer to the realistic idealism which leaders like the late Tom Mboya of Kenya betrayed when he said: 'Intellectual freedom must be maintained for the sake of the country's future.'[1]

But to the critic from the other extreme who wants no inculcation of values at any levels of education, the question might well be: why not promote intellectual and mental independence from the cradle? For a baby and a very young child a complete lack of guiding norms imposes a heavy burden of responsibility. Even for a grown-up the ability to make a choice as between rational alternatives presupposes criteria of choosing. We need to have a yardstick for deciding among, first, an extra bottle of *waragi* a week for the head of the family, as against, second, an extra dress every two months for the wife, as against, third, a better and more expensive school for the third son. All these involve questions of values and, although the grown-up may be exercising his freedom to choose from among them, he cannot escape the burden of creating a scale of priorities. Nor can he escape the burden of being judged by himself, or by others, should his scale of priorities appear to be odd.

The case for providing a foundation for such values to primary-school and secondary-school children is, therefore, the stronger. Our societies may be in the grip of moral flexibility, or changing norms and changing cultures. This is an argument for not having too elaborate a system of indoctrination at any level of education, since the ideology of the state could be transformed overnight. On the other hand, it is also an argument for introducing some degree of inculcation of political values in the educational system.

On Tolerance, Toil and Teamwork

What is the balance which can be struck in this regard? In my opinion there are only three politically significant values which can be inculcated in the educational system and retain relevance regardless of the regime in power. I call these values 'the three T's of training in nationhood'. The T's I have in mind are 'tolerance', 'toil' and 'teamwork'. They are to supplement the traditional three R's of basic education — Reading, Writing and Arithmetic.

By 'tolerance' I do not mean the promotion of a sense of 'brotherhood'. The idea of human brotherhood is a religious idea, and people respond to it more positively when they are listening to a sermon in a church than in their day-to-day lives. It is just not realistic enough to expect people who are otherwise rivals and strongly in competition, and have no connexion of any kind with each other in blood or cultural affinity, to regard each other as brothers nevertheless. Only a few religious individuals, deeply animated by human amity, can transcend notions of ethnic and cultural identification and embrace the human family as a whole. For the majority of people it is fair to ask them to tolerate those who are different from them. It is not as realistic to expect them to treat total strangers and total aliens meaningfully as brothers. Even the Christian imperative of 'love thy neighbour' is a tall order. Even a literal neighbour may be quite demanding — if he plays his gramophone too loud at night, or if his children are boisterous and tend to scream, or if he has a habit of coming to your home to borrow eggs never to be returned.

With children especially, notions of kinship and brotherhood are beginning to consolidate themselves and there is a risk in trying to expand them too far. The critical issue for a society is not how much brotherhood there is but how much tolerance. There is no special credit in being favourably disposed toward your own brother. The real test comes when, in spite of being unable to regard a stranger as your brother, you still succeed in tolerating his unusual and idiosyncratic ways. The educational system should allow for this critical variable in human relations. Our societies need, above all, the capacity to tolerate people of different cultural backgrounds, or different regions and identities, or different political views. Our societies need to be guided not necessarily by the values of liberalism in their totality, like individualism, nor indeed by the institutions of liberalism, like certain types of parliaments and certain types of multi-party systems. But our societies do need to be governed by the liberal rules of the game — the rules which simply say 'live and let live'. The liberal rules of the game permit competing viewpoints and competing interpretations of reality to survive together. The liberal rules of the game prescribe toleration of differences and of pluralism.

Tolerance is, in fact, the most difficult of these three values to be inculcated in children. Children are notoriously intolerant at times, and can be painfully and brutally cruel. What kind of approach should be adopted to foster and build up their capacity to tolerate others is perhaps one of the most important and yet intractable problems in the whole field of child education.

But at the level of intellectual toleration there is a good deal to be said for a system of education which puts a special premium on debating as an activity. The idea of getting schoolchildren to debate among themselves on a variety of fundamental issues has great potential as a teaching device to promote tolerance of differing viewpoints. The training here springs from exposure to radically polarized viewpoints. Every school in Africa must do its best to have a vigorous debating society. The debates should take place several times a term, instead of once or twice a year. By all means combine these debates with the idea of inviting controversial speakers to address current affairs societies, and answer student challenges and expostulations. But controversial speakers should supplement confrontations between students themselves over intellectual issues.

I have had occasion before to discuss the differences between student power in a developed society and student power in an under-developed country. Social reformers and student militants in a developed country are confronted with entrenched values, difficult to dislodge or affect without a massive challenge. Therefore it sometimes makes sense in a developed society for young people to demonstrate in the streets in favour of certain positions, ranging from issues connected with race relations domestically to issues of foreign policy abroad. The young people may be demonstrating against race prejudice in the United States or Britain, or against class inequalities in Japan, or against the war in Vietnam. But behind those policy issues are the entrenched values of a society that has stabilized itself in certain spheres, combined with entrenched institutions of mature political and economic systems. To make a dent on this complex of structures requires, at times, more than a speech. It requires a demonstration of vigorous dissent.

But in situations of the kind confronted by African countries, the real problem is not of entrenched values but of fluid values. The nations are still groping for those social directions we mentioned earlier. There is a mutability of political preferences, some uncertainty regarding ideological positions. In this kind of situation of fluid values, demonstrations are not the appropriate mode of youthful assertion. Instead of demonstrating in the streets, there should be continued promotion of debating as a device to help these young people find their own intellectual resting places. Debating becomes a useful technique in a situation of fluid values, because it helps to sharpen the faculties of deciding between different values, and gradually developing a sophisticated evaluation of different alternatives. Debating is also a critical training in the art of toleration.

The imperative of 'toil', like the other two 'T's, is subject to cultural variations. Attitude to work is conditioned by those cultural factors. President Nyerere in Tanzania has claimed that in traditional Africa everyone was a worker—'a worker' not just as distinct from 'employer' but also as distinct from 'loiterer' or 'idler'.[2] Nyerere sees work in traditional Africa as a factor balancing African hospitality. The tradition of hospitality and support for one's kinsmen could all too easily result in parasitism. The obligation to work is the safety valve against excessive hospitality. As Nyerere put it:

> Those who talk about the African way of life and, quite rightly, take pride in maintaining a tradition of hospitality which is so great a part of it, might do well to remember the Swahili saying *'Mgeni siku mbili; siku ya tatu mpe jembe'* or, in English 'Treat your guest as a guest for two days; on the third day give him a hoe.'[3]

President Nyerere does have a point in this interpretation, but the traditional set-up in most African societies was more complex than that. The incentives to work in traditional Africa were often in the following order: first, the search for the individual's own basic needs and those of his immediate family; secondly, the individual's contribution to the welfare of neighbours and kinsmen if this was customarily expected; and only thirdly, the individual's interest in accumulating more things for himself and aspiring to self-improvement as distinct from self-maintenance. The ordering of priorities is quite significant. It is not correct that the traditional African subordinated his own basic needs to those of his community. His own basic needs came first, the needs of his community and kinsmen came second, and the need for personal improvement came third. The incentive to hard work varied accordingly. Working for personal maintenance made good sense; working hard to meet one's normal or customary obligations to one's kinsmen also made sense; but working hard for some undefined target of self-improvement was in many cases less clearly understood. The phenomenon of 'target workers' in Africa, as they come to the cities to satisfy only certain needs and then go back home, and the phenomenon of workers working fewer hours as soon as they are paid more for the hours they do work, have all been interpreted by varying economic anthropologists as indications of the low priority which self-improvement has in traditional African values if it is regarded as an indefinite process of upward mobility.

The role of schools in dealing with such a scale of values might vary according to the dominant orientation of the government in power. The Kenya government might be inclined to foster and encourage the ethic of self-improvement, since the government is committed to the goal of creating an indigenous entrepreneurial culture and private enterprise. Tanzania, on the other hand, might be inclined to preserve the traditional scale of priorities which put communal work before self-improvement.

But how does the educator know how long Kenya's policies or Tanzania's policies would last? We are back to the difficult problem of trying to decide which values are likely to survive a military coup or an electoral swing. Perhaps educators could investigate ways of transmitting the ethic of work in a manner which attempts to reconcile working for society with working for one's own improvement. The very process of acquiring an education poses the dilemma between education for effective citizenship and education for personal ambition. As we mentioned earlier, the harder it is to acquire an education, the more it will be regarded as a passport to a future life of leisure. Many African children walk long distances every day, and take heavy part-time work, in the endeavour to acquire an education. Because they have acquired their education the hard way, they tend to feel at the end of it that they have 'arrived' and deserve to rest. Thus the educated become, alas, an elite of leisure.

The third 'T' of training in nationhood is 'teamwork', and it is important that there should be opportunities for teamwork at all levels of education. These should range from encouragement of basket-ball and soccer to encouragement of student political societies and social organizations. A few days ago a Ugandan journalist asked if, in the present situation in Uganda, there was a case for banning student activities on the Makerere campus and other educational institutions in Uganda. My answer was that the banning of students' extra-curricular activities would affect the quality of their education. I argued that education was not simply what went on in the classroom, but it was also the experience of being socially engaged and intellectually committed. But behind it all was the further experience of teamwork and collaboration, even in situations where one team has to compete and even quarrel with another. The liberal rules of the game are once again at play — 'live and let live'.

The aim in this entire exercise could be the inculcation of the rules of national integration. Africa is confronted with ethnic pluralism and cultural diversity. The interaction between different tribes could generate considerable stress and tension. The quest is for a system which would permit these groups not only to tolerate each other — which is the first precondition — but also to work with each other in pursuit of shared goals. And even when the groups are in competition, the competition itself should be subject to rules of fair play. Among the least violent societies in the world is England. How much of the British tradition of fair play is derived from the place of games in British public schools?

Eric Dunning, a sociology lecturer at the University of Leicester, has brought out a book entitled *The Making of Football: a Sociological Study* (1966). By football he meant rugby. The history of football goes back to the twelfth century and perhaps even earlier. Prior to the nineteenth century the game was rough and loosely organized. But early in the nineteenth century important changes began to take place. The game began to assume greater sophistication, greater complexity and greater formal organization. Leadership in this transformation of the game was given by seven great public schools of England—Charterhouse, Eton, Harrow, Rugby, Shrewsbury, Westminster and Winchester—the only public schools which were in existence throughout this period of the game.

The period of 1840 to 1960 witnessed the stage when the rules of the game were committed to writing for the first time, and the boys were called upon to exercise much greater self-restraint in their play than had ever been demanded before. Eric Dunning tells us:

> Football became a 'mock-fight' which provided as much as possible the pleasures of a real fight without its risks and dangers, a struggle regulated in such a way that the contestants had much less chance than formerly to inflict serious injury or to use physical violence on each other in earnest. Pleasure in playing was enhanced, henceforward, by the fact that the 'battle' was not fought by brute force alone, but by force transformed by specific skills. Football became at once spontaneous and highly controlled. Ample room was left for inventiveness and the expression of individuality, but barriers—in the form of explicit rules—were set up to ensure that the excitement of the battle did not carry too far.[4]

Dunning compared the evolving system of the English public school and its games with what was happening in Prussian schools. The Prussian schools at the time were highly authoritarian institutions, in which the equivalent of football was 'drill', a regimented activity in which a master barked out the orders and the boys mechanically complied.

> Drill reflected the authoritarian structure of the Prussian schools—indeed, of Prussian society as a whole. Duelling in the German universities provides a further contrast. It represented a far more open outlet for aggressive urges—death, serious injury, and disfigurement were its frequent accompaniments. Football in the English public schools represented a far more constructive means of channelling aggression.[5]

Because the British public schools provided the ruling elite of the country, and because much of the political norms and institutions evolved out of the history of the British elite, the country's entire political culture was affected in a variety of subtle ways by the principles of restraint, teamwork, and fair play which were partly acquired from the football fields of Winchester, Eton, Rugby and Harrow.

Into their colonies the British introduced some of the games which had helped to shape their social and political styles. The most popular game in Africa became soccer. The rules of the game are not internalized overnight, nor is soccer always effective in averting more ferocious forms of aggression. On the contrary, battles have been fought over a referee's decision in Kampala or Lagos, or a linesman's verdict. But the policy-makers of British imperial rule knew what they were doing when they sought to divert the 'natives' with a game of soccer on an afternoon or two every week. The virtues of self-restraint, obedience to rules, team spirit within each side, a spirit of fair play toward the opponents, and respect for the referee — these were virtues which were as relevant in politics as they were in sports. They took time to acquire. But they had to be taught. And the sports stadium was one school of citizenship.

What the experience of British public schools illustrates is that transmission of values is not necessarily a matter of speeches in a classroom or sermons in a chapel. It can be done through media far less obvious — like a game of football, 'sixth form versus school', in nineteenth-century Rugby.

Perhaps more work needs to be done regarding how best to transmit, in African conditions, the three imperatives of tolerance, toil and teamwork. Debating societies and games need to be studied more closely in their sociological and psychological implications. They have too often been taken for granted as mere diversions for young people — 'after all, all children need to play'. Some school games may be better suited for training in tolerance and teamwork than others. If so, which are which? Educational research could pay renewed attention to the study of sports and games, and their comparative efficacy as media of socialization and promotion of national values. If certain games, as yet untried in African schools, are better for citizenship-training than those which are already popular, there is a compelling case for promoting experimentation with the new games. In some situations the gymnasium may be a more effective school of values than an ideological institute can hope to be.

Against the background of recent events in Uganda, we might now look at tolerance, toil and teamwork and ask: what is the relevance of our three 'T's in relation to the training of soldiers in our societies? Two of the values — teamwork and toil — are clearly very important in military training. Principles of discipline, the ethic of solidarity behind one's colours, the principles of organization and command, are all founded on the imperative of teamwork. Toil is also often critical in military life — a great sense of rugged self-reliance is fostered. It is true that, in times of peace, the toil is sometimes contrived. Work is deliberately created to keep the boys occupied. But even that is proof enough that military training puts a special premium on toil as a corollary of discipline. But what about the other imperative of training in nationhood? What about the place of *tolerance* in the life of a soldier? Is there such a place?

Military training is more like drill in the Prussian schools of the nineteenth century than a game of football at Eton. Both drill and football foster teamwork and co-ordination. But drill has less to do with questions of *fair play* than does football. Drill, therefore, is less of an exercise in the discipline of tolerance than a game of football has often proved to be. By the same token, a soldier is trained in the arts of real war, rather than make-believe on a sportsground. In a war the soldier needs to be prepared for toil and for teamwork. But it is very difficult to remember the principles of toleration when one is under fire from enemy guns. Yet we know that in independent Africa soldiers are more often concerned with domestic issues than distant external wars. Somehow or another the imperative of tolerance has to be made more explicit in military training in African countries. Tolerance is needed even more in an army which deals with its own people than in an army sent to fight other soldiers in foreign lands. The promotion of sporting activities between soldiers and civilians is one partial answer. It does not always work, but it deserves to be constantly encouraged.

Then there is the experience of exercising political authority itself. If one were looking for the most important advantage to be gained by soldiers participating in ruling a country, it is the advantage of learning to be accountable to the people for their actions. Until 25 January 1971, the soldiers of Uganda had physical power, and sometimes used that power. They used it in 1966, and to some extent in 1969 following the attempted assassination of President Obote; but at that time the army had power *without* accountability. Then came 25 January 1971. The first suspicion I had that the firing we had been hearing meant a coup, rather than the prevention of a coup or suppression of a plot, came when a student arrived at my house from town. Had he risked travelling through Kampala with all that firing? He said: 'Yes. And what's more, the soldiers are very nice to civilians. They are our friends.' I began to suspect that the power which the Uganda Army had had all along was now about to be linked to public accountability. In short, the army was about to assume supreme authority.

In fact, in the first year after the coup, the Uganda Army went further than most other African armies in this field of tolerance. In relations between the soldiers and members of the government they had overthrown, there was for a while an unmistakable element of magnanimity. Some civilians in Uganda victimized other civilians after the coup; some soldiers killed other soldiers. But between soldiers on the one side and civilians on the other there was more cordiality than ever before.

But the plant of tolerance is a delicate one. Not all the promises of magnanimity in the early days of the Second Republic of Uganda were fulfilled. On the contrary, the situation got more brutal from the middle of 1972. Nevertheless, the emergence of soldiers as rulers was a matter of profound educational significance. We shall now attempt to demonstrate this.

The Decline of the Educated Class

Tolerance sometimes springs from humility. How much humility can be taught effectively at school in conditions where the educated are highly prized? Are conditions of educational scarcity sociologically inhospitable to the promotion of humility in a school curriculum?

It is, in fact, true that Africa approached independence with considerable evidence that it was evolving a power elite based on education. Some societies may have evolved an oligarchy based on birth and ascription, as indeed some African traditional societies did. Other societies might have developed oligarchical systems based on wealth differentials, with the rich exercising power because they were rich. What seemed to be happening in Africa was the emergence of a class assuming critical areas of influence and prestige because it had acquired the skills of modern education.

The elite started by being, in part, the bureaucratic elite — as major positions in the civil service were rapidly Africanized, and the criteria for such Africanization included a high premium on modern western education. But the emergence of an educated bureaucratic elite was accompanied by a slightly less educated political elite. The triumph of anti-colonial movements had thrust leaders into the forefront of affairs, but leaders who would not have attained such pre-eminence but for at least some basic exposure to modern schools. Many of the modern successful leaders, and certainly a high proportion of the politicians, were drawn from the schools where they had previously served as teachers. In East Africa, the most prominent of these pioneers contributed to politics by the schools is President Julius Nyerere of Tanzania. Indeed, the President still carries the name *'Mwalimu'*, signifying teacher or mentor.

In a country such as Uganda, the necessity of educational credentials for national politics was partly derived from the issue of language. Where political power was acquired through communication and interaction with a wide variety of groups, a lingua franca was necessary. And the lingua franca which attained the status of a national language in Uganda gradually became the English language.

A person could become a party official in the local constituency without a command of English, but not a member of parliament. Moreover, the English language in Uganda was not normally acquired in the streets and markets but, in the majority of cases, through exposure to formal education.

It is true that one could reach the heights of political power without a high level of education. But there was no escaping the minimum command of the metropolitan language, and a certain flair for appearing to be educated. In brief, those African countries which did not have an indigenous language widely understood across different ethnic communities were indeed developing a system based on the primacy of the educated class.

It was in this kind of situation that Milton Obote, as President of Uganda, began to lament the inequalities which were evolving in the country, and aspired to raise the mystique of the common man. He was all too aware of the functions of the English language in some areas of national life. But he was also aware of its propensity for conferring certain privileges on those who had acquired an adequate command of it. Obote noted that in the colonial period English was the language of the central administration in Uganda. Many Ugandans learnt the English language in order to serve in the administration. That was in the days of imperial supremacy.

> It would appear that we are doing exactly the same; our policy to teach more English could in the long run just develop more power in the hands of those who speak English, and better economic status for those who know English. We say this because we do not see any possibility of our being able to get English known by half the population of Uganda within the next fifteen years. English, therefore, remains the national language in Uganda when at the same time it is a language that the minority of our people can use for political purposes to improve their own political positions. Some of our people can use it in order to improve their economic status.[6]

But there was one section of the population in Uganda, inter-ethnic in composition, which was not using English as the primary qualification for professional ascent. This section was the armed forces of Uganda. It was in the armed forces that Swahili played virtually its only official role in independent Uganda. The commanding heights of the military profession, unlike any other major profession in Uganda, did not require any special fluency in the English language. Skills of weaponry, courage and efficient military behaviour, loyalty and discipline, counted for more than a command of the metropolitan language. And so the man who came to command the armed forces of Uganda rose to the rank of Major-General, and to the title of Commander of the Armed Forces, with little formal academic education behind him and limited eloquence in the English language. If Obote was looking for a model of social mobility which did not require a command of the metropolitan language, he had it right there in the barracks of his armed forces in Uganda.

Yet, for a while, the implications of this situation escaped the attention of President Obote, in spite of his commitment to the mystique of the common man. Obote was aware that education and western culture continued to widen the gaps between certain sections of Uganda's population. In his *Common Man's Charter* Obote elaborated upon Benjamin Disraeli's concept of the 'two nations'. Disraeli had been concerned about the trend towards polarization in British society, as the nation continued to be divided into two essentially antagonistic 'nations within the nation' — the poor versus the rich. Obote's *Common Man's Charter* took the Disraeli analysis a stage further and related it to the local Ugandan situation. The worry in Uganda was not simply that of a division between the rich and the poor, but also a cultural division between those who had been exposed to western culture and those who had retained traditional ways. Both forms of fragmentation needed to be arrested while the going was good.

> We cannot afford to build two nations within the territorial boundaries of Uganda: one rich, educated, African in appearance but mentally foreign, and the other, which constitutes the majority of the population, poor and illiterate. . . . We are convinced that from this standpoint of our history, not only our educational system inherited from pre-Independence days, but also the attitudes to modern commerce and industry and the position of a person in authority, in or outside Government, are creating a gap between the well-to-do on the one hand and the mass of the people on the other. As the years go by, this gap will become wider and wider. The Move to the Left Strategy of this Charter aims at bridging the gap and arresting this development. [7]

In some societies some families were rich to begin with, and through their wealth they became politically powerful, and through their power as well as their wealth they were able to provide their children with the best education available. But in Africa the trend of causation was reversed. It was through education, at least at certain levels, that some figures managed to enter parliament and organize political parties; it was as a result of capturing political power that they, in turn, proceeded to make themselves rich. In this case, wealth came at the tail end of the career afforded by political power; instead of political power emerging out of the support of wealth.

John F. Kennedy succeeded in being elected partly because he had wealth in his family behind him. A poverty-stricken Irish Catholic family would not have stood a chance of rising to that presidential pre-eminence, regardless of the Harvard education which John F. Kennedy had had. Milton Obote, on the other hand, or Kwame Nkrumah before him, started first by having at least a modest exposure to western education before they could succeed in capturing national power. And it was, at best, only after capturing national power that they could consolidate their economic positions. In fact, Obote himself seemed to have done far less in consolidating his economic position than some of his colleagues in the cabinet. But the main point to be grasped here is simply the reversal of the chain of causation. Economic achievement in Africa's first decade of independence is the fruit of political power rather than the seed from which it springs. But Obote himself fell short of controlling his colleagues in their propensity to consume economically. His *Communication from the Chair* in April 1970 did attempt to curb the special privileges of the civil service. But the civil service was even better educated than the majority of the politicians. And the civil servants' morale could not be reassured if they were forced to make sacrifices, while ministers and other politicians continued to reap the rewards of their own political positions.

A song of the common man in Uganda continued to be sung in spite of those paradoxes and ironies. And then, on 25 January 1971, a modestly educated Lugbara voice haltingly read out to the nation eighteen reasons why the army had taken over power. From a linguistic point of view, that voice which came across Radio Uganda was indeed the authentic voice of the comman man — probably coming from a peasant family in West Nile, with limited exposure to westernism and formal education, and retaining his deep roots within the indigenous soil. Not long afterwards a more educated voice, that of Chief Inspector Oryema of Police, announced that power had been taken over by the armed forces, the police had concurred, and the man in charge was going to be Major-General Idi Amin Dada. Again, from a linguistic point of view and in relation to standards of education, General Idi Amin Dada sounded much more like a common man than ever Obote did. And from a cultural point of view, he was more authentically African than the people whom the *Common Man's Charter* dismisses as 'educated African in appearance but mentally foreign'. In a sense which was at once glorious and tragic, Obote's song in honour of the common man had at last come to haunt him — that Lugbara voice on Radio Uganda enumerating the eighteen charges against the prophet of the common man, and then a new president for Uganda emerging from the womb of the countryside far from the capital, equipped with less than full primary education, but self-educated to some extent. The lumpen militariat had staged their revolution.

Was the change for the better? The answer is in the womb of history. All we can say at the moment is that the supremacy of the educated class has been challenged. This is a class which must remain vitally important for Africa's development. But there was a danger of over-inflation, of excessive privilege, even of arrogance. The new sense of humility of the educated class imposed by political and military challenges may be on the brighter side of recent history. In some parts of Africa, including Uganda, the soldier and the technocrat have yet to learn the spirit of mutual esteem. In other cases, even the spirit of toil is missing. What must eventually be developed are the skills of teamwork, hardened by the ethos of exertion, yet softened once again by that remarkable social lubricant called tolerance.

References and Notes

1. Tom Mboya, *Freedom and After*, André Deutsch, 1963, p. 104.
2. See Julius Nyerere, 'Ujamaa: the basis of African socialism', TANU pamphlet, April 1962.
3. Ibid. This part of the chapter overlaps with chapter 17 in Ali A. Mazrui, *A World Federation of Cultures: an African Perspective*, Free Press, New York, 1976.
4. Eric Dunning, 'The concept of development: two illustrative case studies', in Peter I. Rose, ed., *The Study of Society: an Integrated Anthology*, Random House, New York, 1967, pp. 884-5.
5. Ibid., p. 885.
6. Milton Obote, 'Language and national identification', Opening address delivered before a seminar on 'Mass media and linguistic communications in East Africa' held in Kampala from 31 March to 3 April, 1967. The speech was published in *East Africa Journal*, **IV**, 1 (1967).
7. Articles 21 and 22 of Obote's *Common Man's Charter* (1969). This part of the chapter has been borrowed from Ali A. Mazrui, 'The Lumpen Proletariat and the Lumpen Militariat: African soldiers as a new political class', *Political Studies*, **XXI**, 1 (1973), 1-12.

11 Education and Nationalist Aspirations

At a conference in 1966 to discuss with overseas foundations and other potential donors the next stage in the evolution of the University of East Africa, the head of one of the three constituent colleges enunciated the two principles which must guide that next stage of development. The principles were to be *'relevance and excellence, in that order of priority'*. Should there ever be a conflict between those two principles, that particular university head would rather err on the side of relevance. What is relevant even if not excellent is to be preferred to what is excellent but not relevant. But relevant to what? In this chapter we are concerned with relevance to national purpose and national identity.

The whole concept of modern education in Africa sometimes poses acute problems as to whether or not it really *belongs*. And by the yardstick of nationalist reformers, modern education in Africa suffers from two acute failings. It is both too *foreign* and too *rationalist*. It is too foreign partly because it has emerged from foreign educational and academic traditions, and partly because a high proportion of the educational innovators are still foreign. As for the African university itself, it is too rationalist for reasons connected with precisely its western ancestry. The ethos of western university systems puts a special premium on a form of rationality which aspires to neutral universalism. To be 'scholarly' and to be 'scientific' are, in western terminology, sometimes interchangeable. And to be scientific includes a stance of detachment. But scientific detachment could amount to social disengagement. The equation of detachment with disengagement has sometimes led to demands for rethinking about the role of academics in developing countries. Can Africa afford pure academics?

In February 1969 the Mayor of Kampala telephoned me at Makerere to invite me to take part in a debate at the town hall with the Chief General Service Officer of the Uganda Government, Mr Akena Adoko. What on? The Mayor said it was to be on the subject, 'The role of the intellectuals in the African revolution'. This was the first time that a member of the Uganda Government engaged in a public debate in the town hall with a member of the University community. The public interest was unmistakable. The town hall was packed to overflowing, with loudspeakers for those outside sitting on the lawn.

My definition of an 'intellectual' — which I had given in a public lecture at Makerere not long before the debate — came in for strong criticism on grounds of its being too neutral. I had defined an intellectual as 'a person who has the capacity to be fascinated by ideas and has acquired the skill to handle some of those ideas effectively'. Such a definition was regarded both by Mr Akena Adoko, and by participants in the press controversy which followed, as being one which reduced intellectuals to players in a game of ideas and mental gymnastics. There was widespread feeling that the very definition of an African intellectual should include a moral commitment to national endeavour. My own feeling was that intellectuals were indeed often players in a game of ideas. If we want them to be morally committed, we are prescribing rather than defining. The duty of an intellectual is not to be confused with the definition of an intellectual. In the debate with Mr Akena Adoko I never questioned the assertion that intellectuals in Africa *ought* to be committed. The main thrust of my position was that commitment was not to be confused with conformity. African intellectuals in disagreement with their government were not therefore devoid of social commitment.

What the whole episode illustrated was the widespread view in Africa that the detached rationalism of the inherited academic tradition was unsuited to local needs. The two failings of excessive foreignness and excessive rationalism both needed to be tackled as priorities for educational reform.

Towards Africanization of Syllabus and Staff

One of the most explicitly nationalist criteria of relevance is therefore the Africanization of the syllabus in African institutions. There is a great feeling that first, the staff should be Africanized and secondly, the curriculum should be Africanized. There are times when it is assumed that the curriculum and syllabus cannot effectively be localized unless the staff itself is local. Arguments about the impossibility of empathizing with what is indigenous if the person himself is not indigenous are often to be heard. Up to fifty per cent of the teaching staff of a number of African countries, both French-speaking and English-speaking, is still non-African. The biggest single source of teachers is the former colonial power. But there has been a growing internationalization of this foreign part of the teaching staff, with a high contingent from the United States and other staff from Western Europe, Eastern Europe, Canada and elsewhere. There is also a growing African presence drawn from other parts of the continent. The West Africans in, say, East Africa, might sometimes be credited with a capacity to be sensitized to local problems and local perspectives in the learning process. But the other alien teachers are, on nationalist grounds, sometimes regarded as being incapable — through no fault of their own — of comprehending the local realities and of entering into them sympathetically. With this kind of reasoning the Africanization of the syllabus becomes inseparable from the Africanization of staff. It is a reversal of the old arguments of social anthropology — that a person cannot objectively understand his own culture because he is so much a part of it. He needs the shock of exposure to a culture other than his own. The black nationalist reverses the argument and says he can understand it precisely because he is so much a part of it. Yet many members of the local staff in the schools and universities of East Africa are themselves products of foreign university institutions or foreign academic traditions. The expatriate staff who come to Africa are sometimes almost guiltily eager to try to be relevant. They are all too aware that they are foreigners in a relatively unfamiliar situation and are firmly convinced that some kind of adjustment is now needed on their part. This is particularly true of expatriates who have come to Africa after independence. Those whose tenure of service goes back to colonial days are sometimes less responsive to the winds of change in academic philosophies.

In the case of the newly arrived expatriates there is indeed a self-selection process. Many of them come to Africa partly because they are already members of a liberal school which believes both in making allowances for local sensitivities and in assessing relevance partly on grounds of local orientation. The self-selection process therefore gives the educational institutions of Africa a high proportion of liberal expatriates in at least partial sympathy with the need for Africanization as rapidly as possible.

But the local members of staff are not subject to the same self-selection process and are in any case less activated by semi-guilty desires to bow to local nationalist pressures. Many of the local African staff are indeed in their rhetoric, and to some extent in genuine commitment, believers in the idea of promoting relevance by insisting on local orientation. But a high proportion of the local staff are definitely less radical in their conversion to the need for change than many of the expatriates. And those who are radical are sometimes radical only because the expatriates who are highest in positions of policy-making are in many cases 'old-timers', whose tenure of office sometimes goes back to the reactionary colonial days. Because this segment of the expatriate population is often less responsive to the winds of change than they might be, a reaction is provoked among certain members of local staff. And these become more radicalized in their attitudes than they might otherwise conceivably have been.

But the main point to grasp in any case is that the Africanization of the staff is not by itself a guarantee of accelerated Africanization of the syllabus and curriculum. The local staff, precisely by feeling less vulnerable than some expatriates, with no sense of the guilty outsider, can be more bothered about 'standards' and more resistant to precipitate change. In some cases they are more responsible than some of the more enthusiastic expatriates on the scene. Of some of these enthusiasts, especially at the University of Dar es Salaam, I have had occasion to say the following:

> There is indeed a group of radical academics who have had less faith in the concept of a University than President Nyerere himself. Yet I am not convinced that these radicals — products of distinguished Western Universities — would themselves dream of sending their children to be educated in something like the old Kwame Nkrumah Ideological Institute in Ghana or the old Lumumba Ideological Institute in Kenya. I doubt if any of them would send their children to the Patrice Lumumba University in Moscow. They are all for transforming the University of East Africa into an ideological institute. But if the experience of British socialists is anything to go by, the ultimate academic ambition they have for their children is often admission into Oxford or Cambridge. Indeed, many British radicals send their own children to public schools.[1]

In such cases the local staff do have reason to be more circumspect about the longer-term academic viability of a university than some of the more enthusiastic expatriate reformers. The net result is that localization of staff need not necessarily mean more rapid localization of the syllabus than might have been accomplished by expatriates.

Sometimes the issue of foreign influence in the school and universities of Africa comes up against the market cry, 'New foreigners for old' — and the counter-cry, 'Better the foreigner you know than the foreigner you don't know'. The phenomenon of Americanism and anti-Americanism in the universities of East Africa is, for example, not so very new. One serious manifestation occurred in the Faculty of Law on the campus at Dar es Salaam where there was a student outcry against the Americanization of the law syllabus. A new syllabus which had already been passed by the Senate of the University, and which in some ways was more sensitized to local issues than the old one, was nevertheless denounced by the student body as an alien American intrusion into the academic processes at Dar es Salaam. There are occasions when a continuing British tradition is somehow regarded as less alien than a new American tradition. In such cases local nationalism comes to the defence of an old English pattern established during colonial rule as against a new pattern intruding after independence. At Makerere in Uganda discussions about making coursework assessment relevant toward the final evaluation of a student in a particular course, and discussions about having examinations at the end of each year instead of limiting degree examinations to the final year, sometimes hinged on the issue of whether the syllabus was getting Americanized. And student denunciation of new ways was sometimes couched in anti-American rhetoric. The law syllabus in Dar es Salaam prior to the changes which were about to be enacted that year was substantially British in orientation, though with major changes made by a group of devoted teachers when the Faculty of Law was established. But somehow a diversion away from British standards, in favour of what are regarded as American tendencies, was enough to arouse the nationalist sensitivities of some of the students.

There may be an important logical justification for this kind of attitude to British patterns as against American. After all, time is relevant as a factor in reducing foreignness of an imported idea or an imported institution. What is foreign can become less and less foreign if it remains part of the local scene long enough. As for ideas and values, these may become internalized over a period of time even if they originally started as alien. To the extent that many British ideas and British ways in the educational system, and British prejudices in intellectual patterns, have been part of the local scene for so long, they may in part have become internalized. At any rate their relative familiarity to local people would make them less foreign in appearance than a less familiar new importation from American traditions. In some ways the American tradition may indeed be in spirit more attuned to practical issues in their local environment. The concept of a land grant university for example could all too readily become something sensitized to environmental practicalities. Or the idea of a general education instead of a highly specialized one could in some respects be more relevant to a less developed country than the British tradition of honours specialization. Yet the fact that these American approaches are on occasion more practical does not necessarily elevate them to the status of nationalist relevance. They may be further from that status than a more esoteric British approach. And both are in any case forms of intellectual and cultural penetration into Africa.

Another major consideration in the issue of localizing the syllabus is the simple question of political sensitivity. The new syllabus in law at Dar es Salaam in 1969 included a course on military law. One member of staff of the faculty at Dar es Salaam, on being challenged about such a course, defended it in terms of relevance. He said the military in Africa had become increasingly important as a factor of influence in political and social processes. Strictly from the point of view of relevance, a course in military law might therefore be regarded as pre-eminently defensible. But this was an area of relevance which merged into political sensitivity. It was *too* relevant!

In my own discussions with members of the Uganda Government about the place of political science in a developing country, the issue was now and again sharply posed. On 21 October 1968, President Milton Obote gave a speech in Parliament partly reprimanding me for the position I had taken on the question of the editor of *Transition*, Mr Rajat Neogy, and the local Ugandan constitutional lawyer Mr Abu Mayanja. The President had actually sent me a message in advance to turn up in Parliament to listen to the reprimand. But he went beyond the issue of *Transition* when he started discussing the role of the Department of Political Science. He referred to views about the Ugandan Army which were reportedly made in the discussions at Makarere and which the President regarded as doing less than justice to the performance of Uganda's Armed Forces. The President also referred to a thesis of mine which I had put across at Makerere that the erosion of tribalism in Africa could not be separated from class formation, and that new classes with cross-cutting loyalties might have to emerge before ethnic confrontations in African countries become a thing of the past. President Obote asserted: 'For a Professor of Political Science to say that Uganda must create a class society is to do a disservice to African Nationalism'. [2]

Although this kind of dialogue continued to take place between academics and members of the Government in Uganda under Milton Obote, there was for a while no attempt to interfere with the teaching which was taking place at Makerere or with the views that were expressed. Members of the Uganda Government simply asserted their own right to express contrary views to those which might at times be articulated by lecturers at Makerere. But in any case dialogue between academic intellectuals and members of the government in Uganda was, under Obote, at an all time high, and discussions on various issues took place between groups from both sides. But one African head of government was once all too correct when, with a twinkle in his eye he said to me, 'I would like you to remember, Professor, that there is a difference between being a Political Scientist and being a Politician'. On another occasion, again with an amused look, he asked me, 'Do you teach Politics or do you practise Politics?'. The point President Obote was making was that in certain subjects, and political science is pre-eminently one of them, the quest for relevance becomes a quest for practicality, and the quest for practicality might sometimes blur the distinction between practical politics and academic analysis.

And yet is there really an alternative if the syllabus is to be changed towards local orientation? I indicated to the President that I could teach political science in a most neutral way if I concentrated on topics as distant from the local scene as the committee system in the American Congress, or relations between the Civil Service and the British Cabinet, or on methods of political recruitment in the Soviet Union. But the price of Africanizing the syllabus, especially in the humanities, was to sensitize the syllabus. Teaching military law in Dar es Salaam or the interplay between ethnicity and the class structure in Uganda — though all too relevant to the local scene — was also all too sensitive for that very reason. But the price might well have to be paid if the business of a university was a commitment to understanding some of the most profound problems affecting the societies which the university is supposed to serve.

Towards Africanizing World Culture

But the quest for a reduction of foreigners does not lie in restricting ourselves to the study of only African phenomena. The greater challenge is to study a variety of other intellectual riches but from an African perspective.

Should African students be called upon to study Plato or Rousseau or Marx? After all, neither Plato, Rousseau nor Marx could conceivably be regarded as having had any knowledge of key problems of the Africa of their own day, let alone the Africa of today. One answer which continues to be pertinent is that these were thinkers who attempted to make generalizations not about man in their own geographical area, or about social forces in their own time only, but about man and society at the broadest level of generality. Many of their interpretations have stood the test of time, or at any rate provoked directions of thought which have yielded more fruitful conclusions. It cannot be repeated too often that for those who are called upon to teach European political theory to students outside Europe, there may often be a case for playing down the 'Europeanism' of the theories concerned. This is not in order to make the theories more popular, but in order to see *if* they can be made more relevant. The process might involve tearing the theory out of its historical context altogether, and bringing the logic of all or some of its ideas to bear on a specific situation in perhaps one's own time and one's own area in Africa:

> The object of the exercise being to determine whether the ideas scattered within the theory help in the understanding of the situation, on the one hand, and on the other, whether the situation can lend a new depth to the theory or perhaps expose an old shallowness within it. . . . What can be taken for granted is that ideas can express further ideas if they are systematically referred to one situation after another. To change the metaphor, if an idea is fertile, it may well conceive a different kind of child if it is mated to a different kind of situation.[3]

The first-year course in political theory at Makerere for many years was from Thomas Hobbes to Julius K. Nyerere. But throughout the course there was an attempt to test the ideas of each thinker against experience outside the thinker's own geographical or temporal context. More often than not the test was against African realities. Thomas Hobbes's attitude to foreign missionaries, the question of whether tribal loyalties were the equivalent of 'particular wills' in Rousseau's terms, were the sort of issues which provided occasion in

Makerere classrooms for vigorous discussion of European political thinkers in relation to African problems.

Soon after the difficult events of 1966 in Uganda, a lecturer in normative political theory at Makerere was seeking to apply the Lockean idea of a social contract to the events which had torn up Uganda briefly earlier that year. The 1962 Constitution of the country had been the legal expression of the Independence agreement. The class discussed whether the 1962 Constitution resembled a social contract creating a new society, with the parties to the contract surrendering some of their 'natural rights' for the sake of the compact. Among the 'natural' (or pre-existent) rights of the Baganda was deemed to be the right to the soil of Buganda. Yet, on the basis of the national compact of 1962, Buganda had surrendered her pre-existent right to the area of Kampala to the Central Government of Uganda.

When a social contract of this kind was broken, all rights were supposed to be reverting to their original holders. When Obote abrogated the 1962 Constitution of Uganda, he was in effect dissolving the compact on the basis on which the new nation had come into being. If all rights reverted to their original holders, to whom was the City of Kampala now to go? The Lukiiko, or Legislature of Buganda, interpreted the situation in Lockean terms. The Lukiiko proceeded to issue an ultimatum to the Central Government of Uganda demanding that it should leave 'Buganda soil' by the end of May 1966. But Dr Milton Obote was not playing a Lockean game. He responded by declaring this an act of high treason, and proceeded to deal with Buganda accordingly. [4]

At that moment in time there was indeed a risk that a discussion of the issues of 1966 in those terms could have been too sensitive in a class of several dozen Ugandan students. But although the students were evidently and understandably in disagreement with each other over this or that issue within the situation as a whole, there was no doubt that the use of Lockean ideas to understand recent events in their own country opened up whole new intellectual vistas into the world of their own politics.

But why turn to European political thought for these new vistas? Why not consult the heritage of China or of Hinduism instead? Linguistic considerations are relevant but not central to the problem at hand. More fundamental is the West's cultural and intellectual legendry in the twentieth century. Ideally, one would have wished African educational institutions more cognizant of the *diversity* of the human heritage. The importance of European normative theory for African educational institutions lies not only in the fact that, at least in many of its parts, it can be consulted as a tool for the analysis of African problems. It also lies in the fact that the language of politics in Africa and many of its institutions today have been intellectually influenced by European political philosophy. As John Plamenatz has argued, Europeans have been pioneers not only of the natural sciences, but also of the social sciences as well:

> No one, I think, will contest that the Europeans have devoted more time than other peoples to the systematic study of social institutions, past and present. They have long been accustomed to the idea that societies differ greatly from one another and are all in process of continual change. They have also, more than other peoples, been deliberate reformers; they have often tried to change institutions in order to improve them. This reforming zeal has itself been largely an effect of a closer study of society and social change. [5]

Plamenatz goes on to argue persuasively that Europeans have come nearer than other peoples to creating a vocabulary adequate to the description of social institutions and social change. Both the academic and the practical language of modern politics, he asserts, is European. Wherever political and social institutions are systematically discussed or analysed, they are more often than not discussed in terms of concepts invented in Europe, and the actual business of government is 'everywhere' carried on largely in idioms of European origin.

> To understand the modern world, to explain what is happening to it, and to know how to act effectively in it, a man must be able to think and speak about it in European ways, even when he speaks of Asia and Africa. It may be a pity it should be so, but the fact remains. [6]

Plamenatz exaggerates his case. But there is little doubt that the idiom of modern politics in Africa, even when translated into non-European languages, owes a lot to the original European vocabulary which came with imperialism. Terms like sovereignty, parliament, the vote, constitution, class-conflict, inflation, democracy, common market, nationalism, the state, individualism, socialism, and dozens of others have all become central elements of political discourse at the national level almost everywhere.

We may therefore say that the very language of political priorities now in use in the national politics of most African countries owes a lot to European normative political theory. When a university attempts to raise the level of sophistication in the handling of those ideas, that university is crucially participating in the process of refining and deepening the hybrid political culture of the country it serves. Even the constitution itself is basically a piece of normative political theory. The duty of political science to itself may indeed lie in following the mystique of science. But the duty of political science to society may lie in raising the level of evaluation as between priorities and deepening the language of political discourse. This is to follow the mystique of practicality. And for that mystique normative political theory has a critical significance. [7]

The nationalist task consists in indigenizing what is imported and giving it greater congruence with the realities of its environment. But indigenizing the educational institutions of Africa is in some ways more straightforward than derationalizing them. That other problem of the western educational ethos being too rationalist poses greater challenges than its foreignness. In many ways the rationalist western academic traditions are, paradoxically, committed both to individualism and to universalism. Academic freedom is sometimes defended in the liberal terms of individual autonomy and sometimes in neoscientific postulates of universal objectivity. On one side is the individual scholar and on the other the universe of international scholarship. What is often missing is the intermediate category of the particular society within which the scholar operates. The university is therefore either sub-social in its commitment or supra-social — but seldom adequately social. The process of university education is also itself partly a process of individualization and partly a process of universalization. The individualization takes the form of trying to release the mind of the undergraduate from certain pre-university dogmas. The critical faculty is valued and sharpened in the student, so that he can question, criticize and argue back. Dependence on intellectual authorities is frowned upon, and plagiarism is an academic crime.

Even 'originality' as a virtue is very much in the tradition of liberal individualism. PhD candidates are told that their theses must make an original contribution to knowledge. And there can be no collaboration in the writing of the thesis, or consultation with fellow students in the midst of attempting to answer an examination paper. To learn from the fellow student at the next desk in the examination is to *cheat*. Each one for himself in this competitive world. That after all was what rugged individualism was all about.

But in addition to being a process of individuation, modern education is a process of universalization. Certainly in much of Africa so far modern schools have been the most effective instruments of reducing the cultural gap between people from the former colonies and people from the former metropolitan powers. A new graduate from Makerere University in Uganda is far less different from a new graduate of McGill, Princeton or Oxford than a Ugandan peasant is from a poor farmer in Mexico let alone in North America. I have found that addressing a group of undergraduates at Northwestern University or the University of Singapore is an experience not far removed from addressing a group of students at an African university. But if I were a globe-trotting trade unionist I would find a bigger gap between railway workers in Uganda and railway workers in England than I have found between students in these different countries. That is why I have had occasion to say in another context that it is the intellectuals, rather then the proletariat, that are the most international of all classes.[8] (See Chapter 18.)

In African conditions there is a price to be paid in the cultural field by this role of modern schools as instruments of intellectual homogenization. The ethos of western educational traditions includes a commitment to a form of rationality which seeks to reduce ethnocentrism as a foundation of thought. As we indicated, higher education often put a premium on the virtue of detachment. In Africa detachment becomes suspected of being disengagement.

But the call for derationalization is, from a nationalist point of view, a call for a cultural revival. A wave of modern research interest in African oral tradition and oral history is one step away from the rigid rationalism which had equated historical knowledge with written documentation bearing specific dates. A wave of interest in African oral literature — the enthusiasm for folk tales and romantic superstitions — is also one concession to the demands for derationalization in academic attitudes. And yet the process is still less than fully honest. No village expert on oral tradition is ever appointed to a university lectureship. He does not have a degree from a western university or comparable institution. Okot p'Bitek, former director of the Uganda National Theatre and author of the neo-negritudist poem *Song of Lawino*, has been a leading spokesman in favour of university reform which would make it possible to use local artists more effectively. In a hard-hitting lecture at Makerere he once said: 'You may be the greatest (traditional) oral historian but they will never allow you anywhere near *their* university. . . . I believe that most of our social ills are indigenous, and the primary sources of our problems are native'.[9] Okot also complained that at Makerere there was no department of music, and that if there were Uganda's most gifted drummer would not get a job on the academic staff as instructor or lecturer. The concessions to African culture are still tied to the prejudices of western-derived academic rationalism.

Negritude and Negrology

But in Africa south of the Sahara, as in black America, the theme of *blackness* has to be recognized in its own right as a variable when we discuss nationalist aspects of education.

Sterling Stuckey has asserted persuasively that W. E. B. Du Bois was 'easily the most sophisticated proponent of Negritude until the advent of Césaire and Senghor'. Stuckey has also recommended that there should be a study of Du Bois' cultural views which should, inter alia, seek to determine how the Du Bois variant of negritude differed from that projected by the Harlem Renaissance writers.[10] Du Bois, that towering black American intellectual giant, has in addition to be seen as one of the founding fathers of pan-Africanism.

It is right that the new wave of Black Studies in the United States should explore its links with the negritude movement, for those two waves of intellectualized black assertiveness have a good deal in common. President Léopold Senghor of Senegal, the chief articulator of negritude in Africa, has argued that there is a fundamental difference betweent the white man's tools of intellectual analysis on the one hand and the black man's approach to intellectual perception on the other. As indicated earlier, Senghor has said: 'European reasoning is analytical, discursive by utilization; Negro-African reasoning is intuitive by participation'.[11]

Senghor, partly because of the complexity of his ideological position on culture, is not always consistent in his views on comparative epistemology as between European and Negro-African modes of thought. But it is arguable that the logical conclusion of Senghor's position is that no European or white scholar can hope to understand fully the inner meaning of a black man's behaviour. This is the meeting point between *negritude* as the cultural essence of black civilization and *negrology* as the principles by which the black man was to be *studied*. For both Léopold Senghor and the militant wing of the Black Studies movement in the United States there are indeed certain socio-scientific principles of interpretation without which the black man cannot be adequately understood. The question is whether these principles can be mastered by a scholar who is not himself black. In his address to the Second International Congress of Africanists in Dakar in December 1967, President Senghor intimated that such principles of scholarly interpretation could be mastered by others if those scholars are sufficiently sensitized to the peculiar characteristics of the culture they are studying. But some of the advocates of Black Studies in the United States are more sceptical. For them only black scholars can fully command the principles of negrology.[12]

But if negrology is the science of studying the black man, should it now be sufficiently neutral to be accessible to diverse minds? Senghor would say that such a definition of science is itself ethnocentric. He first quotes Jacques Monod, a Nobel Prize winner, who in his inaugural lecture at the Collège de France in 1967 asserted:

> The only aim, the supreme value, the 'sovereign good' in the ethics of Knowledge is not, let us confess, the happiness of mankind, less so its temporal power, or its comfort, nor even the 'Know thyself' of Socrates; it is the objective Knowledge of itself.

Senghor, after quoting this passage, says he disagrees with it fundamentally. With all due respect to those who hold this 'ultra-rationalist' position, knowledge for its own sake is 'alienated work'. For Senghor, as a child of African civilization, both art and science had a purpose—to serve man in his need for both creativity and love.[13]

Black Studies in the United States are of course also conceptualized in terms of purpose and social function. But what about African studies in the United States? Should Americans study Africa for its own sake? Or should they study it in order to deepen the foundation of relations between Africa and the United States? Or should they study Africa in order to improve relations between whites and blacks within the United States? The second and third motives need not be mutually exclusive, but it may be necessary to decide on priorities and emphases.

There is a danger that if Africa is studied primarily in order to improve relations between whites and blacks within the United States, Africa itself might not be even remotely understood by either the blacks or whites in America. There may be a temptation to concentrate on only those aspects of African studies which are relevant to the domestic scene in America. African history might overshadow all other aspects of African studies. And with all due respect to Dr Stuckey, and to the importance of history, contemporary Africa cannot be understood simply by reference to its history. A proponderance of historians in African studies in the United States today would tend to distort American understanding of Africa as effectively as a proponderance of social anthropologists in African studies in Britain once distorted British understanding of the forces at work in Africa.

Studying Africa for the sake of black-white relations in America may also exaggerate the importance of white-black relations within Africa. Southern Africa might engage a disproportionate share of attention of Americans studying Africa. White-black relations within Africa do indeed remain vitally important. But problems of black ethnicity north of the Zambezi, of the growth of new institutions in new African states, of economic development and changing cultural norms, are at least as deserving of scholarly attention. To study Africa primarily as a branch of American negrology may distort American understanding of Africa for generations to come.

If, as Senghor asserts, all science must be purposeful, American academics should be sure which purposes should be served by which branches of science. Black Studies should indeed be undertaken primarily to add rationality to relations between blacks and whites in the United States — and should therefore be accessible to both white and black students. But African studies in the United States should be undertaken primarily to add rationality to American understanding of Africa. The relevance of African studies for the domestic American scene should be indirect. By helping all Americans to understand Africa better, African studies should by extension also help white and black Americans to understand each other better.

The assumptions of negritude and the principles of negrology might be correct in assuming that complete understanding between groups so deeply divided by history is impossible. But the world of scholarship cannot afford to accept Alexander Pope's poetic assertion:

A little learning is a dangerous thing;
  Drink deep, or taste not the Pierian spring:
There shallow draughts intoxicate the brain,
  And drinking largely sobers us again.[14]

Even a partial understanding of the black man in both Africa and the New World must be, from the point of view of white education, preferable to the ignorant intolerance of yesteryears. A little learning may be a dangerous thing, but a lot of prejudice might be worse.

For Okot p'Bitek the ultimate test of the educational revolution is the re-acceptance of the African dance of passion into the fold of legitimate aesthetics. When he was director of the National Cultural Centre of Uganda, and responsible for the dance troupe 'Heartbeat of Africa', p'Bitek often complained about the long-term effects of the policies of colonial and missionary authorities in discouraging certain kinds of African dances as 'sinful'. This distrust of traditional dancing manifests itself to the present day in some missionary-run schools in East Africa. It is not clear what educational leaders in East Africa can do to reverse the effects of these early educational taboos, but at least one cultural reformer in East Africa sees the issue as symbolic of the whole problem of externally imposed taboos and the agony of cultural deprivation.

On this question Okot p'Bitek and James Baldwin might see eye to eye. They both artistically assume that the body has a special meaning in much of Negro modes of self-identification. James Baldwin tells us about how he stopped hating Shakespeare. At first Shakespeare had stood for him as a symbol of the oppression which had imposed on Baldwin an alien language as a mode of mental experience. But then, particularly as he was reflecting on these issues in France away from the hub of English-speaking activity, Baldwin re-evaluated Shakespeare. He was particularly drawn towards the bard by his unique bawdiness. Baldwin regards Shakespeare as the last bawdy writer in the English language, and he found this a bond between him and Shakespeare precisely because he associated bawdiness with Shakespeare's unabashed preoccupation with things of the flesh. Baldwin had seen this kind of bawdiness before – in things like jazz and its suggestions of sensuality. He felt that most Americans had lost contact with some of these areas of sensibility. Baldwin was here grappling with the old problem of art, its medium, and its relationship to the realities of physical experience. Baldwin was convinced that the English language as an artistic medium could be made to bear 'the burden of any experience', no matter how removed from the areas of propriety of contemporary Anglo-Saxon society:

> In support of this possibility, I had two mighty witnesses, my Black ancestors who evolved the sorrow songs, the blues and jazz and created an entirely new idiom in an overwhelmingly hostile place; and Shakespeare who was the last bawdy writer in the English

language. . . . Shakespeare's bawdiness became very important to me since bawdiness was one of the elements of jazz and revealed a tremendous loving, and realistic respect for the body, and that ineffable force which the body contains, which Americans have mostly lost, which I had experienced only among Negroes, and of which I had been taught to be ashamed.[15]

Conclusion

The crisis of relevance in the modern world now, especially in the arts, is partly a quest to re-establish contact between aesthetics and sensuality. The most dramatic example is in fact in modern drama — the search for sexual candour on the stage. Other branches of literature seem to be also seeking a point of fusion between aesthetic appreciation and sensual responsiveness. This quest partly manifests itself in the themes which are treated and the erosion of taboos about subjecting sex to artistic treatment. But there is also experimentation in sensual styles as well as sensual themes.

We have noted that there was a time in Africa's recent experience when the authority of the Christian missionaries was used to cast a cloud of disapproval on certain kinds of African dancing. And yet the dances were often major examples of fused aesthetic sensuality. The bawdiness which James Baldwin observed in Shakespeare's plays, in jazz, and in the universal attitudes of the average American Black, was all there in depth in some of those African dances.

The crisis of relevance in the western world has now abolished the Lord Chamberlain in England, an institution which had served for many generations the purpose of censuring the English stage. In 1968 London could at last see, without the red pencil of the Lord Chamberlain, displays of the human body in all its nakedness in such presentations as the American play *Hair*. And African dancers themselves, from countries like Guinea and Uganda, found acclaim for their sensual movements in previously stuffy theatres of the western world. Occasionally the women dancers from Africa were mistakenly called upon to cover their breasts, but on the whole the acceptance of bodily movements previously regarded as immodest in stage performances has been one of the great revolutions in assessing the place of the body in the arts.

On the use of the body in performed art, Bob Leshoai, a South African literary figure, talks about the potential of folktales as material for African drama.

Great portions of the story can be told simply in mime action and music and dance. The body, in African dancing, is capable of being used to express and convey ideas that would be quite difficult to express adequately in speech. For example, swaying of the hips, movement of the shoulders, the tempo of the stamping feet and the twitching of the nostrils can say so much to an infatuated suitor as to leave no doubt in his mind about the girl's attitude to him. This is a combination of movements which speak more fluently, adequately and unequivocally than the spoken word. Body movement in African dances is as important as hand movement in the Indian dance.[16]

Here again the gap between aesthetics and sensuality, art and the body, is narrowed. And the crisis of relevance in the world of culture is mitigated as a result.

In East Africa Okot p'Bitek is almost the only one who has carried the revivalist cultural imperative to its ultimate conclusion as a platform of reform. But others also are groping for answers, for a reconciliation between old cultural ways and new educational prejudices. Much of this debate in Africa is still basically either between governments and teachers, or between teachers themselves, or between academics and external advocates of reform. The students are only just beginning to enter the main stream of reappraisal. The range of issues of nationalist relevance is from Africanization of staff to the promotion of African oral literature. But underlying it all is that uneasy feeling that the beast in our midst is foreign in origin and too rational in its supra-social tendencies. Much of the crisis of relevance derives its fervour from just that feeling.

References and Notes

1. See my article 'Tanzaphilia' in *Transition* (Kampala), 6, 31 (1967). Reprinted in Ali A. Mazrui, *Violence and Thought*, Longman, 1969.
2. See *Uganda Argus*, 22 October 1968.
3. See Ali A. Mazrui, *On Heroes and Uhuru-Worship*, Longmans, 1967, p. 3.
4. These issues are discussed also in Ali A. Mazrui, 'Political theory and national involvement in East Africa', *Cahiers d'Etudes Africaines*, IX, 36 (1969).
5. John Plamenatz, *On Alien Rule and Self-Government*, Longmans, 1960, p. 38.
6. Ibid.
7. This material is again borrowed from Mazrui, 'Political theory and national involvement in East Africa', op. cit.
8. Ali A. Mazrui, 'Are intellectuals an international class?', public lecture delivered at Makerere University College, 30 January 1970. Mimeo.
9. Okot p'Bitek, 'Indigenous ills', *Transition*, 32 (August/September 1967), 47.
10. Sterling Stuckey, 'The neglected realm of African and Afro-American relationships: research possibilities for historians', *Africa Today*, 16, 2 (1969), 4.
11. Léopold Senghor, *On African Socialism*, Pall Mall, 1964, p. 74.
12. For an English translation of Léopold Senghor's Address to the Second International Congress of Africanists, see Senghor, 'The study of African man', *Mawazo* (Kampala), 1, 4 (1968), 3-7.
13. Ibid., 7.
14. Alexander Pope, *Essay on Criticism* (1711).
15. James Baldwin, 'Why I stopped hating Shakespeare', *Insight*, British High Commission, Ibadan, 1964, pp. 14-15.
16. Bob Leshoai, 'Theatre and the common man in Africa', *Transition* (Kampala), 19 (1965), 44.

12 Education and Developmental Goals

In the last chapter we discussed nationalist criteria of relevance in relation to African universities. This chapter addresses itself to some developmental criteria of relevance. And in many parts of Africa these criteria are often linked to socialist predispositions.

As a generalization we may say that the practical involvement demanded by nationalism in Africa is a form of *cultural engagement*; whereas the involvement decreed by the needs of radical economic development is a *social commitment*. Cultural engagement seeks the preservation of national distinctiveness, the consolidation of national identity and the forging of appropriate cultural norms. Radical social commitment on the other hand is more activated by poverty than inspired by patriotism. Its definition of relevance includes at the centre a concern for mitigating indigence and reducing economic disparities between groups. The slogan of 'nation-building' in Africa often tends to be tied to cultural engagement — an involvement in the task of reducing tribal cleavages while trying to create a common national heritage. 'Nation-Building' is basically a socio-political slogan. The slogan of 'self-reliance' in places like Tanzania, on the other hand, is a socio-economic slogan which demands involvement in a kind of 'operation bootstrap' to effect economic transformation through self-exertion, without creating economic cleavages in the process.

Nevertheless, it should be remembered that in the African context cultural engagement and social commitment are particularly difficult to separate. The very term 'African socialism' is a fusion of cultural pride and socialist preference. Why use the word 'African' if not to assert a patriotic distinctiveness? Why embrace the slogan of 'socialism' unless you accept its moral respectability? President Julius Nyerere of Tanzania has been known to assert: 'We have no more need of being "converted" to socialism than we have of being "taught" democracy. Both are rooted in our past, in the traditional society which produced us'.[1] This assertion itself is again a fusion of cultural pride and a partiality for social democracy. But while conceding the difficulty of separating social commitment from cultural engagement in the African context, the emphasis in this chapter will be on those

218

aspects of the crisis of relevance in Africa which have a bearing on socialist priorities.

Contemplation versus Commitment

Perhaps the first thing to recall here is Karl Marx's famous saying, 'Philosophers so far have only interpreted the world; the point however is to change it'. The radical movement for university reform has paraphrased Marx by substituting one single word. '*Scholars* so far have only interpreted the world; the point however is to change it.'

We are back here to the demand for a derationalization of scholarship in the sense of reducing its infatuation with the principle of being value-free. Marx himself when he made the above statement was speaking as Marx the revolutionary rather than Marx the scientist. To abandon the principle of detached interpretation for a principle of social commitment is to abandon the scientific principle for the sake of an alternative imperative. Social science was being called upon to be more social and less scientific.

This kind of attitude is not alien to African traditional ways, and provides a meeting ground once again between cultural engagement and social commitment. Much of African traditional life contained both elements. The concept of participation as a basis of tribal membership entailed a firm socio-cultural involvement.

President Senghor's concept of *participation* sometimes also sounds like an alternative to scientific rationalism. Descartes had asserted that the ultimate proof that I exist is that *I think* — in his own famous words, 'I think, therefore I am'. But, as we have noted, African epistemology according to Senghor starts from a different basic postulate. For the African Negro the world exists by the fact of its reflection upon his emotive self — '*I feel*, therefore I am'.

But the idea of emotional involvement, as against the worship of thought, is at the heart of the African challenge to the principles of the western intellectual tradition.[3] Quiet, detached meditation is a respectable exercise in the western scheme of values. Yet meditation can all too easily be, as it sometimes is in Hindu tradition, a form of withdrawal from the real world around you. When an individual withdraws into the privacy of his own thoughts, he may indeed have committed the sin of social disengagement.

In 1967 I had occasion to serve as University Orator at Makerere at the graduation ceremony which awarded a Doctor of Laws to Douglas Griffith Tomblings, a former Principal of Makerere. President Milton Obote presided as Visitor of the College. In the course of my paying official tribute to Tomblings, I referred to what is perhaps the most political of all Shakespeare's plays, and drew attention to the scene in which one character says of another: 'He thinks too much, such men are dangerous'. I said then and still believe that in its bare simplicity, this is a beautiful indictment of excessive thought. This worry about excessive thought goes beyond the mere fear of ideological subversion ostensibly flourishing under the umbrella of intellectual free-play. It can be an attack on the ivory tower approach to learning that we discussed in another context earlier—the approach which, in its extreme, might tend to divorce too sharply the process of thinking from the total process of living. The most persistent moral imperative demanded by reformers is one which would seek to establish for the university a tradition of responsiveness to the practical needs of the moment. There is a deeply felt compulsion to try to avert the risk of having university life reduced to an orgy of thought. It becomes the duty of an African university to try to narrow the chances of producing the type of graduate of whom it could infallibly be said, 'He thinks too much, such men are dangerous'. There is the feeling that students who do not get involved in life outside the university campus will become inadequately sensitive and responsive to the real problems of their country. There is a genuine fear here that attachment to pure intellectual pursuits and to the aesthetics of high culture could fundamentally and perhaps permanently distort an undergraduate's scale of priorities. The right to enjoy a good play, or a good intellectual discussion, becomes elevated above the duty to serve the cause of alleviating national misery.

A related socialist fear which provides a sense of vindication for those who uphold the philosophy of practical involvement is the fear of consolidating an unhealthy class structure in society. There is a feeling that if undergraduates remain secluded from life beyond the campus for three or five years, their divorce from the masses of the people in mental attitudes, as well as in emotional commitment, will become sharper than ever. The students will get more and more out of touch with the masses even if they do go home to the villages for brief periods in the vacation to see their parents. Increasingly, even brief periods in the villages become curtailed as opportunities for vacation work for undergraduates expand with the economy in some cases. An experimental Ford Foundation Scheme to provide vacation employment for African undergraduates, the increasing funds for student research assistants which some departments in African universities now command, the expansion of some opportunities in the private sector of some African economies for short-term helpers with partial university education—all these can so easily aggravate the growing distance between an undergraduate and the village family from which he springs. Even the attempt to make certain courses in the university more practically oriented could have side-effects which reduce contacts with one's home town in a private capacity. For example, a course in public administration at Makerere University once included a period of internship by undergraduates in the public service or comparable administrative experience. Such an internship served a good purpose if it helped to prepare undergraduates to understand administrative problems more immediately and sensitively at a formative period in their intellectual maturation. But the internship did mean living the life of a quasi-administrator during the long vacation, instead of living the life of a member of a village family back home until school opened again. In other words, there are occasions when ideals are in conflict. The task of making students more productive in the vacations, or of making university courses more related to practical professions, might sometimes be achieved only at the cost of widening a little more the more intimate aspects of a student's connexions with the humble family from which he springs.

Yet even serving as a quasi-administrator is a step nearer the masses than writing poetry undisturbed on a university campus. Here again, then, the old philosophy of academic detachment becomes exposed to the charge of widening the social distances between groups of people. Academic detachment as a philosophy of university life might succeed too dramatically in producing 'pure' intellectuals. This, it is assumed by many, would be undesirable in Africa. 'Pure' intellectuals become a class apart. They become identifiable as specialists in the arts of the mind who are reluctant to venture into the skills of the hand. The socialist fear of the distinction between those who work with their minds and those who work with their hands must inevitably result in a profound suspicion of an educational system which values too highly the gifts of the intellect.

African academic reformers are also worried about the rewards which await those who are bright enough to get to university. Lenin once accused 'bourgeois professors' of constantly reproaching the socialists with forgetting the inequality of people and with dreaming about abolishing inequality from the world. Lenin denied that socialists had any such dreams. He said:

Marx not only scrupulously takes into account the inevitable inequality of men; he also takes into account the fact that the mere conversion of the means of production into the common property of the whole society (generally called 'socialism') *does not remove* the effects of distribution and the inequality of 'bourgeois right.'[4]

It is as if both Marx and Lenin agreed that inequality was a self-evident law of nature. This was the inequality of ability and capacity. People were simply not alike—one was strong, another weak; one quick, another slow; one intellectually strong, another, much less so. From this, Marx drew the conclusions that:

With an equal output and hence an equal share in the social consumption fund, one will in fact receive more than another, one will be richer than another and so on. To avoid all these defects, rights, instead of being equal, would have to be unequal.[5]

But what could be fairer than to distribute benefits on the basis of merit?

The answer is that this is an inadequate and imperfect form of justice. To reward natural ability is, at the same time, to penalize natural inability. If you give an extra cake to your bright child, you may be rewarding brightness. But you are at the same time discriminating against your less intelligent children. Privilege and merit are not opposites—a reward based on intellectual merit is one form of privilege. Or so the egalitarian argument would assert. In university life, this must therefore mean that graduates should not enjoy too many advantages arising from the simple accident that they had the mental capacity to do well at school and move to university, or even the sheer good luck to find a place in school when a number of others who might have been brighter have had to do without.

Elites: Labour versus Leisure

It may be true that there is a law of oligarchy in all human organization of any substantial size. Elite formation becomes therefore inevitable. But the issue which still remains to be meaningfully discussed in a given society is what kind of elite the society is going to produce.

Elites can be differentiated by different criteria. But one fundamental distinction which might be made is between an *elite of leisure* and an *elite of labour*. An elite of leisure is usually one which minimizes social commitment and exertion, and is placed in a situation in which it can pursue a life of comfort without worrying about social disapproval. An elite of labour, on the other hand, is one which finds it necessary to justify its elite status by providing effective leadership and by setting an example of hard work through its own behaviour and performance.

A major complaint against the educational system which black Africa has inherited is that it tends to promote an elite of leisure rather than of labour. The syllabus is often geared toward pursuits of a leisurely class, and the attitude at the end tends to promote expectations of white-collar work and minimal office hours. Stanislav Andreski, in his book *The African Predicament*, re-opens in an exaggerated way the old problem about education in Africa—observing once again that education in Africa is 'valued primarily as a means to getting a paper which opens the road to social ascent'. [6]

Among African countries, Tanzania is the one which has perhaps gone furthest in re-examining the fundamental assumptions of education and their implications for social structure and social stratification. Implicit in much of Tanzania's thinking is the simple assumption that an elite of leisure is, almost by definition, basically parasitic. It lives on others. The ideology of Tanzania has therefore included a strong ethos of anti-parasitism. Hard work is what can save a citizen from becoming a *kupe* — a Swahili word which means tick or parasite. Anti-parasitism in Tanzania is older than the Arusha Declaration. It goes back to the slogan of '*Uhuru na Kazi*', or 'freedom and work', which accompanied the country into independence. The slogan was translated into the self-help schemes of 1963 to 1964, and into the regulations about maximum utilization of land in the country as a criterion for possession of land on lease from the state. And finally in October 1966, the ethos of hard work in Tanzania culminated in the start of national service, compulsory for sixth-form and university graduates and for products of comparable educational institutions. National service was to consist, in part, in nation-building forms of toil such as digging and construction. A person was to spend two years in service before starting a regular career.

By the time the national service was launched, Tanzania's ethos of anti-parasitism was assuming certain features of anti-intellectualism. There seemed to be a growing feeling among policy-makers that African intellectuals were becoming basically an elite of leisure, and could therefore be regarded as basically parasitic. They were indeed *kupe*. And one way of changing the situation was to initiate those intellectuals into the rigours of manual labour.

The curious thing is that the ultimate leader in the campaign against the special privileges of intellectuals in Tanzania is himself an intellectual — that is, President Nyerere himself. In this respect Nyerere is reminiscent of Franklin D. Roosevelt. Roosevelt was a millionaire. Yet his New Deal policies were the nearest point to socialism that the United States had ever reached at that time. In a sense, Roosevelt was starting a new movement to squeeze the rich in the interests of the poor. And since he himself was from a rich family, Roosevelt was called a 'traitor to his class'. The Report of the Tanzanian Presidential Commission on the establishment of a democratic one-party state in 1965 referred to Roosevelt's difficulties with the Supreme Court of the United States on the constitutionality of his radical measures to deal with the economic depression. But from the point of view of our concerns today, the real point of similarity between Roosevelt and Nyerere hinges on their attitude to their own respective sectors of society. Just as Roosevelt had attempted to squeeze the rich for the sake of the poor, Nyerere might be regarded as having been trying to squeeze the intellectuals for the sake of the masses. To that extent Julius Nyerere, like Franklin D. Roosevelt, might indeed be regarded as 'a traitor to his class'. But these might well be forms of 'treason' which are creditable to the 'traitors'. They represent a wider loyalty of heroic social dimensions. And perhaps Nyerere's 'treason' to his own class might in historical retrospect be as vindicated as that of Roosevelt.[7]

But why should African intellectuals have acquired tendencies which incline them toward becoming an elite of leisure instead of an elite of labour? One great difficulty is the high prestige which education enjoys in the African continent. The educated as such need not form an elite, even if all societies inevitably do develop an elite. There have been societies where the elite has derived its credentials from birth rather than education, or where the elite is basically a hereditary aristocracy, but some members of this hereditary elite may be well educated and others not so well educated. There have even been societies where the educated have been basically servants of another elite rather than the elite themselves. Philosophers, poets, playwrights, have enjoyed the patronage of royal or aristocratic houses. To some extent technical assistance experts today, or that whole breed of technocrats, sometimes serve in an advisory capacity to the political elites of Africa. In that case science becomes a servant to an elite rather than the basis on which their elite status rests. But on the whole within Africa, education has very often been a distinct foundation of elite status in its own right. One of the great problems of Africa is that people are too often infatuated with education. And the educated acquire a prestige quite beyond that to which they should be entitled. To some extent it is inevitable in societies which are on the whole pre-literate, that those who acquire literacy of any significant degree should thereby have acquired a mark of distinction. But even by the standards of pre-literate societies, Africa's infatuation with modern education is perhaps above average. There is tremendous interest in it, and this in a large measure accounts for the fact that leadership in contemporary Africa has been so disproportionately taken over by those who have acquired education. Of course it is no longer true that the best educated are necessarily the most influential or the most powerful. But they still possess a disproportionate number of the most prestigious positions in societies.

In the old Gold Coast, the word 'scholar' came into being in the middle of the nineteenth century to designate a special type of African. In his book on the political history of Ghana, David Kimble tells us that 'the term "scholar" . . . aroused so much awe among illiterates'. Even a limited knowledge of the English language enabled a person to acquire, at least in the villages, the reputation of being quite knowledgeable about 'modern affairs'. David Kimble draws our attention to the testimony of a missionary in the Gold Coast who, in Kimble's words, 'saw the educated African for what he was worth in his own humble environment'. The missionary was D. Kemp, and he tells us about his experiences and observations in the course of his nine years at the Gold Coast:

> At Abassa I had the pleasure of meeting a catechist. . . . My good friend was 'passing rich' on £20 a year. I suppose he was the only 'scholar' in that town, but he wielded a mighty influence upon all with whom he came into contact. He was the friend and counsellor

of kings and chiefs, and was held in the highest esteem among all men in the villages for many miles around. To such as he, representatives of all ranks of society came to have their domestic, social, and political grievances adjusted.[8]

This phenomenon which the Gold Coast experienced quite early, the rest of black Africa observed not long after. Africa's infatuation with modern education was one of the factors which decided leadership in the nationalist movement during the colonial period, and is now one of the factors which continue to decide social stratification in African countries and resource allocation by governments. The infatuation with education is an important contributory factor to the excessive prestige enjoyed by those who have acquired it. Educational ostentation in Africa, the display of learning and the wrong use or overuse of long words, sometimes have a lot to do with the symbols of status. And this in turn has tended to promote the idea of the educated as an elite of leisure.

National Service and Developmental Socialization

But what changes can be made to the educational system to reduce this tendency? The problem is a difficult one, particularly in view of the high value placed on education by the African masses. One answer would be a kind of academic deflation — a reduction of the high prestige of education in Africa. Yet Africa's hunger for education is something which could be profoundly valuable, and there is a risk involved should we want to reduce this African obsession with education. A more positive strategy is that of developmental socialization — a form of education and upbringing which produces attitudes relevant to national development. One such approach is a national service and other forms of introducing those who are being educated to manual labour and general toil The hope here is that if you introduce those in schools to the rigours of toil you might prevent them from graduating as an elite of leisure and help them emerge instead as an elite of labour. Nigeria and Tanzania are among the countries experimenting with this national service solution.

But as we have mentioned before, there is already a lot of hard work involved in acquiring an education in Africa. There may indeed be too much leisure enjoyed by the educated in Africa after they have been educated, but there is often far too much labour involved on the way toward the status. The problem for the social psychologist is whether there is a connexion between going to school as a test of endurance in Africa and leisurely attitudes at the end of it all. If that is the case then introducing schoolchildren to manual labour as part of the educational process seems singularly irrelevant. The task is to make the acquisition of education less of a struggle, so that the real hard work begins when they go out into the brutal world of adulthood. At the moment the brutal world is that of childhood, while adulthood promises the luxury of restful fulfilment. This anomaly makes developmental socialization difficult to accomplish.

For many Africans, fulfilment might begin on arrival at the university campus. But even at the university, acquiring a degree can often be a lot of hard work. African students are sometimes accused of being excessively preoccupied with preparing for examinations. Such a preparation is a continuation of the pre-university struggle for educational fulfilment. The presumptive elite in Africa is a presumptive elite of labour, while the elite itself can all too often become an elite of leisure.

Another issue involved is the syllabus itself. It can be argued that academic subjects, especially in the humanities, are basically a preparation for a life of leisure and civilized discourse. The learning of history, literature and world affairs can all too easily be a form of education oriented toward the goal of producing gentlemen. As one external observer put it:

> When an African boy is studying British or French constitution or history in the hope of getting a job in the post office he does not expect ever to be able to use the knowledge which he is acquiring with great effort and expense.[9]

Yet education in the humanities could be oriented toward a life of exertion rather than leisure, and might be even more suited to an underdeveloped country than to a highly complex modern society. Manpower planning is sometimes in danger of giving priority to functionally specific categories of training. Some of the manpower projections, for example, calculate in terms of so many architects, agronomists, doctors, economists. In reality much of the educated manpower in black Africa should be functionally versatile rather than functionally specialized. A highly complex modern society might indeed need a whole range of specialized expertise for different jobs in this or that occupational complex. But a developing society, with limited manpower, needs a large pool of people who can be used in different kinds of careers with the same educational background. Such people are pre-eminently the products of the faculties of arts and social sciences and, to some extent, of academic natural sciences. A student trained in history may end up pursuing a career as an administrator, or a businessman, or a teacher, or a manager, or a librarian. A history student would not be wasted in any of these very different categories of positions. But there is a sense in which a medical doctor is wasted in a high administrative job when he could be practising medicine. In other words, to train a person as a medical doctor or an engineer or an agronomist or even a lawyer in the British tradition is to restrict the range of jobs he can be called upon to perform. Any diversion of people trained in this direction for other types of jobs connotes a wastage of expertise, because the particular training involved is of a specialized kind. But a historian would not be wasted in a highly administrative job precisely because training in history is training for functional versatility. Most of Africa still needs specialists, but there is a risk in inflating the importance of manpower projections to a degree which sees all education in terms of specialized categories of careers.

Yet precisely because a developing country needs functionally versatile people, it becomes relevant once again to think of including practical courses in the school curriculum. In the colonial period there was indeed a half-hearted attempt to include some degree of vocational training in government schools here and there. My own school in Mombasa included classes in carpentry which I attended for a while. But the measure was somewhat half-hearted, lacking adequate support from the school authorities and lacking prestige among the students. A more systematic introduction of some degree of vocational training would go some way towards illustrating the desirability of functional versatility. To that extent it could also help the process of developmental socialization.

We have interpreted the national services of places such as Tanzania and Nigeria partly in terms of their being an attempt to introduce the educated to manual labour especially connected with rural development. From that limited perspective, it is not clear that the national service of either Tanzania of Nigeria is fully defensible in sociological terms in black Africa. But such experiments assume greater justification if we look at the national service schemes as being also inspired by a desire to promote functional flexibility within the ranks of the educated. University graduates and products of secondary schools and comparable educational institutions are required under the Tanzanian scheme to serve for two years in the civil service. Part of their time within the service is indeed spent in work for which the graduates are in any case qualified. But the national service was also partly inspired by a distrust of occupational specialization, and certainly by a distrust of the distinction between intellectual competence and manual skills.

The issue of the national service in Tanzania led to the crisis in the government's relations with university students in Dar es Salaam in 1966. A protest by students against the new national service, made with a certain degree of impertinence, culminated in the expulsion of about three hundred students by President Nyerere. The kind of punishment which the President decreed seemed again to be animated by this distrust of intellectual specialization. The President originally sentenced the students to a period of 'working on the family farm' in their own villages. As it turned out, not all the students had family farms to go back to. And the period of punishment was only until the following academic year after all, though the President had at first contemplated a longer sentence. Nevertheless, what matters for us in this analysis is that President Nyerere's conception of penitence was in terms of compulsory exercise in an occupational change. The student of jurisprudence had to try his hand on the wheelbarrow. This is functional versatility on a broad scale.[10]

Functional versatility is a valued principle in Marxist socialism, partly because it is the antithesis of division of labour with all its potential for the emergence of a caste system or a class-system or both. Many national service schemes in the Third World seem in part to be designed to allow for the possibility of students doing manual work and other forms of nation-building activities interspersed with their times of intellectual pursuits at the university. By insisting that under-graduates should be manual as well as intellectual in their attitudes to work and to life, a bridge is created between them and the masses of people in their society. And they themselves are saved from becoming *kupe* — those who are relatively unproductive in themselves and live on others. Indeed much of Tanzania's policy on higher education may become even more oriented towards the task of trying to combat the danger of intellectual parasitism. President Nyerere appointed a 'visitation' or a commission of inquiry into the workings of the University at Dar es Salaam in 1969. There may have been a number of reasons for such an inquiry. But basically Nyerere's academic philosophy continued to be one of concern lest those who have had opportunities to attain higher levels of education should become later in life intellectual parasites, enjoying great social privileges and prestige without giving adequately in return something back to their society.

Uganda's *Common Man's Charter* issued later in the year was also anti-parasitic in aspiration. And in Uganda Obote also appointed a 'visitation' under the chairmanship of Justice Fuad to inquire into the workings of Makerere and submit a report and recommendations. Both the visitation and the national service in these countries seemed animated in part by the ideal of bridging the intellectual gap between different sectors of society.

Then there is the issue of using the national service as a distributive device. Quite often the experiment does seem to demand significant sacrifices by those of the servicemen who are drawn from the professions. It could amount to taxing the relatively fortunate intellectuals indirectly in order to improve the conditions of the poorer citizens. But is the Tanzanian national service, for example, really intended to be in any sense a form of taxing the rich to help the poor? External socialists have been known to make such a suggestion, but Mr Kawawa, then second vice-president of Tanzania, had a different interpretation. He went on record as denying that the scheme was a form of taxing the relatively well-to-do. In a speech to the National Assembly on 3 October 1966, the second vice-president declared categorically: 'To think that the Government is using this scheme as a means of getting money is a gross misconception.'[11] In other words the national service scheme was not intended to be an exercise in distributive justice.

Mr Kawawa suggested that the primary purpose was not so much to save money, but to save the national consciences of the students. The ultimate motivation was to develop certain qualities in the youth of the country. But what great qualities needed to be nurtured? Mr Kawawa enumerated them. The first one he mentioned was courage. The country's future leaders should be trained to be courageous. And yet, ironically enough, the undergraduates at Dar es Salaam in 1966 were penalized as soon as they showed the slightest sign of political courage. It does take courage these days in much of Africa openly to condemn a particular policy of the government. It takes courage for one to stand up even for one's own personal rights. It is so much easier very often to accept and be silent. And yet hundreds of students in Dar es Salaam had their careers temporarily interrupted, were suspended from university studies and put under a shadow because they had the effrontery to challenge authority in defence of what they regarded as their rights. The same government which seemed to be punishing the brave then created a national service to promote bravery. At any rate, so the critics could argue. They could claim that a government killed the great quality of youthful courage so that it could then enjoy the costly experiment of trying to resurrect it.

And yet criticism of this kind misses a good deal of the point of the national service in Tanzania, as indeed in Nigeria. The idea of a national service may be ultimately designed to mitigate some of the habits of intellectual detachment that the educational institutions as now conceived might promote. It introduces an element of practical commitment and utilization of physical labour as part of one's total educational background, as well as reducing the manifold implications of the neat division between those who work with their minds and those who work with their hands.

Conclusion

The central educational value in this whole area of developmental socialization is social commitment translated into active involvement. Underlying this approach is the conviction that those who seek to find intellectual nourishment only from things which are directly intellectual are probably missing deeper nourishment. It is not simply to books and to verbalized ideas in seminars that the human mind responds. It can also respond and expand under the stimulus of things which might not themselves be described as intellectual, but which might nevertheless have a great positive impact on the intellect. It was Dr Samuel Johnson, the great English literary figure of the eighteenth century, who had occasion to say in a poem:

> Deign on the passing world to turn thine eyes,
> And pause awhile from letters, to be wise. [12]

The conviction here is that exposure to life off the campus for an undergraduate might be not merely a contribution to his capacity for practical matters, but conceivably also a contribution to his intellectual maturation and expansion. He lifts his eyes from the page of his book, looks at the world around him, and might become the wiser in the process.

Yet a point to be borne in mind is that intellectualism and involvement can form a circle of mutual nourishment. It is by no means a one-way traffic. Just as experience in the field and villages can have distinctive intellectual value in its own right, so can certain intellectual pursuits lead on to forms of practical commitment. We referred earlier to what we described as perhaps the most political of all Shakespeare's plays, *Julius Caesar*. What we did not mention was that an important figure in Uganda's history, as a student at Makerere, took the title role in the first Shakespearean performance of the Makerere English Department in 1948 of that very same play. And an important figure in Tanzania's history one day came to translate that play into an East African language. *Julius Caesar* was acted live at Makerere in 1948 with Milton Obote as Caesar, and translated into Swahili by Julius Nyerere some years later. It was the character acted by Milton Obote who had occasion to say:

> Yond Cassius has a lean and hungry look;
> He thinks too much: such men are dangerous.

And it was Julius Nyerere who gave the words an African immortality in the Swahili rendering:

> Yule Cassius ana uso njaa na mwembamba;
> Afikiri mno; watu wa jinsiye ni hatari. [13]

What all this would suggest is that even those African leaders who have been brought up on Shakespeare and high culture have been known to develop a commitment to the solution of practical problems in their own countries later in life. President Nyerere is the most intellectual of all English-speaking heads of state in Africa and in some ways the most westernized in the nature of that intellectual orientation. And yet this has not prevented him from becoming a major radical in African affairs, devoted to the ambition of devising urgent solutions to compelling problems. His intellectual preparation in his educational background was not only western, but grounded in the softer humanities. Out of this, and of the personality he possesses, he has devised a circumspect intellectual style, a process of rationalizing moral sensibilities on the basis of a highly developed social conscience. The man who translated Shakespeare's *Julius Caesar* into Swahili is also the man who is committed to the transformation of the educational system of Tanzania in the direction of less stage work and more spade work.

Yet if we think of Nyerere as a living embodiment of the slogan 'Socialism and Shakespeare' we are back to that old interaction between social commitment and cultural engagement in East Africa. Nyerere's translation of *Julius Caesar* was hailed in East Africa partly for reasons of cultural nationalism. Swahili had been called upon to carry the heavy weight of Shakespeare's genius, and had emerged triumphant. Since then Nyerere has completed the translation of one more Shakespearean play, *The Merchant of Venice*. And at least one fellow countryman of his, S. Mushi, has followed the example by translating *Macbeth*. Nyerere, the lover of Shakespeare, is perhaps saying 'Not by bread alone' in emphatic terms. Nyerere the socialist retorts 'Not by the Bard alone either'. The constant interaction between cultural engagement and social commitment is captured in this dual Nyererean sense of involvement.

At the University in Dar es Salaam one feels that there is more than an echo of Marx paraphrased coming from its walls: 'Scholars have so far only interpreted the world; the point however is to change it.'

References and Notes

1. Julius Nyerere, *Freedom and Unity: a Selection from Writings and Speeches, 1952-1965*, Oxford University Press, Dar es Salaam, 1966, pp. 103-4.
2. See Léopold Senghor, *Prose and Poetry*, ed. and trans. John Reed and Clive Wake, Oxford University Press, 1965, pp. 29-35.
3. See Kwame Nkrumah, *Consciencism*, Heinemann Educational Books, 1964, pp. 16-19.
4. V. I. Lenin, *State and Revolution* (1917).
5. Karl Marx, *Critique of the Gotha Programme* (1875).
6. Stanislav Andreski, *The African Predicament*, Michael Joseph, 1968.
7. This is also discussed in Ali A. Mazrui, 'Tanzaphilia', *Transition* (Kampala), 31 (1967), 24-5.
8. See David Kimble, *A Political History of Ghana: the Rise of the Gold Coast Nationalism, 1850-1928*, Clarendon Press, Oxford, 1963, pp. 87-93.
9. Andreski, *The African Predicament*, op. cit.
10. Consult also Ali A. Mazrui, 'Political superannuation and the trans-class man', *International Journal of Comparative Sociology*, IX, 2 (1968), 91.
11. *East African Standard* (Nairobi), 4 October 1966.
12. Samuel Johnson, 'The vanity of human wishes', *Poems*, ed. David Nichol Smith and E. L. McAdam, Oxford University Press, 1974.
13. Nyerere's translation of *Julius Caesar* was published by Oxford University Press in 1963.

PART FOUR

HIGHER EDUCATION AND
NATION-BUILDING

13 The Meaning of Higher Education

Throughout the modern phase of its history, the university as an institution in the world has rested on a basic contradiction. The contradiction lies in the tensions between academic freedom and academic democracy. Academic freedom includes within it the right to hold and to express opinions, the right to teach and to be taught without external interference, the right of access to academic knowledge, and the right to participate in expanding the frontiers of knowledge. Academic democracy, on the other hand, concerns the process of decision-making within an academic institution. How widely distributed is the right of participation in decision-making? How effectively are different interests within the institution represented within the structure of power? How powerful are heads of departments, deans, the vice-chancellor, and administrative committees of the university? What influence do junior staff and students exercise on policy-making? We see here, then, that academic freedom is primarily a matter of freedom from interference, whilst academic democracy concerns the right to participate.

The university as an institution in the West attained a high level of academic freedom fairly early, but until the eruption of the student revolution in the 1960s there was relatively little academic democracy. Western universities were indeed centres of free discussion and lively debates; to that extent they provided the atmosphere for academic freedom. But western universities were also basically hierarchical structures of authority, with institutions which tended to keep out of effective power important sectors of opinion in the university. To that extent western universities were academically undemocratic.

Even academic freedom itself was by no means present from the beginning of the history of universities. On the contrary, it is a relatively recent phenomenon of the West. The history of university institutions was intimately connected at one time with religion and the constraints imposed by religion. Scholarship itself was overwhelmingly oriented towards theological issues, or restrained by theological considerations. Science had to serve God directly — or science could be charged with the sin of heresy. Scientists had to be careful about what they did. Very often those scientists were deeply religious themselves, and shrank from lines of thought which appeared to lead towards irreligious conclusions.

The link between religion and academic life was strong. But the tensions between complete scientific objectivity and considerations of inherited religion entered a new era with the Copernican revolution in the sixteenth century. Copernicus, a native of Prussian Poland and himself a Canon of Frauenburg, propounded the theory that the planets, including the earth, moved in orbits around the sun which was at the centre. His theory was in opposition to the older theory more popular with the Church and associated with the name of Ptolemy. The older theory asserted that the sun and the planets moved around the earth. This was popular with the Church, partly because of the feeling that the planet inhabited by a creature created in the image of God, that is Man himself, should indeed be central to the universe and thus central to the divine scheme of things. Jesus himself had regarded it as important to come to earth and live among men. Why should the Almighty have been preoccupied with a particular creature on that certain speck of dust called the Earth? There was a feeling that the Earth had to be central to creation as a whole. To suggest therefore that it was only one more planet moving round the sun, verged on making a mockery of God's grand design.

Galileo in the following century got into trouble also for promoting the Copernican theory. He himself made important discoveries including the isochronism of the pendulum, Jupiter's satellites, and the libration of the moon. His experiments in physics helped him to prove hypotheses such as the assertion that unequal weights drop with equal velocity. He conducted the experiment from the leaning tower of Pisa. But the Church was breathing down the necks of budding scientists. Galileo's observations before long began to conflict with the Inquisition. In 1633 he was compelled to renounce and repudiate the Copernican theory and was sent to prison. The invasion of Galileo's scientific objectivity became a moving symbol for many scientists in the succeeding generations. But for the time being the scientists had to be careful, lest they too be accused of heresy, or even of witchcraft, and burnt at the stake.

The interplay between the Reformation and the Renaissance was an important moment in the history of freedom of thought. The arts were being liberated from religion, and science had no longer to spend all its time proving that it was not Satan in disguise. But anti-scientism was still an important feature of European civilization. Luther was himself rather hostile to certain sectors of the scientific world.

But then Calvinism in Europe began to transform the fortunes of science. The importance of Calvinism for the growth of capitalism has long been debated, following Max Weber's brilliant thesis in *The Protestant Ethic and the Spirit of Capitalism*. But the link between Puritanism and the growth of the scientific spirit has not been discussed quite as extensively, though it has already found its champions as an academic interpretation.

In England the Royal Society came to be overwhelmingly Protestant, but that was not surprising in the seventeenth century. Catholics had become first an underprivileged majority and then an underprivileged minority, and were not likely to be granted the right of founding a professional association under the auspices of the Crown. What is striking therefore is not that the Royal Society was so overwhelmingly Protestant by the seventeenth century, but that it was overwhelmingly *Puritan*. The men of science were basically non-conformists — neither Catholic nor Anglican in their majority.

The Puritan fascination with science had influenced Cromwell to establish the new English university of Durham, the only new English university to be established between the Middle Ages and the nineteenth century. Durham University committed itself from its birth to the promotion of 'all the sciences'.[1] Cambridge University became more scientifically oriented partly because it was more non-conformist in its religious composition. The origins of the scientific bias of Cambridge in the modern period may well lie in that period of high Puritan influence at Cambridge in the seventeenth century.[2]

In the United States too, the Puritan influence on the growth of the scientific spirit was considerable. Part of the influence came through Cambridge University in England which was described in that period as the alma mater of the Puritans. One author listed twenty leading Puritan clergymen in New England, of whom seventeen were graduates of Cambridge, and only three of Oxford. In Cambridge, Massachusetts, Harvard's educational programme felt this Puritan influence. The sciences in the United States were certainly better upheld in Protestant than in Catholic institutions, but within the Protestant phenomenon the Puritan bias towards science has also been observable.[3]

What was happening then was not a complete break between religion and science. As yet it did not even amount to the secularization of science. What was really happening was the scientification of religion. The full wave of the secularization of science came in the second half of the eighteenth century and continued and grew in the course of the nineteenth century. Jeremy Bentham's establishment of University College, London, as an institution where scholars need not subscribe to the nine articles of the Anglican faith, was itself part of this new assertion of academic freedom in England.

But academic democracy was less fortunate. The organization of universities continued to be hierarchical. The most hierarchical were, on the whole, the universities in continental Europe, followed by universities in England, and the most experimental and relatively democratic were universities in the United States. But even this statement is comparative. None of the liberal universities anywhere in the West has as yet taken academic democracy as seriously as they have academic freedom. The rights to hold and express opinions were eloquently championed, and sometimes eloquently defended. But the right to participate in the decision-making process of the university was more restricted. However, although the United States has been a little ahead in academic democracy than other developed societies, it has sometimes been a little behind in academic freedom. The fortunes of radical scholars in the United States have often been hazardous. During the bad and fearful days of the McCarthy era, scholars who were fascinated by Marx and his values were putting their careers in mortal danger. The anti-socialist tendencies within the American political culture have often erupted into militant intolerance. And seldom were they more intolerant than in the 1950s when socialists were hounded and harassed, and the right to express and hold opinions was drastically curtailed for those on the left of the political spectrum.

And then the 1960s came. In the early 1960s American students were relatively conformist and self-satisfied. Often American students were patriotic in a fighting sense, and even Lyndon Johnson began by enjoying wide student support in his first two years in office following the assassination of President Kennedy. Then the students' revolution got under way. At the University of California at Berkeley student assertion erupted into violence and direct political resistance.

But the militancy of the students' movement, which was democratizing institutions in some of the universities in the West, was in danger of curtailing academic freedom. Student militants frightened some of their fellows who did not agree with them; at times student militants frightened their teachers, who no longer felt confident enough to express their genuine opinions on certain controversial issues. Student agitation may have succeeded in expanding the frontiers of academic democracy in the United States, but for a while the cost was high as academic freedom was diluted. The right of student participation was partially conceded; even the right to choose certain courses, formulate syllabuses, and establish new departments, pre-eminently for Black Studies. These rights were being conceded in the wake of the students' revolution. But concurrently with this development was the curtailment of the right to hold and express opinions. The radicals enjoyed freedom of expression out of proportion to their numbers. The opponents of radicalism retreated into fearful silence.

Town, Gown and Government

But academic democracy can have repercussions for the wider national democracy, just as academic freedom has consequences for political freedom at large. The student revolution since the 1960s has aspired to give the younger generation a say on fundamental issues of national priority, and not merely on issues of the internal administration of university institutions. When students have barricaded themselves in the office of a registrar or a vice-chancellor, the aim has often been to expand academic democracy. But when students have demonstrated in the streets against certain aspects of their country's foreign policy, or in favour of a new basis for allocating the nation's resources, the students have sought to participate in the democracy of the nation itself.

How much of this agitation for expanding the rights of students to participate in national affairs should take place? My answer has been on a fundamental distinction between developed societies and developing countries. As indicated earlier, in developed societies there are entrenched values and institutions, often resistant even to long overdue reforms, often indifferent or hostile to the spirit of innovation, and not always fair to those who dissent from the dominant values of the society. Where values and institutions are so entrenched the case for students' demonstration and students' direct action in defence of certain reforms is clear. Fundamental changes in the society are unlikely to take place merely in response to the verbalized emotions of young people in student newspapers. The very entrenchment of the institutionalized preferences of the society would tend to make change difficult when that change is being recommended merely by young people. But developing countries are in a different predicament. The dominant characteristic of developing countries is not entrenched values and rigid institutions but fluid values and fragile institutions. There is a constant groping for a sense of direction. The rhetoric of socialism is heard on one day, and has become silent and terrified the next day. A Parliament exists this year in effective action; it becomes a rubber stamp the next year; and perhaps dies out completely the third year. Constitutions come and go; bills of rights breathe and expire. The pace of mutability is sometimes frighteningly bewildering. The countries of Africa face the uneven surface of political upheavals. In this situation, student challenges to African institutions and African values need a sense of caution. The whole superstructure of the polity could be endangered by any precipitate action undertaken by one segment of that society. In developing countries, therefore, the role of young people should remain more that of promoting public debate on fundamental issues than of undertaking violent demonstrations directed at values and institutions which still suffer in the agony of fragility.

Yet the issue of fragile institutions and inchoate values in developing societies goes beyond the question of students' responses to the structures of authority. It concerns the whole interaction between the university, the government and society at all levels. Sensitive to the wider political implications of university education, some African governments have been groping for new definitions of academic functions, new principles of academic purpose, new rules of the academic game. Let us now turn more explicitly to the tensions of Africa's own experience.

For seven years—from 1963 to 1970—East Africa experimented with a federal university, with a campus in Kenya, a campus in Tanzania and a campus in Uganda. Then in July 1970 the three constituent colleges of the University of East Africa became three autonomous national universities. Yet the remarkable thing about the University of East Africa was not the fact that it broke up after seven years, but the fact that it ever came into being at all. The University of East Africa was a multinational organization which demanded special academic statecraft to make it viable even for a mere seven years. While it lasted it was a hard-headed and realistic experiment in regional technical co-operation, as well as a dream in the tradition of Pan-East-Africanism.

During those seven years the three countries themselves diverged significantly in ideological orientation. Under the leadership of Julius K. Nyerere, Tanzania rapidly became identified with the radical socialist stream of thought in Africa. Indeed, Tanzania virtually captured the leadership of African radicalism. Uganda wavered for a while. The rhetoric of the ruling party, the Uganda People's Congress, had always included a neo-socialist theme. But the theme did not go much beyond verbal affirmations of socialism for several years. It was not until 1970 that Uganda under the leadership of Apolo Milton Obote really took a turn to the left. The state took over the export and import trade, acquired sixty per cent of the shares in all major industries, proclaimed new standards of self-denial for public servants, and committed itself to a one-party system. But a military coup in Uganda in January 1971 interrupted this process of socialization—and new questions about the purposes of higher education began to be asked. Kenya, under Mzee Jomo Kenyatta, evolved in a very different direction during the seven years of the life of the University of East Africa. The government set out to promote an indigenous entrepreneurial culture. Legislation was passed to support and safeguard a policy of creating a local business class to replace in part expatriate Asians and Europeans in commerce and industry.

The three campuses of the University of East Africa watched these developments. As centres of thought, the university institutions often provided a forum for discussions on these divergent policy preferences. But by the second half of 1966 the East African University institutions were no longer discussing national ideologies merely at a broad level of generality. They had begun to ask fundamental questions about their own role in independent East Africa and the kind of ideals which should govern their work.

The University College, Dar es Salaam, took the lead in this self-evaluation. The crisis of relevance at Dar es Salaam erupted in October 1966 when the three hundred students were expelled from the university by President Nyerere over the issue of national service. The University College began to ask itself 'where have we gone wrong?' Expatriate radicals seized the initiative and tried to engineer a revolution in the very structure of the university. No revolution did in fact take place, but the University College, Dar es Salaam, was never the same again. A crisis of relevance began to haunt it, aggravated by the militant idealism of the Arusha Declaration on Socialism and Self-Reliance proclaimed in February, 1967.

By 1969 President Nyerere appointed the committee of inquiry, the 'Visitation Committee', which by its very existence, activated further self-evaluation within the University College. In January 1970 President Obote of Uganda, as Visitor to Makerere University College, took similar action and appointed a Visitation Committee to inquire into the workings of Makerere and report to him. Again the very appointment of such a committee initiated considerable discussion about the aims and purposes of higher education in a developing country like Uganda. In Kenya no such committee was appointed by Mzee Jomo Kenyatta to go into the functions of the University College, Nairobi. But student activism at Nairobi, and the very transition of the college into a national university, could not but generate similar discussion on issues of relevance.

By 1969 the most vocal among academic theorists were the radical reformers rather than the defenders of the older traditions. And yet it was misleading to go simply by the noise. A profound debate was indeed still under way. It is a debate which continues to touch deeply the workings of these three newly autonomous national universities.

The clash, discussed in the previous chapter on developmental goals, was basically between two academic philosophies. One of these might be called the philosophy of intellectual concentration; and the other the philosophy of practical involvement. The philosophy of intellectual concentration is one which believes that the business of a student at a university must be strictly that of a student. He should concentrate his efforts on intellectual pursuits and attempt to make maximum academic use of his limited stay at his institution of higher training. The philosophy of practical involvement, however, argues from the belief that a student's career is not complete unless he displays a readiness to get involved in some practical affairs of his society. It is not enough that he engages in study and thought; he must also respond to the needs of the masses around him by a display of practical sympathy, and react against the ills of his community and his world with a moral commitment to reform.

The Ethic of Intellectual Concentration

The philosophy of intellectual concentration has had fewer defenders among the more articulate commentators on African education at large. There seems to be a widespread belief that it is wrong for students to live in hazy mists of intellectual detachment and appear unaware of the fact that they are a privileged little group in an underprivileged society. There are more advocates of students establishing links with the outside world, and with youth off the campus, than there are advocates of intellectual withdrawal and retrenchment. But it would be a mistake to assume that the philosophy of intellectual concentration is devoid of solid arguments in its defence. One need not accept it in order to see that it is not bereft of sense and wisdom, at least in some of its aspects.

Why should students concentrate on intellectual pursuits? And what are these intellectual pursuits? To the second of these questions it must immediately be pointed out that intellectual concentration is not the same thing as the life of a bookworm. The term 'bookworm' is usually intended to be derogatory, denoting a hungry attachment to books as books and very often for the sole purpose of preparing oneself for some test which lies ahead. But the philosophy of intellectual concentration is not interested in books for their own sake, but would assert that books are valuable only in so far as they are sources of intellectual nourishment. One turns to a book for information and for ideas in order to give further depth to one's own processes of thought. But the philosophy of intellectual concentration would go on to recognize that intellectual nourishment is not to be found in books alone, but is sometimes found in conversations and discussions with one's companions, and in the whole phenomenon of the meeting of minds with different dimensions and points of contact. The student on an African university campus who is always in the library is a less interesting specimen from the point of view of intellectual concentration than the student who not only uses the library but also the table in the hall of residence, and follows the trend of reasoning in a seminar or tutorial with a sense of mental exploration. The chap who is always in the library is very likely to be a bookworm; the chap who has a multiplicity of intellectual interests, engaged in diverse quests for intellectual nourishment, is a more interesting protagonist of the philosophy of intellectual concentration.

But do not both specimens symbolize the whole tradition of a university being an ivory tower? There is some validity in this accusation. But the question which arises is whether a university in an underdeveloped country can ever help being an ivory tower? In a society in which the masses of the people are barely literate, and where there are very few institutions to compare with the university in technical and intellectual sophistication, a university becomes an isolated oasis in an academic desert. The gulf between the university and much of the society it serves is, to some extent, unbridgeable. By definition there must remain a gap between the concept of higher learning and the concept of pre-literacy. An institution of higher learning in a pre-literate society must therefore be condemned to being, at least in part, something of an ivory tower. This of course is basically a generalization, and we shall come to some qualifications later. What needs to be noted for the time being is the simple fact that the great divide between a university and the masses in an underdeveloped society is to some extent inherent in the situation, and independent of the attitudes of those who are in the university.

Given this fact, what are the implications for the student? One possible stand to take is to insist that the student must make the most of the intellectual opportunities at the university in the limited time that he is going to spend there, particularly given the fact that many of the opportunities will be lost to him forever when he leaves the intellectual oasis for the broader academic wilderness of his country. There are facilities at universities which no African can ever find anywhere else in the country. And many of these facilities may never again be accessible to the student. But opportunities for serving his people by practical involvement in the village are opportunities which will recur time and again in his life. The poverty of the villages will not disappear while the student is busy with intellectual pursuits at the university. But many of these pursuits will indeed disappear from his life when later he finds himself more fully involved with alleviating the poverty of the masses. The moral of this sociological situation is that the student must concentrate intellectually while he has a chance to do so in his brief three to five years at the university.

The level of intellectual expansion which a student's mind can attain will often depend upon the range of stimuli that his mind is exposed to. I have always believed that a student who gets a first class degree at Makerere or Ibadan is likely to have more in him than the student who attains the same standard in London, Paris or New York. This is mainly because the student who does his degree in a developed country has a wider range of stimuli than the student who does it in an intellectual oasis. An undergraduate in Britain is not thrown back on to the resources of the institution for mental excitement to quite the same degree as an undergraduate is in Africa. Most African undergraduates that one knew in Britain some years ago were regular readers of the *Guardian* or *The Times*, both of which were newspapers of greater intellectual sophistication than almost anything which the East African press can as yet offer. The radio that one listened to in Britain was also, on the whole, equipped with a wider range of challenging programmes than are available locally in Africa. The old Third Programme of the BBC had always been something of a highbrow intellectual programme, and only a minority of undergraduates in Britain were likely to listen to it regularly. But even the old Home Service had analyses of world events, and commentaries on intellectual issues which were more sophisticated than anything afforded by the majority of radio programmes in black Africa. Television, too, in Britain had a vastly more rewarding quality than the standard that can as yet be achieved in a technically less-equipped society.

Then there is the value of public debate itself as a contribution to the flow of ideas at the university. There is a sense in which the universities in Africa are becoming greater ivory towers than ever. This is because some of the intellectual feedback which used to come from open public debate outside the university is no longer coming back in quite the same volume. When public issues are vigorously thrashed out at the Clock-Tower in Kampala, or in a Parliament in Zambia unrestricted by threats of curtailment of privilege, or by a press in Nigeria which is not constantly worried about being closed down or having one or more of its editorial staff deported, the excitement of the debates off the campus finds its way onto the campus. Inevitably, students and staff start discussing issues and arguing about matters which were first raised in the hurly-burly of open politics off the university campus.

In Britain these debates are constant. There are two vigorously articulate major parties, the Labour and Conservative Parties, and then there is the Liberal Party. The topics argued about range from the role of trade unions and the race issue in Britain, to the fate of sterling. Many of the domestic issues assume interest for foreign undergraduates, and many of the international issues also become points of discussion among students from overseas, as well as among British students themselves. What is proclaimed by the party leaders, or what is said when some controversial policy is challenged in either Parliament or the press, becomes an excuse for intellectual discussions and debates in colleges at Oxford or halls of residence at Manchester. The colleges and the halls of residence become less of ivory towers precisely because of the openness of articulation and debate outside the college.

But in Africa as the frankness of discourse in the political arena outside has declined so has the stimulus which the universities used to receive from outside their own resources. The vigour of argument in the few years before and immediately after independence helped to maintain the university's interest in some of the larger issues affecting the nation. A clash of views on these issues had an intellectual utility in its own right. Of course, this clash of views had its dangerous aspects and might indeed have been an important contributory factor to those bloodier clashes of latter days in Africa. But whatever the cost of open debates, that debate did mean that African universities were less isolated as arenas of discussion. They were less dependent on themselves. For better or for worse the African universities were stimulated and agitated by some of the arguments that went on in the larger society. At least in this limited area of interplay of ideas between town and gown, the African university in those years was less of an ivory tower than it is now.

When the student is placed in this context, and compared with the student in a developed society, it becomes clearer than ever that an undergraduate in East Africa is more overwhelmingly dependent on his university institution for the kind of nourishment which his mind would need in order to attain intellectual expansion. If, in spite of this handicap of isolation, the student's mind expands enough to get a first class degree at Makerere or Ibadan, he probably has within himself additional intellectual resources which the student who attains a first in Britain might not necessarily have. That is one reason why a first class degree is so relatively rare in many departments of African universities, not because the students are less intelligent than a comparable collection of students in a British institution, nor because the staff are necessarily less qualified than a comparable team of staff in a British university. Many students at African universities show evident signs of having first class minds, but they do not quite attain first class results in their examinations. My own conviction remains that a major contributory factor is precisely the narrower range of intellectual stimuli that a student in an underdeveloped society can ever expect to be exposed to. Given this narrower range, the speed of his intellectual expansion is often the slower as a result.

This seems to be an extra argument for the philosophy of intellectual concentration in Africa. After all, to pursue interests other than intellectual ones during a brief period at university is to dilute even further the one major source of nourishment that a student has. It puts the student at an even greater handicap. In a developed society one could conceive a situation in which an undergraduate develops faster mentally precisely by refusing to be circumscribed within the university circle. An undergraduate in a developed society could thus diversify his stimuli by going out into the larger debates of the outside world. A little activity in party politics off the campus by an undergraduate in Britain, or some involvement in journalistic activities, or participation in controversial pamphleteering, could all have a relevance for his intellectual maturation. But there is a greater risk of sacrificing intellectual expansion for the sake of practical participation if an undergraduate in a much less developed society divides his time at university between pursuits on the campus and other endeavours in the villages.

We mentioned earlier the bookworm spending his time all day in the library. This was not to be taken as a criticism for making as much use as possible of the library facilities at university while one is still there. This is another dimension to the philosophy of intellectual concentration. The world of books in Africa is more narrowly defined. A student who fails to read certain classics in literature or philosophy or economics or science while he is still at Makerere,

Ibadan or Legon might never again have access to these books elsewhere. Makerere is, perhaps, the best and biggest library in East Africa. It is certainly the best and the biggest in Uganda. In fact, the majority of graduates can only hope to have access to much more modest book facilities once they leave this university. If a student does not avail himself of this all too brief exposure to the vast world of books, he might never again get a chance to catch up with the flow of thought in world history.

This problem is aggravated by the issue of reading speed among African undergraduates. On the whole, African undergraduates read significantly more slowly than their counterparts in Europe or the United States. This is partly because they are the first literate generation in the family, and partly because of inadequate school facilities prior to coming to university. It becomes more important than ever that an African student should not be diverted too drastically from the world of books during his brief period of nearness to a major library. Those who subscribe to the philosophy of intellectual concentration as the right option for an undergraduate in a developing country would regard this as an extra element of vindication for the position they have taken.

So far we have presented the case of intellectual concentration as an ethical base for student behaviour. But defensible as this particular philosophy might be, it by no means has a monopoly of rational argument in its support. In fact, as we indicated, most commentators in contemporary Africa have tended to be drawn more towards the rival philosophy of practical involvement.

The Ethic of Practical Involvement

This philosophy of intellectual concentration is often associated with the principle of academic detachment. But although the two beliefs do go well together, they are not logically integrated nor are they always held by the same people. The philosophy of intellectual concentration as so far defined addresses itself mainly to the role of the university as a teaching institution. It is concerned with the best way of enabling a student to make the most of his stay at a university. It does not insist that members of staff should not be actively engaged in matters of practical relevance to the nation. Yet members of staff can be so engaged while students concentrate their energies in their brief three to five years at the university on matters concerned with their own intellectual development.

The principle of academic detachment as a dictum to govern scholarship is a more comprehensive idea than the philosophy of intellectual concentration. The principle of academic detachment seeks to govern the behaviour of the university, both in the way it approaches the business of teaching the students and in its definition of the rightful roles of its staff as scholars. The idea of academic detachment assumes that to be scientific is to be socially neutral. The ultimate purpose of a university must therefore be, not the service of the regime or the society at a particular moment in time, but the pursuit of truth as an eternal question. This of course is a formulation of the principle of academic detachment in its most ideal form. But clearly this is a principle which distinguishes service to truth and knowledge from service to society. Of course, the two may be quite compatible. Yet they have to be differentiated when resources are being allocated and priorities determined. In any case, there are occasions when a particular kind of knowledge is not of any practical interest to society. Indeed, there might be occasions when the cause of disseminating knowledge or revealing the truth comes into conflict with the cause of serving society. There may also be occasions when what society needs is not truth in all its nakedness but truth in the garb of national attractiveness. The study of history especially can, in societies seeking a sense of historical identity, dictate that its purpose is not an unconditional pursuit of the truth but a search for those elements of the truth which would help society to shape its identity. The university has, therefore, to ask itself whether it has a function as a mythmaker where new myths are acutely needed.

There are also occasions when the trouble with a university in Africa is not simply that it is an institution which comes from a foreign country, but also that it is an institution which is derived from the wrong historical period. The age of secularism and of the scientific method in Europe is relatively new. For hundreds of years universities were deeply immersed in the religious mythologies of their period. Graduation at Oxford until the nineteenth century depended on formal acceptance of certain principles of Anglican derivation. Appointment to Fellowships at the colleges until relatively recently presumed full immersion into the socio-religious culture of the dominant groups. Important poets and philosophers in the history of English ideas were expelled or otherwise victimized by Oxford and Cambridge for their heretical formulations.

In short, the idea that a university is ultimately a place which must be governed by the scientific method, and seek to achieve social neutrality, is a relatively recent school of thought. For centuries universities in the western world were indeed engaged in consolidating the myths and values of their own society, as well as in promoting such knowledge as is not in conflict with the most fundamental of those myths and values.

Then the scientific revolution transformed universities in Europe. And later still, the university institution was transplanted from Europe into an environment abroad which is to some extent 'pre-scientific' all over again. Oral tradition, folklore, methods of treating the sick and the insane, ways of maintaining contact with the dead, strong loyalties to tradition, strong bonds of collective conformity — all these elements in the African environment did not seem to belong to the same period of history as the post-Renaissance African university imported into the continent from Europe.

The crisis of relevance then in the universities in Africa is both temporal and spatial. It is temporal because of the need to refashion the university institution in a manner which might make it more compatible with the pre-literate, pre-scientific and pre-national society it is called upon to serve. The university has also to forge relevance in a spatial sense by taking account of the transplantation from one part of the world to another and by adjusting to the environmental variation.

This is what brings in the philosophy of practical involvement. Many regard such a philosophy as being post-modern. It is supposed to be radical, and is therefore presumed to be taking the issue of social commitment beyond the stagnant waters of bourgeois scientism. To some extent there is a post-modern element in this radicalism. What is not to be overlooked is that there is also a pre-modern factor in this quest to relate the duties of the university more firmly to the needs and values of society. It is indeed like going back to the Oxford of the Thirty-nine Articles of religion. Consolidating and fulfilling the values of society becomes as important an aim as enhancing knowledge for its own sake. Indeed, should the two come into conflict, the former duty to society in that pre-scientific age of Oxford had clearly to prevail, at the peril of sanctions.

The aims in Africa today are, of course, not identical with the aims of England before the scientific revolution. In Africa the two paramount aims are the forging of a national identity in each African country and a promotion of socio-economic development. In this book the quest for a national identity is discussed in relation to nationalist criteria of educational relevance. The quest for socio-economic development falls within the developmental and socialist criteria of educational relevance.

Both the imperatives of identity and the imperatives of development have again to be seen in their total perspective. The imperatives of identity were embraced by our early African nationalists when there was very little university education obtainable within Africa south of the Sahara. In the nineteenth century almost all Africans who stood a chance of benefiting from a university education had to go abroad in order to attain it. And the departure of these people to go overseas and learn new ways of thought in foreign surroundings inevitably carried the risk of mental de-Africanization. Some African patriots began to feel, from quite early on, that African local cultures were in danger of being relegated to insignificance if African intellectual leaders looked only to foreign countries for inspiration.

A view began to gain ascendance among African intellectuals in the late nineteenth century that only the establishment of local universities could ultimately save local cultures from the disfiguring effects of foreign influence. African intellectuals of English expression in the nineteenth century, in their anxiety about the long-term cultural effects of colonialism, began to look to the establishment of local universities as a way of preserving their indigenous heritage. Early African scholars like Dr Africanus Horton, Dr Edward Blyden of Liberia and Mr J. E. Caseley Hayford of Ghana were among those who felt that a local African university was what was needed if justice was to be done to indigenous cultures.

Blyden, the towering African intellectual of the nineteenth century, was against modern European studies and strongly in favour of the classics. Blyden thought in terms of establishing in Africa the kind of university which would enable Africans to share in the heritage of Greece and Rome, and link it up with the study of modern African civilizations, without passing through the study of modern Europe. For Blyden only a university which combined Graeco-Roman classics with modern African studies would be capable of broadening African horizons and deepening African roots. The young African mind should drink from the fountains of ancient Greece and ancient Rome, and from the spring of current African civilization, without passing through what Blyden called 'despotic Europeanizing influences which had warped and crushed the Negro mind'.[4] Caseley Hayford of Ghana had ideas after the First World War which were no less revolutionary. He felt that university education in Africa should be given in an African language as soon as possible, and provision should be made for the translation of books and for collaboration in scholarship not only with England but also with Japan, Germany and the United States. In 1920 African intellectuals of British West Africa held their first cultural and political conference. After their meeting, and inspired by Caseley Hayford's views on the matter, they sent a petition to King George V asking that a British West African University should be established 'on such lines as would preserve in the students a sense of African nationality'.[5]

What is significant about the ideas of these early African educational philosophers is not the precise measures they recommended, but the underlying hunger for an institution which would reconcile modern education with African identity. They wanted to make sure that the process of education in Africa was *not* the process of de-Africanization. We may not agree with the details of the measures they were recommending. But there has recently been a resumption of their search for the kind of university which would combine educational changes with cultural continuities.

Conclusion

Developmental criteria of educational relevance were, curiously enough, more warmly supported by colonial policy-makers than by African nationalists in much of the first half of the twentieth century. The idea of vocational training as an educational priority, the insistence that practical relevance should be the guiding principle of educational arrangements in the colonies — all these were arguments more firmly promoted by educational reformers from the colonial powers themselves, than by African nationalist spokesmen in those years.

At the time of the Education Commission of the East Africa Protectorate in 1919 it was already being argued that 'the mere acquisition of knowledge, unless it is made a matter of understanding through practical application to everyday affairs of life, may be found undesirable'. At that time the educational pyramid was still low, and was not as yet oriented towards a pinnacle of university admission. But the commission was nevertheless putting forward arguments in ringing defence of practical relevance.

> Education for natives should be designed to fit them for the common needs of the ordinary life. It is undesirable that any teaching should cause them to look down on manual labor. . . . The bedrock of what the great majority of natives should learn is agriculture, it must be agriculture. . . . The basis of education should be industrial in the widest sense.[6]

A curious development began to be discerned even as early as that. In practice, if not necessarily by calculated design, the beginnings of the education of girls in East Africa were more firmly rooted in practical considerations than boys' education ever was. Missionary education for boys became relatively academic and literary quite early. The foundation was being laid for educational tendencies which finally culminated in producing a literati or literary intelligentsia as the new type of elite in tropical Africa. But the education of women quite early tried to promote not only domestic crafts but also the arts of gardening and rudimentary agriculture. In the words of Anne M. Spencer:

> In general it can be said that over the years in spite of protestations to the contrary, men tended to receive a more academic, literary and urban centered education; whereas women's education had a much more practical, community oriented emphasis. Thus, by implication, boys' education can be seen to have been more elitist in its conception; girls' more egalitarian.[7]

These then are some of the historical antecedents to the debates which have been going on in Africa concerning relevance in education and scholarship. The debates about national relevance find connexions with the beginnings of nationalist movements in Africa, and are an elaboration of the ideas of people like Blyden, Horton and Caseley Hayford. The debates on developmental imperatives find contacts with educational reforms put forward by early colonial educationists. These were debates about the proper line of training for natives in pre-modern societies. The term 'natives' is no longer used now in that sense, and the new term is 'indigenous people'. The temptation to advise what type of education is proper for a pre-modern society or 'backward' country still goes on, but the vocabulary is different. Now the 'practicalists' among reformers prefer to talk in terms of the type of education 'relevant to a developing country'.

Perhaps it is right that debates on education and learning should come in waves, picking up some of the froth which was left by a previous wave, but adding new strength in the sheer momentum of torrential intellectual movement.

References and Notes

1. Consult E. H. Hayward, *The Unknown Cromwell*, London, 1934, pp. 206-30, 315.
2. James B. Mullinger, *Cambridge Characteristics in the Seventeenth Century*, London, 1867, pp. 180-1 et passim.
3. Consult Robert K. Merton, 'Puritanism, pietism and science' in *Social Theory and Social Structure*, Free Press, New York, 1967, pp. 574-605.
4. Edward Blyden, *Christianity, Islam and the Negro Race*, 1887, University Press, Edinburgh, 1967, Chapter 4.
5. For a discussion of the wider political context of these 1920 demands, consult James S. Coleman, *Nigeria: Background to Nationalism*, University of California Press, Berkeley and Los Angeles, 1963, pp. 190-4.
6. *Evidence of the Education Commission of the East Africa Protectorate* (1919), pp. 121, 42-3. Consult also Idrian N. Resnick, *Tanzania: Revolution by Education*, Longmans of Tanzania, Dar es Salaam, 1968.
7. Anne M. Spencer, 'The changing lives of women in Western Kenya, with special reference to friends' education', notes for an MA thesis (Makerere University College).

14 The Environment of Higher Education

Three levels of environment profoundly influence institutions of higher learning—regional, national and international. The regional environment is here defined in terms of a section of one country. Our sense of regional here is therefore sub-national. One question which arises at this environmental level is whether a university is located in, say, the capital city or in a more rural environment. The national environment in African conditions includes the political relationship between the government and the university. The international environment encompasses those problems of cultural and intellectual dependence which are partly derived from the European ancestry of African educational institutions.

The regional environment is important partly because universities are expected to produce manpower which is sensitized to the developmental problems of the society, including the social and economic disparities between town and country. The national environment of a university touches issues which range from ethnicity and race to the psychology of the president in power. We shall also explore in this chapter the historic cultural continuities which condition contemporary African political styles—including the heritage of the elder tradition, the sage tradition and the warrior tradition in Africa's experience. Aspects of the international environment have already been scrutinized in earlier chapters. Other aspects remain to be examined more fully in the last part of the book when we shall turn to international influences which range from the computer to western methodologies. But in this chapter we shall limit ourselves to how the international environment can adversely affect that most sacred of all western liberal values—intellectual freedom itself. But first let us focus on the region and the nation.

The Logic of Location

Successive educational reformers in Africa have argued and protested that African universities are not adequately involved in nation-building. This is a judgement that continues to be widely shared among men of affairs all over the continent. Nor is it simply a case of academics feeling the breath of close scrutiny by external spectators. Sometimes within each university many academics are themselves eager to tear themselves away from a conceptual ivory tower. They feel that the university is a little too distant from the society it serves, and they aspire to reduce that distance. We have been concerned with this problem in a variety of ways. But in this section we are concentrating on the environmental causes of the social distance and social nearness of the university.

The actual physical locality of a university institution in a developing country is sometimes overlooked as a determinant of social distance and social attitudes. Where the institution is located may have a good deal to do with its evolving ethos. This is the political geography of institutions of higher education. For example, all three universities in East Africa are situated in or adjacent to the capital cities of their respective countries. This factor has important consequences in regard to the potentialities of the university for national involvement. It is also pertinent to inquire whether being situated in a capital city makes a university more or less of an ivory tower.

To a certain extent there is an ironic reversal of predicament as between the three universities in relation to the ideologies of their respective countries. Tanzania is clearly the most socialist of the three countries. Its socialism includes the ethos of national involvement for every member of society. National service, partly designed to rescue indigenous intellectuals from being purely academic, is part of Tanzania's clear commitment to this principle of participation. And yet, in sheer physical location, the University at Dar es Salaam has created a distance between itself and the population. It is situated some ten miles out of Dar es Salaam, in an area which does not afford the alternative experience of a real rural exposure. The original location of the University within the city of Dar es Salaam, alongside a genuine dilapidated slum area, was in many ways a sharper reminder of the need for intellectual involvement in nation-building than the present location out in the sedate countryside.

Kenya is perhaps the least socialist in orientation among the three East African countries. Yet the main campus of its University is not only situated within the capital city but has dispersed itself in different parts of it. The University at Nairobi is not a coherent academic community, living together on a shared campus, clearly differentiated in residential location from those who pursue other areas of national endeavour. There is no real equivalent campus of the kind shared by staff and students at Dar es Salaam or Makerere. The staff at Nairobi are scattered in different parts of the city and have to find their way to the University every morning and then join the streams of the rest of the city every evening to return home. And the halls of residence of students are so much part of the centre of Nairobi that special precautions have to be taken to protect the University from an excessive number of uninvited guests turning up for the canteen meals. A system of tickets has been devised because the canteens are near enough to the city to tempt members of the general public to run up for a free lunch or a free dinner. This is in striking contrast to the situation even at Makerere, let alone the more distant University of Dar es Salaam. No elaborate system of identification or tickets is necessary for meals at Makerere for the simple reason that the campus is distinct enough and segregated enough from the rest of the community to ensure that no unwelcome guests can easily stake their claim to a plate in a hall of residence. If a university institution is nearest to communal involvement when it is within the capital city and dispersed in different parts of it, then it is the University of capitalist Kenya rather than the University of socialist Tanzania which comes nearer to the ideal of interpenetration with the rest of the community.

Makerere's situation, like Uganda's own ideological position has been for so long, is intermediate between these two. Makerere is neither in the middle of the city of Kampala nor ten miles away from it. It is on the edge of the city. Contact with city is significant for both students and staff. And some degree of social intercourse does take place between town and gown on an everyday basis. But the University is still basically a community fenced in, with a gate guarded day and night, an appearance of social exclusiveness. It is true that in so far as the staff are concerned there are extensions of the campus elsewhere. But even these extensions tend to be little islands of community living separated from their environment, and quite often literally fenced in.

Makerere has been partially converted to the policy of encouraging more and more students to live off the campus. Historically Makerere has been overwhelmingly a residential institution. To some extent this was inevitable because of difficulties of getting suitable accommodation for students who lived out, because also of problems of public transportation in a city like Kampala, and because of the feeling that communal life for students and easy access to the library were major prerequisites for intellectual development in a situation where the University has few companion intellectual institutions outside of itself.

Yet a residential university could not but emphasize the gulf between town and gown. The university campus inevitably became a separate village, distinct both physically and in terms of prestige and aura of reverence. If Africa's urban universities were now to succeed in breaking the tradition of being overwhelmingly residential universities, and farm out some of their students to live in lodgings and flats off campus, a new form of interpenetration between the university and the wider community in the city would be achieved.

A related issue on the staff side is whether accommodation should be provided for staff on campus. Until recently most African universities have included in their terms of service the obligation to provide housing. This housing has in the main been campus housing. When the staff was almost wholly expatriate, it did not perhaps make much of a difference. Expatriate staff would have been a distinct group whichever locality they were situated in. Certainly during the colonial period it was futile to look for an interpenetration between the local populace and academic expatriates on any extensive scale. But with the increasing Africanization of the staff, the question has arisen of whether to house the staff on campus is not to emphasize afresh the separateness of African intellectuals, at least those who pursue academic careers, from the rest of the population. Quite a number of local members of academic staff have built their own houses off the campus. But instead of living in them they let these houses to diplomats and other highly lucrative tenants, while they themselves live in highly subsidized housing on African campuses.

Nor is it surprising that they should choose to do that. After all if they decided to live in their own houses off the campus, they would not get in cash terms the subsidy which is included in the housing they are entitled to if they choose to live on campus. A member of staff would thus sustain a substantial financial loss every month should he ever decide to vacate his university housing in order to go and live in his own. One possible answer is to change the terms of service for staff to include a housing allowance rather than housing itself. All members of staff would then receive the allowance regardless of whether they lived off or on the campus. But if they lived on campus they would have to pay a full economic rent. And if the house they lived in had a higher rent than their housing allowance they would simply have to supplement that allowance from the rest of their earnings. This might well encourage a number of people to seek housing elsewhere, sometimes opting for smaller houses if this would enable them to save a little of their housing allowance. And many of the East African members of staff might at last return to a life of greater mixing with people outside their own professions, and acquire neighbours other than their own immediate colleagues. It might therefore be said that both the encouragement of students to live off the campus and the encouragement of staff with new housing allowances to seek new homes outside the university community might jointly contribute towards reducing academic exclusiveness in physical location, certainly at Makerere and possibly also at the University of Dar es Salaam.

Again Nairobi seems to have stolen a march over the other two universities in East Africa in promoting greater interpenetration between town and gown. The University at Nairobi started early to encourage members of staff to purchase their own houses. Encouragement went to the extent of providing loans or guarantees for loans while suitable security could be ensured. Kenya, perhaps among the least socialist of African countries, once again exhibited a university philosophy committed to the principle of interpenetration between academics and the wider community.

The Political Economy of Location

But it is not just physical interpenetration which is at stake when a university institution in Africa is within or adjacent to a capital city. Political interpenetration might also be facilitated as a result of location. A university in a capital city is exposed to the country's most central political problems but not necessarily to the country's most important economic problems.

In 1966 Uganda experienced a convulsive moment of national reckoning. The status of the City of Kampala was itself at stake. The Government of the Kabaka of Buganda was challenging the legitimacy of the Central Government of Uganda following the suspension of the Constitution by the head of the Central Government. In this confrontation between the Central Government and the Buganda Region, there followed an attempt by Buganda for what might be called an inverse bid to secede. Instead of saying to the Central Government, 'We are pulling out', as the Ibo had done in Nigeria when they declared Biafra's secession, the Kabaka's Government in the Buganda Region said to the Central Government of Uganda, 'You get off Buganda soil'. As Kampala, the national capital, was surrounded by Buganda and was itself ostensibly on Buganda soil, this was separatism with a difference. It was an attempted expulsion of the nation from the region, instead of an attempted withdrawal of a region from the nation. And Kampala, surrounded by the region, but politically tied to the rival side of the dispute, was momentarily converted into an African 'West Berlin'. Yet Buganda did not have the power to impose a blockade on the city, and in the ensuing confrontation between the Central Government and the Kabaka's Government, the centre emerged triumphant. The Kabaka fled into exile in Britain, and his region was put under a state of emergency and strict central control.

Since the status of the City of Kampala was itself central to the dispute, the dispute acquired extra immediacy for the university community. There was a great sense of nearness to a major national crisis. The firing of weapons in the battle against the Kabaka's palace could be heard distinctly by the university community.

Dr A. Milton Obote, the head of the Central Government, had a protective concern for the survival of Makerere as a major national institution. It appears that he sent a special military unit to surround the college as a way of protecting it from the conflagration which had hit the rest of the country. The need for a protective military cordon of that kind was itself a measure of the immediate vulnerability arising from the very location of the university at the heart of a national crisis.

The 1966 events were only the extreme illustration of the simple proposition that being located in the capital city, though not a guarantee of a genuine exposure to the major economic problems of the country, is definitely a guarantee of exposure to some of the most central of the political problems. Before 1966 Makerere University College was sensitized in another way to political developments in the country. Debates which went on in the city about the rights of the Ganda as against others, or whether the lost counties of Bunyoro should be restored to Bunyoro or remain with Buganda, or whether Uganda should demonstrate against the American Embassy for the stray bombing of a Uganda village by a Congolese plane made in the United States — all these issues which were strongly debated in the city were also taken up in the day-to-day conversations which went on at Makerere. Members of staff could drive down quickly and attend a lively session in Parliament, or a public debate at the Clock Tower in Kampala, and acquire the role of participant observers in this general political discourse. Makerere and Kampala constituted one sub-unit of the political system as a whole.

After the confrontation of 1966, and the resultant proclamation of a state of emergency in Buganda, there was a drastic shrinking of party politics in the country. Political activity did indeed still go on, but the liveliness of public contests went out of Uganda politics. Although political rallies addressed by members of the government still took place in the country at large, political rallies critical of the government were almost a thing of the past. In 1968, when President Obote announced the policy of going into the country to meet the people and addressing meetings there, the leader of the opposition announced his intention to embark on counter-rallies with or without permission. But in the political circumstances this could be no more than a rhetorical threat. Rallies needed to have, by government regulation, the permission of the police. And the permission of the police was all too often withheld if the rally was for the opposition. And now Uganda has become a military state, there is no longer any pretence at organized opposition.

All these factors help to demonstrate that by being situated within or near the capital city a university institution in Africa does become in part a reflection of some of the most central of the political problems of the country. Let us now turn to the other side of the dialectic — whether being situated in the capital city also guarantees exposure to the most important economic problems of the country. On the contrary, is not the capital a little far removed from the economic realities of the populace as a whole?

What can be so easily overlooked is that the capital city or indeed any major African city might, from the point of view of the economic realities of the country itself, be an ivory tower. A university within a big city might therefore be an ivory tower within an ivory tower. The bulk of the population continues to live in rural areas, in ways which might be incomprehensible to a university community unless a systematic attempt is made to understand them. The growth of a city may also give an exaggerated indication of the pace of change in the country. A few impressive buildings emerging, or a new highway in Lagos or Dakar, might afford visual evidence of structural development. Television and the newspapers in African urban centres might also give a sense of participation in the major events of the world and in the civilization of the twentieth century.

The poverty of the urban workers might also create a wrong impression about the degree of poverty in the country. In some countries the African urban worker is basically a member of the relatively privileged class. His style of life and his access to certain benefits, when compared with some of the villagers, indicate an upward rise in the style and quality of living. It may still be very modest by the standards of the business and political classes, but it may nevertheless constitute an important differential between the urban wage-earner and the petty peasant of the countryside.

However, here a warning ought to be sounded. It ought not to be taken too readily for granted that in every African country the rural sector is necessarily more hard pressed than the wage-earning nascent proletariat. There are levels of subsistence in the more fortunate and fertile areas of African countries which afford better nourishment than might be enjoyed by a struggling urban sector. And with the rising threat of general unemployment in many urban centres in Africa, it is not by any means clear that the subsistence sector would in every case be below the wage-earning sector in life-style and material wellbeing. But once we have noted this, the fact nevertheless remains that living in a capital city in an East African country could lead to a gross underestimation of the enormity of the economic difficulties confronting the country. It is such considerations which lead on to the conclusion that the big city itself is, at least in relation to these economic disparities, an ivory tower. And the university which finds itself exposed to the central political problems of the country by being in the big city, finds itself at the same time protected from the economic realities of the rest of the population.

Yet from the point of view of the students, the situation in the large city might conceivably provide a more balanced picture of the nation than would have been the case if the university were situated near a collection of villages further inland. The majority of students do themselves come from villages. And the majority of them go home during at least part of their vacations in the course of the year and resume their lives with their parents and families. For the students there is therefore some exposure to rural realities. And by coming to the city in search of their education they also enjoy the benefits of exposure to central political issues and to the relative sophistication of urban life. A university in a large city in a nation which is still overwhelmingly rural could, for the students that come to it, provide access to a more balanced interpretation of national life.

The movement of students from the villages to the university becomes in effect part of the more pervasive rural-urban continuum in African societies. Sociologists and social anthropologists have analysed this continuum in relation to the migration of labour, and the continuing links that migrants have with their home villages and the rural districts. But a dimension of the rural-urban continuum which has yet to be adequately studied is that which involves the movement of rural children to urban schools and rural youth to urban universities, and rural men to urban professions. The phenomenon of the trans-class man which I have discussed elsewhere, and which involves the anomaly of one person belonging to more than one social class, is seen again when the rural-urban continuum is professionalized and intellectualized.

But the question of whether a university should be deliberately constructed as an academic Brasilia, situated in the bushes of underdevelopment as one way of activating development, takes us to the heart of issues of relevance. How obsessed with the developmental imperative should an academic institution be? What nationalist, socialist or other visions should guide or animate higher education? We come back once again to those major issues of debate in Africa as the crisis of relevance continues to demand soul-searching and self-evaluation in campus after campus.

The State and the Scholar

From our analysis so far it is clear that the regional environment of an institution of higher learning cannot be adequately discussed without reference to the national situation. But the national context covers other issues apart from the physical location of the country's educational institutions. It is to these other national issues that we should now turn.

In places like Nigeria, Senegal, Sierra Leone, Ghana and Uganda, the oldest of the universities enjoyed for a while greater legitimacy than the new independent governments. Some of these educational institutions were older by forty years or longer than the governments. In Sierra Leone, Fourah Bay was older by over a hundred years than the reality of indigenous African government. This had consequences for the comparative legitimacy of the university as against the state. Many local people respected and accepted the university more fully than they sometimes respected or accepted their new political rulers. Consequently, politicians sometimes felt not only intellectually insecure in relation to the university, but also politically uneasy. This was one fundamental interaction between the university and its political environment.

A related interaction is between the university and the wider society. In this latter case the basic raison d'être of the university itself is at stake. How is the university to relate to the society it is supposed to serve? What criteria of service are to be invoked? What is the place of students in all this? We have touched upon some of these issues already. But in this chapter we focus especially on the tensions between governments and universities, between national policy and academic principles.

At the centre of this interaction is academic freedom itself. The elements which add up to academic freedom include relative freedom for universities and similar institutions to determine for themselves what they are going to teach; who is going to do the teaching and, to some extent, who is going to be taught. That involves autonomy to shape the curriculum and syllabus, relative freedom to recruit teachers, and some freedom to admit students by criteria chosen by universities. Then there is freedom for scholars to decide research priorities and research methods, to publish their research findings, and to publicize their intellectual positions. Finally, there is general freedom of expression for teachers and students as a necessary intellectual infra-structure for mental development and intellectual creativity.

I believe intellectual freedom in Africa is up against a dual tyranny. One — a domestic tyranny — the temptations of power facing those in authority at this particular stage of the history of our continent. This is the political tyranny of governments as yet insensitive to some of the needs of educational institutions. The other tyranny is to some extent external. It is the Eurocentrism of academic culture as we know it today. The degree to which the whole tradition of universities is so thoroughly saturated with European values, perspectives and orientations. The very institution of the university virtually became in our type of situation a mechanism of a transmission of European culture in non-European parts of the world. These then are two major tyrannies. Let us reflect on them, beginning with the domestic one.

We are already in the process of discovering that academic freedom needs other freedoms to flourish. Take a simple example. Some time ago I received an invitation to go to the universities of Capetown and Witwatersrand to give lectures. I was torn inside, because I do believe that there is a very strong case for the policy of isolating racist regimes in Southern Africa, at the diplomatic level, and if possible at other levels as well. But I also believe in the free circulation of ideas. Should my preference for the isolation of South Africa be my guiding principle or should, in fact, my preference for the free circulation of ideas be the imperative I should respond to? I wrote to South Africa — to my colleagues there — and said: 'I do not know yet whether I will come, but I have at least three minimal conditions. One — I should be able to say whatever I want. Secondly — I should be able to address racially mixed audiences and thirdly—I should be able to come with my wife if she is interested in coming.' It just so happens my wife is English. I added the last condition deliberately to test the system at its most sensitive point. Now the answer came. In most other societies if I had an invitation to go and I said I would be coming with my wife, of course at my own expense, no civilized societies would say: 'Oh no, you can't. Not with your wife surely!' But the reply came from South Africa. Of course, my colleagues at the universities were very sympathetic and were not responsible for the laws of the country, but their response was to this effect: 'We have been in constant consultation with our lawyers. That you should want to say whatever you want—we can risk it. That you should want to address racially mixed audiences we can virtually guarantee; but that you should want to come with your wife—I am afraid that is impossible. You would immediately be liable to prosecution upon arrival under the immorality laws and would therefore be subject at the very minimum to considerable embarrassment, and at the maximum to actual imprisonment. And we've checked—there is no way out.' My other two conditions, which might have perhaps been the conditions that other illiberal societies might have paid greater attention to, they were able to cope with. But South African society lacked freedom in the important area of individual choice, that of choosing the person one is going to link one's life to, as man and woman, as husband and wife. Because the society lacked that freedom—the freedom to marry across racial lines—clearly an important area of the academic freedom of Capetown University was compromised, and its ability to facilitate intellectual exchanges with scholars from other parts of Africa was considerably circumscribed. So it is clear that academic freedom cannot be regarded as a freedom that is an oasis independent of other freedoms, for it stands or falls to some extent in relation to the other freedoms that the society enjoys.

Within black Africa the dangers are of a different kind from the dangers of Southern Africa still under white control. You might say the tyranny in those societies in black Africa that are intolerant of academic freedom is sometimes derived from first, *the elder tradition*, secondly *the warrior tradition*, and thirdly *the sage tradition*, as they operate in the political systems of those societies. The elder tradition is heavily paternalist, almost by definition. It is particularly strong where you still have the original first president of an African state. The notion of a founding father with prerogatives not just in politics but in opinion-formation is a major component of the total political picture. The elder tradition also carries heavy preference for consensus in the family. The father figure expects that consensus and therefore has a profound distrust of dissent and dispute, even of the kind which is indispensable for a vigorous academic atmosphere. The elder tradition also has a preference for reverence and reaffirmation of loyalty towards political leaders, and that reverence and reaffirmation of loyalty is in turn sometimes hostile to the atmosphere of adequate intellectual independence.

Restlessness against the elder tradition is already evident in some countries, and in others it has already erupted. I was in Ethiopia in December 1973, a few months before the creeping coup started. I was invited to address the student body. An American colleague came to fetch me from my hotel. We arrived at the University. The students turned up, not just in their hundreds but in their thousands. The mass of humanity that was there was surprising for a professorial lecture. When I looked behind me my American colleague had disappeared. The students were singing political songs and he had apparently decided discretion was the better part of valour. I ploughed through this mass of humanity, arrived at the front platform. It was one of the loneliest arrivals of my career, because there was nobody there to meet me. I was bewildered, wondering what to do next, and then saw somebody else struggling to come across, accompanied by some others. It turned out he was my host — the professor of political science there. When he stood up on the platform to introduce me he was immediately shouted down. The students were insisting that the meeting had to be under their sponsorship, or it could not take place at all. My colleague asked me, 'What do you think?'. I said, 'If I were you I would let them preside'. He was worried, presumably about the impact of such a surrender on university opinion of him, but he did capitulate to the situation. What emerged in the course of that address, after the students had taken over the chair and given their speeches, was that these were the most radical African students I had ever addressed. They gave me a fair hearing, listening to me to the end, and after that asked questions deliberately intended to embroil me in their own profound and understandable dissatisfaction with the Ethiopian imperial system as they knew it. They would ask questions like: 'Don't you think professor, that this recent break with Israel by the Emperor is just a gimmick, when behind him American imperialism is still at work?' But question after question came. This was the most direct and most blunt critique of an African government I had ever heard from students anywhere. It is feasible that among the catalysts of radicalization in Ethiopia since then were in fact the students; the soldiers got radicalized partly in response to the students. The coup might have started with a lack of sense of direction on the part of the soldiers, but a sense of direction later emerged as a result of the continuous articulation and reaffirmation of radical policies that the student body was able to put across. If that thesis is correct, then the elder tradition of the Emperor in Ethiopia found its first major challenge from the student body in spite of considerable pressures against academic freedom in that situation.

Kenya has also had a form of restlessness of its own. There has been a heavy elder tradition in Kenya under Kenyatta. He is called Mzee, partly because of respect for his age, but in addition because the orientation of the system includes this elder-revering tendency with all its difficulties in situations where consensus is not achieved. The restlessness in Kenya has not been of the magnitude of student restlessness in Ethiopia, but it is there nevertheless. The restlessness in Kenya was for a while accompanied by the relative independence of the Parliament of that country. Kenya's Parliament was for long the freest Parliament in black Africa. The degree of openness and criticism over the years that was feasible within the Kenya Parliament was not equalled anywhere else in Africa. The report of the select committee concerning the murder of J. M. Kariuki in 1975 pointed a finger at the General Service Unit and its head, as being not merely guilty of covering up, but according to the accusations, conceivably implicated in the murder. The report also expressed reservations about the conduct of the head of the police. That kind of Parliamentary autonomy was not very easy to come by in much of the rest of Africa, but it was feasible in Kenya at that time. Parliamentary freedom in Kenya, along with the students' restlessness, were important catalysts in themselves towards moderating the elder tradition, and potentially towards changing the system in the direction of further tolerance for academic freedom in the years ahead.

The warrior tradition comes in when we are talking about soldiers in power. Its characteristic is not so much reverence, or consensus in the family, but a preference for action. 'We are a government of action', Idi Amin of Uganda would say, 'rather than words'. Now much of the exercise of academic freedom consists of words. Sometimes the words are good, sometimes not so good; but without the words the freedom would be useless. A profound distrust of words under a political system is a distrust of major areas of intellectual activity and certainly a distrust of academic freedom. This potential, or active, anti-intellectualism under the warrior tradition could at times erupt with disastrous consequences. There are times when the soldiers are overawed by the professors. There are other times when they are annoyed by the professorial phenomenon. If you are lucky, and they are overawed, then you as a professor receive reverence; but if things go wrong and the potential anti-intellectualism gets activated, then you had better duck while you can. I remember in a ceremony at Makerere in 1972 Amin was reading his speech and then he suddenly departed from the text, having seen me in the audience. He proceeded to pay a tribute to me in terms which amounted to an admiration of intellectual independence. 'I see Professor Mazrui there. I wish everybody was like him and not just self-seeking politicians. He can speak his mind.' It sounded fairly impressive coming from the warrior president. That evening I was at a party connected with the same ceremony. The Vice-Chancellor, Frank

Kalimuzo, said to me, perhaps unkindly: 'Today the President singled you out for a public tribute. Tomorrow he may single you out for something else.' It now sounds tragic because poor Kalimuzo was singled out for something else; he was taken away from his home and murdered. The murder of the Vice-chancellor was certainly one of the factors which resulted in my own re-examination of my position in Uganda. The warrior may be overawed by the professorial mystique, or the warrior may be annoyed. The professor, or the lecturer, or teacher, has to bear this ambivalence in mind in those African societies where the warrior tradition is at play. Finally, there is in the warrior tradition the element of discipline, partly derived from the military ethos and extended to some extent to the whole nation. This myth of discipline could compromise in a fairly serious way the universities as free institutions.

Let me conclude with a quick comment on the sage tradition. The sage as teacher — but not the teacher in the local school. Under this tradition the president is the ultimate teacher of the nation. A teacher becomes one who wants to make sure that his teachings prevail. Ideology as an exercise in transmitting ideas becomes a monopoly of the centre and an attempt is made to ensure that substantial responsiveness takes place to the ideas that emanate from that centre. Documentary radicalism is sometimes a feature in such African societies where the sage comes out with special pamphlets and charters to announce national directions. That is fair as far as it goes, but it is unfair when alternative schools of thought are not permitted an adequate opening in the totality of the system.

But it is not merely from over-zealous local politicians that academic freedom faces a threat. It is also from the heritage of western academic traditions themselves. Having moved from the regional to the national environment, we must now explore the international intellectual system itself.

African universities still remain instruments for the transmission of western culture, whether they were specifically intended to be so or not. The graduate produced from Makerere or Ibadan or Dakar is a human being who has moved substantially towards becoming a specimen of European tradition. All of us who have been educated at western-type universities, or who are currently at such universities, are at least on our way towards becoming substantially Europeanized. Many of us already are. Clearly academic freedom in the sense of substantial intellectual independence is seriously compromised in a situation where Africans are almost always intellectual followers and almost never intellectual leaders. If the purpose of academic freedom is in part to create conditions for intellectual creativity, that purpose is compromised by the heavy Eurocentrism of academic culture itself. We should, of course, remember that this is not just a peculiarity of academic culture.

Mankind is much nearer to a world culture today than it is to a world government. There are ideologies today that have world-wide believers, Marxism being a pre-eminent example. There are languages that serve the human race as a whole, English and French being particularly functional at the global level. There are legal and moral ideas which are supposed to govern relations among states world-wide; that is what international law is all about. Science and technology are facilitating cultural convergence as they are shared by societies otherwise vastly different from each other. Educational systems are increasingly resembling each other. The next generation of human kind is likely to be a little more culturally homogeneous than the last one. And there are problems which are just beginning to be perceived as global problems. They range from seasonal ones, like inflation, to perennial ones, like resource depletion.

But although we have been evolving a world culture, there is one hitch — that world culture is heavily Eurocentric. International law was born out of European diplomatic history and state system. The most global forms of imperialism were western, and therefore western culture in recent times has spread more widely than any other. If a world language is one which has at least one hundred million speakers, has been adopted by at least ten states as a national language, and has spread beyond its continent of birth, the most convincing candidates for the status of world languages are English and French, both western. The United Nations' charter itself emerged primarily out of western normative concerns and has been struggling ever since to be a little more global. Virtually all the ruling elites of the world are either western or westernized. Even those which are Marxist in orientation have opted for one particular school of western thought — a particular tradition of dissent in western civilization. Almost every educated person in the world has two cultures — his own and western. (If he is himself a westerner, his own culture will be a sub-section of the broader heritage.)

No one is surprised on seeing a Japanese man in western dress, or an African, an Arab, an Indian, or a Chinese man in western attire. But there is something incongruous about a Japanese in Arab dress, or an Indian in Yoruba attire, or a Zulu in an Indian *doti*. The elites of the non-western world imitate the West, but they seldom emulate each other.

From this analysis emerge two conclusions, one positive and the other negative. The positive conclusion is that the human race is indeed evolving a world culture — a potential foundation for the kind of normative consensus without which world reform is impossible. But the negative conclusion is that the world culture which has evolved so far is tragically out of balance — ignoring most of the civilizations of the world, and elevating only the western heritage.

Confronted with that kind of situation then, an African asks: 'How do we escape the tyranny of Eurocentrism? How do our universities become African and not just at best, approximations of western institutions?' The question really is also: 'How do we modernize without at the same time retaining a heavy dependency orientation? How do we modernize without being ipso facto in the process of westernizing ourselves?' In reality, no one has the right answers yet. Some progress is being made; the excesses of Eurocentrism in our universities are in the process of being mitigated. But there is no room for complacency. For years the only language that received any attention at Makerere University in Uganda, for example, was English. There then emerged some interest in French; so Makerere started teaching French. There then emerged some interest in German; and so German was offered. This was followed by a very weak and inconclusive interest in Russian, and that effort was made. In all this time, not a single African language was receiving academic attention either at the degree level or at the level of serious investigation and research. Clearly that was an illustration of excessive Eurocentrism and also a symptom of a wider malaise. The methodologies we follow, whether we are physicists, political scientists, or literary critics are western-derived. Our academic leaders are substantially people who have made breakthroughs in Europe and Europe's extensions — the New World, especially the United States — in that regard. Occasionally we say: 'OK, we are going to do it our way. We are going to take oral tradition seriously. We are going to use oral tradition as material for a new historiography. We are going to ignore the prescriptions previously imposed by Eurocentric historiography.' These are important steps. We have made progress in some of those domains, but at other times we take the easy way out. We are against Europe so we go Marxist. We forget that Marxism is simply another European tradition — a tradition of dissent indeed; a tradition of rebellion; a heresy within Europe, but still an intellectual tradition of Europe. In our groping for intellectual independence we end up embracing an alternative European source of ideas. This external tyranny of Eurocentrism may well be at least as obstinate as the domestic tyranny of African dictators. Both are likely to remain part of the general picture of academic life in Africa for much of the rest of this century. All that one can hope for is at least a realization that we are academic fellow travellers at best — followers basically. We must then resolve to produce academic leaders. And if our universities learn that lesson and proceed to create conditions which would make that possible, the external tyranny will in time be manageable.

Conclusion

These then are some of the elements we have to bear in mind as we assess the impact of environmental factors upon higher learning in Africa. The physical location of a university can be caught up in the dialectic between town and country in African conditions. A university can be at once at the centre of the country's political system, and yet decidedly on the periphery of its economic realities. A university's capacity to respond to the total national predicament could be reduced by the consequences of its precise regional location.

As for the area of linkage between the national and the international environments of higher education, this area lies in the shadow of the dual tyranny which hangs over African scholars, students and the universities to which they belong. The Eurocentrism we have inherited in our educational institutions is still with us. For the time being we seem unable to achieve a paradigmatic revolution in favour of greater intellectual autonomy.

But in addition to this external cultural tyranny there is also the domestic tyranny, basically political. In parts of Southern Africa, this is racist, and affects other domains of national life. In countries ruled by black men this sometimes takes the form of intolerance under the elder tradition; intolerance under the warrior tradition and intolerance under the sage tradition. I hope that Africa will be released from at least aspects of that predicament before the end of this century. Let us hope as we look into the future that Africa's creativity, the capacity to produce paradigms of its own, will result from a greater expression of intellectual independence. The infrastructure of genuine innovation is freedom for the mind. Our institutions of higher learning should find the will to transcend external dependency and the skills to survive domestic pressures, without forgetting the task of genuinely serving our societies.

15 The Political Functions of Higher Education

Perhaps the most fundamental political problems confronting African countries are reducible to two crises — the crisis of national integration and the crisis of political legitimacy. For our purposes, the crisis of integration may be seen as a problem of horizontal relationships. It arises because different groups of citizens do not as yet accept each other as fellow countrymen. The sense of a shared nationality has yet to be forged. Separatism in Quebec or Northern Ireland is a manifestation of a crisis of integration in Canada or the United Kingdom. It bears comparison with secessionist tendencies and ethnic cleavages in parts of Africa.

The crisis of legitimacy, on the other hand, is a problem of vertical relationships. It arises not because one citizen does not recognize another as a countryman, but because significant numbers of citizens are not convinced that their government has a right to rule them. Integration is a problem of neighbour against neighbour; legitimacy, a problem of the ruled against the rulers. A university in Africa has a role to play in contributing to national integration. But it is much more difficult to be sure what contribution a university can make to the consolidation of political legitimacy without risking some of the highest ideals of academic tradition.

Customary Law and National Integration

What is involved in national integration is often a process of cultural engineering, sometimes conscious, sometimes less so. Until recently, most African institutions of higher learning were singularly indifferent to African cultures. And yet processes like nationwide cultural convergence were an inescapable aspect of nation building. Different ethnic groups in a single country may need to find a new nationwide system of values in order to become a viable political community. This need not mean the elimination of subcultures, but the addition of a shared national stream.[1]

The earliest piece of African culture to be taken seriously by colonial regimes was African customary law. Most colonial regimes recognized that, to some extent, ordinary African individuals and families had to be governed with some reference to the values they understood. Most African colonies therefore combined European legal values, principally operating in criminal, and to some extent civil, cases, with customary African law, operating pre-eminently in matters such as marriage, divorce, inheritance and other civil issues. In effect there was a good deal of overlap between the operations of these two legal systems, but the main point for our analysis is that this was a situation where an indigenous universe of legal concepts and an imported universe of legal concepts co-existed with defined boundaries of operation.

What should be remembered is that what went under the name of African customary law was in fact a multiplicity of indigenous systems in each country. The traditions involved were essentially of a tribally exclusive type. It was not a question of the local legal universe being shared by all or most of the groups there. It was a question of highly sectionalized legal areas.

Different Commonwealth African countries have been seeking ways of integrating not only the imported system of law with the local ones, but initially the integration of the local sub-systems with each other. In Uganda in 1964, a commission had indeed undertaken the massive job of taking evidence from all groups on customary provisions on marriage, divorce, and the status of women. Kenya embarked on a similar exercise of accumulating evidence three years later. The object of the exercise has been, in part, to distil out of the multiplicity of tribally exclusive traditions something which could form the basis of a new nationally inclusive common tradition. The hope was to move to a situation in which Uganda law and Kenya law on these matters of marriage and the status of women (and, in the case of Kenya, inheritance) would rest on a new national base, bearing in mind some of the demands of modernization and of national homogeneity. New attitudes to marriage and divorce could let loose other important side effects — ranging from a transformation of marriage patterns to a revolution in the role of women in economic development.[2]

Legal integration of this kind is usually fraught with political difficulties. In the case of Uganda an extra difficulty was the absence of a Faculty of Law at Makerere, with research effectiveness great enough to discern areas of potential legal synthesis on the national scene. The study of customary law in Africa also demands anthropological perceptiveness. Makerere did have a department of sociology with some interest in the sociology and anthropology of law. But there was not enough manpower of both anthropological and legal expertise to be mobilized by the government should the government have decided on a determined policy of legal synthesis.

At the time of the first explorations into the problems of legal integration Kenya did not have a Faculty of Law in the University College of Nairobi either, although one has since been established.

The Kenya Government in its recent attempt to devise a national system on marriage, divorce and inheritance, has used some expertise of varied disciplinary kind. But there is no doubt that the exercise would have stood to gain if there had been in Nairobi a longer established base of legal and anthropological expertise relevant to the task in hand. Sometimes governments do not think of turning to universities for help in national integration simply because the relevant departments in universities have either not demonstrated their relevance or in any case are too weak to be effective for the job.

Total integration of the legal sub-systems within each multi-ethnic African country might be difficult to achieve, and perhaps be not even desirable. But the quest to reduce heterogeneity in matters basic to the lives of the majority of the people must surely be counted as an important feature of national integration. To that extent a university's involvement in this task of legal and customary homogenization is an involvement in the integrative aspects of political development itself. As in the case of merging tribal histories into a coherent national history, the case of legal integration in this sense is one of forging tribal regulators of social behaviour into a national pattern. We are once again in the realm of nationalizing what is sectional. One could cite other examples in the liberal arts, humanities, and the liberal professions, where national integration could be promoted by specific methodological approaches. A university then becomes part of the process of national development by helping to forge, gradually and critically, a new national intellectual culture.

The Ethnic Calculus versus Merit Criteria

But what people are being educated at the university? Which tribal or ethnic groups are going to share this new national intellectual culture? This is where it becomes important to be sure that universities produce an intellectual elite which is ethnically diversified. If there is something in the admissions procedures, or the general distribution of pre-university education, which results in the preponderance of certain tribes as students in the university as against others, there is a serious danger that the university's role in national integration might be compromised. High level manpower in Africa has to be tribally mixed if we are to avoid generating emotions which are nationally dangerous. Opportunities for university entry should therefore be equitably distributed as rapidly as possible between the different sub-groups, not only to ensure that parents within different tribal communities do not feel underprivileged as compared with parents in some other group, but also in order to ensure that the leaders of thought and policy formation who might emerge from a university are not produced on a basis of ethnic imbalance. Sometimes the job of rectifying the ethnic imbalance inherited from the colonial system cannot be accomplished in a year or two. The distribution of education might have been too drastically disproportionate during the colonial period to be immediately restored to equity on attainment of independence. But the problem has to be treated with sufficient urgency if it is to avert certain areas of political disequilibrium.

There was a time when we liked to think of educated Africans as being basically detribalized. But perhaps we should have made a distinction between detribalization and detraditionalization. Detribalization might therefore be defined as a process by which a person loses not only the customary mode of behaviour of the tribe but also any compelling loyalty towards it. But detraditionalization may only mean that a person has lost the sense of conforming to tribal ritual and tribal custom, but still retains an active or potentially active loyalty to his tribe.

Among the most radically detraditionalized of all Africans must presumably be included African academics at universities. But the universities of Ibadan and Lagos before the Nigerian coup of January 1966 were already feeling the internal tensions of conflicting ethnic loyalties between African academics themselves.

The University at Nairobi has at times experienced comparable difficulties. For quite a while the Luo as an ethnic group had produced more academics in East Africa than any other single community. This was not a simple matter of size, since there were other ethnic groups of comparable magnitude, like the Kikuyu or the Baganda. No sociological or socio-psychological study has yet been undertaken to explain the phenomenon of Luo disproportion in academic pursuits in the first decade of independence. Some might even say that it was in any case too early to see much significance in it, since the sample of East African scholars was still rather limited. But the simple fact that the Luo were numerically disproportionate as academics within the University at Nairobi was known to cause some tension. The situation was never as acute as it might have been at the University of Ibadan before the first Nigerian coup when there was a disproportionate Ibo presence in many categories of staff. But there is no doubt that at Nairobi, as was the case at Ibadan, even the most highly detraditionalized of all Africans, the scholars, were still capable of feeling the commanding pull of ethnic loyalties.

In the University at Nairobi, the problem of ethnic disproportion is less conspicuous than the Ibadan case before 1966, but ethnic factors are still significant in Nairobi. It is not clear how the problem can be handled without giving rise to other forms of injustice based on tribe. The criterion of merit is so much a part of the ethos of scholarship that to deny a Luo an appointment on the basis of his tribe would be a fundamental departure from this ethos. What might be less objectionable is the pursuit of ethnic balance in the distribution of good schools and educational facilities rather than in the process of recruitment of staff. One might therefore hope that a more equitable distribution of educational facilities in the country as a whole might, with determination, lead almost of its own accord to a situation of greater ethnic balance in recruitment as well.

In Uganda there is a comparable problem. Can an ethnic calculus be applied to redress occupational imbalance without the risk of incurring other forms of injustice? To discriminate against the Baganda in Uganda when they apply for jobs in government, or when they are available for consideration as judges, simply because they are already over-represented in those professions, does invite the danger of other forms of injustice — just as the temptation to discriminate against the Luo at the University in Nairobi when they applied for jobs as lecturers, and thus ignoring the principle of pure merit in employing them, carried the danger of ethnic victimization. The solution to ethnic disparities in Uganda as in Kenya lies more in improving the lot of the underprivileged than in discriminating against those already privileged. And yet the distinction is useful purely as a guide, and not as a precise measure. Some forms of helping the underprivileged imply discrimination against the privileged.

There are large areas where a difference in attitude could make all the difference in level of fairness. The primary-school results in Uganda from 1969 onwards showed an improved proportion of secondary-school places obtained by Northerners and a declining proportion by the Ganda. In fact, no one had manipulated the school system in order to ensure the seemingly happy result of redressing an imbalance in school places as between the two regions. There was little doubt that Buganda as a region had in previous years sent a bigger proportion of its primary-school products onwards to secondary schools than the Northern Regions had managed to do. Were the results from 1969 therefore to be interpreted as a fortunate reversal of trend in the direction of greater balance? The answer was surely dependent on whether what was happening was an improved standard of educational performance among Northerners or a declining level of performance by Buganda. It seemed to have been both factors, but the more important factor seemed to be a diminishing quality of primary-school education among the Ganda. Part of the problem was older than the 1966 crisis in which the Central Government of Uganda came into military conflict with the Regional Government of Buganda. But from that military confrontation in May 1966 onwards, the region of Buganda was under a State of Emergency, and there seemed to be a void in local leadership during that period. This seemed to have repercussions throughout the educational system, and especially at the primary-school level where the possibilities of mismanagement and commercial exploitation of the local desire for education were particularly marked. The shrinking of a few other areas of opportunity for the Ganda aggravated the tendency to experiment with new forms of occupation. The teaching profession seemed particularly attractive to those with a modicum of education, yet many of them were not educated enough. Primary education also tended to be much more regional in its orientation and less national than secondary education. This was not simply a case of administrative arrangements and local jurisdiction. It was also a case of the age of the children and the necessity in many cases for them to live near home and with their parents while attending day school. The fact that primary education was particularly vulnerable to variations in local conditions in individual districts made Buganda vulnerable to declining standards in that period. The 1969 results therefore made the Ganda fall below the Northerners in sheer eligibility for secondary-school advancement.

Linked to these trends, however, was the general push by both the Obote and Amin Governments to improve opportunities for Northerners in the face of competition from the Ganda. The performance of Ganda undergraduates at Makerere University, on the other hand, seemed to promise disproportionate potential for academic careers in the 1970s. This possibility of a concentration of Ganda in university jobs might be reinforced if opportunities for them in the civil service are reduced by the application of the ethnic calculus, and opportunities for them in business are reduced by the pro-Northern inclinations of both the Obote and the Amin regimes. Makerere might have to face in the days ahead problems not unlike those experienced by Ibadan in the old days of Ibo conspicuousness, nor unlike those which have sometimes introduced tension in the University at Nairobi. The problem of national integration is, in such situations, imported decisively into the university campus itself.

Political Stability and Academic Freedom

But even if the university has its own problems of ethnic cleavage, can it not help in promoting a sense of shared political order in the wider society? What is the university's role in promoting political legitimacy in the country? We have noted that in promoting national integration, or the capacity for people to identify with each other as compatriots and feel a sense of sharing a common nationality, the university can be effective in spite of its own problems. But it is far more difficult to assess what role a university can play in promoting the acceptance of authority patterns and government institutions.

In this case the university is confronting the old problem of 'political obligation' in political philosophy. It is the problem of why and when one obeys or ought to obey the government. Where political legitimacy is fully secure, the citizens do not question the government's right to govern, though they may question the wisdom of this or that government action. When it is not secure, challenges to authority may allow little differentiation between dissent, insubordination, rebellion and outright treason.

In traditional political theory, the problem of political obligation involves a shifting balance between the area of consent in government and the area of compulsion. The area of consent itself has different levels. To take Uganda as an example, one might note that there is a difference between consenting to being ruled by a particular government and consenting to this or that policy of that government. It is possible for an opponent of a particular African government to be in favour of this or that policy pursued by the regime. Thus there were many Ugandans outside Obote's party who supported his toughness against the Kingdom of Buganda although they would not vote for Obote in a general election. In this case they accepted the policy though, given a choice, they would not accept the government.

But even the idea of accepting a particular government, or consenting to be ruled by it has two levels. The more obvious level is in the sense of having voted for the particular ruling party in the last election. Yet there is a sense of course in which even an opposition party, in spite of being in opposition, consented to being ruled by the majority party. The very idea of a loyal opposition implies consenting to be ruled by the constitutional government in power, although reserving the right to disagree with almost every one of its policies. The problem in Africa in the first few years of independence was of trying to ensure that every opposition remained a loyal opposition. It was a quest for a situation in which one could challenge decisions of the government but not the government's right to execute them.

The distinction is a fundamental one but difficult to draw in day-to-day activities in a country. And that is one reason why the university's role in consolidating political legitimacy is so difficult. The problem here is one of forging consensus. Yet there are two levels of consensus. There is primary consensus, which concerns consensus on legitimate methods of policy-making and legitimate methods of implementation and legitimate government institutions. Then there is secondary consensus, which might merely mean consensus on specific individual policies this year, or consensus behind the popularity of a particular leader. It is not the business of a university on the whole to promote secondary consensus — to lend support to this policy or that leader. But it is the business of a university to help in promoting primary consensus, which is the basis of political legitimacy. The continuing problem is how this responsibility can be fulfilled without converting the university into a propaganda instrument to strengthen secondary political consensus instead.

The dilemma is a real one. The difference between a university and an ideological institute is, in a sense, a difference of degree. A university in Africa is in a way one of the most important precipitatory political institutions. And yet in its ethos of academic detachment it is at the same time supposed to be *apolitical*. Governments impatient for change might sometimes be tempted to say: 'In our present state of underdevelopment, we want commitment and not detachment, involved creativity rather than academic objectivity. An institution of such important political consequences cannot afford to be *apolitical* in its ethos.' And yet it is easier to say, 'universities must inculcate and promote national values' than to specify what these values are. What are the national values of East Africa? The days when we could talk glibly about East Africans having common ideals are perhaps over. Ideals now vary not only from one East African country to another, but sometimes also between one generation of East Africans and another.

The most important lesson of the last few years of Africa's history is that African countries are not yet sure where they want to go. The whole question of values and goals is in a state of flux. The business of a university is not to respond automatically to the latest policy declaration from the capital of the country in which it is situated. Nor need it make reckless use of the latitude which the late Tom Mboya gave it in his book — the 'freedom to analyse and expose government policies'.[3] What a university owes the government of the day is neither defiance nor subservience. It is intelligent co-operation.

In its capacity as a source of skills, the university's co-operation is normally a matter of straightforward discussions with the government. But in its capacity as a source of values, the university's role is more complicated. We have already mentioned the tendency of university education to deflate some of the values inculcated at school, and that to teach an undergraduate to be critical of the most cherished values is itself to inculcate a new value — the ultimate value of independent thinking. Can independent Africa do without independent thought? There have been cases of African leaders behaving as if national political independence could not be combined with individual intellectual independence. But at least within the precincts of the university, there are other leaders in Africa who have so far respected the academician's right to be sceptical without being subversive, sympathetic without being subservient.

In the state of flux in which political values in Africa now are, there is a need not only for nation-building but also for *norm*-building. A university in such a situation helps the growth of values best by controlled scepticism rather than by the 'inculcation of national values'. There are no such national values yet. They remain to be built. The starting point must be — to change the metaphor — a greater intellectual sobriety in East Africa. It is to this sobriety that the university might perhaps try to contribute. And primary consensus as an acceptance of new institutional patterns must, in a modern state, be born out of such intellectual awareness.

We might in fact divide politically decisive institutions into two broad categories. One is the category of primary political institutions. These are those institutions whose basic reason for existence is itself political. The more pre-eminent among these are political parties, the legislature, and the executive institutions of government. The second category of politically decisive institutions is the category of precipitatory institutions. These are not themselves directly political in their immediate purposes, but they could have an impact on politics far greater than that exerted by some of the primary political institutions. The military, for example, could — without taking over power — have greater political relevance than a political party. The army's basic reason for existence is less directly political than that of a party. In fact, the army is not normally a primary political institution in that sense. But it has considerable precipitatory potential — and could force major political decisions behind the scenes without actually taking over power. It could easily become politically more relevant than an opposition party. At times, behind the scenes, it could even be more decisive than the governing party itself. It might have been the fear of such massive influence on policy behind the scenes which made Eisenhower, on retiring from the presidency, warn his countrymen of the power of the military-industrial complex in the United States. This complex was, in our terms, becoming a precipitatory political institution of considerable consequence.

A university in Africa might be described as a precipitatory institution of a different but still decisive kind. While the pure sciences in our laboratories augment the riches of scholarship, and the applied sciences promote technological improvements and socio-economic welfare, the humanities have to grapple with problems of values and identity and are therefore the most directly connected with the process of political development. In the process of national integration a university may help to forge a shared sense of historical identity; or help to synthesize different aspects of ethnic heritage, or advise on the integration of local legal systems, or simply produce an ethnically mixed reservoir of high-level manpower. All these in their own way are contributions to the integrative process.

But in the solution of the crisis of legitimacy there might be, as we have indicated, a thin line separating the cause of creating primary consensus for long-term political institutions from the cause of creating secondary popularity for the particular regime in power at this moment in time. And the latter enterprise could easily transform the university into an extension of the public relations department of the Ministry of Information. In order to resolve the dilemma, the role of the African university in resolving the crisis of legitimacy should limit itself to the task of creating that climate of political and intellectual sophistication I have mentioned. When, therefore, a primary consensus does emerge in an African country in long-term support of particular government institutions, it will be a consensus solidly based on informed political awareness and intellectual sobriety.

Perhaps this is where the scientific method moves down from the realm of pure scholarship in the natural sciences to the arena of conflicting social values. A university even in the task of helping the nation to solve its ultimate political crises must somehow retain a point of contact with science as an attitude. Perhaps controlled scepticism is the most important contribution that the natural sciences have made to other areas of thought. Easy credulity is unscientific. Controlled scepticism is a combination of honest readiness to be convinced with a critical evaluation of the evidence. This is what science has contributed to rationality. And it is what the universities of Africa might, in a host of subtle ways, continue to contribute to the intellectual climate of the region they serve.

Perhaps that is the difference after all between a university and an ideological institute. In Ghana under Nkrumah the Kwame Nkrumah Ideological Institute was a primary political institution. In Kenya in 1964 to 1965 the Lumumba Institute was also a primary political institution. But a university in Africa must remain basically precipitatory—something which is contributing to major political changes in the countries it serves but not in itself a primary instrument of politics as such.[4]

The Science of Slogans

A university cannot afford to ignore the ideological rhetoric around it. The university may not propagate an ideology, but it has to take ideology seriously. Against the background of the crisis of relevance, this necessity to take ideology seriously has become greater than ever. Some political scientists have criticized others for writing articles or even books about African political thought when all they have to work with are eclectic African slogans.

First of all, it is not true that contemporary political thought in Africa consists only of eclectic slogans. There is a lot of political theorizing and philosophizing going on which is of profound intellectual worth even in the traditional sense of academic evaluation. But in any case from the point of view of the imperative of social involvement, the political slogan is often more important than the political concept. The place of rallies in the emerging political culture of Africa re-emphasizes the supremacy of the slogan over the concept. A slogan is after all an idea in social action.

The late Tom Mboya of Kenya once described political rallies in Africa as they might appear to outsiders. There was the huge crowd, streaming towards the stadium or an open piece of ground, sitting patiently for hours while a dozen politicians made their speeches. The speakers did not seem to make many new points—or, at least, for every new idea there was a good deal which everyone had heard often before. Mboya went on to describe how the speeches were frequently interrupted by the speaker calling on the crowd to repeat after him a series of slogans:

Uhuru—Uhuru!
Uhuru na Umoja—Uhura na Umoja!
Uhuru na Kenyatta—Uhuru na Kenyatta!

Mboya continued:

The crowd is good natured, it is true, and seems to look on it as a festive occasion. In fact, in front is a women's choir with bark cloth dresses and painted faces and a curious mixture of Western ornaments like dark glasses, and tin cans around their ankles. But what is the point of it all? It may help to boost the people's morale a bit, but don't they get bored after the first once or twice? And why do so many leaders spend so much time at these rallies? [5]

Yet the critical factor here is the factor of participation. A slogan was shouted out, and the crowd collectively responded. The stadium in which this was happening in Nairobi or Kampala was a modern stadium, and the microphone symbolized technology. The politics involved here were supposed to be the politics of modern institutions committed to arrangements which should befit a modern sovereign state. And yet as between the slogan from the microphone and the collective echo from the crowd in the stadium, there might lie a whole eternity of African ritual. As we indicated, politics in traditional Africa was often regarded as inseparable from other social and spiritual arrangements. The political rally, according to Mboya, looked in some way like a festive occasion with people turning up partly to enjoy themselves. The exchange of slogans across the amplifiers had even deeper ritual connotations, almost like a primeval prayer.

Then there is the sheer monotony of it all. There is something profoundly African about certain forms of monotony. The drumbeat, going on and on; the song with a persistent uniformity; the dance which culminates in an ecstatic trance, are all familiar features of African cultural experience. The negritude school was quick to perceive the centrality of monotony in African aesthetics. They regarded it as part of Africa's responsiveness to rhythm. Senghor quotes George Hardy who had written: 'The most civilised African, even in a dinner jacket, still quivers at the sound of a drum'. Senghor asserts that Hardy was right. That sense of the drum has affected African poetry as well. In the words of Senghor:

To blame Césaire and others for their rhythm, their monotony, that is, for their style, is to blame them for being Negroes, West Indian, or African, and not Frenchmen or Christians. It is to blame them for having remained themselves, irreducibly sincere. [6]

This African responsiveness to monotony and rhythm becomes an echo of the regularities of nature and the cosmos. Some of the most symbolic aspects of life and rebirth betray a rhythmic monotony — 'the beating of the heart, breathing, the rhythm of . . . making love, ebb and flow, succession of days and seasons and, in general, all the rhythms of the cosmos'.[7]

The repetitive chanting of slogans in Tononoka Stadium in Mombasa, with all its ritual monotony, might well be assessed against the background of rhythmic regularity within Africa's aesthetic experience. The slogan becomes more important than the concept because the slogan is more immediate to the regularities of nature and the rhythm of the African drum as well as being quite simply an idea in social action.

African scholars have therefore to take some of these slogans seriously. And sometimes out of the living ideas of slogans at political rallies African analysts find themselves constructing new philosophies. In a sense it is a reversal of Lord Keynes' chain of ideological transmission. Keynes once observed that the ideas of theoretical economists and political philosophers, both when they were right and when they were wrong, have often been known to enter the pool of popular beliefs and ideologies and to influence policy-makers in significant ways years after the philosophers have finished with that subject. Keynes said:

Practical men, who believe themselves to be quite exempt from intellectual influences, are usually the slaves of some defunct economist. Mad men in authority, who hear voices in the air, are distilling their frenzies from some academic scribbler of a few years back. I am sure that the power of vested interests is vastly exaggerated compared with the gradual encroachment of ideas. Not indeed, immediately, but after a certain interval, for in the field of economic and political philosophy there are not many who are influenced by new theories until they are 25 or 30 years of age, so that the ideas which civil servants and politicians and even agitators apply to current events are not likely to be the newest. But, soon or late, it is ideas, not vested interests, which are dangerous for good or evil.[8]

Keynes believed in the inter-relevance of economic theory and political philosophy. And he regarded both, at least when popularized, as great influences on policy and social behaviour. For Keynes the striking phenomenon was that out of economic theory and political philosophy gradually emerge the slogans and ideological assumptions of public policy. In Africa sometimes the offspring becomes the parent — out of the slogans of public policy can emerge new economic and political theories. The African scholars can play a critical role in reversing the Keynesian chain of ideological transmission. It is perhaps a case of putting Keynes the right side up on his feet, the way Marx put Hegel.

The slogan is, once again, an idea in social action. The theory should be born out of the action and not the other way around — again echoing Marx's reversal of Hegel. 'It is not the consciousness of men which determines their material being, but their material being which determines their consciousness.'[9]

Conclusion

In the new political theory syllabuses at many African universities, the ideas of black thinkers and African politicians are given a new prominent place. Nkrumah, Kenyatta, Fanon, Mboya, Senghor, Nyerere, Nasser, are all taken as serious subjects of academic analysis. Out of the utterances of men of action comes the raw material of academic philosophizing in some of these classes in the three colleges of East Africa.

As for the monotony of the slogan, it brings us back to a point of contact between nationalism, socialism and science in Africa. We pointed out that the monotonous chanting of slogans at public rallies is in a cultural tradition which includes the monotony of the drumbeat in Africa. What ought not to be overlooked is that monotony is also a characteristic of science and of socialism when it seeks to be scientific. Much of science proceeds by generalization, and generalization relies on regularity. In the philosophy of science the problem of causality has sometimes been defined in terms of David Hume's concept of 'constant conjunction'. The constancy of the conjunction has the monotony of the life cycle as well as of the drumbeat in Africa. Scientific laws are formulated on assumptions of the regularity and general predictability of nature, and sometimes of the cosmos as a whole. Socialism too shares assumptions of monotonous regularity. Certainly Marxism, with its cycle of thesis, antithesis and synthesis, reduces all history to the drumbeat of the dialectic. And the monotony of the class struggle, age after age, century after century, has the constancy of day following night. As for modern socialist precepts of planning, they too assume a tempo of relative regularity in the behaviour of economic phenomena. Without regularity we can never expect what happened before to happen again in similar circumstances. Without regularity linking past experience to future expectation, there can be no prediction, no projection, no prognosis. That is why the art of Africa, in its monotony, reflects nature, symbolizes science and shares a profound attribute with socialism. The slogan at a public rally, the drumbeat at the traditional dance, the experiment in the laboratory, and the new five-year plan, are all slowly merging into a new culture. And the African university is caught up in it all, groping for areas of relevance in this great social adventure of our time.

References and Notes

1. The author's theories of cultural convergence are discussed more fully in the author's two books *Cultural Engineering and Nation-Building in East Africa*, Northwestern University Press, Evanston, Illinois, 1972, and *A World Federation of Cultures: an African Perspective*, Free Press, New York, 1976.

2. Some of these issues are also discussed in Ali A. Mazrui, 'Nationalism, research, and the frontiers of significance', in *Discussion at Bellagio: the Political Alternatives of Development*, compiled and ed. K. H. Silver, The American University Field Staff, New York, 1964, pp. 161-3.

3. Tom Mboya, *Freedom and After*, André Deutsch, 1963, p. 104.

4. See also Ali A. Mazrui and Yash Tandon, 'The University of East Africa as a political institution', *Minerva*, **V**, 3 (1967).

5. Mboya, op. cit., pp. 62-3.

6. See Léopold Senghor, *Prose and Poetry*, ed. and trans. John Reed and Clive Wake, Oxford University Press, 1965, pp. 31, 94.

7. Ibid., p. 31.

8. John Maynard Keynes, *The General Theory of Employment, Interest and Money*, Macmillan, 1936.

9. Marx discusses this materialist conception of consciousness in a number of places, including *A Contribution to the Critique of Political Economy* (1859) and *Theses on Feuerbach* (1888).

PART FIVE

EDUCATION, DEPENDENCY AND LIBERATION

16 The African University as a Multinational Corporation

Many of the characteristics that have been attributed to *commercial* multinational corporations in Africa may apply also to *cultural* multinational corporations, of which university institutions are pre-eminent examples. Almost all African universities in the colonies started as overseas extensions of metropolitan institutions in Europe. Decisions on priorities for development had to respond to the orientations of the parent cultural corporations in Britain, France or Belgium. The cultural goods sold to a new African clientele did not necessarily bear relevance to the real needs of the African market. Skills were transferred without adequate consideration for their value in Africa; other skills were withheld because they did not conform to world criteria of 'excellence' as defined by the parent body.

In this chapter we shall first briefly trace the mode of cultural penetration which resulted in the emergence of the university as its most sophisticated achievement. We shall then raise questions concerning the nature of the cultural and intellectual dependency emanating from this external intrusion into the African universe. We shall then address ourselves to the slow but fundamental process of academic decolonization. After all, both African universities and multinational business in the continent face a fundamental problem—*how to decolonize the process of modernization without ending it*. An examination of African universities, partly on the basis of this analogy with business enterprises, should sharpen the areas of comparison between economic and cultural dependency, as well as between economic and cultural development.

The Imperial Genesis of the Multinationals

The most important factors behind Europe's imperial expansion could be put together in clusters—a cluster of economic motives and a cluster of cultural imperatives. The cluster of economic motives bears out some of the assumptions and theories which go back to Lenin and Hobson. Imperial expansion was in part a response to the emergence of monopoly capitalism in Europe. It was related to Europe's industrial growth, her need for raw materials for the new factories, her desire to create new overseas markets, her quest for new land needed for large-scale plantations of tropical products, her interest in the mineral wealth of distant countries. Industrial and commercial motives converged to create a compelling expansionist drive.

But some of the theorists within the tradition symbolized by Lenin and Hobson underestimated the related cluster of motives, primarily cultural in a broad sense. Notions of imperial greatness were themselves profoundly conditioned by ethnocentrism. And ethnocentrism is in the ultimate analysis a cultural phenomenon. The drive for prestige and international dignity could not all be reduced to considerations of the economic market-place. Cultural variables were at play in defining new roles for the ambitious and the proud. Although Joseph Schumpeter went to the other extreme and denied any causal connexion between imperialism and capitalism, he still fell short of giving due weight to cultural and ethnocentric factors. Carleton J. H. Hayes was a little nearer the mark when he said:

> Basically the new imperialism was a nationalistic phenomenon. It followed hard upon the national wars which created an all-powerful Germany and a united Italy, which carried Russia within sight of Constantinople, and which left England fearful and France eclipsed. It expressed a resulting psychological reaction, an ardent desire to maintain or recover national prestige. . . . Most simply, the sequence of imperialism after 1870 appears to have been, first, pleas for colonies on the ground of national prestige; second, getting them; third, disarming critics by economic argument; fourth, carrying this into effect and relating the results to the neo-mercantilism of tariff protection and social legislation at home.[1]

Images of ruling races and subordinate tribes, theories of social Darwinism, the whole legacy of the white man's burden, were important ingredients in the cultural cauldron of imperialism.

Then there was religious and secular evangelism. The religious side was for a while the more dominant, committed as it was to the spread of the Gospel, the expansion of Christendom. Christian missionaries in Europe constituted a major lobby behind Europe's imperialism. There were parts of Africa which perhaps might not have been colonized, or at any rate might have been colonized later, but for the pressure of missionary and religious groups in Britain and in France. The government of Britain under Gladstone was even veering toward the conviction that Her Majesty Queen Victoria had enough black subjects, but the missionaries felt that Jesus Christ did not have enough black followers. Uganda was annexed partly because of missionary pressure. Secular evangelism was tied to the notion of spreading western civilization, ending ignorance and 'barbarism' in Asia and Africa, and bringing the torch of European enlightenment to 'dark and backward societies'.

These two clusters of factors behind imperialism — the cultural and the economic clusters — changed over the decades. In the economic domain, expatriate business firms, foreign investment, and foreign settlers on productive agricultural land became the major instruments of penetration. In the cultural domain, the church and the school became the major agencies of intrusion.

By the late 1950s, each area was symbolized by a single phenomenon. Economic penetration had for its pre-eminent manifestation the multinational company, be it engaged in mining or cash crops, the importation of goods from outside or the export of colonial products. In the cultural domain, the pinnacle of the structure of dependency was the university, that institution which produced overwhelmingly the coming first generation of bureaucratic and political elites of post-colonial Africa, whose impact on the fortunes and destinies of their countries seemed at the time to be potentially incalculable. The university, like the British Broadcasting Corporation, was a cultural corporation with political and economic consequences. The multinational commercial company was an economic corporation with political and cultural consequences. There was a process of mutual reinforcement in the functions served by these corporate entities. What should be emphasized is simply that the university lay at the pinnacle of the structure of cultural dependency, and the multinational commercial enterprise at the pinnacle of the structure of economic dependency.[2]

But just as the African university has its genesis in European imperialism, so does the commercial multinational corporation. Some of the recent literature on such corporations seems to assume that such international entities are a new thing. But the East India Company was established in the reign of Queen Elizabeth I, and for many decades effectively ruled a substantial part of India before the crown took over directly. Elsewhere in the empire companies in search of natural resources and raw materials were created early.

> From about 1860 onwards manufacturing companies began to establish production facilities outside their own countries, and by 1914 many of today's giants were already operating in several countries. . . . International companies are certainly not a new phenomenon. . . . In the past the main impact of international companies, except in banking, insurance, and finance, was felt in the colonial and semi-colonial territories. The companies themselves were generally involved in trade, the running of public utilities, or the exploitation of raw materials through mining, plantation, and ranching ventures.[3]

In Africa mining — especially in the southern third of the continent — was internationalized from quite early. The gold rush of South Africa, the diamonds of Kimberley, the copper of Katanga and Northern Rhodesia, though each dominated by one western national enterprise, were soon linked to related enterprises across national frontiers.

Elsewhere in the continent the Imperial British East Africa Company held sway for a while. Kenya and Uganda seemed to be on the verge of being actually ruled by the company, in the old tradition of the East India Company. If such companies were not multinational, they were certainly multi-territorial. They had operations in two or three or more colonies, and their headquarters were in the European metropole. Because communications with that metropole were not as developed as they became in the second half of the twentieth century, these old international companies were not as centrally controlled as their modern counterparts. The Imperial British East Africa Company was establishing itself across the seas more than two generations before the full development of the international telephone and telecommunications complex of the period following the Second World War. In those older times there were no instant intercontinental telephone calls, no urgent cables, not even airletters. Centralization of commercial enterprises across continents was not feasible. But these companies were certainly precursors of such commercial octopuses of the future as Unilever, Lonrho, and Anglo-American.

But while the commercial multinational corporation as a phenomenon in Africa ante-dated the full establishment of colonial control in large parts of the continent, the African university as a cultural corporation took longer to evolve. Few policy-makers in Europe doubted that the commercial penetration of 'the virgin lands of Africa' was something 'positive'. Lord Lugard's vision of 'the Dual Mandate' in Africa legitimized the collective exploitation of Africa by Europe as a whole. He regarded the tropics as a 'heritage of mankind' and felt that 'neither, on the one hand, has the Suzerain Power a right to their exclusive exploitation nor, on the other hand, have the races which inhabit them a right to deny their bounties to those who need them'.[4] But the same Lugard who called for the commercial internationalization of Africa's resources was profoundly distrustful of western *cultural* penetration into Africa. He sought to protect Northern Nigeria from Christian missionary education, and was disturbed by the influence of the English language on 'the natives'. He argued that 'the premature teaching of English . . . inevitably leads to utter disrespect for British and native ideals alike, and to a de-nationalised and disorganised population'.[5]

Although some of the institutions in Africa which later became universities were established in the first two decades of the twentieth century or even earlier, actual elevation to university standard mostly came after the Second World War. There was also the anomaly that many of those among imperial policy-makers who wanted to ensure that universities were relevant to African needs and values, were in other respects regarded among the most conservative and least liberal of the time. Here an important difference arose in origins between the movement for higher education in British Africa and such a movement in French Africa. This difference in policy we have noted before in relation to other issues. British colonial policy was profoundly influenced by the doctrine of indirect rule, based substantially on Burkean principles of cultural relativism. Colonial subjects were to be ruled partly according to principles and partly through institutions which had grown up in those very societies themselves. What was at least aspired to was the dictum of Edmund Burke: 'Neither entirely nor all at once depart from antiquity . . . for people will never look forward to posterity who never look backward to their ancestors'.[6]

This kind of reasoning affected some of the initial ideas about the nature of all levels of education in British colonies from the eighteenth century onwards. And even when the movement for African universities gathered momentum in this century, it was possible for an official advisory committee to the British government to emphasize in a statement which became a White Paper in 1925: 'Education should be adapted to the mentality, aptitudes, occupations and traditions of the various peoples, conserving as far as possible all sound and healthy elements in the fabric of their social life'.[7] The committee included among its members Lord Lugard, the architect of the British policy of Indirect Rule in Africa and perhaps the greatest British administrator in the history of the continent.

In French Africa, within the educational domain, the policy of assimilation continued to hold sway even after it had declined in effectiveness in other areas of policy. There were fewer concessions to indigenous cultures and indigenous institutions in countries ruled by France than in those ruled by Britain. While schools in the British colonies used African languages in at least the first three years of primary education, schools in the French colonies continued to be supremely indifferent to the pedagogical case for the use of 'vernaculars'. As for Belgian educational policy for the colonies at the pre-university level, the emphasis on European culture was less than was evident in French policies, but the emphasis on *practical training* was greater than in either British or French policy.

Yet in the conception of a university, in the end the difference between British, Belgian and French policies narrowed considerably. In spite of all the cultural relativism of people like Lugard and James Currie (Currie had once been a director of education in the Sudan), the vision of an African university moved in the direction of creating an institution of higher education based overwhelmingly on the metropolitan country's standards and values. The Asquith Report, submitted to the British Government in 1945, provided a blueprint for higher education in the colonies. The basic assumption of the report was that a university system appropriate for Europeans could still be made to serve the needs of Nigerians, Ugandans and Jamaicans without a major transformation. The stage was set for a significant new level of intellectual penetration by the West into African cultures.

Structural and Organizational Dependency

Structurally, the new universities were for a while integrated with the metropolitan university system. On the whole they were overseas colleges, or official overseas extensions, of universities in Britain and France. Makerere College in Uganda, the University College at Ibadan in Nigeria, and the University College at Legon in Ghana were all overseas extensions of the University of London. They admitted students on the basis of requirements specified by the University of London; they appointed lecturers and professors partly through the good services of the Inter-university Council for Higher Education in London. The syllabuses needed London approval, though there was a good deal of consultation with the African branches. The examination questions at the end of each year were first formulated in the colleges in Africa, then submitted to London for criticism and revision, then some consultation might continue, before London finally approved them. The questions were then printed, put into envelopes, sealed, returned to their African campuses, and opened for the first time at the actual taking of examinations. There were times when changes which were not approved by the local campuses were discovered for the first time at the actual moment when students were taking the examinations, and could not be rectified.

I was involved in the department of political science at Makerere. When the department wanted to introduce Marx for the first time in a course on political philosophy at Makerere, the recommendation had to go to London. London questioned the assumption that Karl Marx was a political philosopher at all. Michael Oakeshott, the distinguished British political theorist, was involved in these negotiations. Oakeshott himself disputed the proposition that Marx was a political philosopher, but in the end he permitted Marx to be included in the syllabus. Not long after, I was teaching that particular course in political philosophy. I encouraged the students to pay particular attention to Marx and Lenin, since there might be more than two questions on Marxism in the final examination. I myself drafted the questions. Three out of a choice of twelve questions were on Marxism. The others ranged from Machiavelli to Rousseau, Hobbes to John Stuart Mill. On the day of the examination in Kampala I was serving as invigilator at my own examination. The parcel of printed examination papers, duly sealed, was delivered to me. It was a solemn occasion, breaking the seal at the time of the examination, and then distributing the papers to the nervous students waiting to see the direction of their fate in political philosophy. I looked at the paper. It was much shorter than the one I had submitted. There was only one question on Marxism. I tried not to betray the shock and anxiety I suddenly felt. I tried to look normal as I distributed the question papers. But in the eyes of some of the students I thought I detected a charge of betrayal. I had promised more than one question on Marxism, and they had given a lot of attention to that promise. Yet here was a paper with a much more restricted choice. According to the procedures of the examination, I could not explain to the students the background to the question papers. I could only complain later secretly to the chairman of my department. Much later we heard from London that the mistake was not really intended as an act of censorship, but had taken place in the printing house. We were assured that the deletion of the additional questions on Marxism was a printing error rather than a deliberate policy decision. Perhaps it was. But the whole experience of an African teacher formulating his examination for appoval by an external university thousands of miles away, and not seeing his questions again until they arrived in a sealed envelope too late for protest at the moment when the students were ready to take the exam, illustrated the low level of control that the teacher had over the course.

The answer scripts by the students were in turn put together, looked at provisionally by the teachers in Africa, but then despatched for authoritative grading in London. A period of waiting ensued, until London returned its verdict on the students in Kampala. Basically the same procedure was followed in the other overseas branches of the University of London, as well as at Fourah Bay College in Sierra Leone as an overseas extension of the University of Durham.

It is true that financially and organizationally these British African institutions were not as integrated with the metropolitan parent universities as the French African institutions were. Makerere and Ibadan were extensions of the University of London only in the manner in which their admission requirements were based on London's standards, their syllabus was London derived, and their degrees were awarded by the University of London. In addition, the lecturers and professors were appointed partly as a result of participation by an inter-university committee in England. The University of Dakar in Senegal, on the other hand, was more deeply integrated with the university system of France. French professors in Paris or Bordeaux could be transferred to teach in Dakar, and French students could spend time in Dakar as part of the same university structure and programme. The overwhelming number of professors at Dakar were indeed Frenchmen, who in turn could be reintegrated back into the French system as part of the same academic universe.

Louvanium University in Leopoldville (later Kinshasa) had a relationship to Louvain in Belgium somewhere between the less integrative formula of the British and the assimilationist assumptions of the French system. On the other hand, there were aspects of the curriculum in Louvanium which were ahead of both the British and the French systems. Zairean students studying at Louvanium from quite early had at least an introduction to African history and literature, African philosophy and psychology. This went further than what was available in the universities in British Africa. In addition, Louvanium offered an option in the Faculty of Philosophy and Letters under the heading of 'Philologies africaines' based substantially on the study of African languages and cultures. In other words, Louvanium was groping toward giving itself some degree of cultural relevance at an earlier stage than most of the other institutions in the African colonies. Belgium's aspiration to make all colonial education practically relevant, and her missionaries' desire to produce African clergy versed in African cultural ways, contributed towards cultural relevance at Louvanium.

On balance, however, the overriding educational goals of all the imperial powers included the desire to make more efficient use of the manpower available in the colonies for purposes defined and chosen primarily by the imperial powers themselves. All the colonial university colleges were mere reflections of the parent bodies in Europe. Like the commercial multinational corporations, they showed a faithful response to external decision-makers in the home countries. They responded to the local environment only within the boundaries permitted by the broader policies of the metropole. They had cultural goods to sell to a new African market—goods marked 'made in Europe'.

The Link between Cultural and Economic Dependency

What ought to be remembered is that a successful sale of cultural goods helps to expand the market for economic goods. This brings us to the direct links between cultural and economic dependency, and therefore between cultural and economic corporations.

During the colonial period the most immediate goal for western education in Africa was to produce culturally relevant manpower. But at least as important an enterprise was to expand a culturally-relevant market for western consumer goods, ranging from toothpaste to automobiles, from ready-made western shirts to canned tuna fish. The significance of an African university for commercial multinationals lay precisely in these two areas of producing manpower and of redefining the market through acculturation. Let us take each of these in turn.

In the earlier stages of the history of western education in Africa, it was the lower level manpower which was needed by the colonial administration and the expatriate companies. By the 1930s in much of British Africa young Africans with Cambridge School Certificates were in great demand for jobs as bank clerks, junior customs officials, assistants to managers in business firms, government administrators, police cadets, teachers, church novices and the like.

By the 1940s some of the companies with foresight were already looking for Africans to take on lower-level managerial roles, but the educational structure was not always keeping pace with these damands. When I completed secondary school in Mombasa, Kenya, in 1948, my headmaster (an Englishman) got me a job with a Dutch multinational corporation, Twentsche Overseas Trading Company. My Dutch employers wanted to train me with a view to making me a sub-manager in due course. But at that time I had no more than Cambridge School Certificate (Grade III). After experimenting with me for two months, my Dutch employers decided that I did not have enough of an educational foundation for rapid training as a sub-manager. Nor was I old enough to compensate with maturity and experience for this educational inadequacy. With apparent reluctance, the Dutch multinational sacked their young African protégé.

What this personal experience illustrated at that point in the history of colonial Kenya was a search among the more sensitive expatriate firms for culturally relevant indigenous manpower for at least sub-managerial roles. The required cultural relevance had to come from a western-based educational structure. The higher the position in the commercial company for which an African was needed, the higher the level of western education normally expected. Before long the highest managerial positions were to require the minimum of a bachelor's degree from the local university. The link between cultural and economic multinationals had by then become direct.

The importance of western education for western investment in Africa grew rather than declined with the growth of African nationalism. Western education had itself helped to stimulate local nationalism, as we shall indicate in the next section, and that same nationalism demanded the 'Africanization' of as many jobs and roles as possible within each enterprise. The history of American investment in Europe was being repeated in the Third World. American companies in Europe discovered early the advantages of employing local managers who understood the needs and sensibilities of the local market and who could serve as a protection against local hostilities:

The U.S. Westinghouse Airbrake was induced to establish manufacturing facilities in France because of stipulations in railway contracts that supplies had to be made locally. Edison built a plant in Germany because it found that 'national feeling' resulted in local supplies receiving preference over imports. In addition governments could in effect force importers to set up local plants by insisting that patents should be worked in order to maintain their validity.[8]

Tugendhat has even gone as far as to suggest that one of the important reasons for the growth of multinationals in the last thirty years of the nineteenth century was itself an aspect of the growth of nationalism within the receiving countries. Governments in different parts of the capitalist world and its appendages introduced tariffs in order to reduce imports of manufactured goods from elsewhere, and in order to foster the growth of their own industries. There were times when the tariffs were actually intended to encourage foreign companies to invest locally, instead of simply importing goods they had manufactured elsewhere. Canada was a classical case in this regard. The Canadian government wanted American companies to establish plants locally instead of supplying the Canadian market from across the border. An earlier version of Canadian nationalism had thus encouraged American investment in Canada—of which a later version of Canadian nationalism became understandably resentful.[9]

With the establishment of local plants came an increasing need for local manpower. Protectionism and nationalism could compel the multinationals to localize higher and higher levels of its staff. As the founder of the Lever Brothers, Lord Leverhulme, once put it in a somewhat exaggerated but suggestive manner:

> The question of erecting works in another country is dependent upon the tariff or duty. The amount of duties we pay on soap imported into Holland and Belgium is considerable, and it only requires that these shall rise to such a point that we could afford to pay a separate staff of managers with a separate plant to make soap to enable us to see our way to erect works in those countries.[10]

But while local personnel recruited for multinationals in Europe or North America are themselves products of the same western civilization (broadly defined), local personnel in Africa need to be partially de-Africanized in advance before they can become culturally-relevant for the multinationals. Hence the same western education which helped to create the new nationalism in Africa has to be called upon to meet the demands of that nationalism. The economic interests of the newly westernized Africans become interlinked with those of the multinationals at some levels. More and more jobs within the multinationals become accessible to the locals. More and more decision-making roles are Africanized. Increasingly the faces behind the managerial desks are local. Increasingly the boards of directors co-opt westernized locals to lend further legitimacy to their operations. What a Dutch company in Mombasa, Kenya, found hard to find as they scraped the cultural barrel in the 1940s, the same Dutch company now succeeds in obtaining more abundantly. The western educational instititutions of Africa have been doing part of their original work successfully—producing culturally-relevant manpower in order to consolidate economic dependency.

The second major area of linkage between cultural and commercial corporations concerns the expansion of the market for western consumer goods. Demand for such goods is, to some extent, culturally determined. The range includes toilet preparations, cosmetics, canned foodstuffs, furniture, wristwatches, soap, cassettes and tape-recorders, ready-made clothing, cigarettes, jam and marmalade, radio and television sets, detergents, lawn-mowers, automobiles, linens, and the like. Some of these goods are an outcome of modernization, but modernization is itself defined in terms of western culture.

Some of the consumer goods were locally produced, but many of the local products were themselves linked to wider multinational concerns. There were also African 'middle-countries' serving the role of middlemen in a regional context. Kenya has often attracted expatriate industries with an eye on the Eastern Africa market as a whole. Goods produced and packed in Kenya have then been exported to, say, Tanzania, Uganda, and more recently Zambia.

The growth of this market for western consumer goods partly depended on the spread of western tastes and life-styles. These were disseminated by a variety of devices, from advertisements to the western demonstration effect as revealed through magazines, films and direct example. But linked to all these other disseminative devices has been the solid core of educated and semi-educated Africans, at once followers of the West and leaders of their own societies in many areas of life.

Some aspects of African culture have reinforced the temptation to emulate and imitate the West. Most of western political and economic culture has been conditioned by the respect given to both political individualism and the profit motive. On the other hand, much of African political and economic culture has been influenced by social collectivism and the prestige motive. Precisely because traditional African society was so collective, the applause of kinsmen in the event of success assumed extra importance to balance the dreaded disapproval of those same kinsmen in case of failure. The conditions of a face-to-face traditional society, influenced by collectivist primordial solidarity, made conspicuous consumption a major method of acquiring prestige. This tendency was strengthened by the traditions of a society without the written word. Publicity as a way of acquiring social prestige could not be obtained through the gossip columns of mass-circulation newspapers and magazines. Fame needed to be spread by a combination of ostentation, large-scale patronage and social hospitality. This quest for prestige increased personal consumption, but it also served as a distributive device. Those who prospered needed to share their good fortune if their name was to become widely known in the villages. The money which in the West would have gone to public relations firms and to the entertainment of editors of relevant columns is thus 'diverted' in Africa and distributed more directly to neighbours.

As the 'European' way of life became part of the measure of social prestige, western consumer goods started to widen their culturally relevant market. In the words of J. Clyde Mitchell and A. L. Epstein in their analysis of social status among working Africans in colonial Zambia (then Northern Rhodesia): 'Success in achieving this "civilized" way of life is demonstrated conspicuously by the physical appurtenances of living. The most important of these is clothes, but personal jewellery (especially wrist-watches), furniture, and European-type foodstuffs are also important.'[11] The pace-setters in all this world of status and prestige were the more educated and more westernized Africans. Some of these later owned mines and not just jewellery, rode in a Mercedes-Benz and no longer on a bicycle, and drank imported liquor and mineral water from Europe and not merely imported foodstuffs.

Some of the more excessive luxuries now seen in Kenya, the Ivory Coast and Senegal may be a declining phenomenon. But there are other aspects of western styles of living which will not be relinquished too readily by the newly educated African elites. Those few leaders that are struggling to control the revolution in consumption patterns risk their own survival in so doing unless they combine these efforts with a revolution in education. Nyerere of Tanzania has been trying to do precisely that. He has appreciated the link between the nature of the personal economic ambition of a Tanzanian and the type of educational system the country has produced. A struggle to control certain aspirations of young people has therefore necessitated changes in the structure of formal socialization. And in order to reduce the widespread taste for western consumer goods, the educational system of Tanzania itself has in the long run to be drastically modified.

It is not clear if Tanzania's efforts to combine educational with economic reform will succeed in the face of considerable domestic and international difficulties. But changes in the University of Dar es Salaam, planned from 1975 onwards, were designed in part to change the type of manpower produced and in part to transform the type of values transmitted. These changes seem to include an assessment of motivation, and not merely intellectual competence, as a basis for admitting students to the University. Some of these new principles of admission were scheduled to be tried out with effect from the 1975-76 academic year. Planned manpower projections as a determinant of how many students are admitted to which courses have been operational for some time. Tanzania has succeeded in drastically reducing the role of commercial multinationals in the economic destiny of the country. Is Tanzania now effectively re-domesticating its cultural multinational, the University of Dar es Salaam? It is too early to predict the final outcome of Tanzania's experiments. What is clear is that a diagnosis has already been undertaken, and it seems to have grasped that there is a link between educational and economic dependency.

The question which now arises not only for Tanzania, but also for Africa as a whole, concerns the dynamics of liberation in the face of such dependency.

Political Liberation and Cultural Bondage

Here we must distinguish three forms of liberation—political, economic and cultural. Political liberation in our context refers to the decolonization process which resulted in sovereign political independence for African states. Today each African country celebrates a day of independence. But independence in this context is purely political. The heavy weight of economic and cultural domination persists. Economic liberation will come when African economies acquire greater autonomy, and when they establish adequate economic leverage on the international economic system as a whole. The economic autonomy will be achieved partly through reorienting African economies away from excessive reliance on the export market and towards greater exploitation of the domestic market, away from excessive reliance on foreign capital and capital-intensive projects and towards more efficient use of surplus labour, and away from indiscriminate importation of foreign goods and towards developing the kind of import-substitution which has genuine developmental consequences. As for cultural liberation, this would come in two stages. One is the stage of some degree of cultural revivalism, involving readiness to pay renewed homage to local traditions and incorporate those traditions into the educational system more systematically. The second stage of cultural liberation would have to consist of cultural innovation, entailing a process of synthesizing the old with the new, and then moving on in independent intellectual directions.

As we discussed earlier the African universities as constituted at birth generated an atmosphere of nationalist restlessness which culminated in a variety of independence movements in the different African colonies. It had happened before in India, as processes of westernization resulted in political assertiveness. In the words of Sir Eric Ashby:

> From the graduates of the universities the currents of nationalism flowed into the press and the people. . . . Africa has stretched the word 'nationalism' to cover new meanings. . . . It, too, was born in America and Britain: in the editorial room of the *African Interpreter* published by African students in the United States, at meetings of the West African Students' Union in London, in Paris cafés. Its sources of inspiration were Jefferson and Lincoln,

J. A. Hobson and the Fabians. It grew into a popular movement in the newspapers and election platforms and gaols of West Africa. [12]

But in his interpretation of the phenomenon in Africa, and perhaps even in his interpretation of India, Eric Ashby assumed too readily that political liberation went alongside cultural and intellectual liberation. He failed to realize that both the Indian and the African universities were capable of being at once mechanisms of political liberation and agencies of intellectual and cultural dependency.

On the Indian front, Ashby first traces the influence of university graduates on the currents of nationalism in the population as a whole, but then sees a return flow, as nationalism from the outside world made the universities 'adapt themselves to the indigenous intellectual climate, with renewed respect they turned back to their own culture'. In the African context too, Ashby saw a black African commitment to indigenous oral traditions and indigenous religions, to indigenous dance and music. On balance, Ashby mistook appearance for reality rhetoric for substance. University graduates in Africa have not been among the major cultural revivalists, nor have they shown either respect for indigenous political institutions or sympathy with indigenous belief systems and modes of entertainment and aesthetic experience. University graduates in Africa, precisely by being the most deeply westernized, were the most culturally dependent. The same educational institutions which produced nationalists eager to end colonial rule and establish African self-government were institutions which were insensitive to the indigenous cultural heritage.

Part of the problem lay precisely in the fact that the African universities were multinational corporations, with their headquarters outside Africa. The requirements of the Faculty of Philosophy and Letters at Louvanium University continued to insist that a Zairean child had to possess a *diplôme homologué d'humanités gréco-latines* as an admission requirement. In West Africa for quite a while no African language could be studied at university level, not even Arabic — but Greek, Latin, and the history of Greece and Rome were firmly placed in the mainstream of the humanities. When the University College at Ibadan in Nigeria was still in a special relationship with the University of London, there were seven one-subject honours schools. Three out of those seven were in classics. Some of the graduates emerging had specialized exclusively in Latin, Greek, and ancient history. [13] At Makerere University in Uganda to the present day no one can take a degree in a Ugandan language. Indeed, several years after independence, the only language taught at Makerere was English. French, German and Russian were introduced before any concrete action was taken towards teaching either an indigenous Ugandan language, or Swahili (widely understood in Uganda and throughout much of Eastern Africa), or Arabic, the most important language of the Nile Valley of which Uganda constitutes a part.

Since then, African linguistics has been introduced as a subject. Students can study the technicalities of Bantu linguistic structure, but the study of either African languages or African literature in indigenous languages is still at best an aspiration at Makerere rather than an accomplished development. What is astonishing is that so many black intellectuals and scholars continue to regard this lack of seriousness about African languages as justified. Recommendations about paying more attention to African languages, systematically building up their vocabularies for certain new areas of national life, and integrating them more fully into the educational system, have often encountered either silent scepticism among many black intellectuals and scholars or outright derision. There are of course a number of other black intellectuals and scholars who are aware of the anomalies of cultural dependency, and have been urging precisely these reforms. But among their most dedicated adversaries in this endeavour are fellow Africans, and not merely expatriate sceptics.

What had happened once again, as in the case of multinational economic corporations, was that a system of values had been distorted — and the metropole had been used as the ultimate reference point. As Irving Gershenberg once put it when discussing the impact of multinational banking corporations on economic change in Uganda:

> A very impressive feature of the relationship between the expatriate multi-national firm and the economically underdeveloped country is that the multi-national has been able to socialize the indigenous to the norms and values of the metropolitan center. What this means in practice is that Black Ugandans are taught to accept the notion that they should act and behave like well-bred Englishmen — these become their significant reference-groups.[14]

Also striking as an omission in the education systems of most African countries is the study of African music and musicology. This factor can all too easily be relegated to the ranks of the frivolous. But in fact dance and song in African societies continue to play a more important sociological role than they now play in the western world. Yet the decision as to which kind of subjects ought to be given priority in Africa is reached as a result of examining what is regarded as important in the western world, with special reference to the particular colonial power which ruled a particular African country. Since in Europe song and dance have substantially become domains of leisure rather than of work and productivity, except among the professional entertainers, educational institutions in Africa have on the whole treated African song and dance as if it were similarly divorced from the work place and the basic social system. To illustrate how important an omission this is in African conditions let us examine a little more fully the roles of dance and song in historical perspective.

The Economic Anthropology of Dance and Song

Dance and song in a highly oral society acquire significant functions in the processes of socialization of the young. Economic socialization is the process by which the young are taught the virtues necessary for the economic survival of the society, and the skills by which these virtues can be reconciled with the need to serve one's own immediate family and proximate kinsmen. Proverbs and songs become ways of enabling the young to memorize the lessons of social commitment and service, and remember with awe the hazards of disloyalty to kinsmen and ancestors. In large numbers of communities all over Africa song and dance are used as part of the process of socializing the young into the work habits of their villages.

> The children of the Chaga tribe [in Tanzania] perform a night-time dance called *shiganu*, which is used to intensify the oral instructions concerning the tribal standards of conduct. For instance, the lazy are spurned in this dance: 'Where were you when we broke the field with the digging stick?'[15]

The Chaga have other dances also intended to drive home the lessons of commitment and responsible conformity, and to deter the potential deviant. The *Iringi* dances, performed for celebration after harvest, circumcision and initiation, are also used simultaneously as functional equivalents of reading out the Riot Act in a British situation. Otto Raum's old account still captures the combination of awe and aesthetic experience.

> The skill with which the offence is gradually revealed can hardly be surpassed. How indelible the impression must be on those who with gyrating arms, clapping hands, and jumping feet emphasise every phrase! But how utterly unspeakable the agony of the child must be at whom the words are levelled![16]

In times of agricultural adversity song and dance are also used, partly as a method of boosting morale in the community, and sometimes as a method of prayer for happier times. While industrialized countries worry about inflation and recession, agricultural communities in villages worry about either floods or drought. Songs of fertility in the fields, songs of prayer for rain or for less water in the fields, serve functions of economic solidarity in situations where the need to share what is available is more compelling than ever. In situations of famine and drought there is always the danger of bitter jealousies and acrimony as families compete for meagre resources. Stealing from each other's storage holes can often become an irresistible drive. The communities need more than ever the constraints of their collective identity, and turn to the songs and dances not merely in quest of cheerfulness, and not merely in pursuit of morale under trying circumstances, but also in order to remain a community.

Europe's colonization of Africa resulted in the partial demise of African dancing patterns. As many schools were started by missionaries, their distrust of African dance had considerable consequences for educational history in African countries. Many outsiders regarded the dance as sexually suggestive and leaning towards sin and potential collective orgies. In the words of Judith Hanna:

> Christian missionaries, supported by European administrators who viewed African dance as licentious, bestial display within the 'civilized' Victorian standards of the nineteenth and early twentieth centuries, were probably most responsible for the modification, suppression, or disappearance of traditional dancing. . . . It was the manifestation of 'savage heathenism' and thus antagonistic to the 'true faith'. Unfortunately, many outsiders failed to recognize that most African dances had universal themes and origins comparable to European folk dances. Nor did they realize that dances involving much pelvic movement or upper torso shimming could be a glorification of fertility related to dire needs: abundant harvests in the face of threatening, uncontrollable natural elements and a large family necessary for work, protection, old age security and a manpower pool capable of replacing the many victims of infant mortality, war, disease, and other vagaries of nature.[17]

Schoolchildren were thus discouraged from experimenting with their own dancing heritage. The educated moved away from traditional dancing and were converted more and more into the imported varieties of ballroom dancing and later rock and roll and related modifications. Traditional African dancing — regarded by most Europeans as 'primitive' — lost the respect of the new westernized Africans.

The university as a pinnacle of this educational system reflected dramatically some of the prejudices of the earlier levels of the educational ladder. For so long there was little interest in African music and dance. Both the specialists in sociology and other social sciences and the specialists in the arts appeared to be supremely indifferent to this particular aspect of African experience. Since then there have been some changes in at least one or two African countries. The University of Ghana and the University of Dakar have led the way in giving African dance a new respectability. Nigerian academic life is also getting to be a little more sensitized to the value of this part of the African heritage. But the university systems in much of the rest of Africa have no provision at all for the study of African music or African musicology as an academic endeavour or even an educational commitment. And even in Ghana, Dakar and Nigeria the university structure does not as yet lend itself to an adequate integration of the sociology of African music and dance as part of the effective teaching programme. A fundamental feature of African cultural life is at best taken seriously only by departments of theatre arts at universities like Ife and Dar es Salaam, departments with only a handful of students, and therefore departments which are not reaching the bulk of the next generation of educated Africans.

In dance we have an illustration of an important aspect of indigenous culture neglected by local institutions. In dance we also have an instance of what was regarded as primitive by European rulers and educators, and came to be accepted as such by the newly acculturated Africans.

Towards Cultural Import-substitution

In the face of all these aspects of dependency, hard new thinking is required. Clearly the university as an institution is in Africa to stay. So is modernity in the sense of social awareness compatible with the present stage of human knowledge and a life-style adequately informed and served by the present stage of technological expertise. The process of modernization was certainly substantially aided by the establishment of western-type educational institutions in Africa, including the university itself. The question arises once again whether modernization can be decolonized without being destroyed.

To a large extent that is what development is all about. One could indeed define development in the Third World as modernization minus dependency. That is the challenging equation of the future of African societies. The tempo of change which should increasingly improve living standards, reduce infant mortality, curtail ignorance and disease, and enhance knowledge of man and his environment, is a tempo which imperialism helped to foster, and which deserves to survive under new conditions. But those aspects of modernization which reduce local autonomy, erode local self-confidence, undermine the capacity of the non-western world to contribute effectively to a genuinely shared world culture should progressively be eliminated. In time the concept of modernization should become increasingly distinct from the concept of westernization. It is because of these considerations that the process of development becomes an equation which subtracts dependency from modernization.

As in the case of commercial multinational corporations, universities have to re-examine what they import, and determine how far import-substitution is feasible if dependency is to be reduced. The business of universities focuses substantially on questions of skills and values. Which skills should more systematically be developed locally? Which values should get sustenance from the educational system?

Two concepts of *relevance* become pertinent — practical relevance and cultural relevance. The practical dimension focuses on issues of skills; the cultural is related to issues of values. In reality, the two dimensions are intimately intertwined, and have a large area of overlap. But it could make sense to distinguish them analytically.

Practical relevance in debates in African universities has concerned itself with whether or not the universities are producing the right numbers of educated personnel for the processes of economic and social development. Is there enough emphasis on producing people skilled in modern agriculture? Is the institution sensitized to the need for veterinarians for pastoral societies in the region? Is there more emphasis on Shakespeare than on rural development in the planning of the university? It is true that many of the African university institutions started more as liberal arts colleges than as training centres for developmentally oriented manpower. Makerere in Uganda had existed for more than forty years before the idea of teaching engineering, or forestry, or veterinary science began to be adequately considered. And when it was, Uganda for a while relied by special agreement on the sister institution in Nairobi, Kenya, for the training of Ugandans in this sphere. The University College of Ibadan was also slow in recognizing the need for engineering, economics, geology, public administration, or even teacher training at the university level. Yet Ibadan had from much earlier courses in Latin, Greek, Christian religious knowledge, and medieval European history. The University College did start teaching science quite early, but once again the focus was on pure science, rather than applied science and technology. The University College in Ghana similarly emphasized theoretical teaching and fundamental research as against developmentally relevant technological courses.

Part of the prejudice was inherited from the metropolitan powers themselves. Practical courses at university level were latecomers in much of Europe, and to the present day have often been placed in separate educational institutions. The universities were reserved for 'pure scholarship' and 'high intellectual culture' rather than practical training. In Nigeria it was not until Dr Nnamdi Azikiwe started the University of Nigeria at Nsukka that something approaching the land grant concept was at last translated into university policy in the country. In Ghana Kwame Nkrumah helped to promote Kumasi as a major centre of technological training in the country. Progress was being made, but much more often as a result of pressures from African governments than of initiatives from within the ranks of academic communities in Africa.

For as long as many of these skills had at best to be acquired outside, the issue of import-substitution in this particular domain had yet to be confronted. The countries imported more foreign experts than might have been necessary had the local institutions been relevantly oriented. This need for outsiders just accentuated the dependency syndrome.

In the wider society there is a continuing tendency to blame all African problems on outside forces and at the same time to seek solutions for all African problems from the outside. This trend, captured neatly by the Ugandan social philosopher, Okot p'Bitek, is a form of dual dependency:

> There is a growing tendency in Africa for people to believe that most of their ills are imported, that the real sources of our problems come from outside. We blame colonialists and imperialists and neo-colonialists; we blame Communists both from Moscow and Peking, and send their representatives packing. We blame the Americans and the CIA. . . . Another, but contradictory phenomenon is the belief that the solution to our social ills can be imported. Foreign 'experts' and peace-corps swarm the country like white ants. Economic 'advisers', military 'advisers' and security 'advisers' surround our leaders.[18]

Okot p'Bitek takes a reverse position, arguing that ultimately both the social ills of Africa and the ultimate solutions for those ills from now on are to be traced to domestic realities:

> I believe that most of our social ills are indigenous, that the primary sources of our problems are native. They are rooted in the social set-up, and most effective solutions cannot be imported, but must be the result of deliberate reorganization of the resources available for tackling specific issues.[19]

My own position lies somewhere between Okot p'Bitek and the trends he is criticizing. Many African problems are indeed indigenous, but there are others which have been created in part by external forces. Some solutions to those African problems need external co-operation or changes in the total world environment, but many solutions could be found from within as a result of what Okot p'Bitek calls 'deliberate reoganization of the resources available for tackling specific issues'.

The worst form of dependency is indeed the dual dependency that blames all misfortunes on external forces and seeks all solutions from outside. But as between blaming ills on external forces and seeking solutions entirely from outside, the latter is a worse form of dependency. If the human psyche had to choose it would be better to blame one's ills on others and yet take concrete action oneself to deal with the situation, rather than accept responsibility for one's ills and look to the outside world for rescue. The worst form of dependency is not the denial of original sin but the refusal to accept personal responsibility for one's own ultimate salvation. The long delays in transforming the educational system in a manner which would enable African societies to take a greater part in solving their own problems has certainly been one of the more obstinate aspects of this particular dimension of dependency.

Also connected with the problem of forging practical relevance is the issue of what kind of emphasis is given in the practical departments and faculties which have already been established. What should a medical school aim to produce, for example? A distinguished professor of medicine, Professor Graham Bull from Britain, captured the problem astutely in a medical journal of West Africa in the year of Nigeria's independence:

> Expenditure should be mainly in the field of public health. Curative medicine is a luxury which must be dispensed very sparingly. . . . Public opinion is sufficiently ill-informed to prefer a hospital to a piped water supply, although the latter will probably save ten times as many lives. . . . British and American medical schools do not provide a suitable curriculum for doctors who are to work in Nigeria and other tropical countries. . . . I was disappointed to find that University College, Ibadan, follows the British system very closely. The training it provides is as good as anywhere in Britain, but it is of the wrong sort. I believe that emphasis on preventive medicine should be very much greater. There is an opportunity here to develop a new approach to medicine which will be unique in providing an example for other developing countries to follow.[20]

Since then medical schools in African universities have indeed developed departments of preventive medicine, but they have not given this particular branch of the profession as much emphasis and support as might be ideal in African conditions. Preventive medicine becomes one out of a dozen or more departments, each jealous of its separate identity, though capable of collaborating in certain areas. A good deal of sound research on tropical diseases does take place, but the promotion of preventive medicine as an academic endeavour is much weaker than African circumstances should dictate.

Then there is the question of whether African medical schools should produce only the type of doctors that could get employment anywhere in the world. Should there be an attempt to have medical training of a more limited duration, designed to produce moderately qualified medical practitioners for large numbers of rural clinics? Again, most African universities have been reluctant to erode their standards. Even the idea of two different types of medical degree is having considerable resistance from universities which range from the University of Zambia in Lusaka to the University of Zaire in Kinshasa.

As for schools of engineering or faculties of technology, there is still a marked lack of interest in the whole phenomenon of intermediate technology. Experiments in using simpler technologies for rural development have been undertaken in societies which range from Mexico to China. Greater exploration of what has been done, systematic research into intermediate technology as a partial answer to some of the more pressing technical problems in rural and urban areas in Africa, could effectively enhance the levels of practical relevance of educational institutions in the continent. But once again, the compulsion to imitate the metropolitan model has been too great for many policy-makers in the African continent.

As for cultural relevance, performance here has at times been even more deficient than in the field of practical relevance. We have already referred to the insensitivity to African languages and the lack of interest in African musicology, dance, song, and even the wider domain of oral tradition. Progress has been made in selective areas. Most African historians now are at least committed to the proposition that oral traditions are proper material for historical reconstructions, and could be regarded in some ways as no less valid than written documents. One historian after another has proceeded to interpret the African past in spite of the lack of written documentary evidence, using instead linguistic evidence, oral tradition, and archaeological findings in a manner which has introduced important new breakthroughs in African historiography. Departments of history in Africa might be leading the way in breaking the stranglehold of intellectual dependency. Western historians working on Africa have in turn shown a responsiveness to these developments, and some of them have themselves made substantial contributions in the new domain of oral history.[21] Departments of literature have also begun to look at oral literature, but their performance in this respect is less impressive than that of departments of history.

As for subjects such as economics, political science, sociology and related fields, there have been changes in what is studied but not in how it is studied. More and more courses on Africa and on development economics are introduced, but there have been few methodological innovations comparable to the use of oral tradition in historiography. Sometimes the furthest that academic reformers in economics and political science will go is to substitute Marxist approaches to political and economic analysis, instead of the standard western techniques. Yet Marxist approaches to the study of African societies, though often adding new perspectives, must nevertheless be regarded as a form of residual intellectual dependency when they are invoked by African scholars. Unless an African scholar dramatically transforms the nature of a Marxist analysis for the understanding of African societies, he has not moved much further along the path of cultural import-substitution. The cultural packages in economics and political science, more so than in history and literature, continue to bear the label 'made in the western world'.[22]

In the face of this inadequate performance in the domain of cultural import-substitution and assertion of local effectiveness, what recommendations might one make for potentially more responsive policy-makers in the future? How is modernization to be decolonized without terminating it? It is to such questions that we must now turn.

Development: the Strategy of Domestication

If development for Africa is the decolonization of modernity, then three major strategies are needed for African development — two of them capable of rapid implementation, and the third for slower but sustained operationalization.

From the specific perspective of this chapter, the first strategy concerns the domestication of modernity, a bid to relate it more firmly to local cultural and economic needs. The second strategy is paradoxical. It involves the wider diversification of the cultural content of modernity. Under this approach the foreign reference-group for an African institution becomes not only the West but also other non-African civilizations. The African university is thus to be transformed from a multinational to a multicultural corporation. The third strategy is perhaps the most ambitious. It concerns an attempt by the African continent as a whole to counter-penetrate western civilization itself. Let us consider each of these strategies, beginning with the imperative of domestication in relation to education.

Until now there has been no doubt that African educational systems have entered deeply into the life-styles of local societies, for better or for worse. In the very process of producing educated manpower, creating new forms of stratification, accelerating westernization and modernization, African educational institutions have been major instruments through which the western world has affected and changed the African universe. Universities were virtually defined as institutions for the promotion of western civilization, at least de facto. The institutions below university level were different stages of the same grand process.

In order to shift this balance, African societies must more systematically be allowed to influence fundamentally the educational systems themselves. It is not enough for an African university to send a travelling theatre to perform a play by Shakespeare or even by the Nigerian playwright, Wole Soyinka, before rural audiences in different villages. This type of endeavour is indeed required, and helps to deepen the life experiences of folk communities in the villages. But the travelling theatre of a university like Makerere is one more form of academic impact on the wider society. It does not by itself constitute a reverse flow of influence.

Similarly, extra-mural departments and even extension services are valued methods of increasing skills and expanding social awareness among rural communities. Like a number of other professors at Makerere University in Uganda I travelled many miles on hard roads to address village schools and village assemblies on the implications of public policies in Uganda and the nature of the political system of the country. That kind of commitment was indeed a way of reaching out to the isolated groups of the African countryside. But once again it was much less an exercise in being affected by the society than an exercise in reaching the society. The social impact was still one-sided.

The first task then toward decolonizing modernity is to enable the influence of the local society to balance that of the western reference group on the dynamics of policy-making and academic vision within the universities. But in concrete terms how is this process to be realized? In order to enable African societies to domesticate the educational systems, four major areas have to be re-examined. These are the requirements for admission of students, the content of courses throughout the educational system, the criteria for recruitment of teachers and other staff, and the general structure of the educational systems.

University admission requirements should be reformed in the direction of giving new weight to certain subjects of indigenous relevance. Social and cultural anthropology ought to become a secondary-school subject, rigorously examinable, and required for entry to university. This should hopefully promote considerably more interest in African cultures in primary and secondary school than is currently the case. Secondly, admission to a university should include a requirement for a pass in a university entry examination in an African language. There were times when many African universities required some competence even in Latin for entry into some faculties; the African university of the future should require competence, formally demonstrated in an examination, of at least one African language regardless of the subject that the student proposes to engage in once admitted.

African dance and music should be given a new legitimacy in all secondary and primary schools, regardless of the sensitivities of the missionary authorities in power. In some societies African dance and music are much more fundamental than games and sports are in British schools. Dance and music should certainly be given equal weight with soccer and athletics in African schools. Investigation should be undertaken into whether dance and music should be competitive, and in what way the ethnic diversity of musicological experience can be made creative rather than disruptive in an African school. These problems are far from insurmountable, and could add a new richness to African aesthetic experience alongside the imported world of sports and athletics.

Progress has already been made in the teaching of African history and African literature. Further progress can be made, including more effective use of oral literature, duly transcribed, as an introduction to the pre-literature aesthetic creativity of African societies.

Such reforms of entry requirements at the university level would, as indicated here, have consequences for the content of education at the sub-university level. The university in turn should re-examine the content of its courses in the different fields, guided in part by permitting indigenous culture to penetrate more into the university, and in part by permitting non-western alien contributions to find a hearing. The quest to convert the multinational into a multicultural corporation has to be pursued with vigour.

Recruitment of faculty will in turn be affected by these considerations. Must all teachers at an African university have formal degrees from western or western-type educational institutions? Or should there be areas of expertise where lecturers or even professors could be appointed without the persistent degree requirement so characteristic of western institutions? Okot p'Bitek was again apt in comparing the recruitment requirements for a university with the electoral requirements for an African parliament. [23] African parliaments have on the whole insisted on competence in either English or French before an African could become a member. A candidate could speak ten African languages, and still be ineligible for membership of parliament if he did not speak the imported metropolitan language. Conversely, a candidate could speak only English or French, and speak no African language, not even the language of his immediate constituents, and he could still be eligible for membership of parliament.

The question arises as to whether there are, for example, specialists of oral history in African societies who can be appointed fully on university academic staffs, and enabled to bear the titles of lecturer, senior lecturer, reader, or professor without having a formal degree. Presumably this might be difficult if these oral historians are completely oral, and are unable to read or write. A compromise situation would be one in which only those oral historians who can in addition read and write might be regarded as eligible. Admittedly, the literary skills are still a departure from ancestral ways in many African societies, but the very readiness to acknowledge competence regardless of formal western-type degrees would be a revolutionary endeavour in African university institutions.

A related area is that of African languages. There are specialists of African languages, who know not only how to use an African language, but also how the language behaves. Some of these constitute superb teachers at university level. I know of at least one, a Kenyan, who spent many years in an American university, teaching Swahili with a sophistication unmatched by many of those who have actual degrees in the subject and in Bantu linguistics. Yet in the United States he could never hope to have a proper tenure appointment, or even a formal rank, since he did not possess a degree. He recently returned to Kenya. The university of his country would not employ him either at that rank without a degree. Yet the same university would be quite capable of appointing a distinguished British Swahilist from the London School of Oriental and African Studies, with a less intimate knowledge of certain African languages than the Kenyan had already proved over several decades.

What all this means is that there is a case for broadening the criteria of recruiting academic staff to include both formal degrees and, where appropriate, indigenous traditional skills adequately demonstrated and capable of being effectively used in either classroom situations or research situations at university level. Clearly there is here a hybrid of cultures at play, and staff recruitment could reflect this dualism.

Departments of sociology could have indigenous specialists in oral traditions; departments and faculties of medicine and preventive medicine could include attention to indigenous herbs, and might even examine the medical implications of sorcery and witchcraft as part of the general training of a rural doctor in Africa. Departments of history, literature, musicology, philosophy, and religious studies could all allow for the possibility of recruiting skills on a different set of criteria from the standard ones which have been honoured in western institutions.

But in addition to all these reforms encompassing student admission requirements, curricula, and faculty recruitment, there must be the broader structural transformation which relates general societal needs to the educational system, reduces the tendency towards a pyramidal educational structure with the university at the top, and with everything below that being no more than a stage toward the pinnacle. Major changes involving a diversification of the content of the curricula of each institution are what the entire agony of the African predicament is crying for.

At the university level, should studies continue to be organized according to traditional western disciplinary categories? Or is there a case for having on one side a school of rural studies, encompassing agriculture, anthropology, preventive medicine in rural conditions, and the like, and on the other side a school of urban studies, sensitized also to the rural-urban continuum, labour migration, ethnic associations, criminology and relevant preventive medicine? These are possibilities that could be considered and explored. Other possible schools could include a school of oral tradition and historiography, a school of languages and oral literature, and a school of religion and witchcraft. These are simply illustrations of potential alternative organizations which could be explored.

What would underlie all these reforms is a form of relevance domestically defined, and relating to both the economic and cultural needs of the society as a whole.

Development: the Strategy of Diversification

The second strategy of development is that of diversifying the cultural content of modernity. This approach partly rests on the assumption that just as economically it is a greater risk to be dependent on only one country than on many, so in culture one foreign benefactor is more constraining than many. To be owned by one person is outright slavery; but to be owned by many masters, who can be played against each other, may be the beginning of freedom. In culture, reliance on one external reference-group is outright dependency. Reliance on a diversity of external civilizations may be the beginning of autonomous creativity.

From the educational perspective of this chapter the African university has to move from being a multinational corporation. From what we have discussed, it is clear that in spite of the fact that African university systems have grown with either structural or other links to metropolitan universities in Europe and North America, in reality the nature of the African university has continued to be heavily uni-cultural. It has been, as we indicated repeatedly, more a manifestation of western culture in an African situation than an outgrowth of African culture itself.

For as long as the African university remained a multinational corporation in this sense, it denied itself the wealth of its own society to a large extent. But in order to become fully a multicultural corporation it is not enough to combine African traditions with the western heritage. It becomes more important than ever that African universities should take seriously the cultures and experiments of other civilizations. The educational system should not simply talk about European history, combined increasingly with African history, but should in addition pay attention to Indian civilization, Chinese civilizations and, most immediate of all in the African situation, Islamic civilizations. Although Arabic is the most widely spoken language in the African continent, the language has received very little concrete acknowledgement in the educational syllabuses of Africa south of the Sahara. It has not even received such acknowledgement from countries bordering Arabic-speaking areas, or countries with large numbers of Muslims among their own citizens. Nigeria has millions of Muslims in its population, and borders countries with millions more, and yet Nigeria's university systems responded earlier to Latin and Greek than to Arabic studies. As for Chinese studies, there is at most an interest in Mao Tse-tung in political science departments these days, but still no interest in Confucius as a more distinctive Chinese phenomenon. The fact that Mao Tse-tung is busy denouncing Confucius is no reason why Africans should not study Confucius, alongside their study of Thomas Jefferson and John Locke.

Mao's China has things to say not only about ideology and economic organization, but also about intermediate technology, intermediate medicine, and new methods of agriculture. A conscious effort to learn more about what is done in China, and attempting to see how much of it is relevant for African needs, could itself help to add technical richness to cultural pluralism. The range of potentially relevant examples is from intermediate mechanization of agriculture to the fine arts, from political philosophy to such traditional medical practices as acupuncture.

A multicultural corporation requires not only a revival of interest in African indigenous traditions, but also a cultural diversification of the foreign component in African curricula. A twin process is then under way. One process is increased Africanization, as the society is permitted to reciprocate the impact of the university; the other process is increased internationalization as the foreign component ceases to be Eurocentric and pays attention to other ingredients in the total human heritage.

An important subject which should be introduced into African secondary schools is the history of science. It is possible that the dependency complex among young African schoolchildren partly arises out of their being overwhelmed by western science. The prestige of the western world, in a continent which is very conscious of the power of prestige, derives disproportionately from western leadership in science and technology. But so great has that leadership been in the last three hundred years that westernism and science are sometimes almost interchangeable in the perception of some young Africans.

In reaction to this western scientific pre-eminence, some Africans have sought refuge in negritude as a glorification of a non-scientific civilization. As noted earlier, Léopold Senghor has defined negritude as 'the sum of African cultural values' informed by their '*emotive attitude* toward the world'.[24] Also dazzled and lured by scientism, other Africans have sought answers in Marxism — partly because it seems to offer Africans the chance of rebelling against the West without ceasing to be scientific. After all, was not the Marxist heritage a scientific critique of the West? These two categories of Africans symbolize wider forces at work in Africa. The negritudist rebels against the scientific West by idealizing his own heritage; the African Marxist rebels against the West by embracing an alternative scientism.

Léopold Senghor, a cultural nationalist, has been denounced by some African radicals as an intellectual primitivist who has tried to reduce African modes of knowledge to pure emotion and has turned the history of Africa into the story of the noble savage. President Senghor has responded to such attacks with similar vigour:

> Young African intellectuals who have read Marx carelessly and who are still not altogether cured of the inferiority complex given them by the colonizers . . . must have read what I have written as carelessly as they had already read the scientific socialists.[25]

Senghor proceeds to deny that he has deprived the African of the capacity to reason and technologically innovate:

> It is a fact that there is a white European civilization and a black African civilization. The question is to explain their differences and the reasons for these differences, which my opponents have not

yet done. I can refer them back to their authorities. 'Reason has always existed,' wrote Marx to Arnold Ruge, 'but not always under the rational form'.[26]

He then quotes Engels, whom he regards as even more explicit on this question in his work 'preparatory to the *Anti-Duhring*':

> Two kinds of experience . . . one exterior, material; the other, interior; laws of thought and forms of thinking. Forms of thinking also partly transmitted by heredity. A mathematical axiom is self-evident to a European, but not to a Bushman or an Australian aboriginal.[27]

This debate between African cultural nationalists and African scientific socialists is likely to continue for the rest of this century. What the two groups have in common is a rebellion against the West and the inferiority complex which had been created by western scientific pre-eminence.

The curriculum in African schools should at some stage reflect these disagreements. But at least as fundamental as the question of whether African culture was traditionally scientific or whether Marxism is a science is the issue of how much western science owes to other civilizations. From the Indus Valley to ancient Egypt, from imperial China to medieval Islam, the West has found intellectual and scientific benefactors over the centuries. As matters now stand, very little of this is communicated to young children in schools in Africa. The cultural pluralism which lies behind the scientific heritage is lost to these young minds, as they continue to be dazzled at a formative period by western civilization on its own. The sense of awe towards the West becomes a foundation for subsequent intellectual dependency. A compulsory paper in all future secondary-school curricula in Africa must therefore put science in its proper historical context, reveal the diversity of the human heritage, and break the dangerous myth of western scientific uniqueness.

Another major change which would need to be introduced into primary and secondary schools concerns the teaching of languages. Each African child should learn a minimum of three languages — one European language, one Asian and one African. The era of learning multiple European languages, some ancient and some modern, while other linguistic heritages of the world are ignored, should come rapidly to an end. The most popular European language in any African country is likely to be the language of the former colonial power. The most popular 'Asian' language in black Africa will probably be Arabic. But in time there may be broader diversification, depending upon which particular school a child attends. Because of the colonial legacy, some African students in former British Africa will need to learn French and some francophone Africans will continue to learn English. Pan-Africanism will need the teaching of an additional

European language for a minority of students. But any additional European language has to be a fourth language — chosen instead of, say, geography or fine art, but certainly not at the expense of either an African language or an Asian one. These linguistic requirements are partly based on the assumption that access to a culture is considerably facilitated by knowledge of its language.

At the university level language requirements should continue in a modified form. Each undergraduate — regardless of the field — should take either an African or an Asian language at an advanced level. In addition he should take a course on a non-western civilization, preferably but not necessarily linked to the language of his choice.

A course on 'great systems of thought' should also be obligatory for all undergraduates in the humanities and social sciences. The systems taught should aspire to be diverse and illustrative of the range of human cultures.

But perhaps the most fundamental of all reforms must be a change in attitude in all departments in African universities away from excessive Eurocentrism and towards a paradoxical combination of increased Africanization and increased internationalization of the content of each departmental programme. It is in this sense that the African university can indeed evolve into a truly multicultural corporation.

Development: the Strategy of Counter-penetration

But domestication of modernity and the diversification of its cultural content will not achieve final fulfilment without reversing the flow of influence back into western civilization itself. There are reformers in Africa who urge only domestication — and some of them would go to the extent of espousing cultural autarchy. But that is a strategy of withdrawal from world culture, whose outcome would be the continuing marginality of Africa in global affairs. In a world which has shrunk so much in a single century, there will be many decisions made by others which are bound to affect the human race as a whole. For Africa to attempt a strategy of withdrawal or total disengagement would be a counsel not only of despair but also of dangerous futility. Modernity is here to stay; the task is to decolonize it. World culture is evolving fast, the task is to save it from excessive Eurocentrism. The question which arises is how this latter task is to be achieved.[28]

This is where the strategy of counter-penetration looms into relevance. If African cultures have been penetrated so deeply by the West, how is western culture to be reciprocally penetrated by Africa? The West has *not* of course completely escaped Africa's cultural influence. It has been estimated that the first piece of carving made by an African to reach modern Europe arrived on a Portuguese trading ship in 1504. African workmanship in leather and probably gold had a much older presence in Europe.

> However, African art burst upon the awareness of the Western world only in the turn of the nineteenth century. Army men like Pitt-Rivers and Torday brought back large collections with good ethnographic description. . . . No one should jump to the idea that Picasso's women who look two ways at once, or anything else about his work, is a copy of something he discovered in African art. There was little direct, stylistic influence, although some can be discovered by latter-day critics. Rather, what happened was that with the discovery of African and other exotic art, the way was discovered for breaking out of the confines that had been imposed on European art by tradition — perspective, measured naturalism, and anti-intellectual sentimentality.[29]

This was certainly an important stage in Africa's artistic counter-penetration into the West.

At least as important has been Africa's indirect influence through its sons and daughters exported to the New World as slaves. Africa's impact on jazz and related forms of music has already been documented. So has the influence of African tales on the literatures of other lands, 'particularly of the Southern United States and the Caribbean area'.[30]

But when all is said and done, Africa's cultural influence on the West has been far more modest than the West's influence on Africa. That asymmetry will continue for at least the rest of this century, but the gap in reciprocity can begin to be narrowed. One approach is to reduce the West's influence in Africa — and the strategies of domestication and diversification should help achieve that. The additional approach is to raise the level of Africa's impact on the West — and counter-penetration is here the relevant strategy.

It is at this stage that Africa will need allies. The continent's most natural allies consist of the Black Diaspora and the Arab world. The Arabs share a continent with black people. Indeed, the majority of the Arabs are within Africa. So is the bulk of Arab land. Black and Arab states share the Organization of African Unity. This organization and the Arab League have overlapping membership. There are possibilities of exploiting this relationship to the mutual advantage of both peoples.

The Arab oil-producers have already started the strategy of *economic counter-penetration* into the West. It ranges from buying real estate in England to controlling a bank in the United States, from acquiring a considerable share in the Benz complex in West Germany to the possibility of extending a loan to Italy. The whole strategy of recycling petro-dollars is pregnant with the possibilities of economic counter-penetration into the West. As a result the West is at once eager for the petro-dollars and anxious about its long-term consequences for Western economic independence.[31]

The Arab oil-producers are already entering the business of commercial multinationals. One important multinational in Africa is Lonrho. Kuwait has entered it vigorously. There is indeed a risk that the oil-producers might start playing a sub-imperial role in Africa. But alongside that risk is an opportunity for a new Third World alliance to counter-penetrate the West. Once again economic power and cultural influence might be linked. The Organization of Petroleum Exporting Countries is heavily Muslim in composition. It includes the largest Muslim country in the world, Indonesia. The largest oil-exporting country is Saudi Arabia, which also happens to be the custodian of the spiritual capital of Islam, Mecca. The second largest oil-exporter is Iran, an increasingly influential Muslim country in world affairs. Two-thirds of the membership of OPEC is Muslim — and that portion constitutes also more than two-thirds of OPEC's oil reserves.

Nigeria, another member of OPEC, symbolizes the three parts of the soul of modern Africa — the Euro-Christian, the Islamic and the indigenous religious traditions. All three are vigorous and strong in Nigeria — and Islam is already the strongest single rival to westernism there.

The rise of OPEC in world affairs — however transient — may herald the political resurrection of Islam. Before the end of this century African Muslims will probably outnumber the Arabs and will be making a strong bid for shared leadership of Islam. It would not be surprising if, within the next decade, black Muslims direct from Africa are seen establishing schools and hospitals in Harlem and preaching Islam to black Americans. The funding for this *Islamic counter-penetration* will probably come from the oil-producers of the Arab world. But since African Islam is distinctive from Arab Islam, and carries considerable indigenous culture within it, Islamic counter-penetration into the United States would also be, in part, a process of transmitting African indigenous perspectives as well.

But at least as important as Arab money for African cultural entry into the West is the black American population. It is the second largest black nation in the world (second only to Nigeria) and it is situated in the middle of the richest and mightiest country of the twentieth century. At the moment black American influence on America's cultural and intellectual life is much more modest than, say, the influence of Jewish America. But as the poverty of black America lessens, its social and political horizons widen, and its intellectual and creative core expands, black American influence on American culture is bound to grow again.

The central task for African universities would have to include a struggle to reach black America. Through black America, Africa should reach much of the rest of America. And by influencing the most powerful country of the western world, Africa would also help to reach the rest of the West as well. After all, much of Western Europe is itself getting increasingly Americanized — and black America has already influenced pop culture in Western Europe simply by being part of America's omnipresence in the western world.

African universities would do well to encourage more and more black Americans to have part of their education in Africa. Here once again Arab money would find a new use in terms of scholarships made available to black Americans to study anywhere in the African continent, north or south of the Sahara. Later, Brazilian blacks, as well as Caribbean blacks, may be similarly encouraged to have part of their education in Africa. There are some American foundations which would also support the idea of black Americans taking a degree in Africa. Even the United States federal government — though its motives would be different — may one day help in funding 'cultural exchanges' between Africa and black America.

These are only some of the media through which Africa might in time restore balance in its cultural interaction with the western world. African universities could play a critical role in consolidating this cultural alliance between itself, the Black Diaspora and the Arab world.

But when all is said and done, we should remember that counter-penetration as a third strategy required for effective decolonization of African modernity is a longer-term endeavour than either domestication or diversification. Counter-penetration would certainly require conditions which make it possible for Africans to innovate sufficiently so that they could begin to teach others a thing or two. This is counter-penetration by the whole African continent into the main-streams of cultural and intellectual skills elsewhere. To some extent it might even be like a chain of transmission beginning with influence from outside into the African rural area, then balanced with influence from the African rural area on educational systems in Africa, stimulated by additional and varied foreign cultural, intellectual, and technical skills, and finally synthesizing these into an atmosphere rich enough to enable Africans to be not just followers of academic trends inaugurated elsewhere, but occasionally pace-setters.

But the full maturity of African educational experience will come when Africa develops a capability to innovate and invent independently and therefore to create a capacity to capture leadership now and again. Full reciprocal international penetration is a precondition for a genuinely symmetrical world culture. As Africa first permits its own societies to help balance the weight of western cultural influence, then permits other non-western external civilizations to reveal their secrets to African researchers and teachers, and then proceeds to transform its educational and intellectual world in a manner which makes genuine creativity possible, then Africa will be on its way toward that elusive but compelling imperative — not only to decolonize modernity, and not even merely to participate in it, but also to help recreate modernity anew for future generations.

References and Notes

1. Carlton J. H. Hayes, *A Generation of Materialism 1871-1900*, Harper, New York, 1941, pp. 218-28. Joseph A. Schumpeter's contribution to the debate is developed in his *Imperialism and Social Classes*, trans. Heinz Norden, ed. Paul Sweezy, Kelley, 1951.

2. For the main issues of the debate on imperialism consult George H. Nadel, ed., *Imperialism and Colonialism*, Macmillan, 1964, and Harrison M. Wright, ed., *The New Imperialism*, D. C. Heath, Boston, 1961.

3. Christopher Tugendhat, *The Multinationals*, Penguin Books, 1971, pp. 30-2.

4. F. D. Lugard, *The Dual Mandate in British Tropical Africa*, Blackwood, Edinburgh, 1926 edn., pp. 60-2.

5. F. D. Lugard, *Annual Reports*, Northern Nigeria, 1900-1911, p. 646. Cited by James S. Coleman, *Nigeria: Background to Nationalism*, University of California Press, Berkeley, p. 137.

6. Edmund Burke, *Reflections on the Revolution in France* (1790), in *Works*, World's Classics edn., 1907, Vol. IV, p. 147.

7. *Education Policy in British Tropical Africa: Memorandum . . . by the Advisory Committee on Native Education in the British Tropical African Dependencies* (1924-25), Cmd. 2374, xxi, 27.

8. Tugendhat, *The Multinationals*, op. cit., pp. 33-4.

9. For a brief discussion of the impact of protectionism on the spread of multinationals, see Tugendhat, ibid, pp. 34-5.

10. Charles Henry Wilson, *The History of Unilever*, Vol. I, Cassell, 1954.

11. J. Clyde Mitchell and A. L. Epstein, 'Occupational prestige and social status among urban Africans in Northern Rhodesia', *Africa*, 29 (1959), 34-9. Consult also Ali A. Mazrui, 'The monarchical tendency in African political culture', *British Journal of Sociology*, XVIII, 3 (September 1967), pp. 231-50.

12. Eric Ashby, *African Universities and Western Tradition*, Harvard University Press, Cambridge, Mass., 1964, p. 3.

13. Ibid., p. 38.

14. Irving Gershenberg, 'The impact of multi-national corporations on the process of development in less economically developed countries: commercial banking in Uganda', paper presented at a conference on 'Dependence and development in Africa', School of International Affairs, Carleton University in conjunction with the Canadian Association of African Studies, held in Ottawa, 16-18 February 1973, p. 3.

15. This dance, and so many others in African societies, go back a number of generations, though they are also subject to modifications. For an early academic account, see Otto Raum, *Chaga Childhood*, Oxford University Press, 1940, p. 223.

16. Ibid.

17. Judith Lynne Hanna, 'African dance: the continuity of change', draft of article commissioned by *Yearbook of the International Folk Music Council*, Vol. 5, 1974.

18. Okot p'Bitek, 'Indigenous ills', *Transition*, 32 (August/September 1967), 47.

19. Ibid.

20. G. M. Bull, 'Impressions of a medical tour of the Eastern and Western Regions of Nigeria', *West African Medical Journal*, n.s. IX (1960), 139-44.

21. A sample of works by both Africans and western Africanists include Bethwell A. Ogot, *History of the Southern Luo*, East African Publishing House, Nairobi, 1967, Basil Davidson, *Can We Write African History?*, University of California, African

Studies Center, Occasional Paper No. 1, Los Angeles, 1965, Jan Vansina, *Oral Tradition: a Study in Historical Methodology* (1961), trans H. M. Wright, Routledge & Kegan Paul, London, and Aldine, Chicago, 1965.

22. Recent pertinent books which have creatively used Marxist categories have included works by both western and Third World scholars. Samir Amin's work on French-speaking West Africa has fallen within this domain. On East Africa consult E. A. Brett, *Colonialism and Underdevelopment in East Africa*, Heinemann, 1972, and Colin Leys, *Underdevelopment in Kenya: the Political Economy of Neo-colonialism*, Heinemann, 1975.

23. Okot p'Bitek, 'Indigenous ills', op. cit., 47.

24. See Léopold Senghor *Prose and Poetry*, ed. and trans. John Reed and Clive Wake, Oxford University Press, 1965, p. 34. The emphasis is original.

25. Senghor, ibid, p. 33.

26. Ibid.

27. Engels as cited by Senghor, ibid, p. 33.

28. Aspects of the Eurocentrism of world culture are also discussed with passion and insight by Chinweizu, *The West and the Rest of Us: White Predators, Black Slavers and the African Elite*, Random House, New York, 1975. Chapters 14 to 16 are particularly relevant. Consult also Ali A. Mazrui, *World Culture and the Black Experience*, University of Washington Press, Seattle, 1974.

29. Paul Bohannan and Philip Curtin, *Africa and Africans* (published for the American Museum of Natural History), The Natural History Press, New York, 1971, pp. 97-8.

30. Ibid., p. 82.

31. This issue is argued out more fully in Ali A. Mazrui, 'The new interdependence: from hierarchy to symmetry', in James Howe, ed., *The United States and Developing World. Agenda for Action, 1975*, Overseas Development Council, Washington, D.C., 1975.

17   The African Computer as an International Agent

The significance of the computer in Africa has to be seen in relation to the three processes with much wider implications — modernization, development and alien penetration. Much of the literature on modernization conceives it as a process of change in the direction of narrowing the technical, scientific and normative gap between industrialized western countries and the Third World. Partly because the industrial revolution first took place in the West, modernization until now has largely been equated with westernization, in spite of rhetorical assertions to the contrary.

Because modernization has connotated a constant struggle to narrow the technical, scientific and normative gap between westerners and others, development has often been seen as a sub-section of modernization. Most economists in the West and in the Third World itself have seen economic development in terms of narrowing the economic gap between those two parts of the world both in output and in methods of production. Most political scientists have seen political development as a process of acquiring western skills of government, western restraints in political behaviour, and western-derived institutions for resolving conflict.

If both modernization and development are seen as a struggle to 'catch up with the West', the twin processes carry considerable risks of imitation and dependency for the Third World. In that imitation lies vulnerability to continuing manipulation by western economic and political interests.

The computer in Africa has to be seen in this wider context. In using the computer is Africa enhancing its capacity for development? Is it facilitating the modernization of management, planning, analysis and administration? Or is Africa adopting instead a technology which is inappropriate to its current needs, expensive in relation to other priorities, detrimental to job creation, and vulnerable to external exploitation?

The debate is already under way in parts of Africa. The leading intellectual weekly journal in East Africa, *The Weekly Review*, carried an article in May 1976, which tried to balance the present costs of computers to a country such as Kenya with the potentialities and presumed benefits in the days ahead. 'Although computers have probably adversely affected Kenya's economy in the fields of job creation and outflow of foreign exchange, it is obvious that their potential has not been exploited to the full for the benefit of society.'[1] But even this relatively guarded statement was soon taken up by another writer as being excessively optimistic about the utility of computers for a country such as Kenya.

> One understands . . . that over 100 such [mini] machines have been bought in Kenya: fifty million shillings for the mini-computers alone. Add to this the cost of the 40 or 50 larger computers, and one must reach a figure of at least Shs. 100 million. Much of the greater part of the work done by these machines could be carried out by human beings. There are large numbers of adequately educated people who with a little instruction could do most of this work, and to whom a job at over a thousand shillings a month is a dream. Think how many of these could be employed with a fraction of Shs. 100,000,000![2]

Stripped of the rhetoric, the author's analysis charges that the purchase of the computers is first a waste of scarce resources; secondly, it aggravates Kenya's balance-of-payments problems; and thirdly, it is detrimental to the struggle to reduce unemployment and underemployment in the country.

The author carries the attack further. He sees the type of technology symbolized by the computer as one which perpetuates the neglect of the countryside as against the city, while aggravating the status of African countries themselves as peripheral appendages to developed industrial states. Mao Tse-tung saw the Third World as a whole as a rural area serving the cities of the industrialized North. Inappropriate technology, when introduced into a Third World country, both maintains the peripheral rural status of the country as a whole in its dependent relationship with the northern metropole and deepens the neglect of the domestic countryside as against the new urban 'civilization'. In the words of one who sees the computer as a symbol of such inappropriate alien technology:

> Most of all we must regret the policy of importing ready-made, highly sophisticated machinery and technical (and technological) complexes, and incorporating these foreign objects into a body ill-adapted to them. Such complexes need correspondingly complex cities and a highly educated elite to support them, and so a dual society is created. Little of the capital goes to the countryside, and so the movement from the country to the city is perpetuated. But for the majority there is nothing. Developing countries, by adopting such complex equipment, commit themselves to dependence on the developed countries, for there are few people who know how to tend the machines. They must, initially at least, come from these countries. And to maintain the alien islands of a foreign technology, to put the machines right when they go

wrong, to supply spare parts, to replace the machines when their useful lives are over, the host country will depend on others.[3]

Again, the rhetoric of the writer often exaggerates and magnifies the problem. The writer is acting as the prosecutor. The accused in the dock is the computer. Like all prosecutors, the writer adopts the posture of an adversary and makes no allowances for mitigating circumstances, let alone for innocence. He knows the computer has its own counsels for the defence, skilful in appealing to the jurors of the marketplace and financially well-provided for the kind of work needed before the brief is prepared. But behind the rhetoric there is indeed a case to answer against the computer when it attempts to invade an economically poor and technologically underdeveloped country.

Yet the computer must once again be examined in relation to those wider processes we mentioned earlier — modernization, development and alien penetration. But these in turn have to be redefined if the Third World is not to be misled into the dark alleyways of technological robbery.

In the last chapter, we redefined development in the Third World to mean modernization minus dependency. Some of the gaps between the West and the Third World have indeed to be narrowed — *but this narrowing must include the gap in sheer power*. To narrow the gap in, say, per capita income in a manner which widens the gap in power is to pursue affluence at the expense of autonomy. To narrow the gap in the use of computers while increasing western technological control over the Third World is to prefer gadgetry to independence.

Somehow each African society would need to strike a balance between the pursuit of modernization and the pursuit of self-reliance. Some African countries would end up more successful in promoting one than the other. It may well be that Tanzania is realizing self-reliance a little more successfully than it is realizing modernization. In that case Tanzania is still falling short of an adequate developmental balance. Kenya, on the other hand, may have had greater success in promoting modernization than in realizing self-reliance. In Kenya's case too the mix falls short of genuine development. In other words, just as self-reliance on its own can never give Tanzania development, neither can modern techniques on their own give Kenya an adequate progressive thrust. The formula for development in Africa is both modernization and decolonization.

But what is modernization? And how do the two processes relate to the technology symbolized by the computer? For our purposes in this chapter the three most important aspects of modernization are:

1. *Secularization*: a shifting balance in the science of explanation and in the ethic of behaviour away from the supernatural to the temporal
2. *Technicalization*: a shifting balance in technique from custom and intuition to innovation and measurement

3. *Future-orientation*: a shifting balance between a preoccupation with ancestry and tradition to a concern for anticipation and planning.

In these three processes the role of the computer in Africa is to some extent related to the role of transnational corporations generally. But here an important distinction needs to be drawn between *the technology of production* and *the technology of information*. The technology of production ranges from the manufacture of shoes to the processing of petroleum. Most transnational corporations are primarily involved in the technology of production. The technology of information ranges from radio and television to computers. If modernization consists of the three sub-processes of secularization, technicalization and future-orientation, the two technologies of production and information relate differently to each.

Historically in Africa it was those transitional corporations concerned with the technology of production that helped to facilitate the process of secularization. On the other hand, it may well be those transnational corporations which have specialized in the technology of information that have gone furthest in promoting the third aspect of modernization — future-orientation. Here the computer, as well as the television set, is involved. Between these two — secularization and future-orientation — lies the intermediate sub-process of technicalization as part of the modernizing process. In its very intermediacy this aspect of technicalization involves both forms of technology — production as well as information. Philips Radio, International Business Machines (IBM), and Bata shoes become part of the same process. The transnational corporations become intimately involved in these aspects of modernization, with all the risks of dependency. Let us now examine the different aspects in closer detail.

Modernization, Secular Education and the Transnationals

One of the positive contributions of western firms to modernization is related to two sub-processes in the Third World — the secularization of education, in the sense of reducing a religious focus, and the practicalization of education, in the sense of promoting greater relevance to concrete social needs.

In most societies almost everywhere education began by having close connexions with religion. Oxford University in England was still insisting that academic appointments be based partly on religious affiliation until the nineteenth century. London University came into being partly in reaction against religious discrimination in the older British universities. Harvard, Yale and Princeton have histories of close intimacy between religion and scholarship. One of the oldest universities in the world, Al-Azhar University in Cairo, still shows a central preoccupation with religion. And Koran schools continue to be widespread in the rest of the Muslim world.

As we indicated previously, in Africa during the European colonial period, Christian missionaries took the lead in establishing schools. Education and salvation were once again closely allied under the imperial umbrella. On the whole one of the consequences of this alliance was to make education more 'literary'. The impact of the multinationals of production on colonial schools was in the direction of both reducing the focus on religion and increasing interest in practical skills. The multinationals contributed to these two trends in five main ways:

1. By helping to create a labour market in which practical skills were needed
2. By becoming an additional secular lobby influencing colonial policy-makers and counterbalancing the influence of the missionaries
3. By the demonstration impact of some of their own training programmes, especially for lower-level manpower
4. By helping to promote a 'consumer culture' in the colonies with its emphasis on materialist tastes as opposed to religious preoccupations
5. By helping to promote urbanization and general labour migration.

At this time computers were virtually non-existent outside South Africa. Other business firms were at work instead. Tensions between these and the misionaries in the colonial territories were sometimes inevitable. Those colonies which had extractive (mining) industries experienced special types of tensions. There were times when the missionaries favoured alternative forms of practical-orientation in education, especially those skills which would help to keep young Africans in their own villages. From the missionary's point of view it seemed that the African who remained in his farming community was more likely to remain faithful to spiritual values than the migrant to, say, the multinational mining industries.

We mentioned earlier the Commission of Inquiry set up by the Department of Social and Industrial Research of the International Missionary Council in 1933, which had as its terms of reference, at the narrowest, the 'effects of the coppermines of Central Africa upon Native Society and the work of the Christian Missions.' The Commission recommended that the 'educational emphasis of Missions should be directed towards preparing Bantu youth to serve the needs of Bantu rather than European society'. There was indeed sincere anxiety that 'Bantu labour' for the coppermines could in certain circumstances be at the expense of 'native society'. The Commission recommended that

the mission societies of the Territories study together the goal towards which their education is directed, define its purpose and visualise the results which they are aiming to achieve. If such study is to be of ultimate value the cooperation of the Government must be secure.[4]

No less significant was the Commission's recommendation that for the sake of rural stabilization 'the syllabuses for the mission schools should be drawn to dignify farming as a vocation'.[5]

In the Belgian Congo (now Zaire) multinational interests, missionaries and the state gradually evolved a working alliance, and much of the emphasis in both missionary and state schools was in time put on practical training. The very readiness of the missionaries in the Belgian colony to promote vocational training helped to satisfy the multinational enterprises and to consolidate a relative missionary monopoly of education in the country until the last decade of Belgian rule. And yet the products of these schools were often *more* vocationally oriented than those of schools in British and French colonies. A major reason was the more successful relationship in the Belgian Congo between the multinationals, the missionaries and the colonial authorities. The practicalization of education could therefore take place without 'excessive' secularization. The emergence of a new semi-skilled African class was thus facilitated by the tripartite alliance. In the somewhat exaggerating but still pertinent words of one observer at the time: 'The encouragement given in the Congo to African skilled workers is turning an African proletariat into a lower middle class. ... [The gulf between 'trade' and 'profession'] will inevitably narrow.'[6]

Even the materialism of consumer culture could be used to justify the direction of imperial policy. The emphasis on vocational training was deemed relevant for spiritual salvation itself. The rationale was that the 'pursuit of moral and social well-being is closely linked with the development of material well-being, the one being the mainstay of the other'.[7]

To some extent Belgian policy merely amounted to a recognition that it *paid* to have certain practical skills. There was also the fear that 'excessive literary education' merely resulted in producing 'discontented political agitators'. At least for a while the Belgian policy-makers seemed to have grasped the significance of the following propositions:

1. People trained in practical skills such as mechanics and engineering generally took longer to politicize ideologically than people trained in the humanities and the social sciences

2. In less developed economies there may be a higher risk of occupational redundancy for those with a purely literary education than for those whose training is partly vocational. Such redundancy carries the risk of discontent and instability

3. Those with a purely literary education are likely to want to move up the educational ladder all the way to university; but since opportunities higher up the literary educational ladder are more

limited than below, the system risks producing disgruntled secondary-school dropouts

4. By contrast, practical vocational trainees are more likely to want to get into their jobs soon and start earning money.

But whatever the precise calculations and machinations which lay behind the Belgian colonial policy, there was no denying the practical results.

The multinational corporations played a major role in promoting such changes, not least because they were often the most important agencies for industrialization, mechanization and commercialization in most of the colonies. What should be borne in mind is the distinction between the multinational industries themselves and the facilities and servicing industries which grow up because of the multinational presence. The Belgian colonial authorities used to boast that the Belgian Congo had the best transport facilities in Africa. The claim was an exaggeration but there was no doubt that impressive progress had been made in this field. The construction of an infrastructure is not always in itself a multinational enterprise, but the need for such an infrastructure is in part often defined in response to multinational pressure. A garage in Lusaka or Nairobi with African mechanics may not itself be part of a multinational firm, but the demand for garage services could have been initially escalated by the needs of personnel employed in multinational enterprises.

In assessing the impact of transnationals on the diffusion of skills in African societies one must therefore bear in mind both the direct and indirect consequences of a multinational presence. The transnational firms may themselves be capital-intensive, but their presence helps to promote labour-intensive infrastructural developments and servicing industries. And these in turn have educational and training implications.

But when all is said and done it is important to remember that building transport facilities and producing semi-skilled artisans is not the be-all and end-all of the task of meeting the practical needs of such societies. These developments create new problems of their own. In the words of the French Report of the Langevin Commission:

> Mechanization, the use of new sources of energy, the development of means of transport and communication, the intensification of industry, increased production, the participation of large numbers of women in economic life for the first time, the extension of elementary education — all these factors have brought about a marked change in living conditions and in the organization of society. In 1880, because of the rate and scope of economic progress, elementary education had to be extended to the working classes. Now, for the same reason, we are faced with the problem of recruiting more and more trained staff and technicians.[8]

The conclusion which the French Commission drew from these new demands of modern economic life was that the educational system needed complete remodelling—'since its present form is no longer suited to economic and social conditions'.

The multinationals have indeed substantially contributed to industrialization and commercialization; in the process they have also contributed to the secularization of education and to the trend towards giving education a greater practical component. But the precise nature of the industrialization and commercialization has itself distorted certain directions of both cultural and educational change. The need for a new adjustment is now becoming more urgent.

Modernization and Technology Transfer

At the centre of that part of modernization which technicalizes society is the process of technological transfer. Again, transnational firms have in fact become the major media of technology transfer outside the military field.

The transfer takes place mainly in four forms. The technology is embodied in, first, physical goods and equipment; secondly, skilled labour; thirdly, know-how which is legally recognized in patents and trademarks; and fourthly, knowledge which is either not patented or nor patentable. Computers are themselves physical goods needing skilled labour, embodying knowledge and designed to generate further knowledge.

G. K. Helleiner sees a consensus emerging among analysts and some planners that the unpatentable know-how with respect to most forms of technology is of greater significance than the patented knowledge.

Technology payments in licensing and collaboration agreements in which patent rights are not involved typically exceed those in agreements in which they are. Knowledge embodied in the patent is, in any case, normally insufficient by itself to permit its efficient working. [As Harry G. Johnson has put it] 'In contemporary conditions, public tolerance and legal protection of commercial secrecy has become more important than the patent system'.[9]

Helleiner regards the effect of patents on technology as being restrictive, but a good deal depends upon the options available in a given situation. There are certainly occasions when commercial secrecy is an inescapable de facto alternative to patented knowledge—and the secrecy can be a worse constraint on technology transfer than the patent. But where the knowledge is indeed made available for local use, an educative process may be under way.

A substantial part of the debate about technology transfer has concerned the issue of appropriateness. And within this issue the distinction between labour-intensive and capital-intensive technology has loomed large. Computers are once again a good illustration of that debate.

The bias in technology transfer by transnationals has on the whole been towards capital intensity. There have been a number of reasons for this bias. Helleiner has drawn our attention to the following, with special reference to the technology of production:

1. Transnational firms have access to relatively cheap capital
2. Unskilled labour is frequently of very low productivity. The wage rate may seem low, 'but it is not cheap in terms of efficiency wages'
3. The heavy protection which the transnationals enjoy reduces the incentive to change to the really efficient labour-intensive techniques
4. The transnational firms have tended to operate in industries (such as minerals processing) in which technology is both capital-intensive and fixed
5. In the manufacturing sector their products — originally designed for richer markets — are standardized and subjected to strict quality control. These controls over standards 'imply relatively capital-intensive and inflexible techniques of production for these particular products although it might have been possible to meet consumer demand for the same basic characteristics through the provision of an alternative product with a more appropriate production technology and/or more flexible quality controls'
6. Labour-intensive technologies tend to be associated with smaller scale production — whereas the multinationals have on the whole preferred to produce on a large scale
7. Shortages of skills in less developed countries make capital a more efficient functional alternative.
8. Labour-relations in less developed countries are at least as uncertain as in the developed states. Labour-intensive techniques increase the risks of disruptions and interruptions
9. Capital-intensive techniques sometimes provide better insurance against unexpected fluctuations in demand than do labour-intensive ones
10. Governments and private purchasers of technology in less developed countries often prefer 'the latest' in technological development as conferring a status of modernity even if the latest technique is less appropriate for the particular developing country than an older method or older model of equipment.[10]

From the computer's point of view what should be borne in mind is that capital-intensive techniques also tend to be *skill-intensive*. Initially, the skilled personnel are imported into the developing country from outside, sometimes in response to demands for 'streamlining' which are generated by computer vendors. The quest for this streamlining in administration may sometimes succeed in reducing inefficiency, but this is sometimes in exchange for increasing the importation of skilled manpower.

In such enterprises which are capital-intensive, in which the technology is complex, the training required for the indigenization of personnel may be substantial. This has implications for the whole problem of the brain drain, especially in situations where a country first adopts capital intensity and then shifts from capital-intensive to labour-intensive techniques. In black Africa the problem is not as yet acute, but both India and Nasser's Egypt had personnel who were well-trained for certain highly technical roles and who then left their own countries when those skilled roles were no longer adequately used at home. A relatively sudden contraction of skill-intensive roles in the country — either because of the consequences of a change in ideology or a change in techniques of management — may result in the transfer of technology in the reverse direction as well-trained engineers, technicians and accountants from the Third World seek the kind of employment in the industrial countries which is more appropriate to their new skills.

> As soon as it is granted that some technology is embodied in human capital, and that it can therefore be transferred internationally through the movement of engineers, scientists and managers, it follows that the 'brain drain' can also be viewed as part of the international technology transfer question. While it is quite customary to consider the role of the multinational firms in transferring technology through human capital from rich countries to poor, it has been less usual, though no less logical, to analyse their role in transferring it in the reverse direction. Their employment of indigenous talent for the pursuit of their own particular interests may deflect it from more socially profitable research and development activity, even if it does not physically leave the country.[11]

On the other hand, there are occasions when the training and education imparted go beyond the particular job with a computer and could make the recipient an innovator in his own right. In the words of Jack Baranson, 'more important than the imparting of technical knowledge and manufacturing capabilities is the ability and willingness to implant indigenous engineering and design capability for continued technological transformation'.[12] This is what Kenneth Boulding would presumably describe as 'knowledge which has the capacity of generating more knowledge in a single head'.[13]

Where the training transmitted in engineering or computer science promotes such self-generating knowledge in a single head, it could indeed contribute to the innovative capacity of a particular sector of a developing economy. But what should continue to be borne in mind is that such a level of knowledge may as likely be diverted towards the brain drain. This particular dilemma of skill-intensity continues to pose problems for the policy-maker. Does it therefore provide an additional argument for shifting from mechanized efficiency to labour-intensive techniques which require lower levels of expertise? As indicated earlier, labour-intensive techniques which follow a period of sustained capital intensity could in any case aggravate the problem of the brain drain by aggravating the problem of skilled redundancy following the shift.

Under the technology of production a distinction does need to be made between modifying factor proportions in an industry already established and selecting new industries or new products on the basis of their being more labour-intensive. Whether labour can be substituted for capital in a particular manufacturing process depends substantially on the product:

> In continuous process industries (chemicals, pharmaceuticals, metal refining, oil refining) and in the production of many consumers' goods and intermediate goods on an assembly line the scope for such substitution is quite limited, except in certain ancillary operations, particularly materials handling and packaging. The main types of activity in which gain (measured in terms of social costs) may be achieved by the substitution of labour for capital are in road-building, irrigation, housing and construction generally and in the production of woven fabrics, clothing, woodworking, leather, some foodstuffs (including foodstuffs for local consumption in local areas), bricks, tiles, and some of the simpler metal products. [14]

The level of training needed for the second category of employment is on the whole less complex than for the first category. Moreover, the less complex skills lend themselves better to in-service or in-plant training than the advanced technical skills. This is a gain if one agrees with the UN Economic Commission for Africa that 'in-plant training is more effective than formal technical training in an academic atmosphere'. [15] There are times when an existing industry which is capital-intensive can be scaled down and in the process be made more labour-intensive, or research could be undertaken to develop unconventional indigenous raw materials. The development or use of new raw materials could itself create new skills in the society. The scaling down of an industry to adjust to the smallness of the market may alter factor-proportions in favour of labour.

One example of scaling down was the plant specially designed a few years ago by Philips N.V. of the Netherlands for the assembly of radios in certain less developed countries.

> The main object of this design was to develop a low cost production unit for smaller volume of output than is typical in Europe; in the process the unit also turned out to be somewhat more labour-intensive. The firm also developed simpler types of equipment which can more readily be repaired or replaced from local stocks. [16]

From an educational point of view, the following propositions have therefore emerged from this analysis so far:

1. Capital-intensive technological processes tend to be skill-intensive. The computer is a pre-eminent example
2. The education required for capital-intensive projects is likely to be at least partly formal, acquired in an academic atmosphere
3. Manpower trained for capital-intensive projects is subject to the temptations of the brain drain partly because the technical skills involved have a market in the advanced economies
4. Labour-intensive processes lend themselves more easily to informal training and education, in-service or in-plant
5. Labour-intensive processes, almost by definition, spread skills more widely in the society and help to democratize education by broadening its distribution.

To the extent that computers have had a bias in favour of capital-intensity, they have been a constraint on educational democratization. The skill-intensity required will tend to aggravate the elitist tendencies inherited from the patterns of education under colonial rule.

The Computer and the Science of Anticipation

The third aspect of modernization relevant to this analysis is, as we indicated, a reorientation towards the future and away from excessive deference to the past and to its ancestral ways. Sensitivity to the future includes an interest in identifying trends, both positive and negative. Positive trends may need to be facilitated; negative ones arrested. A science of anticipation has therefore to be developed. This is what planning is all about.

A major obstacle to efficient planning in a new state may well be the very fact that the country is still under-modernized. Planning needs data on which to base estimates. Yet even basic data such as census figures are notoriously unreliable or imprecise in most new states. Planning in modern conditions needs the help of the technology of information, including the computer. Such a technology requires expertise. New states have a dearth of this expertise. Reliance on foreign experts has serious inadequacies and sometimes hazards for the host country. Planning needs a certain local competence in implementation. The administrators, as well as their political superiors, have yet to accumulate adequate experience for the tasks which planning might impose upon them.

It is certainly true that new states need rapid economic development. It may also be true that national planning is often conducive to faster development. What is often overlooked is that planning probably works best in those countries which need it least; it works best in an already developed economic system with reliable data, efficient managerial expertise and general technical and technological competence. An under-modernized society may well need planning most, but precisely because it is under-modernized it has a low planning capability.

Can the computer help? As a major instrument of the technology of information, can it improve the data-basis of African planning? Can it facilitate that aspect of modernization which is concerned with the future? Strictly speaking, data for African planning cannot be processed by a computer unless those data exist in the first place. The problem of planning without adequate data will not be solved simply by installing additional computers in Zambia or the Congo.

There is little doubt that the computer can assist in the data problem in other ways. Analysing the information which exists can itself yield further information to the planner. Data analysis should yield inferences, conclusions and findings. These in turn augment the body of knowledge available. Two pieces of information analysed in relation to each other often result in additional pieces of information. Processing data is frequently an exercise in augmenting knowledge. It seems reasonable therefore that the computer should be conscripted in the war against poverty, ignorance and disease in an African country. The computer's role as a storage system of information can also be critical for the African planner. Data can be retrieved at relevant moments for measured and well-defined purposes. The computer should facilitate efficient consultation of existing information as well as efficient processing and analysis of what is newly obtained. A computer also aids that aspect of modernization which is concerned with identifying trends, both positive and negative. The science of anticipation can thus be strengthened by greater use of the computer.

But a basic question arises in African conditions. Does the computer *help planning* while simultaneously *harming development*? Is the science of drawing up a rational and well-informed blueprint of planning strengthened by the computer, but at the cost of the actual substance of development? There is certainly evidence to support this paradox. Because of a number of factors, most computers in Africa are unavoidably and grossly underused. Spending a lot of foreign exchange to buy a piece of expensive equipment is one cost. Incapacity to use that piece of equipment adequately is an additional cost. It implies wastage in a situation of scarce resources. Yet the incapacity to use computers fully is due to wider problems of underdevelopment which probably need to be solved first before proficiency in using computers attains adequate levels.

Related to this problem is the whole issue of high vulnerability to exploitation in an industry of high technical know-how. The relatively non-technical buyer is often at the mercy of the highly specialized salesman. Discussing the Kenya situation, Hilary Ouma has observed:

More often than not, the idea of installing a computer originates from computer manufacturers, who are intent on increasing their sales, rather than from company executives. This has meant that feasibility studies on the equipment which are put before firms' boards are more often than not prepared by the computer salesmen themselves. The firms' executives probably do not understand technical computer jargon, leave alone have the ability to translate it into everyday language. [The resulting] excess capacity in expensive equipment can have serious consequences on the economy of a developing country.[17]

This vulnerability to exploitation has a number of anti-developmental consequences. The foreign exchange is depleted not only with the purchase of the equipment but also with the continuing costs of its use and maintenance. The expatriate specialists that are imported command high salaries, large portions of which are paid in hard currency. It is true that developing countries need to import for a while certain types of skilled manpower anyhow. But are computer specialists the most relevant expatriate engineers needed for the time being?

Also anti-developmental in its implications is the economic stratification which takes place between expatriates and locals. In the case of computer specialists this stratification can be particularly glaring. The employers in a developing country are faced with interrelated dilemmas. If the local specialist earns much less than the expatriate for the same job, the foreigner appears privileged and the citizen seems to be a victim of discrimination. On the other hand, if the local's pay is raised to something approximating what the foreigner earns, a new form of stratification is formed among the local people themselves. Again if the local computer specialist is paid a much lower salary than his expatriate counterpart, a morale problem is created — and the local may leave to seek a 'less discriminatory' appointment elsewhere in another field. The expatriate preponderance in skilled computer jobs thus becomes aggravated. On the other hand, if scales for locals are based on international rates, and this attracts better local intellects to such jobs, would this genuinely stabilize the Africanization of personnel? Or would it increase the *international* mobility of the African personnel — and potentially contribute to the brain drain?

Some of these dilemmas are more real than others. What is clear is that a certain number of anti-developmental cleavages open up as computers enter technologically underdeveloped societies. As Ouma puts it with regard to some of these dilemmas of personnel in Kenya:

Expatriates installed the first systems, often with the understanding that they would train local people to take over. But two things happened. First, because most users were government or quasi-government bodies, there was an attempt to fix salary scales for local computer personnel on a level with the then existing salary scales without regard to world scales. While paying expatriate personnel more or less what they asked for, computer users did not seek any independent advice on the remuneration of local computer personnel. The result has been that a local programmer is often paid half the salary of a less qualified expatriate programmer, to take an example of imbalance in the salary structure prevalent in the industry.[18]

Ouma describes the effect as 'disastrous'. The very low salaries paid to local staff have failed either to attract or to retain 'the right calibre of local people' in the computer industry. One consequence is that 'while most of the junior posts—junior programmers, operators and key-punch operators—are held by Africans, there are very few senior local people in the industry'.[19]

Another anti-developmental consequence of the computer takes us to another dilemma. Does the computer in Africa have real automative consequences? Does it reduce significantly the number of employees needed for specific tasks? If so, the computer complicates the problem of job creation, as we indicated earlier.

John B. Wallace refers to evidence obtained in interviews in Nigeria and Uganda which suggests that computers there have no employment impact. But if there is no automative result, is the computer in such nations a case of wasteful duplication? In the words of Wallace:

> Computers are used in these developing countries almost exclusively on tasks for which clerical workers are the next best substitute. If, as the interviewees claimed, there is no employment impact, it is likely that computers are duplicating rather than substituting for clerical resources and that the countries are paying foreign exchange for no benefit, at least in the short run.[20]

Another anti-developmental consequence of the computer overlaps with some of the other considerations mentioned before. The computer does aggravate structures of technological dependency between developing countries and the industrial states which produce them.

In some African countries the computerization of economic life is going faster than in others. Ouma tells us:

> Ten years ago, there was only one computer in the whole of East Africa. Today Kenya alone has over 140 computers, both mini-computers and main-frames and most computer salesmen are of the opinion that the present figure will increase at a very fast rate.[21]

In fact, in Africa as a whole, the speed of computerization is much less spectacular. P. Platon looks at the continent as a whole and estimates that in 1972 there were around a thousand computers in the continent. Half of these were in the Republic of South Africa. D. R. F. Taylor relates this estimate to the original arrival of the computer in Africa in the late 1950s. African independence has indeed witnessed speedy computerization, but the absolute number is still modest. Taylor's estimates for 1975 was 1200 computers in Africa. On the other hand, by 1972 the campuses of the University of California alone were using over two hundred computers.[22]

But although the speed of computerization is modest in absolute terms, and countries such as Tanzania have even attempted decomputerization, the new culture which is coming to Africa with computers cannot but strengthen or aggravate technological dependency. The science of anticipation still has its most elaborate expertise outside Africa. The initial phases of the computerization of Africa carry the risk of a new form of colonialism. Africa could be duly 'programmed'. The 'machine man's burden' looms ominously on the horizon as a new technological crusade to modernize Africa.

The arrival of the computer may indeed be contributing to modernization, but it is also adding dependency. The computer is probably helping to make planning more efficient, but is simultaneously making development more difficult. The science of anticipation is for the time being caught up in the contradictions of premature technological change.

Towards Decolonizing Modernity

If development in the Third World equals modernization minus dependency, how can the contradictions of premature technological change be resolved, and in what way does the computer illustrate these wider issues?

We have described the process of decolonization as involving five processes — indigenization, domestication, diversification, horizontal inter-penetration and vertical counter-penetration. The strategy of indigenization involves increasing the use of indigenous resources, ranging from native personnel to aspects of traditional local technology. But in applying this to the computer we have to relate it to the strategy of domestication as well. While indigenization means using local resources and making them more relevant to the modern age, domestication involves making imported versions of modernity more relevant to the local society. For example, the English language in East Africa is an alien medium. To domesticate it is to make it respond to local imagery, figures of speech, sound patterns and to the general cultural milieu of the region. On the other hand, the promotion of Swahili as against English in Tanzania is a process of indigenization. It involves promoting a local linguistic resource, rather than making an alien resource more locally relevant.

With regard to western institutions in Africa, domestication is the process by which they are in part Africanized or traditionalized in local terms. But with local institutions, the task is partly to modernize them. Thus English in East Africa needs to be Africanized, while Swahili needs to be modernized in the sense of enabling it to cope with modern life and modern knowledge.

Clearly the two strategies of domestication and indigenization are closely related and are sometimes impossible to disentangle. This is particularly so when we apply these strategies of decolonization to computers. The computer is of course more like the English language in Africa than like Swahili. The computer is a piece of alien culture. Can it be domesticated?

I believe it can, but the introduction or expansion of this piece of technology in an African country must be much more carefully planned than has so far been the case. The domestication of the computer would first and foremost require a substantial indigenization of personnel. This would require, first, greater commitment by African governments to promote relevant training at different levels for Africans; second, readiness on the part of both governments and employers to create a structure of incentives which would attract Africans of the right calibre; third, greater political pressure on computer suppliers to facilitate training and co-operate in related tasks; fourth, stricter control by African governments of the foreign exchange allowed for the importation of computers; and fifth, the imposition of at least a fifty per cent import duty on each machine, partly as a disincentive against ill-considered purchases by local firms and partly as one additional source of revenue for job-creating projects in other sectors of the economy.

The indigenization of high-level personnel in the local computer industry should in time help to indigenize the uses to which the computer is put and the tasks that are assigned to it. When the most skilled roles in the computer industry in an African country are in the hands of Africans themselves, new types of problems will in turn be put to computers. The cultural and political milieu of the new personnel should affect and perhaps modify problem-definition. This Africanization of computer personnel should also facilitate in time the further Africanization of the *users* of computer services. What should be borne in mind is that the efficient indigenization and domestication of the computer requires a *gradualist* and *planned* approach.

Diversification, at the broader level of society, means the diversification of production, sources of expertise, techniques of analysis, types of goods produced, markets for these products, general trading partners, aid-donors and other benefactors. This approach—though sometimes inefficient—should help an African country to diversify in its dependence on other countries. Excessive reliance on only one country is more dangerous for a weak state than reliance on half a dozen countries. Reliance on only the West or only the communist world is more risky than diversified dependency on both East and West.

But even if an African country has to deal primarily with the West when it comes to computers, it makes sense to exploit competitive tendencies between western monopolies. In much of English-speaking Africa the International Computers Ltd (British-based) and International Business Machines (IBM of the USA) control the market. But the two are in competition with each other. Just as international business monopolies once facilitated western imperialism, so international business competition could facilitate decolonization—if the victims of imperialism can learn how to exploit the opportunities presented to them.

At least as important an element in the strategy of diversification is to find the right balance between the older manual techniques and the new computer techniques. Computerization should not be allowed to proceed too fast. Where possible manual alternatives should consciously be encouraged alongside computers. And yet it would be wasteful if the computer only duplicated manual clerical work, for example. Between the hypothetical extremity of complete mechanization and the wasteful extremity of complete duplication there must lie a more viable diversified mixture of functions.

The computer is under-utilized in Africa, not merely in terms of capacity or in terms of hours per day, but also in terms of the range of tasks assigned to it. In Kenya nearly half of the minicomputers installed in recent times have been going to banks. A very high proportion of the tasks of computers in Africa are in the direction of clerk substitution.

Even in economic planning the computer in Africa is still greatly under-utilized. I argued in the previous section that the computer can positively help planning, while harming development. If the computers have already been purchased, and are being used in ways which already harm development, should they not at least be made to perform their more positive functions in planning as well? Once again diversification of usage—if handled with care—could extract certain benefits from the computer, while sustaining at the same time its developmental costs.

The next strategy of decolonization is *horizontal interpenetration* among Third World countries. In the field of trade this could mean promoting greater exchange among, say, African countries themselves. In the field of investment it could, for example, mean allowing Arab money to compete with western and Japanese money in establishing new industries or promoting new projects in Africa. In the field of aid it must also mean that oil-rich Third World countries should increase their contribution towards the economic and social development of their resource-poor sister-countries. In the field of technical assistance it would have to mean that Third World countries with apparent excess of skilled manpower in relation to their absorption capacity should not only be prepared but also be encouraged to facilitate temporary or permanent migration to other Third World countries. This last process is what might be called the horizontal brain drain — the transfer of skilled manpower from, say, Egypt to Abu Dhabi or from the Indian sub-continent to Nigeria.

In the field of computers, skill transfers among Third World countries are particularly promising in the short run as part of the process of decolonization. If an African country wants a computer, for the time being it has to buy it from either Europe, North America, Japan or the Soviet Union. Almost by definition, these sophisticated machines are products of highly industrialized economies. But an African country does *not* have to import highly skilled computer personnel from those same industrialized states. As part of horizontal interpenetration, Third World countries must learn to poach on each other's skilled manpower, at least as a short-term strategy. President Idi Amin of Uganda learnt after a while to distinguish between Indians with strong economic and historic roots in Uganda and Indians on contract for a specified period. He expelled almost all of those who had strong local roots — and then went to the Indian sub-continent to recruit skilled professional teachers, engineers and doctors on contract terms. The wholesale expulsion of Asians with roots was basically an irrational act. But the recruitment of skilled Indians on contract was sound. Kenya too should turn increasingly to the Indian sub-continent, instead of Western Europe, for some of its temporary needs for skilled personnel, including the need for computer personnel, pending adequate indigenization. The present pervasive African distrust of people of Indian extraction may be incompatible with the quest for a New International Economic Order.

The final strategy of decolonization is that of *vertical counterpenetration*. It is not enough to facilitate greater interpenetration among Third World countries. It is not enough to contain or reduce penetration by northern industrialized states into southern underdeveloped economies. An additional strategy is needed — one which would increasingly enable southern countries to counterpenetrate the citadels of power in the north.

The Middle Eastern oil producers have already started the process of counterpenetrating Western Europe, and to a lesser extent North America. This vertical counterpenetration by the Middle East ranges from manipulating the money market in Western Europe to buying shares in West German industry, from purchasing banks and real estate in the United States to obtaining shares in other transnational corporations.

Even the southern capacity to impose clear political conditions on western firms is a case of vertical counterpenetration. The Arabs' success in forcing many western firms to stop trading with Israel (if they wish to retain their Arab markets) is a clear illustration of a southern market dictating certain conditions to northern transnational corporations instead of the older reverse flow of power.

The possibilities of southern counterpenetration into the computer industry are modest, but in time petro-dollars could buy a greater say in the ICL and possibly also in IRIS of France. Whether this would make any difference in the receiving countries of Africa is for the time being still hypothetical.

Another question is how far the African computer market, as it expands and acquires greater sophistication, would be able to exert greater counter-influence on the computer industry. This would depend partly upon the extent to which each domestic African market is internally organized and how far African countries using computers consult with each other and possibly with other Third World users on applications of the computer and related issues. D. R. F. Taylor tells us that there is greater awareness and organization on computer-related matters in Francophone Africa than in Anglophone Africa. Gabon, Malagasy, the Ivory Coast, Morocco, Algeria and Burundi have all been experimenting with domestic institutions to co-ordinate informatics. CAFRAD in Tangier has, according to Taylor, played a leading role in organizing and developing such work on computer applications. CAFRAD also held in 1976 the first African Conference on Informatics in Administration.[23] Such consultations on computer applications should be encouraged as part of horizontal interpenetration among African systems of informatics. But the greater sophistication which will in time be acquired should increase the influence of the African market on the computer industry itself.

Yet another element in the strategy of counterpenetration is the northward brain drain itself. On the whole Third World countries cannot afford to lose their skilled manpower. But it would be a mistake to assume that the northward brain drain is totally to the disadvantage of the south. Indian doctors in British hospitals are indeed recruited to some extent at the expense of the sick in India. But those emigrant Indian doctors are becoming an important sub-lobby in British society to increase British responsiveness to the health and nutritional needs of India itself. The American Jews that are not prepared to go to settle in Israel are not merely a case of depriving Israel of skills and possessions which they would have taken there. They also constitute a counter-influence on the American system to balance the influence of the United States on the Israeli system. The presence of Irish Americans in the United States is indeed partly a case of agonizing economic disadvantage for the Irish Republic. But Irish Americans are also conversely an existing economic and political resource for the benefit of the Irish Republic. This is also true of Greek Americans, Polish Canadians, and Algerians in France. Migration from one country to another is never purely a blessing nor purely a curse to either the donor country or the receiving country. The costs and benefits vary from case to case.

As more and more Africans become highly skilled in computer technology and usage, some of them will migrate to developed states. As matters now stand, the costs of this kind of brain drain are for the time being weightier than the benefits for African countries. What should constantly be borne in mind is that the intellectual penetration of the south by northern industrial states must one day be balanced with reverse intellectual penetration by the south of the think tanks of the north. Given the realities of an increasingly interdependent world, decolonization will never be complete unless penetration is reciprocal and more balanced. Part of the cost may well be the loss of highly skilled African manipulators of the science of computers.

Conclusion

We have attempted in this chapter to place the computer in the context of the much wider issues raised by it. The equipment is a piece of modernity in the technological sense. Its functions in a society have identifiable modernizing consequences. The computer helps to secularize the science of explanation, to technicalize analytical approaches to data, and to promote a capacity for estimating the future and planning for it.

But modernization is not development. In the northern industrialized states development should now mean rationalization plus social justice. The rationalization should include a proper balance between social needs and ecological conditions, a proper relationship not only between the individual and society but also between society and nature. Resource depletion and ecological damage has to be moderated by an adequate sensitivity to the future. By its waste and pollution the West has revealed that it is not modernized enough in this sense of adequately responding to the future and making allowances for it. By falling short of standards of justice between classes, races, cultural sub-groups and sexes, the industrial states have not attained adequate standards of development either. But while development in the north equals rationalization plus social justice, development in the Third World must for the time being mean modernization minus dependency.

The computer in Africa probably helps to promote modernization but it also aggravates Africa's technological and intellectual dependency on Western Europe and North America. The computer, were it used more efficiently, would greatly aid the process of African planning. But its consequences are anti-developmental in such tasks as job creation, reducing dependency, conservation of foreign exchange, definition of priorities as between town and country, and devising optimal salary structures for both locals and expatriates.

Africa cannot escape the computer age indefinitely. If for the time being the computer is an instrument for modernization but not for development, can it be made to contribute to both processes? How is the dependency factor to be subtracted from the modernization in order to give us a truly developmental result?

We enumerated the five strategies of decolonization. The computer has to respond to the imperatives of indigenization, domestication, diversification, horizontal interpenetration among Third World countries, and vertical counterpenetration from the south into the citadels of technological and economic power in the north.

But in the final analysis the computer is merely a symbol of much wider forces, ranging from technology transfer to job creation, from the impact of transnational corporations to the process of national planning, from race relations in South Africa or Uganda to the quest for a New International Economic Order.

When adequately domesticated and decolonized the computer in Africa could become a mediator between the ancestral world of collective wisdom and personal intuition on one side and the new world of quantified data and scientific analysis on the other. The sociology of knowledge is undergoing a change in Africa. And the computer is part of that process of change.

References and Notes

1. *The Weekly Review* (Nairobi), 17 May 1976.
2. 'Computers: benefit or detriment?', by a special correspondent, *The Weekly Review* (Nairobi), 7 June 1976, p. 25. Approximately eight Kenya shillings amount to one American dollar.
3. Ibid.
4. *Modern Industry and the African*, Report of Commission of Inquiry set up by Department of Social and Industrial Research of International Missionary Council under Chairmanship of J. Merle Davis, Macmillan, 1933, pp. 338-9.
5. Ibid.
6. Vernon Bartkelt, *Struggle for Africa*, Praeger, New York, 1953, p. 98.
7. M. A. de Vleeschauwer (Belgian Minister of the Colonies at the time), 'Belgian colonial policy', *The Crown Colonist*, XIII (August 1943), 549.
8. Quoted in *UNESCO Chronicle* (Paris), V, 12 (December 1959), 395.
9. G. K. Helleiner, 'The role of multinational corporations in the less developed countries' trade in technology', *World Development*, 3, 4 (April 1975), 163-4. I am indebted to Helleiner for stimulation and bibliographical guidance.
10. Helleiner elaborates on some of these arguments and mentions additional ones. See Helleiner, ibid., 169-71.
11. Ibid., 165.
12. Jack Baranson, 'Comment' in Raymond Vernon, ed., *The Technology Factor in International Trade*, National Bureau of Economic Research, New York, 1970, p. 362.
13. See K. E. Boulding, 'The economics of knowledge and the knowledge of economics', *American Economic Review*, 56, 2 (May 1966), 3.
14. *The Multinational Corporations in Africa* (A document prepared by the UN Economic Commission for Africa), Africa Contemporary Record Current Affairs Series, Rex Collings, 1972, p. 13.
15. Ibid., p. 19.
16. Ibid., p. 15.

17. Hilary Ouma, 'The changing world of computers in Kenya', *The Weekly Review* (Nairobi), 17 May 1976, p. 23.
18. Ibid., p. 25.
19. Ibid.
20. John B. Wallace Jr., 'Computer use in independent Africa: problem and solution statements', in R. A. Obudho and D. R. F. Taylor, eds., *The Computer in Africa.*
21. Ouma, op. cit., p. 19.
22. D. R. F. Taylor, 'The computer in Africa, an introduction', Obudho and Taylor, eds., *The Computer in Africa*, op. cit. Taylor cites also P. Paton, 'L'informatique en Afrique'. *Marchés Tropicaux et Méditerranéens*, 1420 (January 1973) and Mohamed M. El-Hadi, *The Status of Informatics in the African Administrative Environment*, Doc. 75-1, CAFRAD, Tangier, April 1975. Consult also C. Bussel, ed., *Computer Education for Development*, Proceedings based on the Rio Symposium on Computer Education for Developing Countries, Guambara, Brazil, August 1972.
23. Taylor, 'The computer in Africa', op. cit.

18 The African Intellectual as an International Link

We have discussed in earlier chapters the two mystiques of scientism and practicality which sometimes threaten to distort the balanced evolution of university institutions in Africa. We have also related the educational criteria of relevance to both socialism and nationalism.

In some sense it could indeed be said that of the two types of ideologies, nationalist and socialist, it is the socialist dimension which retains contact with the principle of internationalism. Nationalism, on the other hand, appears to be defiantly parochial in its loyalties and commitments. In this chapter we address ourselves to the positive aspects of internationalism.

When applied to the needs of developing countries, both nationalism and socialism are ideologies based on social relativism. Socialism, particularly of the kind inspired by historical materialism, assumed that societies have to pass through different stages before they arrive at socialist maturity. The Marxist stages of ancient, oriental, feudal, capitalist, socialist and communist are, in effect, stages of growth and development. The institutions of each society have to reflect the socio-economic realities implicit in the particular stage of development the society has reached. Where an institution does not so reflect these realities, it should adapt itself if it is to interact meaningfully with the community around it.

Marx himself was a moral relativist, believing that the values of each society derive their validity from the stage of development reached and from the prospect of progress to the next stage. The idea of values which are universally valid to all societies, regardless of the stage of evolution they have attained, may sometimes be propounded by followers of Marx but such an idea is not in itself fully consistent with Marxist theory of historical materialism. The evolutionary nature of Marxist theory is at its heart socially relativist.

Here, then, is a university situated in Africa, but borrowed from a part of the world which has attained a different stage of socio-economic evolution. Even assuming that the ethos of a university in its place of origin is valid domestically, what is to give that ethos validity in another society at a different stage of change? The university in Africa, however western in origin, is therefore called upon by scientific socialism to adapt itself to Africa.

343

To some extent socialism as a political philosophy is a fusion of the two mystiques of scientism and practicality. When Karl Marx proceeded to put Hegel right side up, and insisted on *materialism* as the basis of history, Marx was opting for the mystique of practicality. We have also quoted his famous dictum: 'Philosophers so far have only interpreted the world; the point, however, is to change it'. And we have suggested that a substitution of the word 'scholars' for the word 'philosophers' in this statement would give us the perfect slogan for the crisis of relevance in the modern world. But Marx also saw his whole system of thought as *'scientific* socialism'. He was therefore also wedded to the mystique of scientism.

The dominant schools of socialism in Africa are not Marxist — as both Julius Nyerere of Tanzania and Milton Obote of Uganda once emphasized. But the two mystiques of scientism and practicality are still present. The socialism of leaders like Nyerere and Obote has been based on a presumed fusion between rationality and practicality.

But the problem of education at large is not simply to find the right balance between thought and action. It is also to find the right balance between thought and feeling. This is where socialism, in some of its extreme forms, shows some deficiencies. Socialism has sometimes been accused by its critics of forgetting that Man is a *thinking* animal. The demand for conformity in some socialist countries has sometimes been interpreted as a denial of the right to reflect. And yet socialism does indeed belong to the *rationalist* stream of thought. There are times when the real danger in an African educational system is not the denial of the right to think but the denial of the right to *feel*. When we relate an educational ethic to social toil, we are indeed helping to make thought improve the quality of action. But what about helping thought improve the quality of emotive sensibility?

The arts and humanities as subjects pertaining to such sensibilities are sometimes endangered in an African institution by a presumed irrelevance to practical development. The study of history and literature, the study of social thought and political ideas, the study of fine art — all these occasionally fall under a cloud of potential neglect when manpower projections do not recognize their offerings as being in the forefront of the national need.

Developmental and socialist imperatives become fanatically attracted towards the idea of relating thought merely to action. Fortunately for African countries, nationalism now and again reasserts its own needs; and nationalism does insist on some degree of relation between thought and feeling. The arts in Africa derive their validity from nationalist considerations and the quest for the evolution of identity. The study of African history and the promotion of African literature, the encouragement of artistic creativity, the preoccupation with the task of creating a national heritage are aims which could have been forgotten if the only valid criteria of relevance were developmental ones in the narrow, practical sense. But they are aims which have been saved from neglect and potential extinction by the ambition of a national consciousness in African countries seeking to consolidate itself. President Obote was in agreement with this when he opened the Arts Festival at Makerere University College in 1968 and said that it was within its own creative cultural achievements that a nation's soul resided.

Yet the fusion of thought with feeling must imply a continuing respect for diversity. Creativity as an expression of the individual man or woman requires a permissive atmosphere. But if there is a search for a national identity, should there not be a promotion of ideology in the university classrooms? And yet would not such a promotion of ideology in academic classrooms convert the university into an ideological institute? The answer is, quite simply, that it depends upon how it is done. There has been heated discussion in countries like Tanzania as to whether a university in a socialist country should not become an instrument for the promotion of socialism. Interviewed by the press on this question as long ago as April 1967, I went on record as accepting the proposition that it is the duty of any university in the modern world to *allow* for the study of socialism. This is because socialist ideas have such an important bearing on twentieth-century realities that the university which leaves no room for such study is betraying its function and its duty to remain in touch with reality. But I continued in that same interview to say that this was a different matter from converting the whole university into an institution for the promotion of socialism. I insisted on the validity of the distinction between a university and an ideological institute.[1]

In the press debate which ensued on publication of the interview a number of the critics of my position wondered whether I was honest in assuming that there could be an absence of ideology in any university. Could the study of the humanities avoid having an ideological bias? Was I not simply expressing my own ideological preference when I opposed the promotion of socialism as an objective of the university? I conceded in my reply to my critics, and I reaffirm now, that there is no university in the world which is totally free of ideology. If there were it would be unlikely to be a good university. But a genuine university should not be intellectually monopolistic.[2]

We should draw a distinction between a uni-ideological approach to academic study, a non-ideological approach, and a multi-ideological approach. A uni-ideological approach to academic study is, by definition, monopolistic. It asserts the validity of only one ideology. It is what converts an institution of learning into an institution of ideology. A non-ideological approach aspires to rigorous scientificity. Only subjects such as mathematics and physics are, in reality, close enough to such an ideal. The social sciences, the humanities and the arts have a high normative component in their ethos, and a normative commitment cannot be non-ideological at the same time. A multi-ideological approach is the one which permits maximum interplay between different interpretations of reality. A course in political ideas may indeed be discussing ideologies, and the teacher himself may be lecturing from a particular ideological standpoint. But a real test comes when the work of the students is graded. If the students lose marks in proportion to their divergence from the teacher's ideological preference, the examiner has converted his course in political ideas into a uni-ideological exercise. But if the students are free to take any ideological point of departure in their assessment of, say, the merits or de-merits of nationalization, or the persuasiveness of the Marxist concept of class-struggle, or the desirability or otherwise of parliamentary institutions, and if marks are awarded not on the basis of conformity with particular ideological positions but on the basis of rigour in reasoning, then the course has succeeded in being a multi-ideological exercise.

An insistence on ideological conformity is not a real marriage between thought and emotion. Emotion becomes the dominant partner, using thought not as a marriage partner, but as a prostitute. The conversion of the university classroom into a place for the sole promotion of a particular ideology is an exercise in vulgarity. Only respect for diversity in feeling, and for the principle of creative autonomy can ever do justice to the search for a national heritage in an African country. A non-ideological approach to academic study makes thought the senior partner and eliminates or suppresses feeling. A uni-ideological approach makes emotion the senior partner and discourages independent reflection. Only a multi-ideological approach to the humanities and social sciences could constitute a legitimate basis of matrimony between the mind and the heart in the university context.

There is, then, a residual liberalism in the university ethos which cannot be completely sacrificed without loss. And it is this residual liberalism which maintains a sense of universalism in some qualities of intellectual life. Nationalism and socialism, in their relativist limitations, could retreat into parochial self-sufficiency. But intellectual values continue to have a residual link with the world beyond. It is such intellectual values which have played a part in the internationalization of Africa.

What is an Intellectual?

It is at this level that the debates about the role of the university in East Africa become inseparable from debates about the role of intellectuals. And here I want to refer in more detail to that public debate between myself and Mr Akena Adoko in Kampala in 1969, which was touched on briefly in Chapter 11.

I was invited by the mayor of the City of Kampala to engage in a public dialogue at the town hall with Mr Akena Adoko on the subject of 'The role of intellectuals in the African revolution'. Mr Akena Adoko, Chief General Service Officer or Chief Intelligence Officer of the Uganda Government, was one of the men closest to President Obote, and clearly one of the most powerful political figures in Uganda. The fact that he was interested in engaging in a public debate with an academic was a matter of national interest.

I told His Worship the Mayor that I was already scheduled to give a public lecture at Makerere on the subject 'Are intellectuals an international class?' Would not the theme of this public lecture overlap with the subject of the proposed debate on the role of intellectuals in the African revolution? The mayor replied patiently that what I did at Makerere was my business. But he was the mayor of the City of Kampala, and he wanted the ordinary people of the city to have the opportunity to hear such a subject discussed in their own town hall by people like Mr Akena Adoko and myself.

I accepted the challenge. As soon as the coming debate was announced, there was unmistakeable public interest. When 6 February 1969 came, the debate had indeed become a national event. The subject had seemed so esoteric, and yet the public response was a clear affirmation that there was national questioning about the role of intellectuals. Ordinary people wanted to hear the subject thrashed out in a public confrontation between a man from government and a man from the university. Mayor A. G. Mehta took the Chair. Tape-recorders, television cameras, shorthand notebooks were all poised to record the event for an interested public beyond the town hall.

A major point of difference which arose in the dialogue between Mr Akena Adoko and myself centred on the very definition of an intellectual which touched on the great issue of social commitment. I had defined an intellectual as '*a person who has the capacity to be fascinated by ideas, and has acquired the skill to handle some of those ideas effectively*'. Mr Akena Adoko responded with the assertion:

> I submit with respect to Profesor Mazrui that both legs of his definition are wrong, and that the definition itself, if followed by any would-be intellectual, is very dangerous. . . . The fact is, you cannot divorce intellectual duty from a moral duty. Skilful handling of ideas without regard to their truth is sheer mental gymnastics.

Mr Akena Adoko asserted that the duty of African intellectuals was not only to serve truth but also to serve society and influence changes for the better in society.

> The intellectuals ought to have played a leading role in the African revolution. They ought to have been in the vanguard of the

revolution. They knew long ago the need for a revolution to bring about independence, and they know now the need for a revolution to bring about economic justice. They have the mental capacity to enquire into facts and reasons and the ability to reach conclusions which could strengthen the politicians in their endeavour to mobilize the masses in the attainment of the goals of the revolution.[3]

Mr Akena Adoko reaffirmed his surprise that I should have defined an intellectual without reference to the imperative of truth or obligation to society.

My own response to this counter-argument was that the pursuit of truth was part of the definition of a *scholar* and not part of the definition of an intellectual. It is true that to be scholarly includes the duty to observe rigorously the rules of relevance. A scholar may often be wrong, but his scholarship consists in the conscious attempt to avoid being wrong. Meticulous care in handling the evidence becomes part of the very definition of true scholarship. It is therefore to scholarship rather than to intellectualism that the imperative of truth is definitionally tied.

But intellectuals may indeed be no more than 'mental acrobats', in the words of Akena Adoko. They may indeed often play with ideas for their own sake. Some of the greatest intellectuals in history, including such figures as Plato and Rousseau, have played with ideas and paradoxes partly in the sheer excitement of intellectual brilliance.

In African conditions we may want to say that it is the duty of every intellectual to be socially committed; but to describe the duties of an intellectual is different from defining the intellectual himself. After all, we all agree that it is the duty of every Ugandan to pay his taxes. But it would be an odd definition which asserted that a Ugandan was he who was prepared to pay his taxes. Ugandans who do not pay their taxes are Ugandans all the same, though deficient in social virtue. Intellectuals who are not committed to society nor specially inspired by the pursuit of truth are intellectuals all the same, though deficient in either social or scholarly virtues.

I agree with Akena Adoko that there may be a case at the present stage of national development for saying that academic intellectuals in Africa ought to be socially committed. But social commitment, I asserted, was never to be confused with social conformity.

When we ask African intellectuals to contribute to nation-building we had better be sure that we are not simply asking them to conform. Conformity either with popular opinion or with the government's view may sometimes be a good thing, but it depends upon the regime, the society, and the validity of popular or governmental reasoning.

I said then, and reaffirm now, that sincere political commitment might, depending upon the regime in power, or a specific policy espoused, sometimes demand social criticism rather than social compliance:

> When we ask a creative writer or an academic teacher to be socially sensitive and politically engaged, we should allow for the possibility that he may disagree with the particular government in power in his country or with the particular policy of the government, or with a majority opinion at a particular moment in time.[4]

What Wole Soyinka said of the creative writer might also be said of the academic writer in some fields of social studies:

> Where the writer in his own society can no longer function as conscience he must recognize that his choice lies between denying himself totally or withdrawing to the position of chronicler or post-mortem surgeon. . . . The artist has always functioned in African society as the record of the mores and experience of his society *and* the voice of vision in his own time. It is time for him to respond to this essence of himself.[4]

This is a conception of the creative writer as a sage or teacher. Wole Soyinka sometimes talks as if this particular conception of the role of the artist/writer no longer commands support in Africa. He suggests that the writer is expected now to deny himself independence from 'the mass direction' — that is he must conform with the masses instead of attempting to teach the masses. And yet, in reality, the ordinary people might still look upon the African writer in the way most of novelist Chinua Achebe's readers in Nigeria look upon him — as a kind of teacher. The teacher in African society often has a mystique. That is one reason why President Julius Nyerere is still respectfully referred to in his country as *Mwalimu* or teacher. He has become president of his country, and yet the title of teacher is still a contribution to his stature rather than a detraction from it.

The prestige of the teacher becomes in the modern period intertwined with the prestige of the printed word in the new Africa. The art of writing in its newness commands a sense of awe among much of the population. The academic writer has therefore a grave responsibility in the use to which he puts the prestige of teaching and the prestige of the printed word. But the responsibility is the responsibility to teach as he deems best and not to conform as he deems prudent. The academic intellectual has to be permitted the luxury of intellectual honesty in his classroom and intellectual freedom in his research and publications. Again, an African creative writer captured the spirit and the obligation of the literary and academic intellectual when he said:

> The writer cannot expect to be excused from the task of re-education and re-generation that must be done. In fact he should march in front . . . perhaps what I write is applied art as distinct from pure. But who cares? Art is important. But so is education.

The kind I have in mind. And I don't see how the two need to be mutually exclusive. [5]

But intellectuals are not merely those who put their ideas down in writing. There are others as well, and Akena Adoko was less than just when he suggested that the sin of withdrawal from the African revolution had been committed by the African intellectuals. On the contrary, during that very period of debate in the Kampala town hall early in 1969 the headlines had emphasized afresh what could all too easily be forgotten—the central role intellectuals have often played in different aspects of Africa's transformation. Among the headlines of the time were those concerning the tragic death of Dr Eduardo Mondlane, the late President of the Mozambique Liberation Front (FRELIMO). Mondlane was widely described as a revolutionary intellectual. He was not only a Doctor of Philosophy, but had formerly held an academic appointment at an American university.

The Board of the Faculty of Social Sciences at Makerere University passed the following resolution on hearing of the assassination of Dr Mondlane:

> We the social scientists at Makerere join in mourning our colleague Dr Eduardo Mondlane. A distinguished anthropologist, he left the security of the university to answer the call of his people, and he devoted himself to the struggle against colonial oppression. His commitment inspired us all. Our deepest sympathy goes to his family and to the people of Mozambique in this time of tragedy.

This was a tribute from university social scientists to a colleague who lost his life in a revolutionary cause.

Another eminent African intellectual in the headlines at the same time was the Reverend Ndabaningi Sithole, on trial for his life in Salisbury on charges of alleged conspiracy to murder Ian Smith and two members of his Cabinet. Sithole had suffered already for his convictions and patriotic commitment, having spent several years in restriction. By any definition, Sithole was an intellectual. His book, *African Nationalism*, was a pioneer analysis of the ideological foundations of African nationalist assertion. Like so many other intellectuals, Ndabaningi Sithole attached special importance to ideas as a factor in social change. As Sithole himself put it: 'In our examination of the factors that have given rise to this much-talked-about African nationalism, it is well to bear in mind that all movements of consequence are preceded by ideas'.[6] He had indeed spoken like a true intellectual.

In Dar es Salaam, not far from where Mondlane was assassinated and where many of Sithole's countrymen plot and wait for the moment of Zimbabwe's liberation, there has resided an eminent African intellectual. His name is, of course, Julius K. Nyerere—the leader of an important revolutionary experiment in modern Africa.

It is not often remembered that there are different categories of intellectuals. There is a tendency in Africa at times to think of intellectuals as those people on university campuses. But most people on African university campuses are only one category of intellectuals. That is the category that relates intellectual pursuits to higher learning and commits its mental resources to the arts of teaching and research.

Another broad category of intellectuals is that of literary intellectuals. These need not be attached to the university, but they could be. Literary intellectuals are those who are engaged in a significant way in writing either as a full-time profession, or as a serious pastime. Many eminent journalists belong to this class of intellectuals. So do poets, novelists and playwrights, who may or may not be involved in higher education.

Then there are the political intellectuals. Very often these are the most ideologically engaged of all intellectuals, though they by no means hold a monopoly of ideological commitment. Many people in government, political parties or in higher reaches of the Civil and Diplomatic Service are, to all intents and purposes, political intellectuals. By my definition they are often fascinated by ideas and have evolved the capacity to handle many of them effectively. The ideas that are of most immediate interest to them are inevitably those which concern the polity, the behaviour of man as a political animal, and the intellectual basis of political and administrative organization.

The other broad category of intellectuals in Africa's experience is that of general intellectuals. This category is a residual one in that it encompasses within it those people who are fascinated by and effective in handling ideas, but who do not fall within the other three categories. There are journalists who belong more to the category of general intellectuals than to that of literary intellectuals. And there are civil servants who are more general than political in their orientations. It should be noted that the category of general intellectuals could, with the increasing complexity of a society, be sub-divided to make a whole new category. The general intellectuals include the great majority of those who are consumers of the literary, academic and political output. Many school-teachers and other professional people are general intellectuals. But at the beginning, within this general category must also be included those engaged in the fine arts pending the full intellectualization of creativity. Some art in traditional Africa was intellectual but there was also a lot which was stereotype handicraft.

When art is too social and executed according to a rigid stereotype or ritual, the challenge of ideas remains absent. To that extent the artist or craftsman who does not innovate but simply follows a tradition is not likely to be an intellectual. The few whose work indicates such daring might, for the time being, be included in the broader category of general intellectuals. With the greater individualization of art, and the assertion of artistic innovation, the challenge of ideas begins to affect creativity. Art becomes intellectualized as it becomes individualized. And when a complete school or large enough collection of individualized artists grows in a society it becomes warrantable to define artists as a distinct category of intellectuals, separate both from the general and from the literary. Modern art in Africa is becoming sufficiently widespread and individualized to warrant identification as an emerging, new, distinct sub-class of intellectuals. But because of the newness of modern art in Africa its place in the African revolution is still as yet undecided. Artistic intellectuals are only just beginning to win their autonomy.

The category of general intellectuals might indeed be deemed to be the mother category. Out of the general intellectuals there first broke off a political category; and then a literary one; and then an academic one. The artistic sub-unit is only just beginning to acquire a definition of its own. The process is one of *differentiation* as the group of intellectuals becomes large enough and the criteria of intellectualism become complex enough to permit specialization. But from the point of view of relevance for revolutionary change, we can continue to think mainly in terms of the four initial categories I have mentioned.

There are other reasons apart from revolutionary relevance as to why we need to be specific about the three categories of academic, literary and political — and then group all the rest under a general category. One pertinent consideration is that the three specific categories are the most important in the function of the dissemination of ideas and in the application of ideas to social needs. The academic researchers and teachers at universities, the writers and literary analysts outside the university, the political activists, planners and decision-makers all play a particularly critical role in spreading ideas and giving them social relevance.

The effect of intellectuals on the modern face of Africa's history has been enormous. The twentieth century might indeed be called the golden age of intellectuals in Africa's history. Many of the great movements of change have been initiated or led by intellectuals. We must not forget that the early Pan-African Conferences and nationalist movements in London, Lisbon, New York or Manchester were basically movements of black intellectuals committed to the enhancement of black dignity in Africa and in the rest of the Negro world. There have, of course, always been intellectuals in Africa's experience. But intellectualism before the inauguration of formal schools was more limited in scope. There were indeed many Africans in the villages who were fascinated by ideas and who could handle some of them quite effectively. But there can be no doubt that education expands both the capacity for fascination and the skills of abstract analysis. Formal education in Africa therefore changed the nature of intellectualism fundamentally, from a kind which was grounded in custom and traditional faith to a kind which was affected by secularism and rationality.

From the experience of the Gold Coast and elsewhere in Africa we might say that the first important category of intellectuals in the modern sense produced in Africa was, perhaps predictably, that of general intellectuals. These were people interested in ideas and educated enough to handle them, but impossible to classify at that stage as either literary, academic, or political intellectuals.

What did they become next? It is possible to argue that while in English-speaking Africa the category of political intellectuals came next, in Francophone Africa it was the literary category which emerged first as a distinct group. It has indeed been pointed out often enough that Léopold Senghor of Senegal was a poet, Keita Fodéba of Guinea a producer of ballets, Bernard Dadié of the Ivory Coast a novelist and Cofi Gadeau a playwright, before they held office in their respective states.[7]

But while it is true that these people were writers before they ever held public office, they were politicians. Generally speaking, the colonial situation in both Francophone and Anglophone Africa almost inevitably dictated that the first *specialized* category of intellectuals was the sub-class of political intellectuals. That was why in the beginning of African self-assertion there was often an assumed equation between African intellectuals and African politicians. There developed a so-called colonial office attitude to educated Africans — perhaps typified by an assessment registered in colonial office records in 1875 that the ' "educated natives" or "scholars" . . . have always been a thorn in the side of the Government of the Gold Coast. They have been at the bottom of most of the troubles on the Coast for some years past'.[8] It was partly this kind of status enjoyed by those who were literate which tended to make a politician out of almost every scholar in those early days of African self-assertion. And experience in the Gold Coast, which later became the first black African country to liberate itself from colonialism, was to be repeated in many another African country.

Many of the political intellectuals in those early days were also literary intellectuals. Mensah Sarbah did some writing. Later on so did Nnamdi Azikiwe of Nigeria, George Padmore of the West Indies, Jomo Kenyatta of Kenya. But much of their writing was subordinate to their politics. They were using the pen primarily as an additional element in their political activity. To that extent they were first and foremost political rather than literary intellectuals.

It was not until just before and after the Second World War that a sub-class of African literary intellectuals became more clearly discernible as a distinct group. These were the poets, the playwrights, the novelists and the political essayists. It is true that much of their work (as in the case of the negritude school) was indeed political, but the people themselves were primarily writers rather than politicians. This is the distinction. Political intellectuals can combine their politics with literary activity and literary intellectuals can be occupied with political themes in their writing. But Aimé Césaire, Peter Abrahams and James Ngugi are primarily writers with political commitments, whereas Kwame Nkrumah and Julius Nyerere are primarily politicians with literary inclinations.

But modern Africa is gripped by the doctrine of the primacy of politics. Political considerations often assert their pre-eminence. And so the literary intellectuals are rather unwilling very often to tear themselves away completely from politics as a central preoccupation. Many African literary figures feel they ought to be involved in the task of national regeneration, social criticism and ideological engagements. James Ngugi wa Thiong'o, in a public lecture given at Makerere in November 1968, asserted the need for a literature of social conscience and commitment in Africa; and we have quoted others like Chinua Achebe and Wole Soyinka of similar persuasion. Soyinka spent some time in detention in Nigeria partly because of the extent to which he was prepared to go in his reservations about the Federal Government's handling of the Biafran challenge.

The last category of African intellectuals to assume any important social relevance is that of academic intellectuals. Why have they been the last to emerge? Why did they have to come after an evolutionary process which first produced general, political, and literary intellectuals?

One reason is the degree of education needed for academic appointments. It had to take time before enough Africans were sufficiently trained to be eligible for university jobs. Another reason was the tendency for a colonial system to assume that subject peoples should not be entrusted with jobs entailing high skills too early. But a third reason why the sub-class of academic intellectuals has been the last to emerge in Africa is the simple fact that for many a university career was much less attractive than a political or an administrative one in that political stage of Africa's revolution. The excitement of the nationalist movement, the glamour of independence, the attractions of power and prestige at the centre of national life all helped to divert some of the best African minds away from academic to political and administrative pursuits.

But now Africa has academic as well as political intellectuals. And the nationalism of the latter has already been known to come into conflict with the occasional internationalism of the former. It is to this theme that we must now return.

The Internationalism of Ideas

We have already discussed how the role of intellectuals has become a major issue of political debate in Africa in the last few years. But the international dimension of intellectualism did not become an explicit part of the debate in Africa until the 1960s. In Uganda what brought this dimension to the fore was the detention of two prominent intellectuals, one of whom was the editor of *Transition*, a widely read politico-literary magazine published at the time from Kampala. The ramifications and repercussions raised, among other issues, the simple question of whether there is a necessary international dimension in the behaviour of intellectuals in certain contexts. My position on this particular aspect of the debate has been that there is such a dimension. Indeed, my theme in that public lecture at Makerere on the eve of the debate in the town hall was, quite simply, that intellectuals were in some sense an international class.

But I need to emphasize once again that the loyalty of intellectuals to their own countries is *not* therefore the weaker. On the contrary, we know that the leaders of independence movements in Africa were often intellectuals. The early Pan-African movements were often led by black intellectuals from the West Indies, North America and Africa. There is no doubt whatsoever that among the most passionate nationalists Africa has had, among the most sincere anti-imperialists, among the most consistent anti-tribalists, must surely be included intellectuals. These were also the internationalists who helped to internationalize Africa in a new way.

When we, therefore, say that intellectuals are in some matters an international class, we are asserting that many of their interests as intellectuals are the kinds of interests which cut across national boundaries. But we are also asserting that intellectuals have a highly developed capacity for *empathy*—for seeing a little of themselves in others, even if those others are hundreds or even thousands of miles away.

We have already defined an intellectual as a person who has the capacity to be fascinated by ideas, and has acquired the skill to handle some of those ideas effectively. The ideas may be social, aesthetic, philosophical, political or scientific. But in order to bring out the international element of this human phenomenon, let us relate the issues more specifically to that case study we have mentioned—the detention of two intellectuals in Uganda in 1968, Mayanja and Neogy, and the international stir which resulted from it.

We are facing here the critical question of the affair: Why was there so much external interest in the case of Neogy, editor of *Transition*? In many ways Abu Mayanja was a bigger figure in Uganda itself than Neogy was, but internationally Neogy was a more important figure than Mayanja. Why was this the case? The answer was not unrelated to a remark I made in my original personal statement on the arrest of Mayanja and Neogy. In that statement I had occasion to say, 'There is a sense in which intellectual freedom is indivisible'.

President Obote was right in taking me to task for a certain ambiguity in that particular remark. He took me to task in his speech in Parliament soon after my statement. The term 'intellectual freedom' could perhaps mean 'the freedom of intellectuals'. But that is not what I intended it to mean. By intellectual freedom I meant the freedom of survival for things which are valuable to the mind. The free flow of ideas, the interplay between different interpretations of reality, the dialogue between points of view, the freedom to write and to publish, the freedom to read, to teach and to learn, to hear public lectures even if the speakers are controversial—this is what I meant by intellectual freedom. By it I did not mean a special licence to intellectuals, but a climate which permits society and the educational system to benefit by a relatively unimpeded quest for social understanding and for truth.

In my assertion then that intellectual freedom was in a sense indivisible, I was simply alluding to the great interdependence between nations in scholarship, science and ideas. When a source of ideas in one part of the world is suppressed, it becomes a matter of relevance to people in other parts of the world who might happen to have an interest in that particular intellectual fountain. Great books move from boundary to boundary and free societies permit them to make an entry.

Intellectual freedom means the free expression of ideas and the free dissemination of knowledge, and the right of men to benefit by these. This free flow of ideas and knowledge extends beyond national boundaries. If there was a total suppression of the study of economics in other English-speaking nations of the world, the study of economics in Uganda would suffer. Uganda, therefore, has a vested interest in the freedom of economic scholarship in, say, Britain and the United States. By the same token, the study of medicine in Uganda would suffer if all major medical journals in Britain and America were suddenly suppressed by a conspiracy between the governments of Britain and the United States. These western governments should not, therefore, be surprised if several academic medical men in Uganda were to express concern following such a move. These are, of course, exaggerated examples. The simple point I am making is that men in one part of the world may often have a direct vested interest in the knowledge and ideas produced in another part of the world. In this sense, intellectual freedom has international relevance. It is not simply intellectuals who benefit by intellectual freedom. It is all those who are interested in education or are involved in it. Sometimes the equality of medical care, or the level of economic sophistication, are dependent on freedom to advance the boundaries of these fields of knowledge elsewhere.

Intellectuals are usually among the most articulate members of any society. They talk a lot, perhaps too much. That is one reason why they are often the first to react when intellectual freedom is endangered. Their reaction does not imply that they are the sole beneficiaries of such freedom; it simply proves that they are among the most articulate. The beneficiaries of intellectual freedom are all those who wish to see knowledge advanced and thought enhanced.

Great journals and magazines also acquire an international constituency. It just so happens that *Transition* was indeed an international magazine. A reader in Sweden or France or the United States enjoyed *Transition* and regarded it as one point of contact with intellectual life in East Africa, and inevitably had a vested interest in the survival of the magazine.

This is what differentiates intellectual freedom from other freedoms. Freedom to form a political party, for example, is basically domestic in its implications. Even freedom to form a trade union, in spite of international associations of trade unions, is still very often basically domestic and parochially limited. These things can become of international relevance. But they become of international significance only to the extent to which they impinge upon intellectual freedom and the free interplay of ideas.

Freedom of assembly or whether public meetings can be held in parts of Uganda or not is again very often basically domestic. But banning a public speaker, or a book, or detaining an international writer, or detaining an editor, inevitably has extra-domestic implications. The right of nations to learn from others, the right of readers in one society to await a literary output from another society are compromised in such situations.

Readers of books and magazines include other people apart from intellectuals. We should, therefore, continue to be aware that intellectual freedom is important to other sections of the community apart from intellectuals themselves. It is important to children seeking education; to parents worried about the quality of education their children might receive; to teachers eager to give of the best; to educational planners anxious for diversity. And yet, although intellectual freedom is not the same thing as the freedom of intellectuals, there is little doubt that among those who have a vested interest in intellectual freedom, intellectuals themselves are often in the forefront. When intellectual freedom is suppressed in one part of the world, there may be repercussions from intellectuals in other parts. We might, therefore, say that intellectuals are an international class, partly because the implications of intellectual freedom are international. The consciousness of certain values across national boundaries becomes more highly developed among those who keep abreast of developments within those boundaries of endeavour.

Are Intellectuals an International Class?

A related factor is the sheer question of communication. In many ways, intellectuals are often the most exposed of all classes to international communication. Their reading habits, their interests in certain books and magazines, their awareness of literary and cultural developments elsewhere in the world heightens their sensitivity to what goes on beyond their own borders. A peasant in Busoga is not likely to empathize or identify with a peasant in Singapore. They might not even know that the world is so vast as to include both Uganda and Singapore. And yet *intellectuals* between those two countries might well find areas of mutual awareness. One of the things which impressed me most when I passed through Singapore not long after the great troubles in Uganda of May 1966 was the coverage given to the Uganda crisis in a Singapore newspaper. A feature article of at least one full page was devoted to an analysis of the Uganda situation. But which section of the Singapore population was so interested in Uganda? Interest in the Uganda situation among the readers of that newspaper might be presumed to have resided mainly among the intellectually more sophisticated of the citizens of Singapore.

Some commentators in Uganda at the time of the debate on the *Transition* affair expressed surprise that there should have been international protest about the detention of an editor when the detention of others in Uganda had not sparked off comparable reactions. Again, a major difference might be in the area of communication. Class solidarity among peasants in the world is not of the kind which would make a peasant or small farmer in France react and send a cable of protest to Uganda if a peasant there were to be detained. But a telegram from a French intellectual to Uganda when a major intellectual is detained there is by no means an improbable eventuality. A villager in Uganda might not protest against injustice in Greece, Czechoslovakia or the United States. But an intellectual in Uganda is quite capable of doing so.

One might go further and say that the whole idea of class solidarity at the international level makes far more sense when one is referring to a class of intellectuals than it might if we referred to any other class. No millionaire in India or Africa is likely to react in passionate protest if a millionaire in the United States got into trouble with the authorities. No railway porter in Germany is likely to have the remotest idea of what is happening if a railway porter in Nigeria is victimized. This is partly because the occupation of the railway porter is not one which is likely to have a transnational impact. Nor is the status of a millionaire likely to command the protective anxiety of foreign millionaires much further away. With intellectuals it is different. The advantages they have had in education have given them advantages of communication, and greater access to mass media, and literary sources of reciprocal information have developed their sense of consciousness of what goes on in other parts of the world, and their sense of anxiety about what is wrong with the world.

In at least some schools of Marxism it is constantly maintained that class consciousness is a greater determinant of human behaviour and a more fundamental basis of human motivation than national or racial consciousness. This is the great international dimension of Marxist socialism. It is assumed that those who belong to the same class will, when their consciousness is aroused, empathize and identify with each other more readily than would those who belong to the same nation or the same race. The logical implications of this position would be the expectation that a worker in Uganda will find bonds of sympathy more readily with a worker in Britain or France or Japan than he would find with a landlord or businessman who is a fellow Ugandan. In fact, at the first Internationale of the Communist Party in 1919, European Marxists related socialism and international solidarity so closely that they imagined that only an alliance between workers in the metropolitan imperial countries and workers in the colonies would ever stand a chance of breaking the imperial hold on weaker peoples abroad. We now know that, on balance, it was more the nationalist forces in African countries which broke the imperial control than any significant international solidarity between workers in Uganda or Tanzania and workers in the docks of Liverpool and the factories of Manchester.

And yet was there not a sympathy and identification between nationalist agitators in the colonies and such radical socialists in Britain as Fenner Brockway and Barbara Castle? Time and again colonial nationalists under victimization from authorities did find support and radical defence in their favour among socialists in the metropolitan countries themselves. Was not this a demonstration of the possibilities of comradeship between those who have the interest of the ordinary people at heart?

And yet this is a confusion which verges on being a case of mistaken identity. Solidarity between socialists or radicals is not the same thing as solidarity between workers. Socialist consciousness may indeed be an international phenomenon and yet class consciousness among workers still remains basically parochial.

The Communist Manifesto by Marx and Engels concludes with the rallying cry, 'Workers of the world unite! You have nothing to lose but your chains!'. But, in fact, a global unification of workers has never been a realistic proposition. Ordinary workers are concerned with day-to-day issues affecting their wages and hours of work. These are influenced basically by parochial or domestic considerations within the countries of the workers themselves. There are no effective international controls of wages, salaries and hours of work. A joint exertion by the workers of the world for a joint system of benefits and privilege from labour would not make much sense. But even more important from the point of view of this discussion here is that such a call for workers of India to unite with workers of Brazil, or for labourers in Detroit to find a sudden impulse of unification with labourers in Jinja, is an ambition too remote for serious consideration.

It is true that there have been communist international movements that have captured the attention of international bodies at specific moments in history. It is true that aggrieved radicals in colonial territories found sympathy and support from radicals in metropolitan imperialist countries. It is true that Josiah Kariuki, when detained in Kenya under the Emergency Regulation, and associated with the Mau Mau insurrection, found it meaningful to complain in a secret letter sent to Barbara Castle in Britain about deficiencies and injustice in colonial Kenya.

But when you look very closely at this apparent unity between peoples of different nationalities struggling against capitalist oppression it is not really a unity between workers. It is much more often a unity between intellectuals. British socialists in alliance with African nationalists during the colonial period were often demonstrating not so much pan-proletarianism but simply a kind of *pan-intellectualism*. It was a form of understanding between radical intellectuals in Europe and radical intellectuals in Africa.

When the Communist Manifesto proclaims, 'Workers of the world unite', it is at best simply saying 'radicals of the world unite'. In socialist jargon there is at times a tendency to use the term 'working classes', when in reality what is meant is 'socialist intellectuals'. Certainly the duties which Marxism sometimes seems to impose on ordinary workers betrays a total confusion between radical intellectualism and militant proletarianism. Take, for example, Karl Marx's inaugural address for the Working Men's International Association established on 28 September 1864 at a public meeting held at St Martin's Hall, Longacre, London. Marx concluded his address with again the clarion call, 'Proletarians of all countries unite!'. Did this mean factory sweepers in Manchester or railway porters in New York? Textile labourers in Bombay? Shamba boys in Accra? If so, Marx was assuming a high level of intellectual sophistication among all these different sections of workers. For in that same speech Marx assigned to 'the working classes' what he called

> The duty to master for themselves the mysteries of international politics; to watch the diplomatic acts of their respective governments; to counteract them, if necessary, by all means in their power; when unable to prevent, to combine in simultaneous denunciations, and to vindicate the simple laws of moral justice which ought to govern the relations of private individuals, as the rules paramount for the intercourse of nations . . . proletarians of all countries unite! [9]

Evidently this language was not addressed to the dockworkers of Liverpool or the coolies of Bombay or the African miners in the Copperbelt in South Africa. Nor was the duty being imposed on these people likely to be of the kind which ordinary workers could undertake. To 'master the mysteries of international politics', as Marx put it, is an undertaking for intellectual radicals rather than discontented factory sweepers.

Lenin, the great architect of modern communist Russia, was about as internationalist as Karl Marx in his vision. Perhaps in other things Lenin was less internationalist than Karl Marx, but he was more aware of the revolutionary role of intellectuals than Marx sometimes appears to have been. Lenin also seemed to be conscious of the fact that international socialism is, in the ultimate analysis, a form of pan-intellectualism. Of course, the more orthodox internationalism of classic Marxism was certainly present in Lenin's thought. He did seem to share the belief in a unity between members of the same class which transcended or was supposed to transcend racial or national boundaries. He had led Russia in the great revolution in 1917 and the first few years of consolidation. He could have regarded this as a great patriotic triumph for his country. But for Lenin in this case the larger vision was more commanding. Russia had indeed taken the lead in carrying out the revolution but to Lenin this was merely because she had proved to be 'the weakest link in the capitalist chain'. A great historical role had been thrust upon Russia, not necessarily because of any heroic national characteristics, but simply because of the fragility of this particular link of that necklace of bondage. It is true that even among Leninists this degree of internationality was sometimes attributed to the workers rather than to radical intellectuals. There was still faith that a British worker might, in the final analysis, feel a greater affinity with an Indian coolie than with a member of the British middle class. We might again remind ourselves that two years after the Russian Revolution the Manifesto of the Communist Internationale at its first Congress of 1919 put forward the doctrine that: 'The workers not only of Amman, Algiers and Bengal, but also of Persia and Armenia will gain their opportunity of independent existence only when the workers of England and France have overthrown Lloyd George and Clemenceau'.[10]

Very often when Marxists say 'the workers want this or that' they really mean 'the socialists want this or that'. And when they talk about the socialists in terms of ideological formulations and innovations they really mean the intellectuals among socialists. As we indicated, Lenin was all too aware that international socialism is, at the base, a kind of pan-intellectualism. He once quoted with approval Karl Kautsky's assertion that it was 'absolutely untrue' to regard socialist consciousness as a direct result of the proletarian class struggle. Kautsky went on to say:

Modern socialist consciousness can arise only on the basis of profound scientific knowledge . . . the vehicle of science is not the proletariat, but the *bourgeois intelligentsia* [Kautsky's emphasis]:

it was in the minds of individual members of this stratum that modern socialism originated; it was they who communicated it to the more intellectually developed proletarians who in their turn, introduced it into the proletarian class struggle where conditions allowed that to be done.[11]

Lenin credited the working classes with a capacity for spontaneity but not with an automatic capacity for a socialist consciousness. Ideas of socialist democracy in Russia arose, according to Lenin, altogether independently of this spontaneous growth of the working-class movement; they arose out of what Lenin regarded as a natural and inevitable outcome of the development of thought among the revolutionary socialist intelligentsia. And even further back, the birth of socialism was, according to Lenin, inseparable from the workings of intellectualism:

> The theory of socialism . . . grew out of the philosophic, historical, and economic theories elaborated by educated representatives of the property classes, by intellectuals. By their social status, the founders of modern scientific socialism, Marx and Engels, themselves belonged to the bourgeois intelligentsia.[12]

All these are factors which make possible the phenomenon of pan-intellectualism. Intellectuals often empathize or identify with other classes. There have been intellectuals who have devoted themselves to the cause of peasants, or the cause of workers. But there are other occasions when intellectuals empathize or sympathize with fellow intellectuals. This is where pan-intellectualism attains its purest state — which is not necessarily its healthiest state.

The Internationalism of Students

Student solidarity on an international scale is sometimes a form of pan-intellectualism. Not all students are intellectuals, but a majority of them probably are. The sociological and psychological situation of trying to understand new things, of having to compete for effectiveness in class, of having to read books and express one's ideas in writing, of having to pass academic examinations, of having to redefine one's loyalties — all these tend towards inducing students to be very interested in at least some ideas, and to develop some skill in handling a few of them effectively.

What should be remembered is that some undergraduates are basically only *temporary intellectuals*. When they leave the university they gradually lose their capacity to be fascinated by ideas, or their ability to handle ideas well, or both. And this erosion of their intellectualism is due either to their inner temperament and state of mind, or simply to pressures of other preoccupations.

The fact that there is student unrest in countries which are vastly different in every other way is again an indication of the breadth of this junior school of pan-intellectualism. From Senegal to Mexico, from Germany to Pakistan, from Nairobi to Berkeley, from Kampala to Tokyo, the world has seen signs of student unease about the state of the universe. Sometimes student activity of this kind is the outcome of a demonstration effect. But, as I have argued in another context, political demonstration effect presupposes a capacity to empathize. 'Keeping up with the Joneses' presupposes an ability to identify with the Joneses sufficiently to be able to say: 'What have they got that I have not got? What they can do, I can do!'. It is factors such as these which made German students demonstrate on behalf of Senegalese students by a rowdy show of public disapproval when President Senghor was awarded a special literary prize in Frankfurt in September 1968. It is an even greater capacity to identify which made Makerere students go on a sit-down strike on 29 January 1969, in sympathy with the closing-down of the University College, Nairobi.

As we indicated earlier, in January 1969, the Political Science Club of the University of Nairobi had invited Mr Oginga Odinga, then leader of the Opposition in Kenya, to address a meeting at the University College. The Kenya Government banned the meeting. The students were indignant and asked to see the Minister of Education. When the Minister deferred a meeting the students boycotted lectures. The Kenya Government retalitated by closing down the university. It was this closure which made students at Makerere, in Uganda, also go on strike in sympathy.

The Kenya Government was unwise when it prevented the Nairobi students from having a speaker of their own choice, particularly when the speaker was, at the time, a free and eminent citizen of the country. To deny a university audience the right to hear controversial views was, so the students rightly thought, to attack the very essence of freedom of discussion.

But people do sometimes go too far in defending what is legitimately their right; or they may go too far in exercising these rights. There were many in East Africa at the time who believed that the Kenya Government was wrong to have banned a speech at the college by the leader of the Opposition Party, but also that the students in a country such as Kenya, where political authority was still inadequately consolidated, were wrong to have defied the government so conspicuously.

And yet when the Kenya Government had closed down the university and forcibly sent the students to their homes all over the country, the next step needed was what, at the time, I called 'academic amnesty': an unconditional forgiveness of those whose excesses were motivated by a desire either to exercise or to safeguard academic freedom.

The Kenya Government rose to the occasion and did extend an

academic amnesty to all but the five students who were suspended in February 1969 as alleged ringleaders. Discussions went on in neighbouring countries about the fate of those students. A concern for their future became once again a form of intellectual internationalism at the student level. At Makerere, students discussed behind closed doors what action would be appropriate if those five students were never allowed to return to the University of Nairobi. The possibility of the suspended Kenya students being permitted other educational opportunities in Europe was vigorously pursued by fellow students in London as well as in the neighbouring university institutions. But even these alternative solutions presumed the permission of the Kenya Government to let the students leave the country.

Students with the new radical fervour are sceptical of academic freedom, but they rise to its defence when the challenge is to the right of the students themselves to discuss issues on campus or have speakers of their choice. Some of the earlier convulsions at the University of California, Berkeley, concerned interference with the freedom of discussion on campus. Students reacted strongly to that. In East Africa we had a similar reaction when one of the governments sought to curtail the right of dialogue between students and others.

The events in Nairobi in February 1969 raised an important question about the extent to which students should enjoy not only the right of dialogue but also the right of defiance. Perhaps here we are justified in making a distinction between students operating within consolidated social structures in developed countries, and students operating within fragile social structures in new states.

In the face of the entrenched values in America and Europe, it might make sense that students should resort to demonstrations. Mere speech-making can have no effect on the establishment and its institutionalized preferences. But, as we indicated earlier, the problem in Africa is not of entrenched values, but of unstable values still seeking a solid foundation to rest on. The fact that documents like the *Arusha Declaration* of Tanzania and *The Common Man's Charter* of Uganda are treated as momentous national events is evidence that Africa is seeking, but has not yet consolidated, a new political culture with new political and moral preferences. A document costing one shilling in a bookshop, *The Common Man's Charter*, became an occasion in Uganda for repeated affirmations of new social directions. The *Arusha Declaration* in Tanzania became an occasion for similar drumbeats, and for busy people or tired schoolchildren walking dozens of miles affirming an acceptance of the new blueprint which the President had issued. Only a society still unsure of its values, and eager to create a pattern for moral guidance in public affairs, could treat such blueprints with such earnest fervour.

Where values are entrenched, as in Europe and America, student power may perhaps legitimately be used for demonstrations. The structures are solid, capable of withstanding much of the challenge. And the structures are certainly impossible to affect dramatically without major eruptions of popular questioning. But where values are unsettled, as in Africa, and institutions are fragile, capable of collapsing under strain, student power should be careful how it manifests or expresses itself. On the one hand, student power in Africa is more limited than in North America because it may be more ruthlessly suppressed by a nervous regime. On the other hand, successful challenges of authority even by a student body in Africa could shake the foundation of some of the national institutions.

As argued earlier the role of students in African countries should lean more on the duty to debate than on the duty to demonstrate. Those documents like *The Common Man's Charter* and the *Arusha Declaration* need to be subjected to careful, sympathetic, but at the same time critical, examination. If East Africans are looking for a new political culture they must be sure that every aspect of the proposed new culture is examined before it is adopted and internalized. The search for new values has, of necessity, to include a readiness to ask questions about every proposition. Student days are pre-eminently the days of debate and questioning.

In Uganda before the military coup of 1971, President Obote wanted to extend this culture of debate more firmly to the levels of education prior to university. Obote's idea of student parliaments was a case in point. Student parliaments, as proposed by the President of Uganda, could evolve into institutions for training not only in decision-making but also for training in the use of the critical faculties. Ideas and proposals coming before young people become subject to careful weighing. The quest for a new political culture in Uganda might indeed have to start at the school level, as pupils and students find a role in the evolution of that culture.

If, then, the ultimate public function of students in situations of fragile institutions is the right to debate rather than the duty to demonstrate, the Nairobi episode in 1969 did pose a dilemma. The students' rights to debate had indeed been curtailed by that very action which prevented a major national figure from coming to talk to them. But once that was curtailed, did the students have a duty to demonstrate in defence of their right to debate?

In the ultimate analysis, that was the crux of the matter. In retrospect it remains true that the Kenya Government was not only mistaken in preventing Mr Oginga Odinga from having a dialogue with the students at the university, but also in reacting so strongly when the students engaged in a relatively mild form of demonstration — boycotting lectures for a day or two. If the students had resorted to a stronger kind of demonstration, such as taking over offices or marching on the Ministry of Education, or publicly denouncing the head of state, the challenge would have been of the kind which could compromise the fragile stability of a new state. But the Nairobi students chose their mode of demonstration well. The response of the government was less well inspired.

From the point of view of the international dimension of the crisis of relevance, the significance of the Nairobi academic crisis of early 1969 was not merely in regard to the banning of a speech by an Opposition leader or the suspension of the student leaders afterwards. Academic freedom is perhaps the most intellectual of all liberties and, precisely because of that, it is also the most international of all freedoms.

As students at Makerere and Dar es Salaam worry about their colleagues in Nairobi or Louvanium, as students at McGill, Yale and Berkeley are angry about wars in Indo-China, as students in Japan demonstrate for a vision of a new world, one feels that the torch of pan-intellectualism at its brightest has been passed to the international community of students, for the time being. Like all forms of pan-intellectualism since the Renaissance, this one has also an element of sheer self-satisfied arrogance about it. Sometimes student solidarity merges with international socialism in presuming to 'speak for the workers' in Europe and the 'oppressed' in the Third World. But the student upheaval in the world is, in the ultimate analysis, yet another manifestation of the internationality of intellectualism, and its capacity to empathize with others, even if they are drawn from different social strata or born in different countries.

Conclusion

This, then, is the undercurrent of internationalism in the crisis of relevance as it has manifested itself in Africa. The pressures of nationalist criteria of university relevance, the imperatives of socialist canons of legitimate academic engagement, the demands of full university immersion in the process of development, all engender a sense of acute self-centredness in each society. The university as a transmission belt of new knowledge and new ideas between its own society and the world beyond can also become parochialized under these other pressures.

Somehow contact with the world beyond needs to be maintained if intellectual isolation and academic stagnation are to be averted. This is where a hard inner core of liberalism has to be saved in all this welter of nationalist, socialist and developmental pressures. Africa then becomes open to the breeze of internationalism, with all its diverse smells, both pleasing and offensive.

From the point of view of the free flow of ideas and the free flow of knowledge, the most international of all ideologies is not socialism but liberalism. As a full-blooded domestic arrangement, liberalism might have to be qualified by nationalist, socialist and developmental imperatives. But academic creativity, intellectual values, and scientific innovation do need a residual liberal ethos. The capacity to invent, the right to be creative, the right of dialogue and debate, the pursuit of inner convictions in scholarship, all flourish where some openness and intellectual interaction are still permitted. The crisis of relevance in Africa has to ensure that, when all is said and done, this inner core of openness in university life is not smothered.

References and Notes

1. See *The People* (Kampala), 8 April and 19 May 1967.
2. Consult also Ali A. Mazrui, 'Tanzaphilia', *Violence and Thought*, Longman, 1969.
3. Akena Adoko, 'The role of the intellectuals in African revolution', statement delivered on 6 February 1969 in the dialogue at the town hall, City of Kampala. Akena Adoko's fuller statement was also published later in *East Africa Journal* (March 1969).
4. Wole Soyinka, 'The writer in an African state', *Transition*, No. 31 (June/July 1967), 11. These issues are also discussed in Ali A. Mazrui, 'What is an intellectual?' *East Africa Journal* (April 1969).
5. Chinua Achebe, 'The novelist as teacher', *New Statesman*, 29 January 1965.
6. Ndabaningi Sithole, *African Nationalism*, Oxford University Press, 1959.
7. Thomas Hodgkin and Ruth Schachter [Morgenthau], 'French-speaking West Africa in transition', *International Conciliation*, No. 528 (May 1960), 387.
8. The quotation is a loose rendering of a Minute of 6 February 1875, by A. W. L. Heming, late head of the African Department of the Colonial Office, CO/96/115.
9. See *Selected Works* in two volumes by Karl Marx and Friedrich Engels, Foreign Languages Publishing House, Moscow, 1962, pp. 384-5.
10. Cited in *Survey* (Soviet Affairs), No. 43 (August 1962).
11. Cited by Lenin in *What is to be Done?* See Lenin *Selected Works*, 3 vols., Foreign Languages Publishing House, Moscow, 1960, Vol. 1, p. 156.
12. *What is to be Done?*, p. 149.

19 Cultural Liberation and the Future of the Educated Class

A number of writers have already traced the coming of western education in Africa, the emergence of a modern intelligentsia, the expansion of their role in society, the internationalization of their horizons, and their significance for modern Africa and its new educational and political systems. Let us now attempt to capture the main trends behind the emergence of this modern intelligentsia before attempting to speculate on its future.

We have defined an intellectual as a person who has the capacity to be fascinated by ideas and has acquired the skill to handle some of those ideas effectively. Must an intellectual be socially committed? Social commitment is not part of the definition of an intellectual — however desirable it may be for African intellectuals to be so engaged. Not all educated Africans are intellectuals — a few are ex-intellectuals, having either lost interest in abstract ideas, or permitted their intellectual skills to fall into disrepair. Educated Africans who become very prosperous prematurely are particularly prone to intellectual decay.

If western education has been a liberating experience in Africa, it has also been a case of intellectual dependency. We define intellectual dependency as excessive reliance on an alien reference-group for ideas and analytical guidelines. A disproportionate number of African intellectuals in the twentieth century have been products of western or western-derived educational institutions. Consequently, their universe of ideas has in turn been primarily western-derived. They have manifested both *submissive and aggressive dependency*. Submissive dependency implies compliance uncritically with the reality of being dominated, a tendency to imitate and to be deferential towards the conqueror. Aggressive dependency, on the other hand, is an extreme and irrational rejection of the alien father-figure, a rejection which regards hating the conqueror as the equivalent of self-respect. Both forms of dependency are, by definition, a negation of autonomy and genuine self-confidence. Let us again examine their genesis.

The Secularization of Dependency

Intellectual westernization in the early days in Africa was closely linked to Christianization. As we noted earlier, the missionary schools played a critical role in producing the earlier generations of modern African intellectuals. And many of these aspired to be, or did become, clerical figures or teachers in missionary schools. The lure of the Church was still strong when Kwame Nkrumah was growing up. Like many other budding African intellectuals, Nkrumah wanted to become a priest. In many ways professional preachers and professional teachers enjoyed more prestige in earlier colonial conditions than any other stratum of 'native society'. Intellectual dependency at that stage was heavily sacralized — the educated African was often still a pilgrim in a religious sense, longing for some progress towards both spiritual and material salvation.

After a while, intellectual dependency began to be secularized. The stages were as follows:

1. *The liberal phase of secularization.* This was the phase when western liberalism began to exert greater influence on the political thinking of young Africans than western Christianity. In West Africa Nkrumah and Senghor quoted Rousseau on the general will. In East Africa these were the days when Nyerere was excited by John Stuart Mill's ideas on liberty, the subjection of women, and representative government; young Milton Obote was enjoying the republicanism of the author of *Paradise Lost*, and both were beginning to echo Abraham Lincoln's dictum concerning 'government of the people, by the people, for the people'. Even ancient Greece — as a fountainhead of western ideas of democracy — received the homage of newly westernized young Africans.

2. *The liberal-nationalist phase of secularization.* The transition from fascination with liberal ideas to a new form of African nationalism was smooth. Early African intellectuals were selectively inspired by Jeffersonian language and the American Declaration of Independence. They also admired Mahatma Gandhi and India's Congress Party. The new nationalists appealed to western liberal values in order to gain nationalist concessions. They demanded 'one man, one vote', 'majority rule', 'undiluted democracy', 'freedom of speech' in order to increase their leverage on the pace of decolonization.

3. *The socialist-nationalist phase of secularization.* By this time many African intellectuals had discovered western socialism, the socialist version of anti-imperialism, and the whole debate concerning the link between capitalism and imperialism. Non-alignment and Jawaharlal Nehru loomed large as nationalist symbols with leftist tendencies. There was also a new interest in African socialism and traditional collectivism.

4. *The Marxist phase of secularization.* Socialism can be no more

than a list of related egalitarian values, but Marxism is a system of thought and a method of analysis.

From an intellectual point of view, all these four phases have been linked to continuing dependency. The process was one of secularizing the dependency, rather than ending it. The intellectual world of educated Africans has been witnessing a slow passage from biblical imagery to Marxist dialectics. There is no doubt that the pilgrim within the universe of African intellectualism has been retreating. The question for the 1980s is whether the African patriot has been making any intellectual progress.

Rebellion: Political, Economic and Cultural

Liberalism went well with political rebellion against the West; Marxism may go well with economic rebellion against the West—but both forms of rebellion are compatible with continuing cultural and intellectual dependency. The old days of biblical conformity among Africans were the days of submissive dependency—political, economic and cultural. The liberal and liberal-nationalist phases witnessed escalating political rebellion and agitation against colonial rule, but combined with continuing economic and cultural dependency. Those early political nationalists did not question their intimate economic ties with western economies, nor the dignity of aid and foreign investment. They simply questioned the West's colonial rule in Africa.

The rest of the 1970s and at least the early 1980s will witness rising economic restlessness in Africa and the Third World generally. Marxist explanations of underdevelopment and economic domination will find more and more converts among African intellectuals, though not necessarily among African rulers. The language of economic rebellion—where it occurs—is likely to borrow heavily from the Marxist tradition.

For an African, Marxism is a form of aggressive dependency. The African is still relying on a European intellectual tradition—but this time he has chosen a European tradition of dissent. Among the more superficial African Marxists there is also a desire to 'shock' the ruling classes of the West—comparable to a rebellious child kicking at the father-figure and shouting out obscenities known to be offensive to 'the old man'. There are of course more profound African Marxists, genuinely converted to a new way of looking at the world. Nevertheless African Marxism is a system which has been borrowed, often uncritically and totally, from an alien civilization.

In the early 1980s African intellectuals will indeed be in rebellion against both political and economic domination, but intellectually and culturally they will probably continue to be part of the radical West. The dependency of the mind will continue, as independence in production is sought and, in some cases, obtained.

The Revolution of the Imperfect Acculturates

A perfect product of French assimilation policy is Léopold Senghor, President of Senegal. A perfect result of British indirect rule was Ahmadu Bello, the late Sardauna of Sokoto in Nigeria. Senghor assimilated French culture deeply, and conceived even negritude in French terms. Ahmadu Bello, on the other hand, was a symbol of British insulation of Northern Nigeria from western and Christian influences. Ahmadu Bello signified important cultural continuities from pre-colonial to post-colonial traditions.

On the whole, African militants have come neither from the perfectly westernized African intellectuals like Senghor nor from the almost totally non-westernized leaders like the Sardauna. The militants have tended to come from the diverse middle category of 'imperfect acculturates'. The range in this middle category has itself been wide. Nkrumah was not as anglicized as Kofi Busia, but he was quite near the category of the assimilated. Sékou Touré was not as westernized as either Léopold Senghor or Houphouet-Boigny, or even as westernized as Nkrumah, but he was not far from the category of the assimilated. Among their followers were fellow imperfect acculturates, but further down the ladder of assimilation.

Most of the early African political leaders who were either fully assimilated or nearly assimilated were intellectuals. As already indicated, leadership against the West's *political* domination was captured by this group, especially from the 1930s and 1940s onwards. A staggering proportion of anti-colonial agitators in black Africa were products of western and Christian educational institutions.

The next phase of rebellion concerns *economic* liberation. The proportion of intellectuals in this phase — though still very high — is not as overwhelming as it was in the struggle against political colonialism per se. In the African continent as a whole economic liberators or potential liberators range from intellectuals like Julius Nyerere of Tanzania to religious warriors like Muammar Gaddafy of Libya and Idi Amin of Uganda.

On balance educated Africans out of power have tended to be more radical than educated Africans in power. The struggle for power has been a radicalizing experience for intellectuals, but the exercise of power has often had the reverse effect. Kwame Nkrumah was more Marxist before he returned to the Gold Coast from his studies overseas and after he was overthrown from power in 1966 than he ever was as president of Ghana. Other African intellectuals who got deradicalized in power include Hastings Banda of Malawi (now an ex-intellectual), the late Tom Mboya of Kenya, and indeed Léopold Senghor and Felix Houphouet-Boigny. In contrast, some non-intellectuals, starting as relatively apolitical, have been radicalized in the course of exercising power. The radicalization of Idi Amin is again an outstanding example. By 'radicalism' here we do not mean necessarily socialism or Marxism. Radicalism is a spectrum, ranging from nationalism and anti-imperialism to full-scale revolutionary commitment. African intellectuals out of power, and worried about economic domination by the developed states, are the ones who will increasingly be stimulated and inspired by Marxism. Whether those who succeed in capturing power will remain committed Marxists is one of the major questions for the 1980s.

To summarize the argument so far, those who led the African struggle against political domination were overwhelmingly intellectuals. Those who are leading the struggle against economic domination include intellectuals, but no longer in such disproportionate numbers. On the contrary, there are some notable non-intellectuals who have done more for Africa's economic liberation than the majority of intellectuals.

What about those who are leading or will lead Africa's rebellion against *cultural* domination? Ultimate leadership against cultural domination will initially come overwhelmingly from *non-intellectuals*, and certainly from imperfect acculturates who are much further down the ladder of assimilation than the Nkrumahs and Senghors of African history. We must also remember the authenticity drive by President Mobutu Sese Seko of Zaire. This is probably a sign of what to expect in many other parts of Africa in the 1980s—semi-westernized soldiers, often recruited from rural areas, suspicious of westernized compatriots in their midst, and newly experimenting with cultural revivalism. Mobutu has been forcing the Catholic Church to extend a new dignity to indigenous African names by giving them baptismal validity, while at the same time forging a new relationship between an alien religion and indigenous cultures in an African country. Idi Amin, another extremely imperfect acculturate, has been demanding new respect for African marriage customs, and new respect for African 'superstitions', including the formulation of policies on the basis of dreams. Before long the entire educational systems of places like Zaire and Uganda might—under political pressure—have to respond to the call for greater African authenticity.

Yet clearly Africa's cultural liberation must mean more than just cultural revivalism. The African past cannot be fully restored—and even if it could, it would not be an unmixed blessing in modern conditions. Africa's cultural liberation must mean both revivalism and innovation. The imperfect acculturates wil lead the indispensable revivalist thrust up to the middle of the 1980s and perhaps beyond. But how will Africa proceed to construct a new layer of innovation upon the revivalist accomplishments of the sub-westernized?

The Re-discovery of Liberalism

Another historic opportunity may well present itself for African intellectuals and educated Africans generally. The sub-acculturated soldiers in power — while leading the first revivalist phase of cultural liberation — will also be considerably intolerant of dissent. Many of the new rulers might well be strongly anti-intellectual, and at times brutal towards their westernized compatriots. Under such conditions, African intellectuals may react in two historically significant ways: one section will migrate to other lands, seeking freedom and new opportunities; another section will discover afresh the liberal values of tolerance, pluralism and individualism. Both responses, if they are on a sufficient scale, could be fundamental for the future of the black man everywhere.

First, let us note the difference between the new innovative African liberalism of the 1990s and the old imitative liberalism in Africa two generations previously. When Nnamdi Azikiwe was enthusing over Thomas Jefferson and Julius Nyerere over John Stuart Mill, in the 1930s and early 1940s, they were passing through a period of intellectual imitation of the West, combined with the beginnings of political rebellion. Intellectual hero-worship (be the hero Marx or Mill) runs counter to innovation, which must be the essence of the new liberalism.

Secondly, one must distinguish between liberal institutions and liberal rules of the game. The early liberal institutions which captured the imagination of young African intellectuals included western-style legislatures (starting with the colonial Legislative Council), the western-style party system, the Westminster model of governmental arrangements. By definition, these were clearly borrowed from the political experience of western countries.

The liberal rules of the game are important to liberals and non-liberals alike, for they concern the toleration of those who are against the system and the encouragement of individual effort and experimentation. Many African societies before colonial rule had a high degree of freedom of dissent, although this did not take the institutional form of a free press since there were no newspapers. On the one hand, such traditional societies lacked detention camps and jails within which to condemn political prisoners; on the other, they lacked the mass media. Much of the dissent in traditional societies was tolerated because it was at the level of the individual, without the technology of mass conversion. But whatever the reasons for the toleration, that particular rule of the game among, say, the Nuer or the Ibo or the Kikuyu was profoundly implicit in the political culture of the group. On the other hand, because most of these societies lacked the written word, the heresies of outstanding individuals were not conserved. The oral tradition is primarily a tradition which transmits consensus, rather than heresy, from generation to generation. We shall never know the full range of brilliant thinkers and philosophers in African history simply because the more original they were, the less likely were their thoughts going to be preserved and passed on. Africa's philosophical heritage suffered immensely precisely because outstanding African individualism had no way of communication with succeeding generations.

Imagine Karl Marx operating in a tradition without the written word. While he lived Marx was a heretic in his own western society. Most of the educated elite of Europe had never heard of him as a person. Marx read John Stuart Mill carefully, but Mill (a well-informed man in other ways) was probably unaware of Marx's existence. These two were contemporaries. Marx was clearly much the more original of the two thinkers, but he was also much the lesser known in his own day.

Barely a century later more than one-third of the human race was being governed partly on principles derived from Marxism. For these human beings, it was fortunate that Karl Marx was not merely an oral philosopher, depending for his immortality upon the consensus of his own age and society. Because Marx's ideas were preserved in writing, they were available to enrich other minds in succeeding generations.

But it was also fortunate that Marx lived in a more liberal Europe than Copernicus and some of the old victims of the age of the Inquisition. Had Marx lived in Czarist Russia he would probably have died prematurely — killed as a revolutionary well before his ideas could inspire the Lenins and Trotskys of Russian history. But instead Marx was peacefully working in the British Museum, writing articles for the *New York Tribune*, and being supported by a friend with capitalist interests in Manchester, Friedrich Engels. In addition Marx completed some of the most important contributions to political, economic and sociological thought in human history. A combination of Anglo-Saxon liberalism and the written word was part of the intellectual infrastructure which made the full flowering of this genius possible.

The new African liberalism of the 1990s will also be necessary as an infrastructure for new intellectual innovations among Africans themselves. A new generation of African intellectuals, feeling the neo-Czarist threat of their own regimes, will either follow Marx's example and seek intellectual refuge elsewhere, or attempt to liberalize their own societies from within. Some of these intellectuals might remain culturally dependent, either submissively or aggressively. Western-style African liberals can be as culturally dependent as western-style African Marxists. But by permitting individual Africans at last to innovate in their own way, by tolerating intellectual heresies, by respecting pluralism and the right to borrow from more than one intellectual tradition, the liberal rules of the game could permit even African Marxists to thrive and compete for acceptance.

By this time the non-intellectuals (especially soldiers in power) will have helped to resurrect part of Africa's past. Ancient African values and customs will in turn be struggling for a new mandate in competition with alternative ideas and values, both in schools and in the marketplace. Out of this mixture should emerge *creative eclecticism*, a new intellectual melting pot from which entirely new patterns of ideas might be forged.

Those African intellectuals who have remained in their societies will probably have found a new role before the end of the twentieth century. They will be called upon to shed more decisively their cultural dependency (Marxist and non-Marxist) and play a part in cultural liberation at long last, which until then will have been led mainly by non-intellectuals.

The Black Pilgrim Fathers of the 1980s

The rediscovery of liberalism will probably coincide with the first significant wave of black migration to the Americas since the end of the slave trade. In an important sense it might even be the first *voluntary* wave of African migration westwards across the Atlantic ever. The migrants will not be helpless captives from African villages, rustic and bewildered, but will be some of the most sophisticated Africans in history. The brain drain from Africa will be gathering momentum in the 1980s. The migrants will be either seeking refuge from anti-intellectual military rulers in Africa or new economic or academic opportunities for themselves. They will be inspired by the same range of general motives as migrants from other lands since the *Mayflower*.

Within the western hemisphere itself the issue of black migration has been conditioned either by cultural nostalgia or by economic ambition. Cultural nostalgia inspired 'back-to-Africa' movements, best illustrated by Marcus Garvey's efforts to inspire black Americans and West Indians in that direction early this century. On the whole the nostalgic efforts behind migratory campaigns failed.

Migratory efforts based on economic ambition were inspired less by the East and Africa, and more by the richly developed northern hemisphere. Within the first thirty years of the twentieth century over 300 000 migrants entered the United States from the Caribbean. Most settled in coastal towns and took lowly paid jobs. If the first wave of black immigrants into North America were slaves from Africa, the first *voluntary* wave consisted of poor peasants and labourers from the West Indies. It is the last quarter of the twentieth century which will probably witness the wave of highly-skilled black arrivals once again direct from the African continent, as well as from the Caribbean.

The trend has of course already started, receiving its first major push from the Nigerian civil war, as well as from the racial situation in Southern Africa. Apartheid and the Biafran war between them have served as a catalyst of a new historical phenomenon — nomadic black intellectuals traversing Africa and the world.

The New Bantu Migration

What should be noted is that this intellectual nomadism is indeed partly *intra*-African. In earlier decades of this century it was mainly peasants, petty traders, and the new migrant labourers that crossed territorial borders, seeking to improve their modest economic means. A distinction needs to be made here between *economic refuge* and *political asylum*. When labourers from Malawi pour into the mines of South Africa seeking jobs, they are seeking economic refuge from the poverty and underdevelopment of Malawi. But when frightened Hutu peasants pour into Tanzania running away from a genocidal outbreak in Burundi, the quest is for political asylum.

The first great wave of Bantu migration was probably occasioned and sustained more by economic than by political factors, though it is difficult to disentangle motives across such a vast period of history. The American linguist, Joseph Greenberg, has argued that the Bantu languages spread southward from Nigeria and the Cameroons, while Malcolm Guthrie, the British linguist, has advanced a rival thesis which places the Bantu nucleus in northern Katanga in Zaire. But why was there such an expansion of Bantu-speaking peoples? G. P. Murdock has emphasized the importance of new foods for the expansion of populations and the need to cultivate larger areas. Roland Oliver has suggested that Greenberg's and Guthrie's theses could be reconciled if one saw them as different stages of expansion. The domestication of sorghum, millet and dry rice facilitated both the increase and the spread of population through the eastern and western Sudan. To the south the humid tropical areas later received from South-east Asia the banana, yams and taros.[1] A frontier tradition grew up in Bantu land — 'Go south, young man — and improve your lot!'.

Roland Oliver has also likened Bantu expansion more to the European settlement of Australia and America than to the Teutonic invasion in Europe in medieval times.[2] But even more pertinent as an analogy might be the American expansion westwards. The Bantu, too, had their 'Manifest Destiny' as they extended their frontier, seeking new land to cultivate, new economic opportunities.

Will the last quarter of the twentieth century witness a new Bantu migration within the continent? The late 1980s and early 1990s will probably witness dramatic improvements in communications within the continent. The Lagos to Mombasa trans-continental highway will be only the beginning. After a good deal of hesitation about what to do with their petro-dollars, the oil producers of the Middle East are likely to extend considerable assistance to the task of improving African communications by the end of the decade. Economically motivated movements of labourers and petty traders will cover longer distances, in spite of the resistance of some African governments. Inter-penetration of African populations across territorial boundaries will increase.

But at least as significant as the movement of labourers and petty traders will be the movement of intellectuals and other educated African personnel. Nigeria is likely to establish a 'Peace Corps' of its own, bearing a different name, but designed to serve similar aims of technical assistance to those of the Kennedy experiment. The presence of Nigerian teachers and engineers, economists and even lawyers in African countries far from home will have become a routine phenomenon. Some degree of 'anti-Nigerianism' will have grown up in precisely those African countries benefiting most from Nigeria's wealth and expertise. A new form of aggressive dependency — black aid-recipient against black aid-donor — will have become part of the African scene.

By the middle 1980s a few more African countries will probably have struck oil. Oil will remain important at least to the end of the century, though other forms of fuel will by then also be in use.

South Africa stands a chance of having its main revolution by the early 1990s. With the blacks of South Africa controlling gold, and the Arab world controlling so much of the reserves of dollars, an Afro-Arab alliance would by then be a major factor in the stability of any international monetary system. Zaire, with its human dynamism and material resources, may also become a factor in this world equation.

The possibility of western military intervention either in the Middle East or in South Africa cannot be ruled out. Imperialist habits and gunboat diplomacy die hard. But the chances of a black triumph in South Africa by the 1990s are better than ever. And this black triumph would contribute to the new Bantu migration, partly through the expansion of black immigrant labour in South Africa, and partly through the growing influence of black South Africans in other parts of the continent. Of course not all Africans are Bantu-speaking peoples. We use the word 'Bantu' mainly for purposes of historical analogy with the earlier great movement of African peoples. Once again Nigeria and Zaire as well as South Africa may take the lead in facilitating the movement of their own enterprising citizens into other African areas, but under vastly different conditions.

As for the educated individuals of the smaller African countries, they may sometimes move to neighbouring African countries in response to political pressures in their own societies. We are back here to political asylum as a factor in migration, in contrast to the quest for economic refuge or diplomatic influence. Idi Amin's regime in Uganda may have imitators by the 1980s. Four capitals of the world have lately given refuge to intellectual refugees from Uganda —

Nairobi, Dar es Salaam, Lusaka and London. Other Ugandan refugees are to be found in North America. Those that are in England and North America are precursors of the black Pilgrim Fathers of the 1980s, looking for political refuge and a new life overseas. Those who have moved into professional jobs in Kenya, Tanzania and Zambia are precursors of the new Bantu migration of the coming decades within the African continent itself, much smaller in scale than the historic expansion of the Bantu, but much better endowed in skills and ideas than any other African migration in history.

Conclusion

In brief, sharp strokes we have attempted to portray both the immediate past history of the newly educated class of Africans and their likely future between now and the end of the twentieth century. We traced the Christian impact on the first generations of educated Africans, mainly through the efforts of Christian missionaries. We then attempted to follow the secularization of Africa's intellectual dependency from the Bible to *Das Kapital*. Stages in the process included the penetration of western liberal ideas, the emergence of liberal-nationalist movements, the new fascination with socialist rhetoric, and the triumph of Marxism as opium for Third World intellectuals.

The role of westernized Africans in Africa's liberation has commanded special attention in this book. They took almost undisputed leadership in the phase of political decolonization — the transfer of formal political sovereignty from the imperial power to the new African states. In the phase of economic liberation, educated Africans have remained and will remain important, but they have lost their pre-eminence. Non-intellectuals in military uniform have sometimes done more for the economic liberation of their countries than their intellectual predecessors. In the final phase of Africa's cultural liberation, western educated Africans will take a back-seat for a while, encumbered as they are by westernization, both liberal and radical. The imperfect acculturates like Mobutu Sese Seko and Idi Amin are playing more important roles in Africa's cultural liberation than almost anything being attempted by westernized Africans for the time being.

But Africa's cultural liberation will in turn have two stages. In the stage of partial *cultural revival*, the non-intellectuals will be the decisive actors. But in the process of *cultural innovation*, intellectuals and other highly educated personnel will once again have a chance to lead the way. In time they will probably inject a new vitality into African educational systems and cultural life at large.

By that time educated Africans will have rediscovered the liberal values of tolerance, individual worth, and normative pluralism, under the pressures of their own intolerant governments. Some educated

Africans will remain in their societies, and seek to liberalize and enrich their domestic cultures. Some will be forced to move to other African countries, strengthening inter-African communication and mutual penetration. A third group of educated Africans will constitute the first significant voluntary wave of black migrants to the Americas and to other parts of the western world. These overseas 'exiles' too might enrich their own African cultures from abroad, as well as stimulate afresh the intellectual energies of the Black Diaspora at large. But these black exiles in the western world will find it hardest to escape their cultural dependency on the West, and might alternate between submissive and aggressive dependency in the intellectual field.

What emerges from all this is that the full flowering of Africa's genius in the remaining decades of this century is likely to face two dangers — the tyranny of an omni-present western culture and the tyranny of insensitive and sometimes brutal African governments where these exist. The tyranny of western culture — including its radical Marxist branches — may continue to divert African minds from the challenges of genuine creativity and self-realization. The tyranny of African dictatorships in parts of the continent may continue to frighten a large proportion of potentially original African intellects away from the business of intellectual experiment and discourse. In the past Africa's own oral tradition hampered the task of transmitting brilliant heresies from one generation to the next. In the future it might be African dictators who would stifle the black genius, helped by the commanding presence of a triumphant alien civilization.

But when all these risks are counted and recognized, the prospects for Africa's liberation before the end of the century look brighter now than ever before. Economic liberation is under way, but will inevitably be hard and painful. Cultural liberation might be the hardest of them all. And all three forms of liberation await fulfilment in Southern Africa.

The role of educated Africans in the fourth quarter of the twentieth century will perhaps be less fundamental generally then it was in the third quarter, which might be remembered as the golden age of African intellectuals — supreme in power and prestige out of proportion to their numbers. But while the immediate future will indeed witness further decline in the position of educated Africans and intellectuals in African societies, they are likely to play new roles, linking country to country in Africa, forging new ties with the old Black Diaspora, establishing an African presence in the main streams of technology, scholarship and science in the developed world, and consolidating the foundations for a new era of African creativity and innovation.

References and Notes

1. Roland Oliver, 'The problem of the Bantu expansion', *Journal of African History*, **VII**, 3 (1966), 364, 368-9.
2. Ibid., 362.

INDEX

Abraham, Professor William, 86
Abrahams, Peter, 354
Abu-Lughod, Dr Ibrahim, 136
Academic freedom and political stability, 273-7
Acculturation, definition of, 23
  two dimensions of, 36
Achebe, Chinua, 10, 349, 350n5, 354
Adoko, Akena, 202-3, 246-9
Afar Region, 103
African customary law, 268-70
Africanization in industry, 293-4
African National Congress, 109
African Nationalism (Sithole), 350
African Predicament, The (Andreski), 222
Africa Today (journal), 45
Afrikaners, 91
Afro-Asianism, 129
Aggrey, Dr, 121
Ahriman (satanic darkness), 25
Alexandre, Pierre, 99
Algeria, 115, 118, 135, 136, 173
Ali bin Hemedi, Sheikh, 141
All Africa People's Conference (Accra, 1958), 107
Amin, Field-Marshal Idi, 7, 18-19, 117, 135, 163, 200, 263, 338, 371, 378
Amnesty International, 162-3
Amoo, Anthony William, 86
Andreski, Stanislav, 222, 226n9
Angola, guerrilla movement in, 103, 166
  liberation of, 173
  Russian influence in, 179
Anthropology, 269-70, 300-2
Anticipation, science of, 331-5
Apartheid, 91, 166, 375-6
  see also RSA
Arabic language, need to study, 313-14
Arabs, influence of, 315-17
Ardant, Gabriel, 131
Aristotle, 83, 85, 86, 93, 97-8, 99, 100
Armah, Ayi Kwe, 10

Army life, 15-20
Arnold, Professor Thomas, 82, 94
Arts, the, 344-5
Arusha Declaration (1967), 128, 241, 364-5
Ashby, Sir Eric, 297-8
Asquith Report (1945, on higher education), 289-90
Assimilationist policies, 120
Augustine, St (Bishop of Hippo), 24-5, 108
Authority, challenge to, 273-7
Awolowo, Chief Obafemi, 58, 104
Azikiwe, Dr Nnamdi, 104, 146, 303, 353, 373

Balandier, Georges, 2
Baldwin, James, 215-16
Balewa, Sir Abubakar Tafawa, 146, 164
Balme, D. M., 97-8
Banage, Professor W. B., 36n19
Banda, Dr Hastings, 2, 371
Bantu, new migration of, 376-8
Banyoro, as origin of Egypt, 90
Baranson, Jack, 329
Beautyful Ones are Not Yet Born, The (Armah), 10
Bello, Ahmadu, 371
Bentham, Jeremy, 237
Biafra, Lindt affair, 159-60, 165
  religious support behind, 146
  see also Civil War *under* Nigeria
Bigart, Homer, 52-3
Bissau, guerrilla movement in, 103
  PAGC in, 172-3
  see also Guinea
Black Christ movements, 84
Black Diaspora, 315, 317, 379
Black nationalism and Gandhi, 103-19
Black Pilgrim Fathers of the 1980s, 375-6
Black Studies Movement (US), 212-16
Blyden, Dr Edward, 249-50
Bohannan, Paul, 315n29

Bookworms discussed, 242
Boulding, Kenneth D., 182, 329
British East Africa Company, 288
Brockway, Lord Fenner, 359
Buddha, the, 150
Budge, Sir Ernest Wallis, 89-90
Budo, Uganda, 27, 30-2, 39
Buganda, court at, 29-34, 209, 256-7, 272-3
    see also Ganda, Uganda
Bull, Professor Graham, 305
Bunche, Dr Ralph, 108
Burke, Edmund, 120, 289
Burundi, 136
Busia, Kofi, 18, 371

CAFRAD, 339
Calhoun, John C., 83, 85
Calvin, John, 139
Calvinism, 236
Cambridge University, 235-51
Cameroun, uprising in, 103
Capetown University, 260-1
Carr, E. H., 109
Casablanca group of countries, 136
Caseley Hayford, J. E., 104, 121, 250
Castle, Barbara, 359-60
Central African Republic, military coup in, 163
    military presence in, 18
Césaire, Aimé, 14, 59-60, 84, 124, 278n, 354
Chad, uprising in, 103
Children, having many, 28
China, see Russia and China, influence of
Chou En-lai, 181-2
Christianity:
    in African diplomacy, 153-68:
        on combat and compassion, 163-7
        on man and kinsmen, 155-7
        politicization of life, 157-63
        summary and conclusion, 167-8
    influence of, 1-2, 24-8, 33-4, 108-9
    see also Church and state; Islam; Missionaries; Religion
Church and state, 143-7
Churchill, Sir Winston, 30-1
Classics, languages of the, 98-100
Coleman, James S., 3, 52, 104
Colonialism:
    alternatives to tutelage of, 43-7
    and oratory, 69-73
    as cultural experience, 23
    education during, 1-4
        and its relevance, 47-52

influence of French revolution on, 120-1
nationalist (French) movements and, 121
writers evolved from, 8-9
Colton, Joel, 95
Combat and compassion, 163-7
Commercial corporations, influence of, 292-7
Commission of Inquiry by the Department of Social and Industrial Research of the International Missionary Council, 49-50, 324-5
Commitment versus contemplation, 219-22
Common Man's Charter (Obote), 199-200, 228, 364-5
Communication from the Chair (Obote), 200
Communism, effects of Russian, 170
    in France, effect of, 120-1
Communist Manifesto (Marx and Engels), 359-61
Community development projects, 163
Compassion and combat, 163-7
Computers as international agents, 320-41:
    modernity, decolonizing, 335-40
    modernization, secular education and transnationals, 323-7
    and technology transfer, 327-31
    summary and conclusion, 340-1
Concentration, power of intellectual, 241-6
Confucius, study of, 311
Congo (Brazzaville), 136, 157
Congo, Republic of, see Zaire
Consciencism (Nkrumah), 86-7
Contemplation versus commitment, 219-22
Convention People's Party, 148
Copernicus, 236
Cosmopolitans, theory and aims of, 129-30
Counter-penetration, strategy of, in development, 314-18
Courage, training to attain, 229
Cox, Richard, 110
Creative eclecticism, emergence of, 375
Crowder, Michael, 147
Cuba, Afro-Asian Conference in (Havana, 1966), 129
    influence of, 179-80
Cultural matters:
    and economic dependency, link between, 292-7

bondage and political liberation, 297-9
dependency, 13-15
engagement, 218-22
import-substitution, 302-6
liberation and the future of the educated class, 368-79:
  Black Pilgrim Fathers of the 1980s, 375-6
  new Bantu migration, 376-8
  rebellion, political, economic and cultural, 370
  re-discovery of liberalism, 372-5
  revolution of imperfect acculturates, 371-2
  secularization of dependency, 368-70
  summary and conclusion, 378-9
rebellion, 370
Curriculum, Africanization of, 203-8
Currie, James, 289
Curtin, Philip, 315n29
Customary law and national integration, 268-70

Dadié, Bernard, 11, 353
Dahomey, military coup in, 163
Daily Nation (newspaper), 6
Dancing:
  economic anthropology of, 300-2, 308
  the art of African, 216
Dar es Salaam, University of, 252-4, 296-7; see Tanzania; Universities
Darkness and light, 25
Davidson, Basil, 92
Davies, Chief H. O., 104
Dayal, Mr Ambassador, 53
Decolonization:
  strategies for, see Counter-penetration; Diversification; Domestication
  of modernity, 335-40
DeGraft-Johnson, Dr J. C., 89
Dei-Anang, Michael, 87
Dependency, secularization of, 368-70
Descartes, René, 86, 124
Detraditionalization, 271
Detribalization, 271
Deutscher, Isaac, 174
Development, Chinese model of, 174-9
  counter-penetration of, 314-18
  diversification of, 310-14
  domestication of, 306-10
  educational goals for, see Education and development goals
  Russian model of, 171, 175-6, 179-81

Dia, Mamadou, 131, 147
Dike, K. O., 139
Dini ya Misambwa (Masinde), 60, 84
Diop, Cheikh Anta, 86, 92
Discourse on the Origin of Inequality (Rousseau), 124
Diversification, strategy of, in development, 310-14
Djibouti, 103
Domestication, strategy of, in development, 306-10
Dress, Western-type, 14-15
Dual Mandate (Lugard), 82, 288
DuBois, W. E. B., 93, 212
Dunant, Jean Henri, 164

East Africa:
  and the impact of the Greeks, 87-91
  Education Commission of (1919), 250
  Federal University, experiment of, 240
  part of the old classical world, 88-9
East African Community, newspapers in, 5-7
Economic matters:
  and cultural dependency, link between, 292-7
  rebellion, 370
Educated class, cultural liberation of, see Cultural liberation
Education:
  Africanization of syllabuses, 203-8, 226
  and development goals, 218-31
    contemplation versus commitment, 219-22
    labour versus leisure, 222-5
    national service and socialization, 225-9
    summary and conclusion, 229-31
  and nationalist aspirations, 202-17:
    negritude and negrology, 212-16
    syllabus and staff, Africanization of, 203-8
    world culture, Africanizing, 208-12
    summary and conclusion, 216-17
  and political change, 187-201:
    educated class, decline of, 197-201
    limits of indoctrination, 188-90
    tolerance, toil and teamwork, 190-7
  and politics, effects of each, 1-4
  and salvation, 23-40
    Ganda and the Japanese, 32-4
    cultural schizophrenia, origins of, 27-9
    desocialization of education, 29-32
    techno-cultural gap, 24-7
    closing the gap, 35-40

and sovereignty, 42-61
  alternatives to colonial tutelage, 43-7
  colonial education and relevance, 47-52
  educational policy to political experience, 55-7
  mass literacy or elite-formation, 52-5
  political to cultural, progress through, 57-61
  curricula changes needed, 312-18
  desocialization of, 29-32
  from policy of, to political experience, 55-7
  how much and what type, 52-5
  political and journalism, 4-8
  secular and modernization, 323-7
  see also Higher education; Schools; Teachers; Universities
Egypt, 91-4, 134, 136
  see also Nile
Elder tradition, 261-3
Elite:
  decline of, 197-201
  labour versus leisure, 222-5
  politics of literary, 8-12
Engels, Friedrich, 137-8, 140, 149, 150, 313, 374
English language, command of, 30, 197-8
  see also Languages
Epstein, A. L., 296
Eratosthenes, 88
Eritrea, uprising in, 103
Ethiopia, 179, 181, 262
Ethiopianism, 84-5
Ethnic calculus versus merit criteria, 270-3
Ethnocentrism, doctrine of, 94, 98
Eudoxe, 93
Eurocentrism, 264-5, 314
Euro-Christian gap, 155, 167
Excellence after relevance, 203, 216

Facing Mount Kenya, 60
Fair play, 196
Fallers, Lloyd A., 33
Family planning, 163
Fanon, Frantz, 10, 103, 119, 280
Fodéba, Kéita, 11, 353
Football and teamwork, 194-6
Fourah Bay University, 259-60, 291
France, effect of internal political moves in, 173-4
  1789 revolution, effect of, 120-1

Francis, Dr Ngombe, 19
Francophone writers, 11-12, 14
Freedom fighters, 166-7
FRELIMO, 172-3, 180, 350
Freymond, Jacques, 166

Gadeau, Cofi, 11, 353
Gal, Roger, 54
Galileo, Galilei, 236
Gallagher, John, 96
Gamesmanship, 194-5
Ganda peoples, 29-34
  and Japanese, 32-4
  and Uganda, 209, 256-7, 272-3
Gandhi, Indira, 105
Gandhi, the Mahatma, 103-19, 369:
  in black history, 103-8
  limits of doctrine of, 111-17
  sociology and, 108-10
  summary and conclusion, 117-19
Garvey, Marcus, 121, 375
Gayaza High School, Uganda, 26
Gershenberg, Irving, 299
Ghana, as a member of the Casablanca group, 136
  Islam in, 148
  military coup in, 164
  nationalism in, 105, 111-12
  oratory in, 74
  percentage of teachers entering politics in, 3
  ratio of children attending school in, 44
  scholarship in, 224-5
  teaching of dancing in, 301
  universities of, 259-60
  see also Nkrumah, Kwame
Ginwala, Miss, 6-7
Government:
  challenge to authority of, 273-7
  town and gown, 238-41
Gowon, General, 18
Gown, town and Government, 238-41
Greece, impact of ancient, on African thought, 81-100
  Africanization of, 97-8
  East Africa, Nile and the Middle East, 87-91
  negritude and, 83-7
  philosophy of, 94-7
Greenburg, Joseph, 376
Grundy, Kenneth W., 170-1
Guerrilla movements, 103, 170-2, 173, 174
Guinea, 126-8, 134, 136, 172-3, 175-6
  see also Bissau; Touré, Sekou
Guns, Mao's faith in power of, 171-4

Guthrie, Malcolm, 376
Gutteridge, William F., 163-4

Habari za Mwezi (newspaper), 4
Hailey, Lord, 50-1
Hamites, origins of, 93
Hamlet (Shakespeare), 14
Hammarskjöld, Dag, 45, 160-1
Hanna, Judith, 301
Hardy, George, 278
Hasan Al-Banna, 143n15
Hassel, Kai von, 50
Havana Conference (1966), 129
Hayes, Carleton J. H., 286
Hayford, *see* Caseley Hayford
Hegel, George W. F., 279-80, 344
Helleiner, G. K., 327-9
Herodotus, 93, 97
Herskovits, Melville J., 95
Higher education:
  environment of, 252-67:
    logic of location, 252-6
    political economy of location, 256-9
    state and the scholar, 259-66
    summary and conclusion, 266-7
  meaning of, 235-51:
    introduction, 235-8
    intellectual concentration, 241-6
    practical involvement, 246-9
    town, gown and government, 238-41
    summary and conclusion, 249-51
  political functions of, 268-80:
    customary law and national integration, 268-70
    ethnic calculus *versus* merit criteria, 270-3
    political stability and academic freedom, 273-7
    science of slogans, 277-80
    summary and conclusion, 280
  see also Education; Schools; Universities as multinational corporations
Hindus, philosophy of, 111-12
Hobbes, Thomas, 126-7, 290
Hobson, John Atkinson, 285-6, 298
Hodgkin, Thomas, 84, 121, 126
Hodgson, Marshall G. S., 89, 95
Horton, Dr Africanus, 249-50
Hoskyns, Catherine, 156-7
Houphouet-Boigny, Félix, 371
Humanitarianism in African diplomacy, *see* Christianity in African diplomacy
Hume, David, 280
Huntingford, G. W. B., 90

Hyder, Dr Mohamed, 98

Ibadan University, 248, 290, 303
Ideas, internationalism of, 354-7
'If' (Kipling), 71-2
Imperial genesis, 285-90
Imperialism, the Highest Stage of Capitalism (Lenin), 73
Indian National Movement, 103-5
  see also Gandhi, the Mahatma
Individual, the, and populism, 121-3
Indoctrination, limits of educational, 188-90
Industry, influence of corporations on, 292-7
Infant mortality, 28-9
Informatics, co-ordination of, 339
Inheritance, Islamic law of, 140-1
Insurance, policies of, 29
Intellectual:
  definition of, 203
  power of concentration and the, 241-6
  the African, as international link, 343-67:
    as international, 357-62
    internationalism of ideas of, 354-7
    internationalism of students, 362-6
    summary and conclusion, 366-7
International Congress of Africanists, 83
Internationalism of ideas, 354-7
International links, *see under* Intellectual
International Red Cross, *see* Red Cross
International pragmatism, 179-81
International relations and populism, 129-31
IRA, tactics of, 144
Ireland, conflict in Northern, 144
Iringi dances, 300
Islam, 89
  and radicalism in African politics, 134-51
  and a tradition of rebellion, 149-51
  and Marxism, 137-9
  and modernity, 142-3
  and political structure, 147-9
    anti-cumulative aspects of, 139-42
  separation of religion and politics, 143-7
  see also Christianity; Church and state; Religion
Issas region, 103
Ivory Coast, 296
Ivory towers, universities as, 243-5, 257-8

Japanese and Ganda, 32-4
Jefferson, Thomas, 373

Jennings, Sir Ivor, 49
Jesus Christ, 106, 109, 150, 236
Jews, prejudice against, 125
Jinah, Mohammed Ali, 105
Johnson, Harry G., 327
Johnson, Dr Mordecai, 106
Johnson, Dr Samuel, 229-30
Johnston, Governor (of Uganda), 30
Journalism and political education, 4-8
Judeo-Christian philosophy, 84-5
Julius Caesar (tr: Nyerere), 74, 219, 230-1
Juries, 65

Kabaka of Buganda, influence of, 29-34
see also Buganda; Ganda and Uganda
Kalimuzo, Frank, 264
Kariuki, J. M., 263, 360
Karume, Abeid, 134, 151
Kasavubu, Joseph, 163
Katanga, migration from, 376
secession of, 42, 156, 161
Kaunda, Kenneth, 2, 107-8, 110, 113-14
see also Zambia
Kautsky, Karl, 361
Kawawa, Rashidi, 134, 229
Kelly, John, 144
Kemp, D., 224-5
Kenya:
computers in, 320-1
customary law in, 269-70
detentions in, 162-3
divorce laws of, 269-70
import of luxuries to, 296
inheritance laws of, 269-70
Lands Title Ordinance, 140
marriage laws of, 269-70
newspapers in, 5, 7
per capita expenditure on education, 43-4
pre-eminence of Luo people, 271
Ugandan refugees in, 378
University of, 253-4
restlessness in, 263
women, status of, in, 269-70
see also Kenyatta, Jomo
Kenyatta, Jomo, 5, 7, 43, 58-61, 67-8, 75, 108, 117, 280, 353
Keynes, John Maynard, 279
Kimble, David, 224
Kimble, George T., 48n24
King, Martin Luther, 106, 108-9, 116
King's College, Budo (Uganda), 27, 30-2, 39
Kinsmen and man, 155-7
Kipling, Rudyard, 70-6, 155

Kiryankusa, Mr, 121-2
Kitandawili (riddles), 66-9
Kitching, Rev. A. L., 26
Klein, Martin, 147
Koran, 138-9
see also Islam
Krushchev, Nikita, 3
Kuper, Leo, 109

Labour *versus* leisure, 222-5
Lagos/Mombasa Highway, 376
Lamizana, General, 18
Langevin Commission, 54, 326-7
Languages, ancient classical, 98-9
impact of French and English, 69-73, 197-201, 265-6, 298, 309, 313-14
see also English language, command of
teaching native African, 309-10, 313-14
Latin language, 98-9
Law, African customary, 268-70
syllabus in, 206
Leakey, J. S. B., 88
Legislative Councils, 73-4
Legon University (Ghana), 290
Legum, Colin, 166
Leisure *versus* labour, 222-5
Lenin, Vladimir Ilyich, 73-6, 127, 151, 170-1, 174, 221, 285-6, 361
Lenshina, Alice, 113-14, 122
Leshoai, Bob, 216-17
Leverhulme, Lord, 294
Levy, Reuben, 142
Lewis, Bernard, 147-8
Liberalism, re-discovery of, 372-5
Liberation:
Chinese model of, 171-4
political and cultural bondage, 297-9
Libya, 136, 182
Life, politicization of, 157-63
Light and darkness, 25
Lindt, August, 159-60, 165
Linguistics, 299, 313
Lipset, Seymour Martin, 55
Literacy, as mass or elite formation, 52-5
Literary elite, politics of, 8-12
Locke, Rovan G., 170n
Lofchie, Professor Michael, 141
London, Colonial University dependence on University of, 290-1
Ugandan refugees in, 378
Louvainium University (Kinshasa), 291-2, 298
Luganda language, 99
Lugard, Lord, 82, 288-9

Lumumba, Patrice, 54, 134, 160-1
Luthuli, Chief Albert, 2, 108
Lwamfafa, J. W., 71

Macbeth (tr: Mushi), 231
Machel, Samora, 13
Machiavelli, Niccolò, 290
Macpherson, Margaret, 99
McNeill, William H., 95
Mahdism, tradition of, 149
Mair, Lucy, 85
Makerere University, 235-51, 253-4, 256-7, 290, 298, 303, 346-7
  see also Universities
Malawi, under-development in, 376
  see also Banda, Dr Hastings
Mali, 136
Man and kinsmen, 155-7
Mandela, Nelson, 110
Manicheans, 25
Man of the People, A (Achebe), 10
Mao Tse-tung, 170-1, 178, 181-2, 311, 321
Marriage across racial lines, 261
Martin, David, 19
Marx, Karl:
  and cultural liberation, 374-5
  and internationalism, 343-4
  as political philosopher, 290-1
  on Hegel, 279-80
  on ownership of property, 140, 208
  on science, 312-13
  religious views of, 137, 208
  views on world changes, 219, 221
Marxism, Islam and radicalism in African politics, 85, 137-9
  Russia's influence and, 171-4
Masinde, Elijah, 60, 84, 122
Materialism, the demon of, 27
Mathew, Gervase, 88
Mathu, Eliud, 14
Mau Mau insurrection, 60, 68, 103, 117-18, 360
Mauritania, 135, 136
Mayanja, Abu, 355-7
Mazrui, Professor Ali, 13, 23n, 170n, 205, 206-7, 208n3, 260-1, 290-1, 293, 345, 346-8, 349
Mboya, Tom, 43-4, 55, 71, 75, 111, 189, 275, 277-8, 280, 371
Meanings, double, 66-8
Mecca, 138
Mehta, A. G., 347
Mengo School, Uganda, 30-2
Merchant of Venice, The (tr. Nyerere), 74, 231

Merit criteria and ethnic calculus, 270-3
Meritocracy and militocracy, 15-20
Middle East, impact of ancient Greece on, 87-91
Migration:
  new Bantu, 376-8
  to the USA, 375
Military training and fair play discussed, 196
Militocracy and meritocracy, 15-20
Mill, John Stuart, 123-4, 290, 373-4
Mirambo, Chief, 4
Missionaries, influence of, 1-2, 4, 24, 25-7, 47-50, 153-4, 168, 286, 301, 323-5
Mitchell, J. Clyde, 296
Mitchell, Sir Philip, 140
Mobutu (Sese Soko), Joseph Désiré, 13-15, 57-8, 61, 163, 372, 378
Modernity:
  counter-penetration of, 314-18
  decolonization of, 306-10, 335-40
  diversification of, 310-14
Modernization, 323-31, 335-40
Mombasa/Lagos Highway, 376
Mondlane, Dr Eduardo, 350
Monod, Jaques, 213
Mormons, 146
Morocco, 136
Morris, Colin, 107
Motion of Destiny, The (Nkrumah), 100
Mozambique:
  Chinese influence in, 178-9
  Cuban influence in, 180-1
  FRELIMO in, 172-3
  guerrilla movement in, 103, 166
Mphahlele, Ezekiel, 125-6
MPLA, 179-80
Msimulizi (newspaper), 4
Muhammad, Prophet, 138, 142, 149-50
  see also Islam
Muigwithani (newspaper), 5
Multinational corporations:
  business of, 320-31
  universities as, *see under* Universities
Munno (newspaper), 7
Murray-Brown, Mr, 75
Music, 299, 300-2, 308
Muslim League, 104-5
Muslims, *see* Islam
Musoke, Mr, 122
Muzorewa, Bishop Abel, 2
Mwiri College, Uganda, 99

Nairobi University, 253-5, 271-2
Names, changing euro-hebraic, 58

Namibia, guerrilla movement in, 103
National integration and customary law, 268-70
Nationalism, black, and Gandhi, 103-19
education and, *see* Education and nationalist aspirations
Nationalist, The (newspaper), 7
National service, 225-9, 253
Nations, building of, by USSR and China, 174-9
Naville, Marcel, 160
Negritude, 13-14, 58-61, 83-6, 124-5
and negrology, 212-16
Negrology and negritude, 212-16
Nelson, Danny, 7
Neo-colonialism, the Last Stage of Imperialism (Nkrumah), 73
Neogy, Rajat, 207, 255-7
New International Economic Order, the quest for, 338, 341
New Nations (Mair), 85
Newspapers, influence of, 4-8
Ngugi wa Thiong'o, James, 10, 354
Nigeria:
  and the Red Cross, 159-60, 165-6
  civil war in, 105, 159, 164
  export of skills from, 377
  Islam in, 135-6, 145-6
  its own 'peace corps', 377
  Lindt affair, 159-60, 165
  military coup in, 164
  nationalism in, 104-5, 111
  national service in, 225, 227
  newspapers in, 5
  percentage of teachers entering politics, 3
  pre-eminence of Ibo peoples, 271
  relations with OPEC, 316
  song and dance in, 301
  Universities of, 259-60
Nile region and the impact of the Greeks, 87-91, 96
Njonjo, Charles, 13
Nkrumah, Kwame, 1-2, 73-4, 81, 83, 86, 98, 99-100, 106-7, 111, 121, 134, 148, 158, 164, 174, 280, 354, 369, 371
Non-violence, policy of, 103-19
Numeiry, President, 7
Nyerere, Dr Julius, 6-8, 38-9, 74, 117, 125, 128-30, 176-8, 192, 218, 223, 230-1, 350, 354

Oakeshott, Michael, 290
OAU, resolution of, to break diplomatic ties with Britain, 136

Obote, Dr A. Milton, 7, 19, 75, 99, 134-5, 163, 198, 206-7, 230, 256, 365
O'Brien, Conor Cruise, 156
Ocaya-Lakidi, Dent, 23n
Occultism, 19
Odinga, Oginga, 137, 363, 365
Ojukwu, General, 165
Oliver, Professor Roland, 89, 94, 376
Omar, Caliph, 141-2
OPEC, economic effects of, 316
Orators, emergence of modern, 64-76:
  from Kipling to Lenin, 73-6
  in a pre-literate polity, 64-9
  the colonization of, 69-73
Ordinariness, cult of, 127-8
Ormuzd (godly light), 25
Orwell, George, 114
Ouma, Hilary, 332-4
Oxford University, 235-51

Pacifism, 103-19
Padmore, George, 353
PAFMECA, 110
PAGC (Guinea-Bissau), 172-3
Pakistanism, 104-5
Palmer, R. R., 95
Pan-African Freedom Movement (PAFMECA), 110
Parental immortality, 28
Parkes, Henry Bamford, 87
Participation, concept of, 219
Parti Démocratique de Guinée (PDG), 126-8
Partition policies, 105, 111
p'Bitek, Okot, 10, 28, 67, 212, 215, 217, 304, 309
PDG, 126-8
Peasantry as vanguard of revolution (Mao), 171-2
People, The (newspaper), 7, 99, 345nl
Periplus of the Erythrean Sea, 88
PhD theses, 211
Philosophies of intellectual concentration and practical involvement, 241-9
Pilgrim Fathers of the 1980s, 375-6
Plamenatz, John, 19, 56, 131, 209-10
Plato, 93, 99-100, 208, 348
Platon, P., 334
Political liberation and cultural bondage, 297-9
Political rebellion, 370
Political science, place of, 207-12
Politicization of life, 157-63

Politics:
  and education effects of each, 1-4
  and higher education, *see* Higher
    education, political functions of
  and religion, separation of, 143-7
  changes in, and education, 187-201
  and education and journalism, 4-8
  experience in, from educational policy,
    55-7
  healthy debating in, 244
  impact of foreign language on, 67, 70
  instability of, 187-8
  militarization of, 163-7
  progress towards through cultural
    experience, 57-61
  radicalism and Islam, *see under* Islam
  stability of, and academic freedom,
    273-7
  structure of, and Islam, 147-9
  the place of political science in, 207-12
  see also Orators
Politics (Aristotle), 97
Pope, Alexander, 214-15
Populism, 120-32:
  African, 121-3
  and the individual, 123-6
  and international relations, 129-31
  and society, 126-9
Positive action, philosophy of, 106-7,
  111-12
Practicality and scientism, 344
Prejudice, 125
Press, role of the, 4-8
Prisoners of war, 166-7
Property, Islamic views on ownership of,
  140
*Protestant Ethic and the Spirit of
  Capitalism* (Weber), 236
Protestantism, 236-7
Proverbs discussed, 65-6, 68
Public health, expenditure on, 305
Public schools, example of British, 194-5
Punt, 90
Puritanism, 237
Pwani na Bara (newspaper), 4
Pye, Lucian W., 17
Pygmies of the Congo, 37-8
Pythagoras, 93

Qaddafi, Colonel Muammur, 182, 371

Radicalism and Islam, *see under* Islam
Radio, impact of, 70
  programmes, 243-4
Rahman, Mujibur, 105

Rassemblement Démocratique Africaine
  (RDA), 121
Raum, Otto, 300
Reading speed, problem of, 246
Rebellion:
  and Islam, 149-51
  political, economic and cultural, 370
Red Cross Organization, 157, 159-68
Relevance:
  and excellence, 202, 216, 248
  practical and cultural discussed, 302-6
Religion:
  and academic life, 235-7, 247-8
  and politics, separation of, 143-7
  see also Christianity; Church and
    state; Islam; Missionaries
Rhetoric, see Oratory
Rhodesia:
  guerrilla movement in, 103
  liberation fighter of, 173
  UDI in, 114-15, 118, 136
  see also Smith, Ian
Riddles discussed, 66-9
Robinson, Ronald, 96
Romans, civilization of the, 82, 94-6
Roosevelt, F. D., 223
Rousseau, Jean-Jacques, 35n17, 120-32,
  208, 290, 348:
  and African populism, 121-3
  populism and the individual, 123-6
    and international relations, 129-31
    and society, 126-9
  summary and conclusion, 131-2
Royal Society (London), 237
RSA, *see* South Africa
Ruge, Arnold, 313
Rugumayo, Edward, 39

Sage tradition, 261, 264
Saloway, R. H., 111-12
Sao Tomé, guerrilla movement in, 103
Sarbah, Mensah, 353
Sardauna, Sokoto of, 371
Sartre, Jean-Paul, 84, 124-5
Satan, 25
Satyagraha (passive resistance), 111-16
Schizophrenia, origins of cultural, 27-9
Scholar and state, 259-66
Schools:
  Africanization of staff in, 203-8
  attendance numbers in Zaire, 48
  boarding, 26-7
  missionary, 24
  primary and secondary, indoctrination
    in, 188-90
  public, example of British, 194-5

see also Education; Higher education;
    Universities
Schumpeter, Joseph, 286
Science and religion, 235-7, 247-8
    introduction of history of, 312
    of anticipation, 331-5
    of slogans, 277-80
Scientism and practicality, 344
Secessionist tendencies, 268
Secularization of dependency, 368-70
Seligman, Professor C. G., 93-4
Senegal, import of luxuries to, 296
    Islam in, 145-7
    teaching of dancing in, 301
    universities of, 259-60
    see also Senghor, Léopold
Senghor, Léopold, 11, 13-15, 58-9, 85-6,
    94, 124, 129-30, 145, 147, 213,
    214, 219, 278-80, 312-13, 353,
    363, 371
Separatism, 268
Sex, sin or moral, 26
Shakespeare, William, 74, 215-16, 219,
    230, 307
Sierra Leone, Universities of, 259-60
Singapore, 358
Sithole, Rev. Ndabaningi, 2, 350
Slogans, science of, 277-80
Smith, Ian, 114-15, 136
    see also Rhodesia
Social commitment, 218-22
Social Contract, The (Rousseau), 127
Socialism:
    discussed, 344-5
    influence of Russia and China on,
        174-9
Socialization and national service, 225-9
Society and populism, 126-9
Sociology of Religion (Weber), 142
Soldiers, 15-20
Somalia, 134, 179˙
Song, economic anthropology of, 300-2
Soul, journey of the human, 25-6
South Africa:
    Bantu Authorities Act, 110
    black migration to US from, 375-6
    boycott on goods from, 116
    freedom fighters in, 166
    Gandhism in, 109-10
    Group Areas Act, 109-10
    guerrilla movement in, 103
    liberation fighters in, 173
    populism in, 122
    revolution by 1990, 377
    Separate Representation of Voters
        Act, 110

see also Apartheid
Soviet Union, see USSR
Soyinka, Wole, 13, 307, 349, 354
Spencer, Anne M., 250
Stalin, Marshal Joseph, 171, 174
Standard, The (newspaper), 6-7
Stanleyville, rescue operation at, 156-7
State:
    and church, 143-7
    and the scholar, 259-66
Stuckey, Stirling, 212
Students:
    internationalism of, 362-6
    militancy and, 238-9
    power of, 191
Sudan, 134-6, 164
Sunday Nation (newspaper), 6
Sundkler, B. G., 84
Swahili language and technical terms,
    98-9
Syllabuses, Africanization of, 203-8, 226

TANU, 128
Tanzania:
    anti-parasitism in, 223, 228
    Chaga peoples of, 300
    Chinese influence in, 176-8
    combination of reform in both educa-
        tion and economics together,
        296-7
    diplomatic break with UK, 136
    education in, 222-3
    expulsion of students in, 241
    indigenization in, 335-6
    influx of Hutu into, 376
    Islam in, 145-7
    national service in, 225-9
    newspapers in, 6-7
    oratory in, 74
    radicalization in, 176-7
    radical socialism in, 240
    support for Obote from, 134-5
    TANU and the Arusha Declaration,
        128
    technology and, 176-8
    Ugandan refugees in, 378
    Uhuru na Kazi policy, 223
    see also Dar-es-Salaam, University of;
        Nyerere, Julius; Ujamaa
Taylor, D. R. F., 334-5, 339
Teachers:
    Africanization of, 203-8
    attraction by politics of, 2
    prestige of, 349

see also Education; Higher education; Schools; Universities
Teamwork, need for, 190-7
Techno-cultural gap, 24-7, 35-40
Technology, 176-8:
  faculties in, 303-6
  transfer and modernization, 327-31
Telli, Diallo, 86-7
Tennyson, Alfred Lord, 73-4
Theatres, travelling, 307
Things Fall Apart (Achebe), 10
Thiong'o, Ngugi wa, *see* Ngugi, James
Third world, concept of, 129-30
Three T's, philosophy of the, 190-7
Toil, call for, 190-7
Tolerance, need for, 190-7
Tomblings, Douglas Griffith, 219
Tomlin, E. W. F., 112
Touré, Sekou, 131, 148, 151, 172, 371
Town, gown and Government, 238-41
Trade Unions, 158
Training for nationhood, 190-7
Translation (journal), 355, 357-8
Transnationals and modernization, 323-7
Trevor-Roper, Professor Hugh, 94
Trial by jury, 65
Trial of Dedan Kimathi, The (Ngugi), 10
Tribal welfare system, 155
Tshombe, Moise, 156, 161
Tucker, Bishop Alfred, 90
Tugendhat, Christopher, 294
Turnbull, Colin M., 37-8

UAR, 136
Uganda:
  Asian expulsion from, 338
  customary law in, 269
  delays in introducing lessons on engineering, 303
  detention of Mayanja and Neogy, 355-7
  divorce laws of, 269-70
  Egyptians descended from, 89-90
  Islam in, 135
  marriage laws of, 269-70
  military presence in, 18-19
  missionary activities in, 286
  national service in, 228
  newspapers, 7
  occultism in, 19
  People's Congress of, 122, 240
  percentage of teachers entering politics, 3
  political detainees in, 163
  radio in, 200
  refugees from, 377-8

  Russian influence in, 180
  status of women in, 269-70
  tolerance in, discussed, 195-6
  uprising in, 103, 196
  use of English in, 197-201
  see also Amin, Idi; Buganda, court at; Ganda and Uganda; Kabaka; Obote, Milton
UGCC, 148
Ujamaa, policy of, 8, 61, 180
UNCTAD, 129
UNESCO, 43-7
UNITA, 179-80
Universities:
  as multinational corporations, 285-318:
    cultural and economic dependency, link between, 292-7
    cultural import-substitution, 302-6
    dance and song, economic anthropology of, 300-2
    imperial genesis, 285-90
    political liberation and cultural bondage, 297-9
    strategy of, in development:
      counter-penetration, 314-18
      diversification, 310-14
      domestication, 306-10
      structural and organizational dependency, 290-2
  housing at, 254-5
  rationalism of, 202-17
  see also Education; Higher education; Schools; Teachers
UNO, 161, 166-7
  see also Hammarskjöld, Dag
Upper Volta, military coup in, 163
USA, racial situation in, 116-17
USSR and China, influence of, 170-83:
  building nations and socialism, 174-9
  domestic revolution and international pragmatism, 179-81
  Marxist revolution and Maoist liberation, 171-4
  summary and conclusion, 181-3

Verwoerd, Henrik, 91
Victorian Age, 26
Visitation Committees (to universities), 241
Voice of Uganda, The (newspaper), 7

Wallace, John B., 334
Warriorhood, 15-20
Warrior tradition, 261, 263-4
Watson, Tom, 31

Weber, Max, 139, 142, 236
Weekly Review, The (journal), 320-2
Wheeler, Sir Mortimer, 88-9
'White Man's Burden, The' (Kipling), 70, 155
Witchcraft, 19
Witwatersrand University, 260
Wordsworth, William, 73
World Council of Churches, 167
World Federation of Cultures: an African perspective, A (Mazrui), 13
Writers, a product of Colonialism, 8-9

Youth, facilities for, 163

Zaire:
    changing euro-hebraic names, 58
    literacy in, 48-9
    Louvainium University, 291-2, 298
    military uprising in, 42, 160-1, 163
    missionary influence in, 325-6
    modes of dress in, 14-15
    quest for sovereignty in education in, 42-57
    school attendance figures, 48
    white hostages in, 156-7
    see also Lumumba, Patrice; Mobutu, Joseph
Zambia:
    consumer goods on offer in, 296
    Kaunda's views on Gandhism, 113-14
    Lumpa Church in, 113-14
    populism in, 122
    pro-Obote stance by, 134
    Ugandan refugees in, 378
    see also Kaunda, Kenneth
Zanzibar, 135-6, 141, 151, 158, 162, 176
Zimbabwe, *see* Rhodesia
Zolberg, Aristide R., 18